GLOBAL ISSUES

WOMEN'S RIGHTS

GLOBAL ISSUES

WOMEN'S RIGHTS

Second Edition

Natasha Thomsen

Foreword by Kathryn Cullen-DuPont

✓Facts On File
An Infobase Learning Company

GLOBAL ISSUES: WOMEN'S RIGHTS, SECOND EDITION

Facts On File, Inc.
An imprint of Infobase Learning
132 West 31st Street
New York NY 10001

Library of Congress Cataloging-in-Publication Data

Thomsen, Natasha.
Women's rights / Natasha Thomsen ; foreword by Kathryn Cullen-DuPont. — 2nd ed.
p. cm.
Includes bibliographical references and indexes.
ISBN 978-0-8160-8379-4 (alk. paper)
1. Women's rights. 2. Women's rights—United States. I. Title.
HQ1236.W652525 2011
305.42072—dc23   2011018483

Text design by Erika K. Arroyo
Cover design by Salvatore Luongo
Diagrams by Jeremy Eagle
Composition by Hermitage Publishing Services
Cover printed by Yurchak Printing, Landisville, Pa.
Book printed and bound by Yurchak Printing, Landisville, Pa.
Date printed: January 2012

Printed in the United States of America

10 9 8 7 6 5 4 3 2 1

This book is printed on acid-free paper.

To the memory of Rosa Parks (1913–2005)
and all who advocate self-development.

CONTENTS

PART III: Research Tools

List of Graphs, Maps, and Tables

Foreword

Individual women have taken their own and other women's rights seriously throughout recorded history: Enheduanna, the daughter of the Sumerian king Sargon and history's earliest author to be known by name, tells, in a ca. 2300 B.C.E. poem, of her efforts to be delivered from exile and restored to her rightful position; Empress Theodora (497–548) used her power in Byzantium to pass laws that outlawed trafficking in girls and gave women greater equality in divorce proceedings; English writer Mary Astell (1668–1731) proposed a women's college and expanded opportunities for women in her *A Serious Proposal to the Ladies* (1694); and during the American Revolution, Abigail Adams famously, but unsuccessfully, urged her husband, John Adams, to secure rights to women in the new republic.

It was in the 19th century, though, that women first began organizing to demand recognition of their rights. And these rights—first fought for in the United States and Europe, but now demanded in countries all around the world—speak to the very humanity of the world's women. While not all these rights are at risk in every country, in no country is every one of these rights fully secured to women and girls: the right to be free of selective abortion and female infanticide; the right of the girl child to equal nutrition and education; the right of girls to remain unmarried during childhood and, in adulthood, to have a right of approval over any marriage; the right to legal and social equality for lesbian and transgendered women; the right to be free of sexual assault, both within and without relationships, including marriage; the right of women to reproductive health care and to a determination of their own maternity; the right to their own children; the right to work and have ownership of their wages; the right to own and inherit property; the right to equal religious participation; and the right to vote and participate in civil affairs.

When women began to demand their rights, there was widespread ridicule. Following American women's inaugural event, the Seneca Falls Convention of 1848, for example, one newspaper editorial had this to say about the idea of women seeking rights in their own person, as opposed to seeking favor through a connection with a male representative of their society:

> *A woman is nobody. A wife is everything. A pretty girl is equal to ten thousand men, and a mother is, next to God, all powerful. . . . The ladies are resolved to maintain their rights as Wives, Belles, virgins, and Mothers, and not as Women.* (Philadelphia Ledger and Daily Transcript, September 26, 1848)

Certainly, no 19th-century government considered women's aspirations for equal rights when setting its domestic agenda or when shaping its foreign policy. That is not the case today.

Women's rights are currently affecting domestic agendas worldwide. France and Turkey are struggling to balance their states' secularism with the desire of many Muslim women to wear the *hijab* (a struggle that centers on the governments' view of the *hijab* not only as a religious symbol but a symbol of women's subordination, which is opposed to many Muslim women's view of the veil as not only a symbol of devotion but, in feminist terms, a less objectifying garment than contemporary Western choices for women). China is working to prevent the selective abortions that have followed its One-Child Policy and which, every year, result in the birth of at least 1.5 million fewer girls than demographers would expect. A Congolese military court has recently sentenced a high-ranking officer to 20 years in prison for ordering, among other things, the rape of women in the eastern Democratic Republic of the Congo town Fizi. Italian president Silvio Berlusconi faces trial on charges of paying an underage girl for sex, and thousands of Italy's women have demonstrated in the streets to protest their president's treatment of women and the status of women in their county. In the United States, the White House Council on Women and Girls recently released the report "Women in America: Indictors of Social and Economic Well Being"; it presents a thorough evaluation of the status of women in many areas of American life, including health, education, employment, and role in the family, with the stated goal of gathering facts that may underpin the setting of goals for the future of American women.

Women's rights have also become an international and foreign-policy consideration. As this is written, the Taliban's willingness to respect women's rights is an issue as the United States and its allies approach the 2104 target date for removal of combat forces from Afghanistan. The United States also reviews every country's efforts to combat human trafficking, including the 80 percent of trafficking that victimizes women and girls, with a view toward, among other things, imposing sanctions on countries not working to eradicate the practice. United Nations (UN) member states are also focusing on women's rights: The unanimously adopted UN Millennium Development Goals, intended to end poverty by 2015, include achieving gender equality and improving maternal health as two of its eight goals, while also incorporating parity for women in its goals for education, nutrition, and HIV/AIDS prevention and treatment.

With this revised edition of *Global Issues: Women's Rights*, Natasha Thomsen has given readers the information they need to understand all of these issues, and more, in their historical and cultural context. Thomsen begins with an overview of women's rights issues around the world. Her discussion of what is at issue when we speak of women's rights makes clear how the question of those rights arise in every aspect of human life. Thomsen thoroughly and thoughtfully assesses the current worldwide status of women's civil, political, and legal rights, including suffrage; property and inheritance rights; women's right to educational access; their social and economic rights; employment rights, including measures taken to address sexual harassment and the needs of working mothers; the rights of women in the military; reproductive rights ranging from contraception to surrogate motherhood; the right to refuse female genital mutilation or cutting; the right to be free from violence, whether in the home or in a war-torn country; the rights denied in the practices of female infanticide and human trafficking; and the rights of women in the word's religions.

Thomsen then turns to an international history of women's struggle to secure these rights. Beginning with European and American women's individual and unified efforts in the 19th century, she proceeds to discuss the founding of the first international women's rights organization in 1904 and the early 20th-century founding of women's organizations in countries such as China, Egypt, India, Mexico, and Japan. Tracing the women's rights movement through the middle of the 20th century, she explores the efforts of newly organizing women to advocate for peace after World War I, the role of Allied- and Axis-nation women in World War II, and the impact of World War II on women's struggle for their rights. Thomsen's international history of the continuing struggle for women's rights concludes with a well-researched discussion of women rights as a truly global concern. She details the founding of the United Nations, the then-status of women within its founding nations (only 30 of the 51 founding nations, for example, granted women suffrage when the UN was founded in 1945), and UN initiatives to focus on women's rights. Those efforts, explored in depth, began with the 1946 UN Commission on the Status of Women and have included, among other initiatives, four world conferences on women, held over two decades (1975 in Mexico City; 1980 in Copenhagen; 1985 in Nairobi; and 1995 in

Beijing). As Thomsen discusses, these efforts have also resulted in the treaties intended to guarantee women's rights, including the 1979 Convention on the Elimination of All Forms of Discrimination Against Women (CEDAW), as well the founding of international organizations to allocate resources to women, including the United Nations Development Fund for Women (UNIFEM).

Despite all these efforts, many goals for women's rights were not met by the beginning of the 21st century, and Thomsen sets forth both the work that remains and the continuing struggle to complete that work. Her discussion is a far-reaching one, ranging from the growth of women's studies programs worldwide and their impact on individual women to the unanimous adoption by UN member nations of the UN Millennium Development Goals, which, among other things, target gender inequities as part of a landmark effort to eradicate poverty.

Following her overview of the women's rights issues and the international history of the women's rights movement, Thomsen closely examines women's rights in five countries: the United States, France, China, Afghanistan, and the Democratic Republic of the Congo. Each country's history and current status of women's rights is provided with well-researched and sensitive attention to the influence of culture; the differing viewpoints, if applicable, of women from different religious backgrounds; and the issues currently at the fore of the women's rights struggle in each country. Examining the United States, for example, Thomsen presents American women's many successes in their struggle for equal rights, including the winning of suffrage, the passage of property and equal credit laws, the passage of equal employment and educational opportunity laws, and a legal recognition of reproductive freedom. At the same time, she also explores the failure to ratify the Equal Rights Amendment, the low percentage of American women in elective office, the United States' position as the only developed country not to have ratified the UN Convention on the Elimination of All Forms of Discrimination against Women, and the continuing legislative and other challenges to legalized abortion.

Thomsen's discussion of women's rights in France, China, Afghanistan, and the Democratic Republic of the Congo is equally insightful and well-researched, and it includes a nuanced discussion of the most fraught women's rights issues facing each of these countries. Moreover, each of these discussions is set within its historical and cultural history. These difficult and often painful issues include debates in France about some customs affecting immigrant women, such as polygamy and female genital mutilation or cutting, as well as the wearing of the *hijab* by Muslim immigrants or French-native converts. They include the consequences in China of a state-mandated one-child policy, a policy that has not only resulted in 1.5 million "missing girls," but has also led to an increase in human trafficking as men face a "bride shortage" and resort to illegal means of securing a wife. They include the impact on Afghan girls and women of the Taliban legacy of being kept from education, free movement, and medical care that might be provided by a man—and the prospect that the Taliban may become part of the Afghan government after U.S. withdrawal from that county. They also include the experience of an estimated 5.4 million women in the Democratic Republic of the Congo, who have been targeted for rape and violence as part of a military strategy. In every one of these difficult but necessary discussions, Thomsen provides her reader with sufficient background to understand not only these issues but the societies from which they emerge.

Thomsen's text is augmented by primary source documents, ranging from contemporary newspaper and periodical accounts to legal documents and public speeches. In addition, *Women's Rights, Second Edition* contains resources to help the reader with further research, including brief biographies of key players, a "Facts and Figures" chapter that presents global statistics and statistics about the United States, France, China, Afghanistan, and the Democratic Republic of the Congo; a list of relevant organizations and agencies; an annotated bibliography; and an especially helpful guide on researching the women's rights movement. Women will surely continue to struggle for their full and equal rights, and the reader of this book will be well equipped to continue following that struggle.

Natasha Thomsen's *Global Issues: Women's Rights* will give any high school or college student and any interested person a thorough and sound understanding of women's rights around the world. I sincerely hope it gains the large readership it—and its subjects, the world's women—deserve.

Kathryn Cullen-DuPont
Brooklyn, New York

List of Acronyms

ACW	African Centre for Women
AD	active duty
AERA	American Equal Rights Association
ATA	Afghan Transitional Administration
AWSA	American Woman Suffrage Association
BLS	Bureau of Labor Statistics (U.S.)
BWOA	Black Women Organized for Action
CCDF	Child Care Development Fund
CEDAW	Convention on the Elimination of All Forms of Discrimination against Women
CIS	Commonwealth of Independent States
COYOTE	"Call Off Your Old Tired Ethics"
CSCE	Conference on Security and Co-operation in Europe
CPTP	Civilian Pilot Training Program
D&E	dilation and evacuation
D&X	dilation and extraction
DOB	Daughters of Bilitis
DOMA	Defense of Marriage Act
ECOA	Equal Credit Opportunity Act
ECPs	emergency contraception pills
EMILY's List	Early Money Is Like Yeast's List
ENDA	Employment Non-Discrimination Act
ERA	Equal Rights Amendment
EEOC	Equal Employment Opportunity Commission
EU	European Union
FACE	Freedom of Access to Clinic Entrances
FGM	female genital mutilation
FMLA	Family and Medical Leave Act
HIV/AIDS	human immunodeficiency virus/acquired immunodeficiency syndrome

IAW	International Association of Women
ICCPR	International Covenant on Civil and Political Rights
ICESCR	International Covenant on Economic, Social and Cultural Rights
ICPD	International Conference on Population and Development
ICW	International Council of Women
IDP	internally displaced person
IED	improvised explosive device
IGOs	intergovernmental organizations
ILO	International Labour Organization
INSTRAW	United Nations International Research and Training Institute for the Advancement of Women
IPV	intimate partner violence
IUD	intrauterine device
IWSA	International Women's Suffrage Alliance
LDNs	least developed nations
LGBT	lesbian, gay, bisexual, and transgender
MDGs	Millennium Development Goals
MP	member of parliament
MULPOC	Multinational Programming and Operational Centre
MWPA	Married Women's Property Act
NACW	National Association of Colored Women
NAF	National Abortion Federation
NASA	National Aeronautics and Space Administration
NATO	North Atlantic Treaty Organization
NAWSA	National American Woman Suffrage Association (1890)
NBFO	National Black Feminist Organization
NCVS	National Crime Victimization Survey
NCL	National Consumer's League
NGO	nongovernmental organization
NOW	National Organization for Women
NWP	National Women's Party
NWSA	National Woman Suffrage Association
OECD	Organisation for Economic Co-operation and Development
OSCE	Organization for Security and Cooperation in Europe
PaCS	Pacte civil de solidarité (civil solidarity pact)
PICW	President's Interagency Council on Women
PPFA	Planned Parenthood Federation of America
PPP	purchasing power parity
PRC	People's Republic of China
STDs	sexually transmitted diseases
UIFSA	Uniform Interstate Family Support Act

List of Acronyms

UNDP	United Nations Development Programme
UNESCO	United Nations Educational, Scientific and Cultural Organization
UNICEF	United Nations Children's Fund
UNIFEM	United Nations Development Fund for Women
UPAA	Uniform Premarital Agreement Act of 1983
USAID	U.S. Agency for International Development
VA	Veterans Administration
VAWA	Violence against Women Act
VOCA	Victims of Crime Act
VTVPA	Victims of Trafficking and Violence Protection Act of 2000
WASPs	Women's Airforce Service Pilots
WCTU	Woman's Christian Temperance Union
WHO	World Health Organization
WILPF	Women's International League for Peace and Freedom
WITCH	Women's International Terrorist Conspiracy from Hell
YWCA	Young Women's Christian Association
YWHA	Young Women's Hebrew Association

PART I

At Issue

1

Introduction

WOMEN'S RIGHTS: THE ISSUES

The call for women's rights began at different times in different countries, often coinciding with the demand for other rights, such as political freedom or economic reform. Countries redefining their futures have repeatedly kindled women's aspirations, beginning in the early 17th and 18th centuries in Europe and the United States, followed in the 19th and 20th centuries in many African, Asian, and Latin American countries as part of their struggle for independence, and into the 21st century in some countries of the Middle East.

The issues women have been dealing with have been similar worldwide but varied by the pace of change allowed by political climate and cultural beliefs. What began as largely a political and legal awareness by women in the suffrage movement, which fought for the right to be represented by vote, evolved into social and economic rights that included the rights of employment and reproduction rights, and the balance of these two domains.

Civil, Political, and Legal Rights

Women the world over have been foremost concerned with winning the right to vote in their countries. This basic power would then enable them to participate in elections of local officials and, in turn, have a voice on legislative issues that would affect their lives. Although women have played a role in various wars throughout history—from Bodaceia in the first century c.e. to the French Revolution, through World War II, and now in Iraq and Afghanistan—they did not have a significant part in the political process that caused or ended these wars. Women's demands for political participation enhanced their influence in other aspects of society, such as property ownership, inheritance rights, and access to higher education.

WOMEN'S RIGHTS

SUFFRAGE

The privilege of political and legal equity has been hard won where it is in effect. In 1893, New Zealand became the first country to grant women the right to vote, yet in other countries the struggle for suffrage and the right to stand for elections as a candidate continues even today. Although most accounts of how suffrage movements succeeded describe peaceful protests— such as picket lines, marches, and peace rallies—in many instances women were the victims of perpetrators of violence. In Great Britain and the United States in the early 1920s, for example, hunger strikes turned into forced feedings and marchers shattered windows.

One of the first aims of the United Nations once it began its existence after World War II was to extend suffrage rights to the women of all member nations. In 1952, the General Assembly adopted a resolution urging such action. By the 1970s, most member nations complied with the act, although subtle forms of discrimination persisted.

For example, although some countries in Asia and Oceania—such as Bangladesh, Pakistan, India, Indonesia, Sri Lanka, Philippines, and New Zealand—have had a large number of female heads of state and have enjoyed universal suffrage for decades, cultural barriers have often prevented women from fully exercising their voting privileges and penetrating political realms. In other countries, the right to vote has not always been continuously assured once it was won. The Taliban government in Afghanistan did not recognize women's suffrage during its time in power from 1994 until its fall in 2001 at the hands of international troops. Even now, warlords defend traditional views in rural areas of that country, making it difficult for women to reclaim their rights. An amendment to Kuwait's election law in a decision made in May 2005 enfranchised Kuwait's women over the age of 21 with the vote and the right to stand for election. The parliamentary elections were held in June 2006, and although none of the 27 female candidates was elected at the time, 60 percent of the Kuwaiti electorate was female. The situation improved by 2009, when four women were elected to the Kuwaiti legislature, becoming 8 percent of the parliament.

More recently, three Gulf Cooperation Council States, once resistant to political change, have begun to incorporate it. In the United Arab Emirates (UAE), a federation of seven states, where the parliament is officially appointed, neither men nor women have the right to vote or to stand for election in the country's 40-member Federal National Council (FNC). However, since 2005, an electoral college of 6,689 persons was established that includes 1,189 women (17 percent), and one woman was appointed to the FNC.[1] In Bahrain, where women have struggled to exercise their right to

4

vote since the country's constitution was amended in 2002, the first woman was elected to the lower house of Parliament in 2005. By 2009, 25 percent of the seats in Bahrain's parliament were held by women.[2] Both in Bahrain and the UAE, female judges were appointed in 2006 and 2008, respectively.[3]

In Saudi Arabia, men took part in the first local elections ever held in that country in 2005. Women were still not allowed to exercise the right to vote or stand for election, even though the election law of Saudi Arabia does not explicitly deny them that right. In 2011, the absolute monarchy announced it would allow women the right to vote and run in municipal elections.[4] The next municipal elections are scheduled for 2015. Oman restricts the privilege to vote to a certain number of citizens, mostly male. Brunei still does not allow women the vote. Restrictions in Bhutan (one vote per family) and Lebanon (optional voting for women, who must have attained a certain level of education) make it impossible for women to vote in large numbers.

The concept of political accountability to women has become a priority to most governments around the world. Perceived, in part, as a democratization of society, it is a conceivable way for women's issues to become matters of general public interest. With electoral system reforms, there has been in some countries an increase in the use of quotas as a way to guarantee fair representation by women at different levels of government.[5]

EQUAL RIGHTS

With the establishment of suffrage for women, the next logical step was to demand civil rights in other areas of living: from property ownership and job opportunities to financial and social rights. Depending on the country, this effort has mushroomed into a range of issues that include family leave and access to medical care.

The idea of equal rights for men and women, although starting with a simple premise naturally ensuing from the right to vote, would prove to be difficult in its interpretation. For example, some women's rights activists in the United States consider the Equal Rights Amendment a threat rather than an advantage, believing that the act could be used to fight the need for special employment considerations for pregnant women and mothers. The Equal Rights Amendment was first introduced to Congress in 1923, but it was not passed until 1972. It failed to win ratification by its 1982 expiration deadline and has been reintroduced a number of times since then, but without success.

One of the first steps toward equal rights of men and women has often been the establishment of equal opportunities in employment, as seen in the United States with the amendment of Title VII of the Civil Rights Act in 1964 and the establishment of the Equal Employment Opportunity Commission

(EEOC). Affirmative action, a policy to ensure equal representation by women, ethnic minorities, or other disadvantaged groups in the workplace, was put in place by the EEOC. It began when the then-president, Lyndon B. Johnson, issued two executive orders, 11246 and 11375, requiring government contractors and educational institutions receiving federal funds to "correct the effects of past and present discrimination."

In the United States, opponents have characterized affirmative action as "reverse discrimination." Many see enforced hiring of individuals, not solely for their skills, but also for filling of what they view as de facto quotas based on their sex or ethnicity, as counterproductive.

The concept of affirmative action was taken up by governments around the world as a way to obligate society to provide opportunities for minorities and women, especially within managerial-ranked positions. Denmark followed a more radical approach by adopting the 1988 Equality Act, which established equal rights of the sexes. Since 1997, the European Court of Justice has upheld the use of affirmative-action programs for women in the public sector, establishing a legal precedent for the nations of the European Union (EU). Since 1996, the EU has been tracking the application of the principle of equality—"gender mainstreaming"—to the national law of member states.[6] Australia and Great Britain have also implemented equal employment legislation that is largely responsible for women's access to management-level positions.

PROPERTY OWNERSHIP AND INHERITANCE RIGHTS

The ability of women to own property is also a right applied with varying degrees of cultural acceptance worldwide. The adoption of the Convention on the Elimination of All Forms of Discrimination against Women (CEDAW) on December 18, 1979, by the United Nations (UN) General Assembly has been a driving force behind asserting women's property rights. This "Treaty for the Rights of Women" has received ratification, as of October 2010, by 186 of the 192 UN member countries. The United States has signed but not ratified the treaty.

In order to own property in some Arab and Islamic countries such as Saudi Arabia and Iran, women are required to have either male proxy representation or permission from a male relative. In Afghanistan, a woman's right to inheritance varies depending on the application of the Islamic law in different regions, from only the trousseau (personal possessions of a bride) to a portion of the father's land. On the other hand, under Islamic law, Muslim women have, for the most part, been able to retain their own belongings and could even specify conditions in their marriage contracts, such as the right to divorce if their husband takes another wife. In contrast, until the late 1800s women's property in Western societies was given to their husbands when they married.

Property ownership is also a central issue in countries with a large rural population. In Kenya, where two-thirds of the population is rural, women receive the rights to land through husbands, fathers, and sons. Privatization during colonial rule in the 1950s led to land registration, making the process more difficult for a woman to exercise tenure over property registered in her husband's name. In China, inheritance and property rights apply equally to men and women, but in practice, they are dependent on various factors. Often, land is owned by the state but rights to its use is extended to a family, a right that becomes nebulous if the husband dies.

Property ownership is also linked to the issues of severe climate changes and migration. The World Health Organization (WHO) estimated that more than 140,000 excess deaths had occurred annually by 2004 from extreme climate condition changes since the 1970s, in which women often withstand the worst of disease and poor health.[7] In addition, displaced and refugee women are often challenged without the proper paperwork to recover property lost during sudden evacuations.

ACCESS TO EDUCATION

Education has been among the first priorities of the women's movement in most countries. In the United States and Europe, women's access to education was limited to primary schooling until the late 1800s, except among the rich. When political rights proved extremely difficult to attain, women rallied for the right to enter higher educational institutions. By the 1950s, women in Europe and the United States had access to a college education, but domestic duties were still expected to be their priority. This emphasis shifted in the 1970s, as women won political and legal rights to the same jobs as men but were often required to have had more education than men.

Women from other nations joined this rally for the fundamental right to be educated as the movement increasingly became more international. By the end of the 20th century, women had access to higher education in most countries around the world with the exception of some Asian and African countries. Women's poverty, disease, and illiteracy in sub-Saharan, Asian, and Latin American countries have been perceived as a direct result of their lack of education, leading to the universal "Education for All" program within the Dakar Framework for Action and the UN Millennium Development Goals (MDGs). The programs seek to ensure that "by 2015 all children, particularly girls, children in difficult circumstances and those belonging to ethnic minorities, have access to and complete free and compulsory primary education of good quality."[8]

By the dawn of the 21st century, girls' primary school enrollments had significantly improved, especially in some of the lowest-income countries of sub-Saharan Africa, and South and West Asia. Gender and educational quality measures are increasingly visible in national education plans. With improved access to education was a decrease of the illiteracy rate among women, giving them better employment, health, educational, political, economic, and cultural opportunities. Eradicating illiteracy is considered a strategy of human rights by Human Rights Watch, a privately funded nongovernmental organization (NGO) founded in 1978. Almost a fifth of the world's adult population, an estimated 771 million, is illiterate, and two-thirds of them are women.[9] The United Nations Literacy Decade (2003–12) is focusing on women's literacy as a crucial element in establishing gender equality and ending poverty and "gender apartheid."

Social, Employment, and Economic Rights

Today, more women are employed in the world than ever before in the history of humankind. In addition, the role of women substantially changed in the latter half of the 20th century because of wars, decolonization, and lifestyle changes. The decolonization that was achieved by the national movements of the 20th century led to reforms that often included the liberation of women from traditional boundaries of home and responsibilities and their right to take on duties as far away from home as the military front.

SOCIAL CHANGES

More women were being paid for work in the latter half of the 20th century than ever before, including married women who had children. One possible reason for this trend is the increase in job opportunities for women associated with greater educational attainment. The other is that men are not making as much as they did in the past, in proportion to the increase in cost of living, leading to the need for more income.

As women began to enter the workforce in greater numbers, their traditional role and duties did not adjust as quickly. Women struggled with the need to balance duties at home and in the workplace and to define themselves as either "housewives" or "working women."

Women's social roles have changed as a result of their new participation in the workplace, concerns about job discrimination, and managing of dual careers. By the same token, men's roles in many societies have also changed, expanding to include domestic responsibilities and gender awareness in nearly all aspects of living.

Some cultures are dealing with radical changes to custom because of the country's liberation or women's enfranchisement, and women stake out a variety of positions in response. For instance, the practice by Muslim women of wearing burqas has led to debates inside Muslim countries and foreign powers on the privileges of wearing them. When France passed a law in 2005 that forced young Muslim women and girls not to wear their traditional head scarf to schools, it stirred heated public debate, as many women argued that a woman should have the right to choose the customs she wants to follow. Meanwhile, in Afghanistan, where women had to wear the burqa by law under the Taliban, the debate is around women not having to wear them, if they so choose.

Another area of social change involves the choice of using a married or "maiden" (also "birth") name. In most Muslim countries, women have traditionally been allowed to keep their own surnames after marriage. But in countries where this right is dictated by common law and does not require legal action, such as England, the United States, and much of Canada, choosing to keep one's birth name was rare until the mid-19th century. The act itself has grown to be more of a practical issue with the emergence of the professional woman who uses her maiden name professionally and her married name socially. This trend shifts as each generation of women reconsiders its social and professional priorities. In a 2009 survey among women in the United States, 71 percent of respondents took their spouse's last name, holding steady from 2000.[10] Meanwhile, hyphenated surnames dropped from 21 to 8 percent.[11] Chinese and Korean women keep their maiden names after marriage, although Chinese women who live abroad might insert their husbands' surnames as a middle name. A married woman in Taiwan also uses her maiden name and appends her husband's name only when she wants people to know her marital status.

Most countries consider age 18 the legal minimal age for marriage for both men and women, which is also upheld by the UN Committee on the Elimination of Discrimination against Women. However, in some countries the legal minimal age is ignored as a result of poverty and traditional customs. The tradition of early marriage is most common in South Asia and sub-Saharan Africa and is often tied to lower education enrollment of girls in primary education, higher poverty rates, birth rates, and death rates, as well as being found in countries with a higher incidence of conflict and civil strife. This is the case in the Democratic Republic of the Congo (DRC), Niger, Afghanistan, Congo, and Mali, where more than half of girls ages 15–19 years are married.

Sometimes considered as "forced marriages," international organizations are watching this tradition closely. For example, the Organisation for Economic Co-operation and Development (OECD) reported on early marriages that occur before a girl is 20 years old as one of several indicators concerning gender treatment in developing countries. The world marriage database maintained by the UN Department of Economic and Social Affairs (UNDESA) Population Division reported 71.8 percent of girls in Bangladesh and 56.3 percent of girls in India were married by the age of 19 in 2008, even though it is illegal in both countries for girls under the age of 18 to be wed.[12] In Yemen, half of all girls are married before they are 18, and well over a third before they are 15. Attention to the problem was raised by a news story in 2010 that showed how an 11-year-old girl found a means for winning a divorce.[13] In Niger, where marriage is governed by custom and many communities begin to marry their children at puberty, 77.6 percent of all girls were married by the age of 19.[14]

THE "WORKING WOMAN"

Although women have been part of the labor force since humankind began, a woman's role has traditionally been largely associated with domestic duties of family care and child rearing. This perception began to change with industrialization, as women began to spend part of their time at paid work outside the home. France was among the first countries to engage women's participation in the labor force during the Industrial Revolution. The role of the so-called new woman at the end of the 19th century in Europe and the United States continued to evolve at a rapid pace during World War II and the 1950s.

In 1972, the assertion of Title VII of the Equal Employment Opportunities Act in the United States made it clear that employers could no longer discriminate in their hiring and employment practices on the basis of sex. Meanwhile, opponents of this act argued that problems with children were rising because of mothers who were no longer "on the job."

The idea of the "working woman" did not become an accepted notion in China until after 1949, when the socialist government began implementing measures to assist mothers with the double burden of home and work. With increased mobility, women—even in rural areas—are today participating more in industry and having a greater say in family decision making.

The urban, skilled, and educated woman who arose in Afghanistan in the 1950s and 1960s suffered a series of severe setbacks with the Soviet invasion in 1979, the subsequent civil war, and the establishment of the Taliban government in 1996. Even today, since the removal of the Taliban by international security forces in 2001, professional women are challenged by strict Muslim rules that tend to safeguard tradition.

The image of women in Muslim countries is diverse, however. Sheikha Lubna al-Qasimi (1958–) has been serving as the United Arab Emirates minister for foreign trade since 2004, the first woman in her country to hold a cabinet post. She maintains that 30 percent of management positions and between 30 and 40 percent of the country's wealth are in the hands of women, and more than 70 percent of higher education students in the Middle East are women.[15]

African nations have followed a different trajectory, often being under colonial rule—especially sub-Sahara Africa—until the 1950s and '60s. Women were often subject to native customs that disempowered their property rights and education. Here, women have known a largely rural lifestyle, with limited professional opportunities within a patrilineal and patrilocal community.

Of the estimated 3.179 billion workers in the global labor force in 2009, 1.2 billion, or 40.5 percent, were women, an increase from 39.9 percent in 1998.[16] However, women still face higher unemployment rates, at 6.3 percent in 2008, as compared to a rate of 5.9 percent for men; receive lower wages than men; and represent 60 percent of the world's 550 million working poor.[17] The gender gap has narrowed with the recessionary pressures from the global financial crisis that began in December 2007. In 2008, unemployment increased by 4.9 million people, reaching 33.7 million people; men accounted for 65 percent of that increase.[18]

When looking at what occupations women now hold, the picture varies widely in different parts of the globe. Services surpassed agriculture (37.5 percent) in 2007 as the primary sector of global employment. Except in Asia and Africa, the world has been shifting toward the service and industry sectors, which currently account for 40.4 and 22.1 percent, respectively, of global employment opportunities.[19] Within the service sectors, women still primarily perform community, social, and personal services while men secure the better-paying jobs in finance, business, and real estate. The potential for women in industry to thrive on better wages and skill development is also limited by the fact that employers still prefer to hire male workers. Now, less than five years from the MDG of achieving parity by 2015, many estimate that most regions in the world will not reach this goal. Furthermore, it is estimated that it will take five years for the total labor force to return to pre-crisis levels of unemployment. Of note was that young people, ages 15 to 24 years, are experiencing a high unemployment rate, at 14 percent.[20]

According to a 2009 report by the International Labour Organization (ILO), the trend of women's activity in the labor market varies by country. Overall, the trend of increased rates of young women's labor force participation noted in the 1980s and early 1990s has slowed in the non-EU countries of central and eastern Europe; the Commonwealth of Independent States (CIS) countries of Armenia, Azerbaijan, Georgia, Kyrgyz Republic, Moldova, Uzbekistan, and Tajikistan; East Asia; and sub-Saharan Africa; and even stopped in regions of Southeast Asia and South Asia. The number of working women actually increased in Latin America and the Caribbean between 1998 and 2008, from 44.2 percent to 52.6 percent of the employment to population ratio, as well as in the Middle East, where female participation grew from 20.5 percent of the labor force population in 1998 to about 24.7 percent in 2008.[21] In North Africa, the growth was even greater, from 22.6 in 1998 to 27.0 in 2008.

In most economies, women still tend to earn about 17 percent less than what men earn for the same job.[22] In lower-paying industries, women earn less than male workers, with the discrepancy depending on the country. In many economies, male workers might earn between 8 and 20 percent more than women earn for the same job, even though these professions are generally considered typical for women.[23] Furthermore, most women on average occupy more of the lower-paying positions in services and agriculture, while fewer women than men work in industry, a pattern that contributes to a significant wage disparity between the sexes.[24]

Alongside these changes evolved different perceptions of the working woman, with her expectations growing beyond just equal pay and social benefits. She was also seeking stature. Although women still represent a small portion of management levels and few receive high salaries equal to those of their male counterparts, they are nevertheless more present in the workforce than ever before worldwide.

Beginning in the 1980s, women in management have been most noticeable in industrialized nations. In the United States, England, and Australia, more women have been able to make their way into management positions under enforced equal opportunity laws, but not without being challenged by office politics and status quo management. Issues such as sexual harassment and difficulty in achieving a balance with home management and child rearing have also contributed to the slow rate of growth.

In the United States, 43 percent of female legislators, senior officials, and managers were women in 2009, while within the European countries, between 30 and 36 percent of women held these positions. Most European Union countries have enacted legislation for equal opportunity, but the level of enforcement varies by country. Still, high-profile positions, such as network news anchors, are starting to become available to women all over the world, and this trend may lead to more opportunities for women to hold influential positions.

At first, it was believed that women's lack of access to managerial positions was due to their lack of work experience in general. Now that women have over 25 years of exposure, it has become apparent that the problem has more to do with entrenched customs. Although the number of business degrees conferred upon women in the United States may have slightly declined at the bachelor degree level between 2002–03 and 2007–08, from 50.5 to 49.0 percent, respectively, 44.5 percent of master's degrees in business were conferred upon women in 2007–08, up from 41.0 percent in 2002–03. The number of degrees conferred upon women at the doctorate degree candidate level grew significantly by 93.1 percent.[25] Numbers have peaked at 44 percent in medical and law schools. Among the reasons more women are not pursuing degrees in business may be a lack of female role models, incompatibility of careers in business with work/life balance, lack of confidence in math skills, and a lack of encouragement by employers, according to one study.[26] Nevertheless, women's ability to share and delegate power, a skill developed from raising families, has been cited as a reason why they may make naturally good managers.

SEXUAL HARASSMENT

In hand with increasing employment has risen the opportunity for discrimination against women in the workplace. As women have fought to establish themselves within the workplace, they have also had to define inappropriate behavior that affects them physically and emotionally as sexual harassment. In spite of legislation to protect women against sexual harassment, a pattern has emerged by which women often do not report cases because of fear of losing their jobs or positions.

The ILO recognized the implications of sexual harassment as a labor condition that negatively impacted women and their work performance in a 1985 Resolution of the International Labor Conference. Since then, sexual harassment is considered a form of violence, discrimination, and health risk, defined in CEDAW's General Recommendation 19, Article 11, to include

such unwelcome sexually determined behavior as physical contact and advances, sexually colored remarks, showing pornography and sexual demand, whether by words or actions. Such conduct can be humiliating and may constitute a health and safety problem; it is discriminatory when the woman has reasonable grounds to believe that her objection would disadvantage her in connection with her employment, including recruitment or promotion, or when it creates a hostile working environment.[27]

In spite of international support from the ILO and the UN, many countries still regard sexual harassment, alongside domestic violence, as taboo subjects, with no national legislation in place to address them. About a third of industrialized global economies had laws on sexual harassment by 1992, while others classified sexual harassment under wrongful dismissal, tort, and criminal laws. A 2003 report from UNIFEM revealed that 14 of 186 countries (7.5 percent) had specific legislation and 45 countries (24 percent) had nonspecific legislation in place to address sexual harassment.[28]

Australia, Canada, Denmark, Ireland, New Zealand, Sweden, the United Kingdom, and the United States are among countries that have equal employment opportunity laws. In the United States, where the Equal Employment Opportunity Commission has jurisdiction over sexual harassment cases, this issue won center stage in the 1990s as a series of high-profile sexual harassment cases made their way into the public eye. One poll in the United States indicated that four of 10 women were being victims of some kind of sexual harassment at work and nearly half of all women said they could perceive evidence of it at some point during their professional careers. This is about on par with similar reports of an estimated 40 to 50 percent of employed women in the European Union.

This percentage is lower in Denmark, where the Equal Treatment Act has been in effect since 1978 and the Gender Equality Act since 2003 to reinforce the protection. There, an estimated 15 percent of women have experienced some form of sexual harassment on the job.

In China, although a law exists to deter sexual harassment, a woman's fear of losing her job frequently overrides her legal right to report incidences. This is also true of women in most countries.

Japan, Switzerland, the United Kingdom, and the United States have applied tort law—a legal wrong for which the court usually offers remedy, such as monetary damages—to sexual harassment cases.

Criminal law in some countries applies to extreme cases of sexual harassment, such as assault or indecent behavior. France is among the few countries to have passed a criminal law related to sexual harassment.

WORKING MOTHERS AND CHILD CARE

With improved day care facilities and job protection under family leave legislation in many developed countries, marriage and children seem to have less of an effect on the percentage of women who are paid workers today than they had in the 1950s. As a result of the growth of the labor market, competitive trade, and increased pace of industrialization, this trend has now become global, radically changing women's lives the world over. Women are increasingly dependent on child care services and maternity benefits.

Beginning with the French *école maternelle* at the turn of the century, and the Russian model for state support to working mothers during World

War I, day care services today range from sophisticated ones in Scandinavia and continental western Europe to basic and mediocre ones in the United States, Canada, the United Kingdom, and Japan. The quality of available care is often tied to economic factors, which include the total salary the two parents must earn to be able to afford better care.

In most countries, women's maternity benefits are left to private enterprise and some legislation at the government level. Child care is often an essential component of government-based health care systems in nations with a social welfare tradition—including the states of the former Soviet Union (USSR), Europe, Latin America, and Asia—where child care and working women are supported by politics, family, and society. Women in Canada are protected by a government-based medical system that gives them up to 18 weeks of maternity leave with employment insurance maternity benefits for 15 weeks, depending on the province. Most European countries, especially the Scandinavian countries, also offer paid leave. Women in Denmark receive up to 60 weeks' paid leave compared with 16 weeks in France, Netherlands, and Spain.[29] By comparison, the United States requires only 12 weeks of unpaid leave. In addition to Papua New Guinea, Lesotho (South Africa), and Swaziland, the United States has no national maternity program.

PERSONAL FINANCE AND MICROCREDIT

While cultivating their roles as a provider, women were finding fewer reasons for being declared a dependent of family or spouse and began seeking financial independence. Women's desire to do business and be self-reliant also meant having access to and control over their own credit and bank accounts.

In the 1970s, women around the globe began to organize themselves into associations of entrepreneurs or bankers in order to enhance their economic status and have an impact on economic policies. The right to have their own credit cards and bank accounts without a husband's approval was granted to married women in the United States in 1974. The ability to borrow money for investment led to economic improvements for women and often to positive social change in general as women used their newfound economic freedom to the benefit of their families. "Women's banks"—whereby women are encouraged to put their funds in a bank that will support fellow women's investments in small businesses—were started in the 1970s in different parts of the globe. Implementation of women's banks was especially successfully in India, where female trade union workers and poor self-employed women were forming their own banks. The successful paradigm in India was later implemented in Africa in the 1990s. One experience in a small suburb in the

Republic of Benin saw its bank membership grow in 1992 from 15 women to 2,000 women, with a combined $20,000 in savings and $40,000 in loans, and a 99 percent reimbursement rate.[30] A similar trend arose in Japan in the late 1990s as an alternate mode for women whose needs to finance businesses were overlooked during times of recession or in the name of traditional banking approaches. Another example is Women's World Banking, founded by the former World Bank executive Nancy Berry. It has made a difference to many women, including a farmer in Kenya who now exports roses and a Bosnian woman who now owns three food shops. With some 18 million women worldwide receiving microfinance loans, the United Nations dubbed 2005 the Year of Microcredit. An initiative launched in 1997 by 137 countries at the Microcredit Summit in Washington, D.C., reported achieving a goal of reaching 154.8 million people in the world by the end of 2007, of whom 109.8 million were women.[31] One measure of success to be implemented soon after was the progress of small business owners beyond the $1 per day income. The financial crisis in 2008 and 2009, with attendant fluctuations in gas and food prices, had a sobering effect on microfinancing—from discontinuation of credit, inability of clients to repay their loans from lost business, and microlenders profiting from inflated interest rates.[32] Political competition has also interfered, such as between Sheikh Hasina, a female Bangladesh prime minister, and Nobel Peace Prize winner Muhammad Yunus, a passionate advocate for microfinancing through his establishment of the Grameen Bank.

The African Centre for Women (ACW) organized a meeting in Kampala, Uganda, in 1994 to evaluate the establishment of an African bank for women. The meeting was attended by high-level experts invited from Burundi, Cameroon, Ghana, Kenya, Mali, Nigeria, Sierra Leone, Uganda, and Zimbabwe. Their expertise ranged from finance and banking to economic planning and improvement of women's access to financial resources. Observers from the United Nations Development Programme (UNDP), the United Nations International Research and Training Institute for the Advancement of Women (INSTRAW), and the Lusaka-based Multinational Programming and Operational Centre (MULPOC) also attended. The feasibility study conducted during the meeting helped to establish the base for a financial institution that could cater to specific needs of African women at all economic levels, defined the mode of operation, and identified financial sources for getting it started.

Climate change has also contributed to a growth in female-run businesses and collectives from Mali to Bangladesh to Nepal. Women share resources—financial, technological, and knowledge-based—in farmer's clubs and land purchases to overcome poor living conditions.[33]

Introduction

ENROLLMENT IN THE MILITARY

Women's involvement in the military was not part of international discourse until 1961, when the first North Atlantic Treaty Organization (NATO) Conference of Senior Women Officers of the Alliance with delegates from Denmark, the Netherlands, Norway, the United Kingdom, and the United States took place in Copenhagen, Denmark. Since then, the committee has grown with the NATO alliance, in which 25 nations are represented today. Iceland is the only country missing since there is no military in that country.

Since the end of the cold war era in the early 1990s, many nations have considered doing away with male-conscription armies and maintaining volunteer armies of men and women. In the countries where military personnel include females, women often occupy noncombatant roles as physicians, lawyers, pilots, paratroopers, military police, air traffic controllers, heavy equipment operators, photojournalists, and forklift operators.[34] Canada, Belgium, Denmark, and Norway began allowing women to choose their occupations, including combat in the army, in the 1990s. In Britain, women were allowed to join air and sea combat units, but not ground units.

Debates turn around women's ability to fight, gender integrated training, provocation of discipline problems among male members by the presence of women, and the question of whether women add to or detract from the capacity of its armed forces. The issue of equal rights becomes enmeshed with issues of military strategy.

Italy was the stage for a conference about this topic in 1992 as it was the only NATO country at the time to prohibit women from active duty (AD), although they were allowed to participate in the other roles mentioned. Italy is still reluctant to allow women to serve in positions that might bring them nearer to combat within the armed forces. In 2005, 1 percent of Italy's armed forces were women.[35] The U.S. Department of Defense defines AD as full-time duty soldiers and sailors. Members of the reserve components and national guard may serve on AD or training duty but are considered separate parts of the military.

In recent years, women's enrollment in military service academies for officer training and service in active combat has sparked public debate in several countries, including the United States, Australia, Canada, Algeria, Zimbabwe, and Nicaragua. Although women traditionally had to fulfill military service requirements in Israel, they can be exempted for religious, physical, or psychological reasons. NATO has been closely examining the process of integrating women into its armed forces since the late 1970s.[36]

The way wars are fought is changing, however, with the added element of terrorism, which does not discriminate by gender. The recruitment of women as suicide bombers in terrorist plots within the Palestinian/Israeli conflict is one example of how women's role in war is changing.[37] In the more recent conflicts in Iraq and Afghanistan (2002–2010 and 2001–present, respectively), enough U.S. female soldiers have suffered casualties that they are being trained to handle firearms while they do their "support" jobs as drivers, medics, and the like.[38]

Gender Roles, Family Health, and Sexuality

An unprecedented number of social choices now exist for women in developed countries. This, in turn, has dramatically altered the roles women and men adopt in every aspect of life—from how wars are fought to lifestyle choices. The progress made by developing and medium-developed nations will no doubt accelerate to include many of these choices, even at the risk of radically departing from tradition.

HUMAN RIGHTS

The core right of a person to own his or her body is taken for granted in many countries now. However, not so long ago women were thought of as property, or "chattel," of their fathers or husbands. This notion persists in some nations and is upheld by tradition in many African cultures. Some, such as the Taliban in Afghanistan, defend the tradition in the name of protecting women and girls from societal pressures or defacement.

Whether women should have a choice over the destiny of their bodies is also still very much debated. A woman can choose where and how to experience childbirth—in the home or hospital, as a cesarean section or vaginal birth. She can also elect to terminate pregnancy prematurely or use her reproductive capacity as a means of income and/or to benefit others, as is the case with surrogate motherhood (often referred to as "womb for hire," but sometimes involving family members or friends without financial remuneration). The rights and access to these choices vary, not only from country to country, but according to cultural and religious preferences. Choice is not always an option, with women dying or experiencing obstetric fistula from lack of skilled medical assistance to perform C-sections in rural Africa, in Asia, and the Middle East.

DEFINING ROLES WITHIN THE FAMILY AND THE WORKPLACE

The family has evolved dramatically in developed countries since the 1970s, causing gender roles to be redefined. Higher education and increased job opportunities have caused both women and men to delay marriage. Smaller households, delayed childbearing, declining birth rates, increased divorce and single parenthood, and family mobility are all contributing factors as well. In eastern Asia, western Europe, and most developed countries, there are few early marriages (below 2 percent of the population), with the average age for first marriage between 25 and 30 in 2000. In transitional economies in eastern Europe and central and western Asia, most women are marrying in their early 20s, a trend that has been maintained since the early 1990s. Young people are marrying at an older age than their parents in nearly every country of the world.[39]

With the increasing number of women in the workplace since the latter part of the 20th century, the role of man and woman, or husband and wife, in the family setting has changed dramatically since the 1950s. As women have increasingly occupied the workplace, they have expanded their roles from child rearing to sharing the identity of "breadwinner," or earning income outside the home, with men. By the same token, men are participating more in child rearing, albeit still not to the same extent as women. This transition has been more evident in some countries than in others. For instance, Denmark leads the way as a model for the modern couple's equal division of labor. There, men and women spend nearly the same amount of time with housework and caring for family members (three hours per day), with a one- to two-hour difference between them, while couples in other countries average between four and six hours per day, with women still doing the majority of the work.[40]

As a result of these changes, comparing male and female behavior and physical gestures became a topic for scientific, social, and economic study that often centered around the question of whether it is a person's (biological) sex or (socially determined) gender that shapes his or her behavior. At the start of the 21st century, men's studies developed into a formal academic area of study in Western countries, focusing on men's roles in the workplace and family as well as men's health and masculinity.

The UN proclamation of 1994 as the Year of the Family around the theme "Family: Resources and Responsibilities in a Changing World" was largely an attempt to preserve some of the values of family structure, while bearing in mind the need for gender roles to evolve. These issues were explored at the International Conference on Population and Development in that same year.

ACCESS TO MEDICAL CARE

An issue that moved to the forefront in the 1990s and early 2000s for women around the globe is access to health care. This ranges from access to basic care such as immunizations and screenings for pregnancy, human immunodeficiency virus/acquired immunodeficiency syndrome (HIV/AIDS), and other sexually transmitted diseases (STDs), to more sophisticated tests to diagnose heart disease, breast cancer, and bone density.

The socioeconomic consequences of women's low access to health care, especially to HIV treatment, have been magnified in developing countries. Even though the annual number of AIDS deaths globally has declined from a peak of 2.1 million in 2004 to 1.8 million in 2009, the number of infections in women is growing in certain countries.[41] Worldwide, 52 percent of the 32.8 million adults living with HIV were women in 2009.[42] Sub-Saharan Africa is the most affected region, with 68 percent of all people living with HIV—the majority being women, at 60 percent—and 72 percent (1.3 million) of total AIDS-related deaths in 2009.[43]

The United Nation Children's Fund (UNICEF) reported in 2005 that, worldwide, about 1 percent of pregnant women were HIV-positive, with a 35 percent chance that their child would be born HIV-positive if no prevention measures were taken. By 2008, it was estimated that there were 42,000 deaths due to HIV/AIDS among pregnant women.[44] The percentage of women receiving antiretroviral care to prevent mother-to-child transmission has significantly increased between 2005 and 2009, from 15 to 50–80 percent respectively, especially in sub-Saharan Africa, where it is most needed.[45]

High prevalence rates were also occurring in heavily populated countries such as India and China, where the number of people living with HIV infection in 2009 was estimated at 2.4 million and 740,000, respectively.[46]

Countries that have been conservative in acknowledging the presence of AIDS, regarding it as taboo for public discussion, such as in the Caribbean and Latin America, are beginning to emerge with public campaigns and greater support from churches. These countries are coming to terms with having one of the highest rates of adults and children living with HIV in the world, at 240,000 and 1.4 million, respectively, in 2009.[47] The price of waiting has been paid by the spread in Caribbean countries of HIV among women and girls, who make up the majority of people living with HIV. The percentage of the population with HIV who are women and girls grew from 24 to 57 (137,000) between 1990 and 2009. AIDS is considered the primary cause of mortality for adults under the age of 50 in Caribbean countries.[48]

The problem also exists in developed countries. In the United States, 1.2 million people live with HIV, and as in sub-Saharan Africa, the rate of infection among women is increasing, with women accounting for 27 percent of annual new HIV infections and 25 percent of those living with HIV. Sharing injected drugs and having unprotected sex are the two leading causes. African Americans and Hispanics in the United States, who represent a little more than one-quarter of all people in the United States, account for 63 percent of people living with HIV reported in 2006, according to the U.S. Centers for Disease Control and Prevention.[49] New HIV infections occur disproportionately by race, ethnicity, and gender in some countries, such as the United States, where 45 percent of 2006 infections were in the African-American population, with black females being 19 times more likely to acquire HIV than white women. Similarly, a growing proportion of new infections are occurring in women in Canada and Europe as a result of unprotected sex.[50]

Prevention and education can make a marked difference in outcomes involving HIV and AIDS. A pregnant woman can decrease the chances of passing HIV to her baby by 50 percent by taking antiretroviral drugs. Her receiving the drugs thus has a disproportionate effect on preventing infection among children.

While high-income countries rate ischemic heart disease, cerebrovascular disease, lung cancer, lower-respiratory disease, and breast cancer among the 10 leading causes of death and disability for women, low- and middle-income nations report these and HIV/AIDs as the leading cause of death.[51]

The quality of medical care and access to it varies from country to country. Additionally, women's access to health care services is influenced by social customs. Prohibitive factors include women's low societal status and not being allowed to receive treatment from male practitioners. In some countries, the government enlists the help of women to administer basic services. In Iran, Women Health Volunteers is a network of 100,000 women who directly aid the government by providing health and hygiene services (i.e., vaccinations and family-planning supplies) in urban areas like Tehran.

In most countries, their access to health care and benefits is largely related to economic stature. Health disparity—or the unequal treatment of women based on social, economic, and ethnic background—is being discussed on an international scale by the World Health Organization and other international organizations, as one of the eight MDGs adopted at the 2000 Millennium Summit. This discussion appears to have had some influence on maternal mortality. The estimated 358,000 maternal deaths that occurred worldwide in 2008 were a 34 percent decline from 1990 levels. However, sub-Saharan Africa still bears the burden of most of these deaths, at 87 percent (313,000). Eleven countries (Afghanistan, Bangladesh, the Democratic Republic of the Congo, Ethiopia, India, Indonesia, Kenya, Nigeria, Pakistan, Sudan, and the United Republic of Tanzania), made up 65 percent of all maternal deaths in 2008.[52]

SELF-DETERMINED REPRODUCTIVE RIGHTS: ACCESS TO CONTRACEPTIVES

The development of contraceptives and access to them has allowed women of reproductive age across the globe to exercise their rights to reproduce and have children or abstain from having them. With the advent of safe and efficacious methods of family planning since the 1960s, the use of contraception—including female sterilization, the intrauterine device (IUD), and oral contraceptives—has steadily risen to 62.9 percent among married and partnered women worldwide.[53] The initial reservations of the 1970s about the Pill and the IUD have been relieved by decades of research from the pharmaceutical industry, governments, and independent organizations, which are now moving in the direction of offering increased options to women. This trend has, in turn, been perceived as a means for empowering women by giving them better control over their lives.

On the other hand, heavily populated areas, such as Africa, India, and China, have also introduced contraception as a coercive means to control the population. Women's groups rallied for greater emphasis on strategies that encouraged people's participation in programs to exercise their voluntary rights to use contraceptives. Curiously, the 1994 International Conference on Population and Development in Cairo, Egypt, did not emphasize contraceptive use, in spite of the growing AIDS epidemic. Condoms, for instance, are considered an important and effective measure in HIV prevention—a fact that was acknowledged by the Vatican's Pope Benedict in a November 2010 interview when it was stated "condoms may be acceptable in some limited circumstances."[54]

By 2005, contraceptive use by women who were married or in a partnership varied dramatically by region and wealth distribution within the region. As many as 106 million married women in developing countries were still lacking access to contraceptives.[55] Contraceptive access has been slow, if not stagnant, in the world's least developed nations (LDNs)—largely made up of sub-Saharan, Asian (including Afghanistan), and Oceanian countries, and Haiti; as a result, the fertility in these countries averaged 103 births per 1,000 women ages 15 to 19 compared with the global rate of 52 births for that age group. In Europe, anywhere from 56 to 69 percent of the female population of reproductive age used contraceptives.[56]

A major factor in contraceptive use is wealth. On average, the poorest women are four times less likely to use contraception than the wealthiest. Access to contraceptives, however, is also tempered by cultural and religious beliefs both within the United States, where an estimated 95 percent of women have used some form of birth control during the course of their life, and worldwide. Several new methods are being developed, including male hormonal products, which are adding to the choices available in wealthier nations.

The global fertility rate is at 2.5 children, and family size has fallen about 50 percent with the widespread use of contraception in both developing and developed countries as of 2009.[57]

Introduction

INVOLUNTARY EUGENIC STERILIZATIONS

Another means of controlling reproduction is sterilization. In women this procedure is usually done by tying the fallopian tubes (tubal ligation). Although the right to choose sterilization as a form of birth control is an issue in some countries, it is involuntary sterilization, usually employed by the government as a means to control birth rates, that has received public scrutiny.

In the United States, the issue of forced sterilizations was highly publicized in the 1920s with the case of *Buck v. Bell.* In 1924, the state of Virginia adopted a statute authorizing the compulsory sterilization of the mentally retarded for the protection and health of the state. Carrie Buck was a dependent in the care of the state of Virginia. In 1927, the Supreme Court decided that it was in the state's interest to have her sterilized. Virginia's eugenics law was partially repealed in 1974 and completely repealed in 1979, but *Buck v. Bell* has yet to be overturned.

During the reign of Indira Gandhi (1917–84), India used forced vasectomies, a form of sterilization, on fathers; that policy led to public resentment of family planning in that country that persists today. Family planning has since focused on women, with sterilization and contraception programs, but educational campaigns have been hampered by illiteracy and poverty.

SURROGATE MOTHERHOOD

Ten to 15 percent of married couples worldwide are unable to have children. As a solution to being unable to reproduce an offspring, surrogacy, also known as "womb for hire," has become one of many assisted reproductive technologies. Surrogate motherhood dates back to biblical times, when Sarah, the wife of Abraham, could not have children in the first decades of her marriage. She gave her handmaid, Hagar, to her husband to produce a child.

Assisted reproduction has become a field of science that includes the technologies involved in surrogate motherhood. The act of a woman's bearing a child for an infertile woman or couple is slowly gaining acceptance. Ethical issues are numerous: from the pros and cons of using excess embryos from medical research, to the possibility that the surrogate will decide to keep the baby, to the legal question of handing over a child after delivery for a fee.

In the United States, surrogate mothers are paid between $10,000 and $15,000 for their services, in partial payment if they miscarry, and nothing if they withdraw from the agreement. Commercial surrogacy—considered illegal and regulated by states in a variety of manner—is when a couple pays a fee to a woman in exchange for her carrying and delivering a baby.[58] This is different from gestational surrogacy, the more common of the two, when the surrogate is impregnated with the egg of another woman and fertilized by the sperm of the intended father (or donor) prior to implantation, a process known as in vitro fertilization. In the case concerning "Baby M" in 1987, the New Jersey Supreme Court upheld the maternal right of a surrogate mother who refused to surrender her baby and ordered that custody and visitation be arranged as if following a divorce. With this decision, limits on surrogacy contracts and custody rights were defined.

European countries also have specialized laws to cope with surrogate motherhood. Italy considers the mother to be the woman who gives birth to the child, regardless of the source of the egg. A similar law in the Netherlands makes it difficult for commissioning parents to have custody over their surrogate-born child.

In 1995, Israel's High Court of Justice overturned a 1987 law barring surrogate motherhood and now allows it with strict supervision. Restrictions include that the surrogate mother must be a full citizen of Israel, preferably not married, and not a relative of either of the commissioning parents.

Opponents of surrogacy feel that bearing a child for others in exchange for large sums of money may be a coercive, if not attractive, option for poor women. They perceive surrogacy as a form of baby selling that takes advantage of women's economic situation and should be banned.

ABORTION RIGHTS

The earliest documented right to abortion dates back to the 1327 Twinslayer's Case and 1348 Abortionist's Case in England, which helped establish a common law authorizing termination of a pregnancy at any time, when the judges—in pre-Reformation England all Roman Catholic—refused to make causing the death of a fetus a legal offense. Abortion before the "quickening"—when the fetus moves or kicks in approximately the 21st week—was never punishable under English common law, nor considered a moral problem.

In mainland Europe and the United States, abortion was not regulated by the state until the 19th century. In the United States, opponents of abortion and birth control have accused Margaret Sanger, the nurse who pioneered family planning and founded birth control clinics in the early 1900s, with eugenicism and racism. The 1973 *Roe v. Wade* case was the first court case decided by the U.S. Supreme Court to establish a woman's constitutional right to an abortion in the first trimester of pregnancy, and it is still being debated today. The decision, written by Justice Harry Blackmun and based on the residual right of privacy, struck down dozens of state antiabortion statutes, but the right to abortion has been meeting resistance in other ways.

Introduction

An ongoing concern of women's organizations in the United States is how the Supreme Court might handle abortion cases in the future. In 1976, the U.S. Congress barred the use of federal funds to reimburse the medical expenses involved in abortions under its Medicaid program, except when the woman's life is endangered by a full-term pregnancy or in the case of rape or incest. Abortion was also one of the central issues during the 2009–10 health care reform debates within the U.S. Congress before legislation was passed that excluded it from the public health care option.

In the same year *Roe v. Wade* was decided by the Supreme Court, abortion became a bargaining chip when discussed in the context of foreign aid. Congress amended the Foreign Assistance Act, sponsored by Republican senator Jesse Helms from North Carolina, prohibiting the use of U.S. foreign aid funds for abortion. In August 1984, at the International Conference on Population in Mexico City, the U.S. delegation, headed by James Buckley, announced that the United States would not authorize funding of foreign NGOs that provide, refer, counsel, or advocate for abortion. The executive branch policy stayed in effect until 1993 and became known as the Mexico City Policy, later dubbed the "Global Gag Rule" by its opponents. The ruling has affected family planning services around the globe, including not only clinics in Kenya that depended on abortion as a way to control multiple births in Kenyan families, but other clinics that refer patients to outside abortion services. Of concern in Asia, Africa, and Latin America is the one in 10 pregnancies that will end in unsafe abortion.[59]

In China, on the other hand, the government encourages the use of abortion as part of its one-child policy to control the population increase, leading to resentment among people who view the government's policies as an imposition on their lives. In France, abortion is covered by the government-based health care system, in spite of a population that is largely Catholic.

According to the Guttmacher Institute, family planning and reproductive health have lost priority as development issues since the International Conference on Population and Development in 1994. Reproductive health was noticeably absent from the eight goals discussed at the UN Millennium Development Conference in 2000.[60]

SAME-SEX ROLES AND RELATIONSHIPS

Gay rights have moved beyond the social arena into political and legal fields with sufficient success that legislation establishing civil rights has been awaiting ratification by the courts in many countries since the latter half of the 20th century. Although a variety of sexual orientations—bisexual, transvestite, and transgender—are publically known, no others have tried to establish civil rights in the same way.

Still considered taboo in many countries for even a public debate, gay rights have moved to the news in other countries as supporters have fought for the right to same-sex marriages and other sociopolitical and economic benefits afforded to opposite-sex couples. By the end of 2010, same-sex marriage, which affords the same legal rights and benefits as marriages between heterosexual partners, swept across many countries and states: Belgium, Canada, the Netherlands, Spain, Norway, Sweden, South Africa, Argentina (the first Latin American country), Portugal (unusual for a predominantly Catholic country), Iceland (with its openly gay LGBT prime minister, Johanna Sigurdardotter), and the U.S states of Massachusetts, Connecticut, Vermont, New Hampshire, Iowa, and the District of Columbia. In June 2011, New York passed legislation to make same-sex marriage legal. Rhode Island and Maryland recognize same-sex marriage but do not conduct ceremonies. The state of California passed a same-sex marriage referendum in June 2008, but it was repealed in November of the same year.[61] Civil unions and other forms of partnerships for gay couples have been legally established in many different countries and with varying amounts of benefits.

In 1989, Denmark became the first country to introduce civil partnerships, establishing for same-sex couples the same privileges as for married heterosexual couples, with few exceptions, one of which is adoption. This paved the way for other European nations to allow civil unions for same-sex partners. In France, the National Assembly passed an equality law in 1999 known as the civil solidarity pact (*pacte civil de solidarité*, or PaCS). It permitted same-sex partners to be joined in a civil union contract in order to organize their common life. The couple is required to register a common declaration with the local court where they are resident. The contract makes them eligible for joint taxation benefits after three years. The tenant's lease can be transferred to one partner if the other leaves their common home or dies. A partner who does not have social protection (health benefits) may enjoy the other partner's social protection. The law does not address lineage, adoption, or custody roles. In March 2009, however, the Danish parliament initiated a bill that permitted equal adoption rights for same-sex civil partners and married couples, a decision that was formalized in May 2010 (effective July 1, 2010), thus joining Iceland, Norway, and Sweden as countries in which same-sex couples are able to "adopt jointly."

In the United States, political activism for lesbian rights first emerged around 1970, in the wake of the feminist movement, which then divided over whether to associate women's gay rights with its campaign. The Stonewall uprising of 1969 is considered the initiating act of the modern gay rights movement. Youths protested on June 27 by throwing bricks at local police during a routine raid of the Stonewall Inn, which catered to gay and lesbian customers in the Greenwich Village area of New York City. The fact that gay rights are now part of the platform of the National Organization for Women (NOW) has helped, however, to make the movement more mainstream, so much so that it is today a subject of television plots and films. Activism for sexual freedom and basic legal, political, social, and economic rights has led actors and politicians to reveal their private lives in the name of making a difference.

On the other hand, gay marriage or civil unions are challenged by traditional and fundamentalist views in Asia and Latin America, where religion has a greater influence over society. After winning by a majority in 2009, a law went into effect in March 2010 making Mexico City one of the first Latin American cities to break with tradition and legalize same-sex marriage, followed by Argentina in July. Resistance to the landmark legislation considered gay marriage as unconstitutional and outside the protection of family rights. Mexico's Supreme Court countered in August 2010, when it ordered the country's 31 states to recognize same-sex marriages performed in the capital as legal contracts, upholding the concept and definition of family as "open." The law also granted gay couples the right to adopt children. It is expected to be challenged in court.

Furthermore, civil unions are permitted in Brazil. In India and most African countries, homosexuality is still considered illegal. Although gay marriage is recognized in South Africa, anti-gay practices ("corrective rapes" of lesbians) occur. A zero-tolerance policy by the Chinese government means homosexual practices are treated as a mental illness. Since the late 1990s, Chinese psychiatrists have debated the classification of homosexuality in the Chinese Classification of Mental Disorders. After the People's Republic of China's (PRC's) rise to power in 1949, any open display of or discussion about gay or lesbian orientation was suppressed. Urban life has evolved somewhat to accommodate gay nightclubs, and the Internet has provided some room for discussion, but still with much restraint. Although the Chinese parliament has proposed same-sex marriage legislation since 2003, as of 2010 the bill had not passed.

TRADITIONAL PRACTICES: FEMALE GENITAL MUTILATION

Female genital mutilation (FGM), also known as female circumcision and female cutting, is the practice of cutting any part of the female genitalia for cultural (rather than medical) reasons. There are three kinds of FGM:

1. Clitoridectomy: the cutting of the "hood" or tip of the clitoris, leaving the muscles and nerves intact.

2. Excision: the cutting away of the entire clitoris and the labia minora. This ensures that because of the destruction of muscle and nerves, the woman does not experience pleasure during the sexual act. However, the entrance is not restricted.
3. Infibulation: the entire clitoris, the labia minora, as well as at least two-thirds of the labia majora are cut away. The two sides of the vulva (external genitalia) are then sewn together, leaving just enough room for a matchstick to pass through. If a finger can pass through, the hole is considered too large.[62]

Over 40 Muslim and non-Muslim countries—mostly the sub-Saharan Africa countries of Egypt, Sudan, Somalia, Ethiopia, Kenya, and Chad—practice some form of circumcision of men and women for cultural, social, and economic reasons. FGM is perceived as a cultural custom among various religious groups and is not itself a religious rite. Clitoridectomy and excisions are practiced in Chad, countries of West Africa, Kenya, and Tanzania. Excision is most common in Kenya and much of Africa, often done without anesthesia and with a blunt knife or a razor blade, by a woman.

Medical consequences of a practice perceived by many as a violation of women and girls that adversely affects their health and well-being include infection, hemorrhaging, trauma, and death, not to mention the psychological trauma that lives with them for the rest of their lives.

As immigrants move to the United States, they take with them their customs. According to the Centers for Disease Control and Prevention in Atlanta, Georgia, an estimated 168,000 girls and women in the United States had been circumcised as of 1990. The U.S. Congress and several states have outlawed the practice of infibulation since 1996. Similar laws have been passed in Europe, New Zealand, and Australia, as well as in a number of African countries.

Violence against Women

Violence is a major and growing public health problem across the world, takes many forms, and is subject to cultural interpretation. International organizations such as the World Health Organization (WHO) have played a key role in addressing the connection between women's development and violence, especially during wartime and with domestic partners. The adoption by WHO of Resolution WHA49.25 in 1996 drew attention to the serious consequences of violence—in both the short term and the long term—for individuals, families, communities, and countries and stressed the damaging effects of violence on health-care services, evidence for which was documented in a highly publicized multi-country study in 2005.

The United Nations now includes "interpersonal violence in the home, violence against women in public space, trafficking, violence in post-conflict situations and harmful gender-based practices" in its definition of violence against women.[63]

Advocacy about the extent of violence against women and its damaging consequences has intensified in the 2000s, relying on better statistics and case studies. The International Centre for the Prevention of Crime has tracked integrated strategies and programs from around the globe to provide guidance about programs, policies, and practices that have proven effective in promoting women's safety. An international campaign from the Women's Global Leadership Institute—16 Days of Activism against Gender Violence—annually runs from November 25th (International Day for the Elimination of Violence against Women) until December 10th (International Human Rights Day) to emphasize the connection between violence and human rights.

The Council of Europe has led a campaign entitled "Stop domestic violence against women" since 2006. Amnesty International, the human rights organization, has led a campaign, "Stop Violence against Women," since 2004. UNIFEM has been using the Internet for a "Say No to Violence against Women" campaign since November 2007.

A 2006 report by the UN Secretary-General Ban Ki-moon emphasized violence against women as a human rights violation and as an obstacle to achieving gender equality, one of the 2015 MDGs.[64]

PORNOGRAPHY AS FREE SPEECH

The UN Resolution of December 17, 1993, on pornography was an early opportunity to evaluate the connection between violence and women. The word *pornography* is derived from Greek and means "writing about prostitution." Pornography as an act of free speech is complex and polarizes around several viewpoints, ranging from consent and self-choice to prevention of violence.

Antipornography laws have been advocated by religious fundamentalists and feminists who believe the public portrayal of women in explicit sexual conduct provokes violence toward women and is socially demeaning, thus violating their civil rights. Those who support antipornography laws see pornography as a form of violence that "glamorizes the degradation and maltreatment of women and asserts their subordinate function as mere receptacles for male lust."[65]

In the literature and research studies on the topic, the definition of what constitutes pornography and the way it is measured vary. The definition ranges from explicit sexual images to coercive images.[66] The only link research has consistently shown between violence against women and pornography are the common elements of sexual repression and aggression. Whether the violent act was committed as a result of the sexual fantasies that were inspired by the pornographic images or was a result of unrelated emotional or psychological causes has not been measured consistently. For example, a 2006 study in Denmark using 200 randomly selected young Danish adult males (100) and females (100), aged 18–30 as a representative sample, suggested that violent pornographic material did not induce changes in the experimental group when compared with the control group. Attitudes toward women, sexism, rape, myth acceptance, acceptance of interpersonal violence, and gender stereotypes did not change as a result of watching hardcore pornography, although doing so did cause emotionality and negativity.[67] The United Nations has encouraged further evaluation of the bearing of pornography and prostitution on men's violence against women.

The legal boundaries for pornography involving children are more established, including the universally accepted Convention on the Rights of the Child (1989, ratified by 193 countries, except Somalia and the United States) and its Optional Protocol on the Sale of Children, Child Prostitution and Child Pornography (2000, signed by 118 countries as of October 2010).

GENDER-BASED VIOLENCE: RAPE AND DOMESTIC ABUSE

The World Health Organization reports that 10 to 69 percent of women worldwide have been physically assaulted by an intimate male partner at some point in their life.[68] Within Japan alone, 10 percent of women reported physical abuse by a close relation and 57 percent suffered a combination of physical, psychological, and sexual abuse. In other countries, such as Mexico, over 50 percent of physically assaulted women were also sexually abused by their partners. In Nicaragua, 40 percent of women of reproductive age have experienced violence by a partner, of whom 31 percent reported its occurrence during one or more pregnancies.[69] A 1995 study by the Pan American Health Organization of 500 women and 1,000 service providers in 10 countries in Latin America, called La Ruta Crítica (Critical Path), identified two factors that led women to seek help: recurrence or severity of violence and fearing for one's life or that of the children. Economics was an important factor as well, in whether women felt they could support themselves.[70]

A 2005 landmark study on domestic violence sponsored by WHO, which began interviewing more than 24,000 women in 1997 from rural and urban areas in 10 countries (Bangladesh, Brazil, Ethiopia, Japan, Namibia, Peru, Samoa, Serbia and Montenegro, Thailand, and the United Republic of Tanzania), is the first survey of this scope to be done outside North America and Europe.[71] The survey found that 25 to 50 percent of all women physically assaulted by their partners suffered physical injuries as a direct result. These abused women were twice as likely as nonabused women to have poor health, including physical and mental problems, even years after the violence took place. Symptoms included suicidal thoughts and attempts, mental distress, and physical symptoms such as pain, dizziness, and vaginal discharge.

Although this issue may have been present since the dawn of time, it is only recently that women have created means by which to litigate against it in some countries. In most countries, there are still cultural as well as legal barriers that prevent women from seeking protection against physical violence and rape.

Acts of violence against women include rape and sexual assault. In the United States, which has one of the highest rates in the world, it was estimated that as many as 1.3 million women were victims of physical assault by intimate partners in 2007.[72] Under the Victims of Crime Act (VOCA), 7.8 million people reported themselves to be victims of violence in 2007–08, 46 percent of whom were victims of domestic violence; the majority of cases took place at home.[73]

There was an increase in legislation to protect women during the 1990s and law enforcement has taken a more active role in domestic disputes in some countries. There has also been an increase in the number of women's and children's shelters and rape crisis hot lines.

In the United States, rape is treated as a violent felony and tough sentences await repeat offenders. Since 2004, under the Crime Victims' Rights Act, domestic violence is also punishable as a federal offense, thereby mitigating against previous weakness of state-based jurisdictions.

WAR AND VIOLENCE AGAINST WOMEN

War, or armed conflict, as a form of collective violence, is a context for a variety of forms of violence against women, from rape, forced labor, death, and exposure to communicable diseases such as HIV/AIDS and infections. Nearly 19 percent of global violence-related deaths, or 301,000 deaths in 2002, resulted from war, in which the majority occurred in low- to middle-income countries.[74] Sixty to 70 percent of those deaths were among people not engaged in fighting and included women and children.[75]

Rape was frequently used as a weapon of war in recent civil wars in the latter half of the 20th century to terrorize and break up communities. Conflicts in Somalia, Bosnia-Herzegovina, the Democratic Republic of the Congo (DRC), and Kashmir have caused human rights activists to watch closely and insist that rape cases not be dismissed as private crimes or as commonplace. An estimated 10,000 to 60,000 women were raped in Croatia and Bosnia-Herzegovina alone between 1992 and 1995. Bangladesh, Liberia, southern Sudan, and Uganda have also reported high incidences of war-related rape cases. As many as 250,000 to 500,000 women were raped during the 1994 genocide in Rwanda.[76] The severity of rapes has been extreme enough in the DRC, where 27,000 rapes took place in just one year (2006), to be considered war injuries.

Given the psychological impact on those who survive and their families, much has been needed in the way of developing programs to cope with displaced families and women. UNIFEM has been implementing training programs for law enforcement officials in handling rape crimes, and NGOs in war-torn areas have been active in providing remedial action, but more efforts are needed on an international scale.

FEMALE INFANTICIDE

Infanticide, mutilation, abandonment, and other forms of violence against children date back to ancient civilizations. In some countries, the pressure to control populations and the low status of the girl child has led to illegal means of killing female babies. Sex-selective abortions, or "missing women," have been noted in Afghanistan, India, China, and Pakistan.[77] In China, where the one-child (Planned Birth) policy is in effect, and India, where sterilization is encouraged after birth of a third child, the perception is that male children provide more revenue for the family. The act of female infanticide—the abandonment and killing of female infants—has been increasing in South Asia as a way to alter the man/woman ratio. The World Health Organization has identified a pattern of fatal abuse of children that is more prevalent in low-income countries.[78]

The issue of female infanticide was raised at the Beijing Conference in 1995 and has continued to garner interest as one form of child abuse. The practice continues in India and China and among the Inuit of Canada and North America.

HUMAN TRAFFICKING AND PROSTITUTION

Human trafficking is defined as "the recruitment, transportation, transfer, harboring or receipt of persons, by means of the threat or use of force or other forms of coercion, of abduction, of fraud, of deception, of the abuse of power or of a position of vulnerability or of the giving or receiving of payments or benefits to achieve the consent of a person having control over another person, for the purpose of exploitation," by the Protocol to Prevent, Suppress and Punish Trafficking in Persons, Especially Women and Children, which supplements the United Nations Convention against Transnational Organized Crime. Involuntary trafficking is illegal in most countries and 117 countries have signed the treaty since its adoption in 2000 and enforcement in 2003. The number of countries with anti-trafficking legislation has more than doubled between 2003 and 2008. Estimates from 2006 about humans being trafficked from 127 origin countries for exploitation in 137 destination countries appear to be holding in 2009, reinforcing human trafficking as an acknowledged global problem.[79] An increase in recognizing human trafficking as a criminal offense is expected to lead to better accountability for the actual number of offenses. Of countries registered with the United Nations Office on Drugs and Crimes, 21 percent have experienced an increase in convictions during the 2003–07 period.[80]

Sexual trafficking is especially prevalent during wartime violence and economic difficulty, when women are deceived, coerced, or kidnapped and enslaved into prostitution. The greatest incidence of trafficking occurs in Asia, for origin, transit, and destination, with China and Thailand ranking highest. Africa is a significant source of origin for victims of trafficking. Central and southeastern Europe are origins for women who are then exploited in western Europe. The Commonwealth of Independent States (11 former Soviet Union countries) and Latin America are significant providers of the international traffic that takes women to western Europe and North America. Oceania (New Zealand and Australia) and the United States are mostly destination countries for the international slave trade.

Trafficking is distinguished from prostitution, a profession in which a person offers to provide sexual services in return for money. Prostitution is legal in many countries, including in the Netherlands, where prostitutes are taxpaying and unionized professionals. On the other extreme are countries such as Iraq, where prostitution carried the death penalty until the United States–led invasion in 2003. The liberal laws tolerating prostitution in some western European countries have made it difficult to distinguish traffickers who exploit young girls and women in global networks against their will from prostitution rings. The protocol implicates prostitution in trafficking in the following way: "Exploitation shall include, at a minimum, the exploitation of the prostitution of others or other forms of sexual exploitation, forced labor or services, slavery or practices similar to slavery, servitude or the removal of organs."

Although no accurate numbers exist, the estimated number of individuals who are trafficked worldwide is between 600,000 and 2 million a year, with women and young girls being nearly 80 percent of victims.[81] The sex trade represents the third-largest source of illicit revenue worldwide, after arms and drugs, at profits of between $5 billion and $7 billion a year. As of 2006, as many as 50,000 girls were taken into the United States each year. In eastern Europe, 500,000 women have been forced into commercial sex.[82] Of the 61 countries that reported figures about trafficked victims in 2009, women (66 percent) and girls (13 percent) were the majority of victims being trafficked, while others reported that boys (9 percent) and men (12 percent) also were among those being trafficked.[83]

Religion and Spirituality

The relationship between women and religions is complex. Reflecting women's general status in society all major religions were traditionally male dominated, and many religious leaders have contributed to the spread of misogyny, the hatred of women. The adherence to sacred texts and customs, and their traditional interpretation, has also made it difficult for women to modify the way they are treated by religions. Beginning in the 20th century, the possibility of religious freedom took on several forms, from the stance of choosing not to adhere to a faith (agnostic or atheist), to a modification of traditional religious modalities (freethinkers), to adoption of an individual or gender-based spirituality, better known as "new age." All major religions have had remarkable spiritual woman leaders such as Rabia al-Adawihay (712–801), a great Sufi mystic; Hildegard von Bingen (1098–1179), a German nun renowned for her talents in mathematics, science, medicine, music, and theology; Muktabai (d. 1297), a Hindu saint; and Mother Teresa (1910–97), an Albanian nun who founded the Missionaries of Charity in India.

The women's movement has been supported by some religions more than others. Protestant sects sympathetic to female emancipation—primarily Quakers and Unitarians, who believe in the equality of men and women before God—gave rise to many of the leading women suffragists in Europe and the United States. Mary Wollstonecraft, author of *A Vindication of the Rights of Woman*, was influenced by the Unitarian Church in Europe. Susan B. Anthony, Lucretia Mott, and Alice Paul were all raised as Quakers.

Women's role in all the major religions of the world has improved significantly over the past few decades. The efforts have concentrated on gaining access to leadership roles, analyzing and reinterpreting religious history and sacred texts, and creating innovative forms of religious and spiritual practices.

LEADERSHIP ROLES IN RELIGIOUS WORSHIP

Some scholars argue that male dominance in world religions may have been a relatively recent development considering the role of women in mythology and antiquity. A gradual decline in the importance and status of women has been documented for the Judeo-Christian tradition, Hinduism, Buddhism, and Islam.

Introduction

Lucretia Mott was recorded as a Quaker minister in 1821, and Antoinette Blackwell was ordained a minister by the First Congregational Church in 1853. It was not until the United Methodist Church began to ordain women in the 1980s, however, that female clergy began to serve in numbers. The Anglican and Episcopal Churches followed suit in the 1990s. By 2001, over 1,000 women were serving as ordained ministers in the Southern Baptist Convention. The authorization of female priests and bishops by the Methodist Church is evidence of women gaining more power within the church.[84] Nevertheless, women in the clergy have been faced with issues similar to those in other domains, namely, unequal pay and requirements, as women have often had to have more education to do the same task.

U.S. federal labor statistics indicate that the number of women who describe themselves as "clergy" increased from 16,408 in 1983 to 65,268 in 2008. As of 2008, 14.8 percent of the clergy in the United States were female.[85]

The percentage of female graduate students at 229 North American Christian schools of theology rose from 10 percent in 1972 to 30 percent in 1997. In some schools of theology, more than 50 percent of the students are women.[86]

Within the Lutheran Evangelical Church, the national church of Denmark, 40 percent of all priests were women by 1995, the year the first woman became bishop.

The Roman Catholic Church, the faith of about 25 percent of the U.S. population, continues to bar women from ordination worldwide.

Although Orthodox Judaism does not permit female rabbis, more liberal Jewish movements have begun to allow them in recent years. Reform movements in Judaism have also put in question traditional rituals that separate women from men in prayer. In the United States in 2006, Dina Najman was made spiritual leader—not as a rabbi, but as a *rash Kehillah* (head of congregation)—of a modern Orthodox community in New York City that adheres closely to Jewish law.

Within Buddhism, it was believed that Buddha not only established an order of *bhikhsu* (monks) but, albeit reluctantly, one with female *bhuksuni* (nuns). In instituting the order, he affirmed that women could attain spiritual enlightenment, an unusual concept for its time. At the same time, however, he imposed rules on the *bhuksuni* that were designed to maintain their subordinate status within the Buddhist religious community. Buddhists of diverse traditions and schools from around the world joined together in 1998 for an international and ecumenical ordination in Bodh Gaya, India. One of the goals of the ceremony was to reestablish the order of nuns in Sri

Lanka, Thailand, Tibet, and India, where no nuns had been ordained for over eight centuries.

In recent years, some Muslims have argued that women should be able to lead mixed congregations as well as single-sex ones in prayer; they support their arguments with passages from the Qu'ran and the hadith. Most Islamic schools allow women to lead a congregation of women; however, women are currently not allowed to lead mixed congregations. In 2005, the Islamic scholar Amina Wadud (1952–   ) led a mixed congregation in prayer in New York, the first time such an event garnered international attention. In response, the Assembly of Muslim Jurists in America reiterated the traditional view that women cannot deliver the Friday prayer.

FEMINIST SPIRITUALITY

Women's spirituality became popular in the late 20th and early 21st centuries, in what is often called the "new age" movement. The term describes alternative spiritual practices that combine Eastern and pre-Christian Western traditions and were developed in response to the restrictive tenets of established religions. Popular practices include meditation, channeling, reincarnation, use of crystals, psychic experience, and holistic health.

As part of the movement, Neopaganism, or new religious movements, has also gained in popularity. The largest Neopagan belief in the United States is Wicca, an Earth-based faith that depends on celebrations of the seasons and recognizes divinity in the female form. Its contemporary origins are attributed to Gerald Gardner, a civil servant in Great Britain, whose activities in the 1930s caused the movement to spread to many parts of the globe and to include men.

RELIGIOUS SCHOLARSHIP AND HISTORY

Around the same time, women scholars within the major religious traditions began to reconsider the scriptures, interpretations, and practices of their religion from a feminist perspective. Religious history has largely been preserved through sacred texts, which recount the prophesies, tales, and founding philosophies upon which a religion or spirituality is based. The impact of sacred and religious texts on gender roles has been considerable worldwide. Men have been key players in creating these texts, both oral and written, and maintaining the knowledge of the original language in which they were written. In the few pre-19th-century religious texts authored by women, such as Catherine of Siena in 14th-century Italy, the Indian saint Mahadeviyakka in the 10th century, and the Arabic poet Rabi'ah (c. 644), wisdom is often couched within folklore myths, poems, dialogues, and letters.

Introduction

Feminist theology has been particularly strong in the Christian and Jewish traditions. Among its goals have been reinterpreting sacred texts, changing the language and images used to describe God, studying female religious leaders in history, and increasing the role of women among the clergy and religious authorities.

Monitoring Women's Rights

The contemporary women's movement has expanded its agenda from the early focus on the freedom to vote within each nation to a new emphasis on holding governments accountable for the hard-won freedoms and rights.

These freedoms are liberties that need to be protected with care. Holding countries accountable for signed treaties and agreements has become an important issue. The ability to monitor progress for the welfare of women and men is subject to the capacity and willingness of countries to report data accurately.

During the 1995 UN conference on women, the Beijing Declaration and Platform for Action highlighted the importance of the ability to monitor countries' commitments; participating countries agreed to provide yearly reports to the United Nations and to allow human rights and women's advocacy groups as well as the United Nations's own Department of Economic and Social Affairs to monitor their activities.

Strengthening the ability of countries to gather and report statistical information has been an important goal in the first decade of the 21st century. The results from the 1995–2004 period were cause for concern: Among the 204 countries that reported statistical information, only 54 percent were able to supply some data about wages, birth, and death by sex. Europe had the highest ability to submit data and Africa the lowest.

Recognizing the important role statistics are playing in countries' accountability, the United Nations celebrated World Statistics Day for the first time in October 2010.

Where Is the Women's Movement Headed?

That women have not been newsmakers for the majority of time that life has been recorded by books, newspapers, magazines, and movies indicates that people have still much to discover about women's history.

The women's movement evolved largely around a variety of causes—decolonization, national liberation, civil rights for all races and creeds, world peace, gay and lesbian rights, educational access, equal employment and pay are some—that contributed to the movement as a whole. Much of the emphasis so far has been on establishing those rights, something that is still happening today in different parts of the globe. Gender balance is now a strategy that encompasses the women's movement and promotes gender equality through quotas.

Other aspects of the struggle now are fulfilling the rights that have already been achieved and finding a voice that fits with being a woman in these times. The rights women seek are also for children and men, and are expanding to what women wish to safeguard in the world. Many organizations—including the Girl Scouts—are calling out to girls and women to consider careers and lifestyles in which they can influence, or change, public policy by the choices they make.

INTERNATIONAL HISTORY OF WOMEN'S RIGHTS

The demand for women's rights first became vocal in the late 17th century and 18th century, but it did not become a visible part of life until the 19th century revolutions in Europe. Although the movement arose separately in the United States and Europe, the common goal of achieving women's independence caused woman in these countries to appreciate each other's efforts and coordinate efforts to make a greater impact.

One of the earliest women who attempted to "move" other women about rights was the British author and feminist Mary Astell (1668–1731). She pleaded for greater opportunities for women in her *Serious Proposal to the Ladies,* written in two parts between 1694 and 1697, which offered a scheme for a women's college, an idea that turned out to be before its time and subject to public ridicule.

During the American Revolution in 1776, Abigail Adams admonished her husband, John, future vice president and president of the United States, to include women's rights in the new republic, else "there will be another revolution." It was not until the 1789 French Revolution that women rallied in support of women's rights.

In 1792 in England, Mary Wollstonecraft published *A Vindication of the Rights of Woman,* which was translated into several languages and gave impetus to the movement worldwide. She addressed political emancipation for women when others around her limited their demand for rights to men. Although this stirring text opened the door for the women's movement, women's suffrage did not become the focus of the movement for another 50 years. One reason why liberal and socialist groups generally opposed women's suffrage was the claim, mostly by men, that women would vote conservatively. Conservatives, in turn, viewed suffrage as being entirely incompatible with the "women's sphere."

Introduction

The First International Movement

The 1830s and 1840s was a time of social and radical reform, and leaders of the movement in Europe and the United States began to demand voting rights for women. However, the movement's agenda diversified quickly as it became evident that there were other issues that could be addressed in the short term, including economic independence for single women and improved legal position of married women.

In Europe, the rise of the Saint-Simonians and Fourierists in France inspired women to be *femmes libres,* or free women, believing they would lead the world into social and sexual freedom. This movement was opposed by some feminists, who said they would find their path to emancipation through religion, not sexual freedom. In Germany, the feminist Mathilde Franziska Anneke (1817–84) stated that her fellow feminist Louise Aston (1818–71) was exiled from the country for rejecting the religious faith, yet men were treated much less harshly for their resistance. The Chartist movement petitioned the vote for all men in England in the 1830s and 1840s and stimulated the same notion in women, yet while the men's movement was tolerated, the women's demand was not.

In the United States, Ernestine Rose (1810–92), a rabbi's young daughter who advocated married women's property rights, and Lucretia Mott (1793–1880), a promoter of racial equality and international women's rights, were early voices in the movement in the 1830s and 1840s. Mott was denied entry to a conference on antislavery in the United Kingdom because she was female. This pushed her onto the path of demanding equality for women and minorities. Public speeches by Frances Wright (1795–1852) and the Grimké sisters—Angelina Grimké Weld (1805–79) and Sarah Moore Grimké (1792–1873)—were conscious raising, as were publications by women: Mathilde Franziska Anneke's *Women in Conflict with Social Conditions* and Louise Otto's (1819–95) *Song of a German Maiden* among them.

A series of revolutions in 1847 and 1848 across Europe released a fury of women's rights activities. During this time, feminists began to reach out to one another for inspiration and help, mailing articles and books to each other across the ocean and translating each other's works into their native languages. By 1847, many women considered themselves compassionate about issues concerning women—propelling the international women's movement into existence—although the first known use of the term *feminist,* was not documented until 1895.[87]

Elizabeth Cady Stanton (1815–1902), a judge's daughter with a flair for dramatics and a belief in coeducation, and Mott stood up to the limitations placed on them. They planned what came to be known as the first Women's

Rights Convention in Seneca Falls, New York, in 1848. For that occasion, *Declaration of Sentiments* was drafted by Stanton to describe the key grievances of the day, including "the duty of the women of this country to secure to themselves their sacred right to the elective franchise."[88]

Stanton's high profile among women suffragists attracted Susan B. Anthony, who was then a schoolteacher and working with the temperance movement; they met in 1851 and developed a lifelong friendship of mutual support, often with Anthony taking care of Stanton's nine children so the latter could concentrate on speechwriting. Anthony's organizational and strategic strengths, which caused her to be nicknamed "Napoleon," complemented Stanton's eloquence in public speaking.

Along with suffrage, women focused on establishing economic independence and property rights. Together, Stanton and Anthony secured the first laws in the New York state legislature guaranteeing women rights over their children and control of property and wages, which gave impetus to the movement in other countries over the next two decades. In 1856, the British women Barbara Smith Bodichon (1827–91) and Bessie Raynor Parkes (1829–1925) advocated women's property reform through their newspaper, the *English Women's Journal*. The German feminists Louise Dittmar (1807–84), Louise Aston, and Anneke took radical positions on property and other rights in 1865 in the General Association of German Women. Canadian women began to lobby for similar rights. Canada's first suffrage groups—the Woman's Christian Temperance Union (WCTU), founded by Letitia Youmans (1827–96) in 1874, and the Toronto Women's Literary Club, led by the physician Emily Howard Stowe (1831–1903) in 1876, and later by her daughter, Dr. Ann Augusta Stowe-Gullen (1857–1943)—were moving beyond charitable and religious work to focus on suffrage. The Toronto Women's Literary Club became the Toronto Women's Suffrage Association in 1883, then the Dominion Women's Enfranchisement Association in 1889, paving the way for and inspiring women's leagues in other Canadian territories.

Preparing for the Next Wave

In the United States, the Civil War of 1861–65 subdued the focus on women's rights as energy was put into preserving the Union and defeating a secession attempt by slave-owning states. In 1863, Anthony and Stanton coorganized the Women's National Loyal League to support Lincoln's government and emancipation policy during the war. American women served in the conflict as nurses or spies. The Thirteenth Amendment, ending slavery throughout the United States, was passed in 1864 and ratified in 1865. The Fourteenth Amendment, stating that "[a]ll persons born or naturalized in the United

States . . . are citizens" and extending suffrage to black men, was passed in 1866 and ratified in 1868. Anthony and Stanton opposed granting suffrage to freed men without also giving it to women, and many woman suffrage sympathizers broke with them on this issue.

In 1869, Anthony and Stanton organized the National Woman Suffrage Association (NWSA). Three years later, Anthony led a group of women to the polls in Rochester, New York, to test the right of women to the franchise under the citizenship clause of the Fourteenth Amendment. Anthony's arrest, trial, and conviction on charges of unlawful voting received front-page attention, as did her refusal to pay the sentenced $100 fine.

Meanwhile, other factors were fueling the movement. An early supporter of women's liberation was the English philosopher and economist John Stuart Mill (1806–73). As a member of the British parliament, he advocated women's right to vote in the name of proportional representation. He addressed the rights of women in his 1869 book *The Subjection of Women* and wrote articles on the subject for the press. His work was translated into Danish, inspiring the movement in Denmark.

Women were applying for higher education by the mid-19th century, following pioneers like the British-born Elizabeth Blackwell (1821–1910), who, in spite of being turned down by 29 medical schools, was finally admitted to the medical department of Geneva College in upstate New York. She graduated from Geneva and attained full status as a physician in 1849. Universities had been associated with men and monasteries since the 12th century, and women were admitted only to colleges, often single-sex schools. Nielsine Nielsen (1850–1916) was among the first women to apply to and be accepted in medical school at the University of Copenhagen in Denmark in 1874. Women were required to take an entrance exam and could obtain degrees at the university in most subjects, except theology.

Through the late 19th and early 20th centuries, the women's rights movement emerged with renewed intensity from the seeds of previous attempts and expanded in a ripple effect throughout Europe. In 1868, the activist Maria Goegg (1826–99) founded the International Association of Women (IAW) in Geneva, Switzerland, which then grew to have divisions in Italy, Portugal, France, Germany, England, and North America. Women's suffrage and better education for girls and women were IAW's priorities. At the same time in France, the Society for the Amelioration of Women's Condition was pioneered by Léon Richer (1824–1911) and Maria Deraismes (1828–94) to create better access to education, divorce, and property rights for married women. Both Danish and Swedish women also founded organizations to solidify rights for women.

These endeavors were not without resistance, however. IAW collapsed in France after the defeat of the Paris Commune in 1871; the new conservative government associated women's rights with a socialist regime. Another attempt by French feminists in 1878 to convene as the International Women's Rights Congress in Paris turned into a decision to deny women suffrage by the 220 mostly male delegates.

The International Council of Women (ICW) was founded in Washington, D.C., in 1888, formed by Anthony and Stanton with contacts made while in Europe, to work on women's issues on a broad front. However, the ICW's leader from 1893 to 1899 and from 1904 to 1936, the Scot Lady Aberdeen (1857–1939), was reluctant to advocate women's suffrage, believing women's household duties were primary.

Twentieth Century: Women Network

During a conference of the ICW in Berlin in 1904, a special organization, the International Women's Suffrage Alliance (IWSA), was founded to focus on the struggle for suffrage across the globe. It hosted meetings in Copenhagen (1906), Amsterdam (1908), London (1909), Stockholm (1911), and Budapest (1913) before World War I. By then, it had added labor, prostitution, world peace, and equal rights to its agenda.

In the early years of the 20th century, although national movements were occurring separately, women were making contact with one another individually, inspiring and influencing each other. Events that occurred in the United States involving female factory workers who marched against substandard conditions in New York City in 1857 drew the attention of the second International Conference of Socialist Women in Germany in 1910 through the German labor leader Clara Zetkin (1857–1933). The conference designated International Women's Day in recognition of women's fight for universal rights (but the United Nations did not decide upon the specific date of March 8 until 1975, during International Women's Year). A women's uprising in Russia along the Afghan border in the 1920s inspired Afghan women to commemorate the occasion on International Women's Day many decades later.

The British suffrage movement was a radical model for the women's movement leading up to World War I. The English suffragettes Hertha Ayrton (1854–1923) and Emmeline Pankhurst (1858–1928) and her two daughters, Christabel (1880–1958) and Sylvia (1882–1960), applied near-violent pressure for women to vote out Winston Churchill, the prime minister of England at the time, upsetting "the whole orderly conduct of life."[89]

Introduction

The French suffragists Madeleine Pelletier (1874–1939) and Caroline Kauffmann (1840–1926), riled by their experience in British demonstrations, resuscitated the movement in France. Pankhurst's American friend (and suffragist daughter of Elizabeth Cady Stanton) Harriot Stanton Blanch (1856–1940) invited Annie Cobden-Sanderson (1852–1944) to speak of her experience of imprisonment in British jails, which no doubt influenced American suffragists Alice Paul (1885–1977) and Lucy Burns (1879–1966). Paul and Burns participated in the British suffrage demonstrations and were both arrested in London. Undeterred by the experience, they applied the same techniques to the American struggle when they returned home. The South American Bertha Lutz (1894–1976) also tried to take militant techniques to Brazil from her visit to London, where women marched in picket lines, chained themselves to fences, or endured hunger strikes in prison in the name of winning the right to vote.

By contrast, Carrie Chapman Catt (1859–1947) used a more missionary style as she traveled with Dr. Aletta Jacobs (1854–1929) from the Netherlands through the Philippines, Palestine, Indonesia, and Burma in 1911 and 1912, trying to induce suffrage movements in developing countries.

Despite these efforts, when World War I began in 1914, few women in Europe, other than in Finland and Denmark, were allowed women's suffrage. For the next several years, women's rights organizations put their efforts into supporting the war and filling jobs vacated by men at war. Women in the United States and western Europe, each in their own way, questioned their limited rights in democratic societies that claimed they were going to war for democracy. The founding of the Women's Peace Party in 1915 by Jane Addams (1860–1935) was also part of a trend in which several women's organizations rallied for peace during the war. Jacobs helped found with Addams the International Congress for the Future Peace. The journalist and lawyer Crystal Eastman (1881–1928) established the National Civil Liberties Bureau to protect conscientious objectors to the war.

One of the larger European organizations—the International Conference of Socialist Women—and the Euro-American International Women's Congress met in 1915 to advocate peace. Women from 12 countries met in the Hague, the capital of the Netherlands. U.S. delegates campaigned for America not to enter the war, and it did not until 1917. In 1919, the delegates from the International Women's Congress formed a new organization, the Women's International League for Peace and Freedom (WILPF), in Geneva, Switzerland, led by Addams.

By the war's end in November 1918, women had been moving into white-collar jobs as secretaries, postal service clerks, and telephone operators, as well as such trades as plumbing. Public perception of women's ability, dress, and appearance shifted dramatically. Women were finding out about contraceptives as an option for sexual freedom and self-determination. Although women would soon be again alienated from job opportunities as men returned to the workforce, countries initiated suffrage in record numbers after the war.

After the war, women had the opportunity to meet with the 14 allied country representatives at the Paris Peace Conference in 1919 and to provide proposals for the newly formed Covenant of the League of Nations and ILO. This set a precedent for women's organizations to observe the intergovernmental agencies at work regularly and provide recommendations, helping them to gain experience in international affairs and networking. The covenant included statements about reasonable working conditions for men, women, and children and the prevention of human trafficking. It also specified equal opportunity for employment within the league. For the ILO constitution, women proposed statements that were radical for the time, including an eight-hour workday, an end to child labor, and equal pay and minimum wages.

The movement that was formerly dependent on middle-class women in North America and Europe now began to accommodate a more diverse social and multicultural population of women. African-American women, impacted by racism in the United States, formed their own alliance in 1920, the International Council of Women of the Darker Races. In the same year, Ayrton and Pankhurst befriended the two-time French Nobel physicist Marie Curie (1867–1934), who returned their support by lending her name to petitions to free suffragists from British prisons. While British property-holding women over the age of 30 had gained suffrage in 1918, it would not be until 1928, with the second passage of the Representation of the People Act, that suffrage was granted equally to men and women in Britain. Concurrently, American women were granted their right to vote on August 26, 1920, with the 19th Amendment to the Constitution.

Women gathered in countries such as Egypt, India, China, and Japan to form their own organizations. Delegates attending IWSA conferences were raising issues that were of concern to Muslim women. South American and Pacific Rim countries also began to host movements. The first Pan-American Woman's Conference was called by the IWSA president Catt in Baltimore, Maryland, in 1922. Organized by the Pan-American International Women's Committee, the Mexican Feminist Party cofounder Elena Torres (unknown birthdate), the Brazilian activist Bertha Lutz, and the Chilean Amanda Labarca (1886–1985) were among the 2,000 delegates, who included Canadians and Americans, to be inspired from the conference for the next two decades. The Brazilian Women's Suffrage Alliance and the Pan-American Association for the Advancement of Women emerged in the wake of this occasion.

Latin American women also united with Spanish women to form the International League of Iberian and Hispanic-American Women in the 1920s. Led by Paulina Luisi (1875–1950) from Uruguay, the league represented the sentiment that South America did not depend on missionary feminist zeal, as portrayed by Catt.

Women tried very hard to use their newfound voices for world peace. The WILPF grew to 50,000 members by 1926 and was advocating control of fascism and imperialism through pacifism, an approach, others argued, that would not be effective.

Throughout the 1920s and 1930s, women persisted with campaigns to be sure their rights would not be neglected by the League of Nations, which gradually implemented international legal protection of rights for specific minorities and women. During this period, many of the international NGOs that would later play an important part in the forming of the United Nations were formed. The League of Nations ended with the outbreak of World War II, as did, temporarily, much of the contact among different women's movements.

During the 1930s, Joseph Stalin in the Soviet Union and Adolf Hitler in Germany found ways to limit women's rights through governmental rule. In Russia, abortion was banned, and, although women had previously won the right to vote, the one-party system did not allow them to exercise their voice. National Socialism in Germany was vehemently opposed to women's rights. Although it tried to limit the number of women in the workforce, the men's call to arms required that women take on their jobs, even in civil service positions.

World War II (1938–45) transformed women's working experience. In the United Kingdom, unmarried women were drafted into the military. The United States implemented a women's auxiliary for the armed forces. Germany's voluntary labor service also drew out young women from the home. By the early 1940s, an estimated 90 percent of unmarried women and 80 percent of married women were employed in some form of service in the United States and Europe. Shift work, day care, and increased pay rates were policies new to the workplace to accommodate needed women workers. Social equality was first felt, finally, in a time of crisis.

As a result, women were given suffrage toward the end and after the war in Russia, Germany, France, Hungary, Italy, Portugal, Croatia, and Romania. At the same time, the return of men from war and the need to find jobs for them led to an emphasis on family values and women in the home. During the 1940s and 1950s, unmarried women began working in "female" jobs, such as nursing and teaching. In the United States, these professions were considered "male" jobs until the mid-1800s, when women began to assert their stature and access to educational training. On the other hand, married women often left the workforce to have children and returned on a part-time basis, if at all. Although the particulars varied by country, the trend to reemphasize domestic priorities for women was global.

Women's Rights: A Global Affair

From its inception, the women's rights movement has been fostered by national and international influences. After World War II, the founding of the United Nations in 1945 as a mediator for world peace was expected to include women's participation. Yet, of the 51 founding member states, only 30 granted women equal voting rights with men or allowed them to hold public office. On the other hand, the United Nation Charter specified equal rights for men and women in a way that no previous international legal document had.

In 1946, the UN Commission on the Status of Women was established to secure equal political rights, economic rights, and educational opportunities for women throughout the world. U.S. delegate Eleanor Roosevelt's (1884–1962) authorship of the Universal Declaration of Human Rights, which would be adopted by the General Assembly in 1948, was one example of women's new presence at the forefront of the international scene. It was also an early example of the as yet futuristic concept of gender balance.

During the first 30 years of the United Nations's work on women's rights, it struggled with some of the same issues that the women's movement in general faced, mainly the challenge of expanding the concept of gender equality from a minimal and basic legal and civil right into a socially and politically accepted idea. By the 21st century, countries also needed to establish mechanisms to gather data on the status of women around the world, a task that is still being worked on today.

Over time, it became increasingly apparent that laws, in and of themselves, were not enough to ensure the equal rights of women. Although the ILO adopted a convention for equal pay for women in 1951 for enforcement in 1953, the resolution would be ignored for another two decades. The Equal Remuneration Convention ratified nations to enforce among all men and women workers the principle of equal remuneration for work of equal value. The convention has been ratified by 162 nations, including most of Europe, Canada, South America, and the United Arab Emirates in 1997, but not the United States, which is still cautious over how comparable worth of work between men and women is to be measured.

Introduction

In the 1960s and 1970s, the women's movement flourished at national levels, beginning in the United States alongside the Civil Rights movement, then spreading to Europe, where it gained momentum with the trade unions. University students began to call for a change to the status quo in all aspects of life, and the rebellious character of the young people manifested itself in demonstrations and riots in 1968. Many marched against the U.S. involvement in the Vietnam War, advocating peace. Women, still considered supporters and not leaders in this wave of change, began to take independent positions, demanding social and economic liberation and recognition. This took the form of the women's liberation movement, also known as "second-wave feminism," which, in turn, grew at an international pace, involving women from all social and economic strata.

WOMEN AND THE UNITED NATIONS

As the movement became international, the United Nations responded by designating 1975 International Women's Year and holding the first of what would evolve into four world conferences on women, in Mexico City (1975), Copenhagen (1980), Nairobi (1985), and Beijing (1995). These international conferences empowered the movement by strengthening the web of communication. The exponential increase of conference attendees was another indication of the growth of the movement into a global one.

In Mexico City, 6,000 women from NGOs and 133 government delegations (113 were led by women) attended. One focus of discussion was the effects of colonialism, which was reflected in the World Plan of Action. It was here that INSTRAW and UNIFEM were established. The Mexico City conference also led to the proclamation of 1976–85 as the UN Decade for Women.

At the time of the UN world conference on women in Copenhagen, the cold war and apartheid preoccupied the program. The Copenhagen conference adopted a World Program of Action calling for women's participation in politics and decision making, and for the elimination of discrimination in law and policy. It encouraged governments and international institutions to conduct more research and to collect gender-based data. It also introduced CEDAW to the 1,326 delegates from 145 states and 8,000 women who attended as NGOs. The convention, which had been adopted at the end of the previous year by the General Assembly, provided strategies and set specific goals aimed at improving women's participation in social, economic, and political activities.

The women's movement was redefining itself as one for global gender equality with the Third World Conference on Women, in Nairobi, Kenya, in 1985, marking the end of the United Nations Decade for Women. Among the 15,000 women from NGOs and 157 government representatives, the sentiment was that, although many gains had been made during the past decade, statistics indicated that these benefits were only reaching a minority of women. Action statements concerning new approaches to the same problems—equality, development, and peace—were drafted and issued as the Nairobi Forward Looking Strategies for the Advancement of Women, focusing on three areas: constitutional and legal steps, equality in social participation, and equality in political participation and decision making.

By the time of the Fourth UN World Conference on Women in Beijing, China, in September 1995, it became clear that the focus needed to be on gender equality and human rights, a position that would draw international attention to itself and make use of the new World Wide Web, the Internet.

In addition to the 5,000 representatives of 2,100 NGOs and 189 government representatives, 30,000 women participated through the independent NGO Forum '95, and many thousands more took part through the Internet. All told, 47,000 people participated at this landmark event.[90]

The conference unanimously adopted the Beijing Declaration and the Platform for Action as an agenda for empowerment, highlighting three main areas: economic advancement, equal rights and access to health care and education, and violence against women and girls. Women's involvement in armed conflict and access to health care was of critical importance at the time. The Platform of Action also called to public awareness the important economic role that women migrant workers play, including domestic workers, who contribute their remittance to the economy of their country of origin and participate in the labor force of the country of destination.

The platform identified 12 critical areas for action:

- Poverty
- Education and training
- Health
- Violence against women
- Armed conflict
- The economy
- Women in power and decision making
- Institutional mechanisms for the advancement of women
- Human rights of women
- Women and the media
- Women and the environment
- The girl child

Introduction

In 1997, the 15 EU nations adopted the Amsterdam Treaty, which confirmed equality of men and women as a fundamental right in the EU. Both the treaty and any legislation toward "gender positive action to compensate for discrimination against women"[91] were intended to assert women's rights for "effective equality" and "obligation of result" in the newly expanding EU.

To give momentum to political commitments to achieve women's empowerment and gender equality, a UN special session was scheduled in June 2000 by the General Assembly and the Division for the Advancement of Women, entitled "Women 2000: Gender Equality, Development and Peace for the Twenty-first Century." Also known as "Beijing+5," the special session reviewed the progress made in the five years since the Beijing Platform of Action was adopted. It provided the opportunity for governments and participants to share strategies and study obstacles encountered in the implementation of the Beijing Platform for Action.

Between September 6 and 8, 2000, heads of states and governments gathered at the United Nations Headquarters in New York to reaffirm their faith in the organization and its charter "as indispensable foundations of a more peaceful, prosperous and just world," in what has become known as the Millennium Declaration.

Certain fundamental values were asserted by the countries present, including freedom and the right to live "in dignity, free from hunger and from the fear of violence, oppression or injustice." A major step for all nations was to agree explicitly on the value of equality: No individual and no nation must be denied the opportunity to benefit from development. Finally, the equal rights and opportunities of women and men were to be, in some manner, assured.

That equality for women was now perceived as a vehicle by which a nation could measure its development for both genders gave it new legitimacy. The assembly ratified this notion in 2000 with the following statement: "To promote gender equality and the empowerment of women as effective ways to combat poverty, hunger and disease and to stimulate development that is truly sustainable." It was here that the member nations pledged to combat all forms of violence against women and yet again to implement the CEDAW, established in 1979.

On October 31, 2000, the United Nations Security Council passed Resolution 1325 on Women, Peace and Security. Women's organizations and peace groups around the world made it clear that governments needed to be held accountable and to honor commitments made through this and previous resolutions. The UN International Day for the Elimination of Violence against

Women is now observed on November 25 in countries worldwide. Although it is overshadowed in the United States by the Thanksgiving holiday, it is often used to publicize local work at the community level with women in other countries. In the latter half of the 20th century, women's movements in all parts of the world found a voice through events like Women's Day.

Women's full participation in the peacemaking and peace-building process is a criterion from Resolution 1325 that international organizations are using to measure improvement or declines in women's conditions and rights, especially in regions of conflict. For instance, UNIFEM provided oversight for coaching and preparation of female representatives from women's groups so they could attend the post-2006 election peace processes in the DRC. However, few women attended because they could not afford to travel, and of the few who did, their role was greatly diminished by prevailing attitudes. Today, sexual violence persists.

A 2010 study of the Indonesian province of Aceh, Colombia, Israel, Liberia, Sri Lanka, and Uganda highlighted evidence that Resolution 1325 has not been effectively implemented in countries where there were insufficient public educational campaigns, numbers of women integrated into the decision-making bodies, and support from aid donors to pay for women's expenses so they could afford to travel to these processes.[92] These are issues that UN Women, an entity created in July 2010 by the UN General Assembly as part of its "reform agenda," is expected to tackle.

The Dakar Framework for Action adopted at the World Education Forum in 2000 also highlighted the role the United Nations Educational, Scientific and Cultural Organization (UNESCO) could play in eradicating poverty and achieving the MDG of universal primary education by 2015 by joining its agenda with the movement for gender balancing.

GENDER BALANCE

A conference commemorating the 10th anniversary of the UN's Fourth World Conference on Women was held in Beijing in March 2005 to review advances and objectives since 1995 globally and in China. At "Beijing+10," member nations declared solidarity with "gender mainstreaming" and planned to take recommendations of this conference to the Millennium Summit 2005.

At the convening of the General Assembly in September 2005, further goals were stated in the Millennium Document, adding the promise of education, especially for females: "for eradicating illiteracy, and [to] strive for expanded secondary and higher education as well as vocational education and technical training, especially for girls and women."[93]

Member nations were explicit about their positions of continued support of the 1995 Beijing conference as well as pursuance of gender equality in education and other areas such as property ownership, equal access to reproductive health, employment, and "productive assets and resources" such as land, credit, and technology. The 2005 World Summit promised to eliminate all forms of discrimination and violence against women and "the girl child," especially during and after armed conflicts. Another area that was featured was the "increased representation of women in government decision–making bodies, including through ensuring their equal opportunity to participate fully in the political process."[94]

THE MOVEMENT EVOLVES

During the three decades following its passage in 1979, CEDAW would become the subject of outreach by more than 190 national NGOs. Known as the "Treaty for the Rights of Women," or the international "Bill of Rights" for women, it shaped the passage and enforcement of national laws in many countries. The treaty consists of a preamble and 30 articles that define what constitutes discrimination against women and set an agenda for national action. The treaty requires regular progress reports from ratifying countries, but it does not impose any changes in existing laws or require new laws of countries ratifying the treaty. It lays out models for achieving equality but contains no enforcement authority. In December 1999, an Optional Protocol to the Convention was entered into force, enabling women victims of sex discrimination to submit complaints to an international treaty body and making the convention as effective as other international human rights instruments by providing individual complaints procedures. As of September 2009, 90 states have become parties to the Convention's Optional Protocol. Responsibility for servicing the Committee on the Elimination of Discrimination against Women—a body of experts who monitor the convention's implementation— was transferred to the Office of the United Nations High Commissioner for Human Rights in Geneva, Switzerland, in January 2008.

The United States is one of only eight member states—and the only developed country—that has not ratified the treaty. Opponents of U.S. ratification of CEDAW have raised fears about the ways it might affect the United States' ability to grant or withhold rights to its citizens. Some believe ratification would give too much power to the international community, with treaty provisions superseding U.S. laws and violating U.S. sovereignty.

The enforcement of women's rights is now closely watched through a variety of international agencies and NGOs. The United Nations holds member nations accountable through statistics-gathering efforts and regular meetings of the Commission on the Status of Women, which has focused on two "emerging issues" every year since the implementation of the Beijing Platform for Action.

Amnesty International and Human Rights Watch also appoint delegations to monitor on-site elections and to provide testimony to the implementation or absence of women's rights in countries around the globe.

OECD has been analyzing and tracking the MDGs, taking gender into account. For instance, in order to achieve the first goal of eradicating poverty, women will need to have greater control of natural resources, land, and credit. Or for universal education, there would need to be better controls in regarding women's decision-making power and a shift in the percentage of married women ages 15 to 19. In order to improve health, measures would first need to address the violence incurred by women, both from war and such tribal practices as female genital mutilation.

International women's organizations, such as WILPF, continue to advocate enhanced participation and development of women, including equal participation of women and men in decision-making processes at all levels. They send delegates to attend and address meetings of the Commission on the Status of Women at the United Nations every year.

The efforts of women's movements are continuing in countries where these rights are only now seeing the light of day, such as Afghanistan, where women have been fighting to keep their rights under the threat of conservative Islam. In the United States, the emphasis is on equal pay, and protecting reproductive rights, social security, pensions, and secure employment. Meanwhile, domestic violence is a growing concern across the globe, made visible by a 2005 report from the World Health Organization.[95] The severe and continuing problem of violence against women was newly underscored by the UN's October 2006 presentation of the Secretary-General's in-depth study on all forms of violence against women.

At the September 2010 MDR meeting, it was acknowledged that violence continues to be a "blight on humanity" everywhere and not adequately addressed, in spite of the increase in initiatives. In many ways, violence is clearly an obstruction or limitation to progress being made in many of the development goals, especially in countries where civil war or ethnic rivalry persist, such as Afghanistan, Iraq, and the Democratic Republic of the Congo.

WOMEN STUDYING WOMEN

The growth of women's studies programs paralleled the growth of women's conferences. Beginning in the late 1960s and early 1970s, courses formalized into degree programs in the United States and Europe, soon followed by women's studies programs in Australia, New Zealand, Taiwan, India, South Korea, the West Indies, and Japan. With the international conferences, the field of women's studies moved across borders in the 1980s into other parts of the world, including the Philippines, Thailand, South Africa, Puerto Rico, the Dominican Republic, China, and Eastern Europe. By the 1990s, it had reached Malaysia, Vietnam, the Czech Republic, Slovakia, and Uganda.

The programs have helped to dispel the image of a monolithic women's movement and have proved invaluable for observing the evolution of the women's movement from one about women's rights into one about gender equality. In the past few years, some programs have been changing their names to reflect this shift in perception. In addition, programs have helped bring about accountability that is outside of the political arena and offered another market for statistics gathered by international organizations and NGOs. Women's history classes have also become part of some public school curricula in the United States.

One common element to most programs, whether a course, an undergraduate degree, or a doctoral program, has been the analysis of power and ways it is handled by gender and ethnicity within any given country. More important, women's studies programs have helped women to understand that "every issue is a woman's issue," a concept inspired by the U.S. congresswoman Bella Abzug (1920–98) and, in some way, a wedge to keep progressing forward.

[1] U.S. Department of State. Country profile of United Arab Emirates (March 6, 2007). Available online. URL: http://www.state.gov/g/drl/rls/hrrpt/2006/78865.htm. Accessed October 23, 2010.

[2] IPU. "Women in National Parliaments, Situation as of 31 July 2010." Available online. URL: http://www.ipu.org/wmn-e/classif.htm. Accessed September 24, 2010.

[3] Sanja Kelly. "Women's Rights in the Middle East and North Africa 2010," Overview Essay: Hard-Won Progress and a Long Road Ahead. Freedom House. Available online. URL: http://www.freedomhouse.org/template.cfm?page=384&key=270&parent=23&report=86. Accessed October 23, 2010.

[4] Sanja Kelly. "Women's Rights in the Middle East and North Africa 2010," Overview Essay. BBC. "Women in Saudi Arabia to vote and run in elections" (September 25, 2011). Available online. URL: http://www.bbc.co.uk/news/world-us-canada-15052030. Accessed September 26, 2011.

[5] United Nations Development Fund for Women (UNIFEM). "Progress of the World's Women 2008/2009," p. 23.

[6] EUROPA. "Gender Mainstreaming in EU Policies: European Commission Reports Significant Progress." March 4, 1998.

[7] World Health Organization (WHO). "Climate Change and Health." Fact sheet number 266 (January 2010). Available online. URL: http://www.who.int/mediacentre/factsheets/fs266/en. Accessed December 23, 2010.

[8] Christopher Colclough, et al. "Rights, Equality, and Education for All." EFA Global Monitoring Report 2003/4, UNESCO, 2003, p. 44.

[9] Colclough, et al. "Rights, Equality, and Education for All." Executive summary.

[10] Indiana University. Press release, August 11, 2009. Presenting research at the American Sociological Association annual meeting, "Mapping Gender Ideology with Views toward Marital Name Change." Available online. URL: http://newsinfo.iu.edu/tips/page/normal/11558.html#7. Accessed on December 22, 2010.

[11] Amanda Bower. "It's Mrs., Not Ms. In a Return to Tradition, More Brides Are Taking Their Husband's Name." *Time*, May 29, 2005.

[12] United Nations, Department of Economic and Social Affairs, Population Division (2009). World Marriage Data 2008 (POP/DB/Marr/Rev2008). Available online. URL: http://www.un.org/esa/population/publications/WMD2008/WP_WMD_2008/Data.html. Accessed January 7, 2011.

[13] ABC News. Child Bride Escapes Life of Abuse (January 2, 2011). ABC News. Available online. URL: http:labcnews.go.com/WNT/video/child-bride-escapes-life-abuse-12525083. Accessed October 20, 2011.

[14] United Nations, Department of Economic and Social Affairs, Population Division (2009). World Marriage Data 2008.

[15] "Quand les femmes assument leur pouvoir." *Le Figaro*, October 12, 2007, 18.

[16] Central Intelligence Agency (CIA). *The World Factbook*. 2010. Available online. URL: https://www.cia.gov/library/publications/the-world-factbook/geos/xx.html. Accessed October 19, 2010.

[17] International Labor Organization (ILO). "Global Employment Trends for Women." March 2009, p. 9.

[18] ILO. "Global Employment Trends for Women." March 2009, p. 9.

[19] CIA. The World Factbook, 2010.

[20] United Nations. "Keeping the Promise: A Forward-Looking Review to Promote an Agreed Action Agenda to Achieve the Millennium Development Goals by 2015." Report of the Secretary-General, February 12, 2010, p. 5.

[21] ILO. "Global Employment Trends for Women." March 2009, p. 9.

[22] UNIFEM. "Who Answers to Women? Gender and Accountability" (2008/09), p. 55.

[23] ILO. "Global Employment Trends for Women." Report, March 2009, p. 18.

[24] UNIFEM. "Who Answers to Women? Gender and Accountability" (2008/09), p. 57.

[25] National Center for Education Statistics (NCES). Table 301. Degrees in Business Conferred by Degree-Granting Institutions, by Level of Degree and Sex of Student: Selected Years, 1955–56 through 2007–08.

[26] "Study Finds 'Opportunity Gap' for Women in Business Schools." Press release, Center for the Education of Women and Catalyst Business School. University of Michigan, Ann Arbor. The University Record Online (May 22, 2000). Available online. URL: http://www.umich.edu/nurecord/9900/May22_00/8.htm. Accessed January 21, 2006.

[27] UN Division for the Advancement of Women. "General Recommendations Made by the Committee on the Elimination of Discrimination against Women" (May 19, 2006). Available online. URL: http://www.un.org/womenwatch/daw/cedaw/recommendations/recomm.htm. Accessed December 23, 2010.

[28] UNIFEM. "Who Answers to Women? Gender and Accountability" (2008/09), p.76.

[29] "Maternity Benefits—European Study Shows Wide Variations." Press release, Mercer Human Resource Consulting, May 10, 2006. Available online. URL: http://www.mercerhr.com/pressrelease/details.jhtml?idContent=1221340. Accessed June 5, 2006.

[30] Mauricette Mongbo. "Low-Income Women's Bank in Benin: Social and Economic Empowerment." Brandeis University, Waltham, Mass. Available online. URL: http://www.gdrc.org/icm/wind/benin.html. Accessed January 30, 2006.

[31] State of the Microcredit Summit Campaign Report 2009, pp. 1–3. Available online. URL: http://www.microcreditsummit.org/state_of_the_campaign_report/. Accessed February 2, 2011.

[32] State of the Microcredit Summit Campaign Report 2009, p. 30–31.

[33] United Nations Fund for Population Activities (UNFPA). "The State of the World Population 2009," p. 55–57.

[34] The following Web site lists male and female personnel available for military service by country: Central Intelligence Agency. The World Factbook. Available online. URL: https://www.cia.gov/library/publications/the-world-factbook/fields/2024.html. Accessed December 23, 2010..

[35] "Percentage of Military Service Women in NATO Countries Armed Forces, 2001–2005." Datenquelle: Office on Women in the NATO Forces. December 4, 2006. Available online. URL: http://www.nato.int/issues/women_nato/perc_fem_soldiers_2001_2006.pdf. Accessed December 23, 2010.

[36] Committee on Women in the NATO Forces. "Gender Mainstreaming: CWINF Guidance for NATO Gender Mainstreaming." Report, 2007. Available online. URL: http://www.nato.int/issues/women_nato/index.html. Accessed December 23, 2010.

[37] Tim McGirk. "Moms and Martyrs."Time, May 14, 2007, Vol. 169, No. 20.

[38] Tim McGirk. "Crossing the Lines." Time, February 27, 2006, p. 38.

[39] United Nations. The World's Women 2010: Trends and Statistics. New York: United Nations, p. 14.

[40] United Nations. The World's Women 2010: Trends and Statistics, p. 17.

[41] Joint United Nations Programme on HIV/AIDS (UNAIDS). "2010 UNAIDS Report on the Global AIDS Epidemic," p. 19.

[42] UNAIDS. "2010 UNAIDS Report on the Global AIDS Epidemic," p. 23.

[43] UNAIDS. "2010 UNAIDS Report on the Global AIDS Epidemic," p. 25-26.

[44] WHO. "Trends in Maternal Mortality: 1990 to 2008," 2010, p. 1.

[45] UNAIDS. "2010 UNAIDS Report on the Global AIDS Epidemic," p. 28.

[46] UNAIDS. "2010 UNAIDS Report on the Global AIDS Epidemic," p. 110.

[47] UNAIDS. "2010 UNAIDS Report on the Global AIDS Epidemic," p. 20.

[48] UNAIDS. "2010 UNAIDS Report on the Global AIDS Epidemic," p. 20.

[49] CDC. "HIV in the United States, Fact Sheet." July 2010.

[50] UNAIDS. "2010 UNAIDS Report on the Global AIDS Epidemic," p. 50.

[51] Etienne G. Krug, Linda L. Dahlberg, James A. Mercy, Anthony B. Zwi, and Rafael Lozano, eds. "World Report on Violence and Health." Report, World Health Organization (WHO), 2002, p. 286.

[52] WHO. "Trends in Maternal Mortality: 1990 to 2008," 2010, p. 1.

[53] UN Department of Economic & Social Affairs. "World Contraceptive Use." Population Division, October 2009. Available online. URL: http://www.un.org/esa/population/publications/contraceptive2007/contraceptive2007.htm. Accessed October 4, 2010.

[54] Sylvia Poggioli and Steve Inskeep. "Vatican Clarifies Pope's Comments on Condoms." NPR (November 22, 2010). Available online. URL: http://www.npr.org/2010/11/22/131504280/pope-comments-on-condom-use. Accessed January 9, 2011.

[55] UNFPA. "The State of the World Population 2009," p. 22.

[56] UNFPA. "The State of the World Population 2009." Monitoring ICPD Goals: Selected Indicators, p. 80

[57] UNFPA. "The State of the World Population 2009," p. 91.

[58] Grayce P. Storey. "Ethical Problems Surrounding Surrogate Motherhood." Report, Yale–New Haven Teachers Institute, 2000.

[59] Alcalá. "State of World Population 2005," p. 35.

[60] Duff G. Gillespie. "Whatever Happened to Family Planning and, for That Matter, Reproductive Health?" *International Family Planning Perspectives* vol. 30, no. 1 (March 2004): 34–38.

[61] Human Rights Campaign. "Marriage Equality & Other Relationship Recognition Laws." April 2010. Available online. URL: http://www.hrc.org/documents/Relationship_Recognition_Laws_Map.pdf. Accessed January 7, 2011.

[62] Joanna Francis. "Making a Wave." *Template Times,* February 1, 2006, p. 2.

[63] UN-HABITAT. "Global Assessment of Women's Safety. Preliminary Results 2007."

[64] UN. "In-depth Study of all Forms of Violence against Women."

[65] Mrs. Coomaraswamy, UN Special Rapporteur on Violence against Women. "Human Rights: Women's Violence." United Nations Department of Public Information, DPI/1772/HR, February 1996.

[66] Neil M. Malamuth. "Pornography and Sexual Aggression: Are There Reliable Effects and Can We Understand Them?" *Annual Review of Sex Research,* Vol. 11 (2000): 26–91.

[67] Gert Martin and M. Hald. "The Effects of Exposure to Pornography: An Empirical Contribution to the Porn Debate." *Journal of Sex Research,* University of Aarhus, Denmark (February 2006).

[68] Krug, Dahlberg, Mercy, Zwi, and Lozano, eds. "World Report on Violence and Health," p. 89.

[69] Kajsa Asling-Monemi, Rodolfo Pena, Mary Carroll Ellsberg, and Lars Ake Persson. "Violence against Women Increases the Risk of Infant and Child Mortality: A Case-Referent Study in Nicaragua." *Bulletin of the World Health Organization* 81, no. 1 (2003): 11.

[70] Krug, Dahlberg, Mercy, Zwi, and Lozano, eds. "World Report on Violence and Health," p. 109.

[71] Claudia García-Moreno, Henrica A. F. M. Jansen, Mary Ellsberg, Lori Heise, and Charlotte Watts. "WHO Multi-Country Study on Women's Health and Domestic Violence against Women: Initial Results on Prevalence, Health Outcomes and Women's Responses." Report, World Health Organization, 2005.

[72] National Coalition Against Domestic Violence. Fact sheet, 2007.

[73] Office for Victims of Crime, US DOJ. "Report to the Nation, Fiscal Years 2007–2008." VOCA VICTIM Assistance—Chapter 5, 2009, p.21. Available online. URL: http://www.ojp. usdoj.gov/ovc/welcovc/reporttonation2009/ReporttoNation09Part2.pdf. Accessed December 25, 2010.

[74] Krug, Dahlberg, Mercy, Zwi, and Lozano, eds. "World Report on Violence and Health," p. 10.

[75] Krug, Dahlberg, Mercy, Zwi, and Lozano, eds. "World Report on Violence and Health," p. 218.

[76] Krug, Dahlberg, Mercy, Zwi, and Lozano, eds. "World Report on Violence and Health," p. 218.

[77] Organisation for Economic Co-operation and Development (OECD). Selected GID Indicators, 2007. Available online. URL:http://www.oecd.org/dev/gender. Accessed on September 23, 2010.

[78] Krug, Dahlberg, Mercy, Zwi, and Lozano, eds. "World Report on Violence and Health," p. 60.

[79] United Nations Office on Drugs and Crime (UNODC). "Trafficking in Persons—Global Patterns." Report, 2006, p. 17.

[80] UNODC. Global Report on Trafficking in Humans. February 2009, p. 37.

[81] International Federation for Human Rights (FIDH). "Women and Migration," 2007.

[82] UNFPA. "Trafficking in Human Misery." Available online. URL: http://www.unfpa.org/ gender/violence1.htm. Accessed December 23, 2010.

[83] UN Office on Drug and Crimes (UNODC). Global Report on Trafficking in Humans. February 2009, p. 11.

[84] Michael P. Harris. "Hour of Decision for Women Priests—The Church of England Considers the Ordination of Females." *Time*, March 2, 1987.

[85] U.S. Bureau of Labor Statistics. "Women in the Labor Force: A Databook." September 2009. Table 11. Employed Persons by Detailed Occupation and Sex, 2008 annual averages, p. 30.

[86] Caryle Murphy. "A Chorus of Amens as More Women Take over Pulpit." *Washington Post*, July 25, 1998, p. B.01.

[87] Merriam-Webster Dictionary. "feminism." Available online. URL: http://www.merriam-webster.com/dictionary/feminist. Accessed December 23, 2010.

[88] E. C. Stanton, S. B. Anthony, and M. J. Gage, eds. Seneca Falls Declaration. *History of Women's Suffrage*, Vol. 1, 1887, p. 70. Available online. URL: http://usinfo.state.gov/usa/info usa/facts/democrac/17.htm. Accessed December 20, 2005.

[89] Denis Brian. *The Curies: A Biography of the Most Controversial Family in Science*. New York: John Wiley & Sons, 2005, p. 149.

[90] "The Four Global Women's Conferences 1975–1995: Historical Perspective." United Nations Department of Public Information Bulletin. DPI/2035/M, May 2000. Available online. URL: http://www.un.org/womenwatch/daw/followup/session/presskit/hist.htm. Accessed February 1, 2006.

[91] Antoinette Fourquet. "Women's Rights and the European Union." Women and Law in Europe. January 1997. Available online. URL: http://www.helsinki.fi/science/xantippa/wle/wle13.html. Accessed November 30, 2005.

[92] Sanam Naraghi Anderlini. *What the Women Say: Participation and UNSCR 1325. A Case Study Assessment.* Massachusetts Institute of Technology. Center for International Studies and the International Civil Society Action Network, October 2010.

[93] Office of the Spokesperson. "Message from Mr. Koïchiro Matsuura, Director-General of UNESCO, on the Occasion of the International Day for the Eradication of Poverty" (October 17, 2005). United Nations Educational, Scientific and Cultural Organization. Available online. URL: http://portal.unesco.org/en/ev.php-URL_ID=30221&URL_DO=DO_TOPIC&URL_SECTION=201.html. Accessed May 25, 2006.

[94] "2005 World Summit Outcome." United Nations General Assembly, September 15, 2005, p. 18.

[95] García-Moreno, Jansen, Ellsberg, Heise, and Watts. "WHO Multi-Country Study on Women's Health and Domestic Violence against Women: Initial Results on Prevalence, Health Outcomes and Women's Responses," 2005.

2

~

Focus on the United States

The establishment of political rights for women in America, Europe, Australia, and New Zealand in the early part of the 20th century set a precedent for the rest of the world. This pattern persisted with women's pursuit of higher educational, employment, and social rights in the middle of the 20th century, which women of the 21st century are now seeking ways to enforce. The concerns are far more diverse now, as industry and technology spawn issues never before considered, from access to advanced forms of health care screening and contraceptives to the policing of live pornographic feeds over the Internet.

Women in America are now aware of the interdependence one issue can have with another, whether it is poverty, health, violence, or equal pay. They also are becoming more aware of the impact one country can have on another and global issues. By the same token, women elsewhere are struggling with and discovering new identities, yet retaining their independent cultural features.

HISTORY OF THE U.S. WOMEN'S RIGHTS MOVEMENT

The rights described in the first U.S. constitution, written in 1787, were intended for male property owners; women were denied most legal rights and expected instead to be treated according to social custom and English common law. Although unmarried women had the right to own property, that property usually passed to their husbands upon marriage. They could not vote, keep their own wages, or even have custody of children.

Abigail Adams (1744–1818), the wife of the future vice president and president John Adams, and Mercy Otis Warren (1728–1814) pressed for the inclusion of women's emancipation in the Constitution, but the issue would not be considered seriously for another 45 years. Women began, one by one, to break the barriers of public silence in the early 1800s; they spoke out on property and civil rights, suffrage, and education. The historical event that contributed most to the initiation of the women's movement in the United States was the Seneca Falls Convention of 1848, when Elizabeth Cady Stanton (1815–1902), Lucretia Coffin Mott (1793–1880), and other women met at Seneca Falls, New York. There, they issued a declaration of independence for women, called *Declaration of Sentiments*, demanding full legal, educational, and commercial opportunity; equal pay; the right to earn an income; and the right to vote.

The Sentiments were modeled after the Declaration of Independence and just as the Declaration's authors had more than 70 years prior, the authors of the Sentiments highlighted 18 grievances. Grievances included married women's being considered legally dependent ("civilly dead") and women's not being allowed to vote or to have property rights (although they had to pay property taxes). Husbands had legal power over and responsibility for wives to the extent that they could imprison or beat them. Divorce and child custody laws favored men with the "ownership" of children, household belongings, and land. Most occupations, including all those in the fields of medicine, law, and politics, were closed to women, and when women did work, they were paid only a fraction of what men earned. Women were not allowed to receive an education, and colleges and universities would not accept women as students. The situation was even worse for African-American women.

Civil Rights

Frances ("Fanny") Wright (1795–1852) wrote *A Plan for the Gradual Abolition of Slavery in the United States without Danger of Loss to the Citizens of the South* in 1825 and became one of the first American women to lecture before "promiscuous audiences" (audiences that included both women and men). Maria Stuart (1803–79) advocated rights for black women of the North. The Grimké sisters from South Carolina began lecturing crowds in 1836 about slavery. Angelina Emily Grimké (1805–79), converted to the Quaker faith by her elder sister, Sarah Moore Grimké (1792–1873), became an abolitionist in 1835 and wrote *An Appeal to the Christian Women of the South*. With her sister, she began speaking around New York City and became an orator of considerable power.

Also a Quaker, Mott in her early activism focused on racial equality and international women's rights. She aided fugitive slaves, and in 1833, after a meeting with the American Anti-Slavery Society, she organized the Philadelphia Female Anti-Slavery Society. The refusal to recognize Mott and other women formally as delegates because of their gender at London's World Anti-Slavery Convention in 1840 fueled her actions in the United States.

Property Rights

Another area that gained early attention by women's rights advocates was property rights. The first-known advocate for women's land rights was the colonial Maryland landowner Margaret Brent (1601–71). An active businesswoman and lawyer, she pleaded legal cases on numerous occasions on behalf of Governor Leonard Calvert of Maryland and Lord Baltimore. In 1648, she made her mark as a suffragist when she argued that she should be awarded two votes for a voice in the colonial assembly's counsels—as a landowner in her own right and as holder of a power of attorney for another landowner—but she received neither.

Until the Married Women's Property Act (MWPA) in 1839, women who married in the United States automatically turned over all their property to their husband. Early activists such as Ernestine Rose (1810–92), the daughter of a rabbi who immigrated to the United States in May 1836, petitioned for married women's property rights in New York State, aided by Paulina Wright Davis (1813–76).

In 1839, Mississippi became the first state to pass MWPA, and Maryland followed soon after, in 1843. After 12 years of campaigning, New York finally passed the law in 1848. It became a model for many states because of the increased protection it afforded women from husbands' creditors.

Suffrage

Although women put their ambitions for suffrage on the backburner during the Civil War (1861–65) and focused instead on the campaign against slavery, they fully expected that women's right to vote would be part of the civil rights for which they were fighting. However, the Thirteenth Amendment, which prohibited slavery, and the Civil Rights Bill of the Fourteenth Amendment granted rights to slaves and citizens, but the right to vote was extended only to black men, not to white or black women.

Two women pivotal to the movement were Stanton and Susan Brownell Anthony (1820–1906). They met in 1851, and their relationship evolved into a lifelong commitment to each other's role in the movement. Stanton and Anthony formed the National Woman Suffrage Association (NWSA) in 1869 to fight for amendments to the U.S. Constitution that would enfranchise women. In the same year, Lucy Stone (1818–93), Julia Ward Howe (1819–1910), and Josephine Ruffin (1842–1924) organized the

American Woman Suffrage Association (AWSA) in Boston, Massachusetts, to promote change in individual state legislatures for women's suffrage. The AWSA membership base was more conservative than NWSA's and did not campaign on issues such as employer discrimination and easier divorce for women. In 1870, the AWSA founded the *Women's Journal,* a magazine edited by Lucy Stone.

Abby and Julia Smith (1797–1878 and 1792–1886, respectively), two Glastonbury, Connecticut, sisters in their 70s, received international publicity for their refusal to pay taxes unless they were given the right to vote in town meetings in 1869. Abigail Duniway's (1834–1915) weekly Portland, Oregon, newspaper, the *New northwest,* founded in 1871, also became a vehicle for women's suffrage.

With the text of the Fourteenth Amendment and a copy of New York State's constitution in hand, Anthony voted in the presidential elections on November 5, 1872, with other women following her lead. Three weeks later, she and three election inspectors were arrested and brought to trial, which lasted until 1874 and enabled the issue to become newsworthy as the trial of Susan B. Anthony. The trial also highlighted that women were not allowed to serve as jurists at the time.

Meanwhile, Virginia Minor (1824–94) had also tried to vote in the 1872 presidential election in Missouri. Her husband, Francis Minor, filed suit when his wife was turned away at the polls by the voter registrar. The couple petitioned for their case to be heard by the Supreme Court, and their appeal was accepted. The Court ruled that, although Virginia Minor was a citizen, the Fourteenth Amendment did not guarantee her right to vote. (The Fourteenth Amendment would not be interpreted as protecting women's rights until the Supreme Court's 1971 decision in *Reed v. Reed.*)

Congress passed a constitutional amendment that enfranchised women in 1878, but the act would not be ratified by the states for decades. The campaign labored on in the postbellum years, and many of the activities are recorded in a multivolume work, *History of Woman Suffrage,* authored by Stanton, Anthony, and Matilda Josyln Gage (1826–98), that was later published in 1881, 1882, 1886, and 1902.

Upon being admitted to the Union in 1890, Wyoming became the first state to grant suffrage, followed by Colorado in 1893, and Utah and Idaho in 1896. With the right to vote, women's insistence on access to higher education, trades, and professions, and married women's rights to own property were gaining public awareness and acceptance.

The two suffrage groups, NWSA and ASWA, united in 1890 as the National American Woman Suffrage Association (NAWSA). Carrie Chapman

Catt (1859–1947) was named its president in 1900. She left in 1904 to care for her ill husband and upon his death in 1905 became involved with the International Women's Suffrage Alliance. Meanwhile, Ida B. Wells-Barnett (1862–1931) organized a national movement for black women. Presidency of NAWSA was assumed from 1904 to 1915 by Dr. Anna Shaw (1847–1919), under whose leadership membership grew from 17,000 to 200,000 women.

Inspired by the British example, increasing numbers of African-American and working-class women joined the movement during the opening decade of the 20th century, leading to a more diverse movement, socially, economically, and politically.

A younger generation of suffragists, including Alice Paul (1885–1977) and Lucy Burns (1879–1966), picked up the struggle for a federal amendment to the constitution for women's suffrage with renewed energy after 1912. Largely inspired by the high media coverage of Emmeline Pankhurst's prison hunger strikes and protest marches in Britain, Paul and Burns organized a large-scale parade on March 3, 1913, in Washington, D.C., the day before Woodrow Wilson's inauguration. The parade of 8,000 women was the largest of its kind ever seen in the U.S. capital and was Paul's first attempt to arouse public support for women's rights on a broad scale, with floats and banners and an audience of a half-million people.

After trying in vain to coordinate her efforts with Chapman, who had returned to NAWSA, in 1913 Paul created the Congressional Union for Woman Suffrage, which was renamed the National Women's Party in 1916. Under Paul's leadership, picket lines, marches, and hunger strikes became prominent tactics used to pressure the government and President Wilson to grant women the right to vote. In the climate just before the nation entered into the throes of World War I, the tactics did not garner much public support.

Another influential woman during this time was Emma Goldman, who advocated free speech, birth control, women's equality and independence, and union organizations. She was imprisoned for two years for criticizing mandatory conscription of young men into the military during World War I. Deported in 1919, she participated in international social and political events, including the Russian Revolution and the Spanish Civil War, until her death in 1940.

On January 9, 1918, President Wilson endorsed the amendment allowing women to vote. The amendment was not passed, however, until 1919, pending ratification by two-thirds of the states (32 of 48 states). The 32nd state to vote for constitutional ratification was Tennessee. In a historic moment, the young state legislator from Niota, Tennessee, Harry T. Burn, changed his intended vote to support the amendment, at the urging of a note from his mother. Ratification allowed 25 million women to vote and the Nineteenth Amendment to the Constitution to become law on August 26, 1920.

In 1919, when ratification of the Nineteenth Amendment seemed imminent, Catt had renamed the National American Woman Suffrage Association the League of Women Voters to educate women about their newfound voting freedom, especially pending employment legislation. Women were divided about which strategy to pursue: demanding equal standing with men or protective legislation that would control the number of hours women could work per week and prevent them from entering certain risky occupations. The Women's Bureau of the Department of Labor formed to gather information about women's conditions at work and to lobby for the protection of women workers from abusive and unsafe conditions.

After the ratification of the Nineteenth Amendment in 1920, Paul continued to fight for woman's equality in the United States and abroad. In 1938, she founded the World Woman's Party, based in Geneva, Switzerland. Her international work included a demand for equality of the sexes in the preamble to the United Nations Charter. In 1923, Paul introduced a draft of the Equal Rights Amendment for the Constitution, called the Lucretia Mott Amendment, at the 75th anniversary of the Seneca Falls conference. Now that women had won suffrage, guaranteed equality under the Constitution was Paul's next goal. The amendment was finally passed by Congress in 1972, but it failed to win ratification.

Other Fronts

At first American women focused on property, civil, and voting rights, but as they became aware of how long it might take to effect change, they also turned their attention to other areas of life, from work opportunities, to quality of life, to birth control.

EMPLOYMENT RIGHTS

An important social activist who focused on employment rights was Florence Kelley (1858–1932). She began to advocate labor reform as early as 1894, when she persuaded the Illinois state legislature to change existing child and women labor laws and limit the workday for women to a maximum of eight hours. The Illinois Association of Manufacturers repealed the legislation in 1895. Kelley then established the National Consumer's League (NCL) in 1899; its main objective was to implement a minimum wage and limited working hours for women and children.

The idea of protecting women and children from labor exploitation through law eventually became a source of conflict with equal rights advocates, who thought a strategy that demanded special protection for women would ultimately backfire in the fight for equal access to labor opportunities.

EDUCATION

As efforts to gain suffrage were thwarted, some women began to focus on education as a way to advance change. In the early 19th century, girls and young women were allowed to attend grade school, academies, or seminaries but were not expected to go beyond that stage, having their domestic and marital duties to occupy them. The wife of a male school headmaster, Emma Willard (1787–1870), asked for funds from the New York State legislature in 1819 to open a women's college. The state refused her request, and she was forced to use her own funds to open the Troy Female Seminary, in 1821. Among its graduates was Elizabeth Cady Stanton.

In 1833, Oberlin College in Ohio became the first college in the United States to admit women, coeducating them with men. The first all-women college to offer a bachelor of arts degree in a variety of disciplines was Mount Holyoke in 1837 in South Hadley, Massachusetts, founded by Mary Lyon (1797–1849), a former assistant principal of Ipswich Female Seminary, which she had found limiting in its ambitions for women, given its missionary focus.

Access to education varied according to one's social, racial, and economic background. The Morrill Act of 1862 provided land grants for colleges where men and women could receive basic technical and agricultural training to pioneer the West. This happened along with generous land development accommodations from the Homestead Act, which granted 160 acres of public land to citizens who would purchase the land after living on it for five years.

Three private colleges in Ohio—Antioch, Oberlin, and Hillsdale (which later moved to Michigan)—and two public universities—the University of Iowa and the University of Utah (formerly Deseret)—admitted women before the Civil War. The war caused fewer male students to enroll, making some postsecondary institutions more amenable to admitting women.

By 1870, eight state universities accepted women. While coeducation was not allowed by the more established universities, expensive all-women colleges, called "sister schools," began to flourish in the late 1800s. They included Vassar in 1865, Wellesley and Smith Colleges in 1875, Radcliffe College in 1879, Bryn Mawr College in 1885, and Barnard College in 1889. By the turn of the century, 15 percent of college alumni were female. However, their limited access to specialized training in medicine, law, politics, and education, in turn, affected their ability to become physicians, lawyers, politicians, and college professors.

Women's demand for higher education was fueled by the appearance of some home appliances (such as mechanical carpet sweepers, kitchen gadgets, glass jars, canned food, and public laundries) and the development of electricity, which freed women from their full-time domestic duties. The phonograph, the radio, and the telegraph, alongside the increasing availability of reading material for women that informed them about the world, also stirred women's ambitions. The growth of primary schools led to a shortage of teachers that fed the demand for educated personnel. Another impetus to educating women was the increase in the range of jobs that women could pursue that began during the Civil War. Although it remained limited (including domestic servants, agricultural laborers, seamstresses, milliners, teachers, textile mill workers, and laundresses), the increase of the number of women in the workforce contributed to social awareness that education might better prepare them to work.

The decades following World War II saw an explosion in the number of male students who entered higher education institutions due to the return home of veterans under the GI bill. As service benefits applied only to men, women's enrollment in colleges declined during the 1950s. During the 1960s and 1970s, all-male institutions of higher education—from the Ivy League, such as Dartmouth, Princeton, and Yale, to other elite colleges and universities, such as Amherst, Haverford, Wesleyan, Williams, Bowdoin, Colgate, Hamilton, Lafayette, and Lehigh—opened their doors to women in accelerated numbers because of social and legislative changes.[1] Women's colleges began to merge with all-male or coeducational institutions. Declining enrollment and financial problems in women's colleges caused some to close, as they could not keep up with the increased competition in higher education. Although the number of women's colleges decreased from over 200 in 1960 to 83 by 1993, women's enrollment in higher education regained momentum in the 1960s and 1970s. In 1970, 68 women enrolled for every 100 men, and in 1978, the ratio was 100 women for every 100 men. By the 1980s, female students outnumbered male students, 110 to 100.[2]

STANCE AGAINST ALCOHOLISM

The temperance movement spurred on by women's groups in the 1870s was a precursor to the Prohibition era of the 1920s. The Woman's Crusade of 1873–74 had opposed the manufacturing of alcohol and operation of saloons, forcing some owners to close their doors and engage in another line of work. Catt noted at the time that the liquor industry was a powerful opponent of women's suffrage—with good reason.

Women who had gained the right to vote in 16 states were largely responsible for the launch of the Prohibition era, as in 1917 they used that power to pass the Eighteenth Amendment, banning the manufacturing and selling of alcohol in the United States.

THE BIRTH CONTROL MOVEMENT

Although the first birth control clinic was founded by a Dutch physician, Aletta Jacobs (1854–1929), in 1878, in Amsterdam, the birth control movement in America would have to wait for several more decades. In 1873, public morality had already culminated in the Comstock Act, which classified information about birth control—including rubber condoms, diaphragms, chemical suppositories, vaginal sponges, and medicated tampons as well as classical techniques of rhythm and withdrawal—as immoral. The notion of a woman's right to own her body and control her own reproduction and sexuality was a novel concept of the women's movement. One of the leading birth control reformers was Margaret Sanger (1879–1966), a public health nurse. She gave up her New York practice in 1912 to focus on the distribution of information about contraceptives. Arrested for distributing obscene material, she managed to flee to England, where she founded the National Birth Control League. During World War I, she returned to the United States, where she opened the first birth control clinic in 1916 but was arrested and received a 30-day jail sentence in a workhouse in 1917 because she was deemed "a public nuisance," as she later wrote in an article for the October 1931 issue of *Birth Control Review*.[3] Nevertheless, an American judge ruled in 1918 that contraceptive devices could be used legally to prevent disease.

The birth control movement emerged as a more widely recognized cause once the drive for suffrage reached its culmination in 1920. This meant women needed to be educated about birth control methods such as contraceptive suppositories and the decision to become a mother. The National Birth Control League became the American Birth Control League in 1921 and later was renamed the Planned Parenthood Federation of America in 1942. Prior to that, a 1936 Supreme Court decision declassified birth control information as obscene material. Throughout the 1940s and 1950s, legal suits occupied birth control advocates, but the movement still made strides and resulted in the U.S. Supreme Court's striking down the last remaining state law (in Connecticut) to prohibit married couples' use of contraceptives in 1965. (Unmarried women's right to contraception was recognized by the Supreme Court in 1972 when it struck down a Massachusetts law.)

The Stock Market Crash of 1929

The Depression era that was initiated in the United States by the stock market crash on October 29, 1929, caused the federal government to urge women to leave job opportunities to male heads of households. Nevertheless, during the administration of President Roosevelt (1932–45), the first lady, Eleanor Roosevelt, worked hard to represent women's rights in the workplace, often urging her husband to employ women in government positions. He made Francis Perkins (1880–1965) the first female cabinet member as secretary of labor. Mrs. Roosevelt also extended her support to minority men and women. Mary McLeod Bethune (1875–1955) became the Negro affairs director for the National Youth Administration during Roosevelt's administration.

World War II

The advent of another world war meant women were enticed back into the labor market to make up for the shortage of men in both civilian and military jobs. From 1939 to 1945, over 6 million women were estimated to be employed outside the home. Women's percentage in the workforce grew from 25 percent in 1940 to 35 percent in 1945 with nearly 19 million women employed outside the home by the end of the war.[4] Of those, three-quarters were married, a majority were over the age of 35, and more than a third had children under the age of 14.[5]

Women now held nontraditional jobs in the blue-collar sector: in shipyards and airplane plants, as welders and crane operators. The famous Rosie the Riveter was the icon—inspired by real women—for Americans in the 1940s who assembled bombs, built tanks, welded hulls, and greased locomotives. As men were shipped to the front lines, women moved into assembly lines, enticed by higher wages and a propaganda poster featuring a muscle-bound Rosie the Riveter exclaiming, "We Can Do It!" Leading up to World War II, women with nursing skills or medical expertise began to serve as flight attendants, as they were better able to cope with airsickness and emergency landings. During the war, however, with many registered nurses needed in the armed forces, the requirement for flight attendants having medical experience was relaxed.

Almost 400,000 women served in the armed forces in 1939, mostly the army and navy, in noncombatant jobs as secretaries, typists, and nurses.[6] However, some were involved in military activities, namely, the Women's Airforce Service Pilots (WASPs), who were responsible for ferrying airplanes to strategic points. Nancy Harkness Love's (1914–76) Women's Auxiliary Ferrying Squadron and Jacqueline Cochran's (1910–80) Women's Flying Training Detachment trained women to work within the United States and

Great Britain. The Women's Army Corps tried to recruit women with the claim that it could offer 239 kinds of jobs for women, including radio repairing.[7]

Of the thousand or so women who enlisted in the flying programs, 38 women pilots in the WASP program were killed in service, while drawing $250 a month as army employees. Jacqueline Cochran wrote in her final report that this "was slightly less than that of a 2nd Lieutenant with flight pay." She also noted, "There was no promotion or advancement in pay depending on length of service," meaning veterans were paid the same rate as inductees.[8] During their flying careers in World War II, she and other women lived a military style of life and were expecting to be commissioned as officers in the Army Air Forces. But not until 1977 did President Carter sign a bill that granted the women veteran status, and even so, without full benefits. In 1984, they were awarded World War II Victory Medals and Theater Service Medals. In 2010, President Obama awarded the Congressional Gold Medal to the WASPs.

In spite of the mounting evidence that women were competent in the workplace and in the battlefield, the American government promoted women's war work as a temporary response to an emergency.

The 1950s: The Silence before the Storm

War-weary Americans were eager for the resumption of traditional life. Although the women's movement did not disappear, it became more subdued. Several lesbian organizations in the United States were founded in the early 1950s, including the Daughters of Bilitis, a name inspired by a poem by the Frenchman Pierre Louys about women in love. Founded in 1955 in San Francisco, California, it had a growth in membership sufficient for a national convention in 1960. However, even by the time of its third convention in the 1970s the discussion of lesbian rights was still considered taboo and separate from women's rights.

Images of women's freshly found domestic bliss in television series like *Blondie* or *Father Knows Best* were offset by the reality of women's struggling to find work during peacetime. In further contrast to media images of traditional family life, the number of single mothers and divorced women also started to increase.

The 1960s and 1970s: Women Go Professional

In the 1960s and 1970s, feminism experienced a rebirth in the United States. Several influential leaders emerged to become icons for this second wave of the women's liberation movement (a term coined in 1968), including Betty

WOMEN'S RIGHTS

Friedan (1921–2006), Bella Abzug (1920–98), Shirley Chisholm (1924–2005), and Gloria Steinem (1934–   ).

In 1963, Betty Friedan published *The Feminine Mystique,* which emerged from her survey of colleagues at a 20-year college reunion, inspiring women to seek fulfillment beyond their roles as homemakers. The best seller documented the impact that limited life options and emotional and intellectual oppression had on middle-class educated women.

Bella Abzug, a female politician from New York, founded Women Strike for Peace in 1961 and the reformist New Democratic Coalition later. Known for her wide-brimmed hats and New York chutzpah, Abzug vocally opposed the Vietnam War, made herself a bitter enemy of President Nixon, and became the first Jewish congresswoman. She was elected to the U.S. House of Representatives from New York in 1970 and became a leader of the House antiwar movement and a vigorous proponent of women's rights. Abzug founded the National Women's Political Caucus with Friedan and Chisholm in 1972.

After her loss in a Senate primary in 1976 and in a New York City mayoral primary in 1977, Abzug went on to found and head the Women's Environment and Development Organization and to take a more active role in international women's affairs.

As far back as 1872, professional and political women repeatedly sought nominations through major and minor political parties to run as presidential and vice-presidential candidates during presidential election years. Chisholm, the first black woman to become a congresswoman, was a founding member of the Congressional Black Caucus in 1969. She also became the first black woman to run for president in 1972. She addressed social, economic, educational, and political issues affecting black women through the National Political Congress of Black Women, which she also founded. However, it was not until 1984 that a woman's name would appear on a national ballot as a vice-presidential candidate, when Geraldine Ferraro became Walter Mondale's running mate.

The media became a vehicle for the women's movement when Gloria Steinem founded *Ms.* magazine in 1971. While few women journalists were covering politics, Steinem took up the political beat. She also founded the National Women's Political Caucus, the Women's Action Alliance, and the Ms. Foundation for Women.

During that era, activism was also fueled by younger college women who participated in the antiwar and Civil Rights movements but found themselves hampered by domestic gender issues and legal and social barriers in education, political influence, and economic power. A component of the movement was the use of "consciousness-raising" as a tool, for example, by the Redstockings, who in 1969 combined education with social revolution to produce alternative think tanks and strategies toward winning women's rights, and the Women's International Terrorist Conspiracy from Hell (WITCH), which combined spontaneous street theater with protest to gain attention to women's causes.

Other organizations began to address the needs of specific subgroups, including those of blacks, Latinas, Asian Americans, lesbians, welfare recipients, business owners, aspiring politicians, tradeswomen, and professional women.

EMPLOYMENT

At the urging of Esther Peterson (1906–97), director of the Women's Bureau of the Department of Labor, in 1961, President Kennedy convened the Commission on the Status of Women and named Eleanor Roosevelt as its chair. The report issued by the commission in 1963 documented discrimination against women in virtually every area of American life. State and local governments quickly followed suit and established their own commissions for women, to research conditions and recommend changes that could be initiated.

In that same time period, Kennedy signed Executive Order 10925 on March 6, 1961, heralding legislation that would hold federal government contracting agencies accountable for employment practices not based on "race, creed, color, or national origin." Although the "affirmative action" and "nondiscrimination" order did not specify gender, its impact upon women and minorities in the workplace, in the United States and abroad, continued for decades.[9]

Several federal laws improved the economic status of women at this time: The Equal Pay Act of 1963 required equal wages for men and women doing equal work; the Civil Rights Act of 1964 (Title VII) prohibited employment discrimination based on sex, race, religion, and national origin by any company with 25 or more employees; and a Presidential Executive Order in 1967 prohibited bias against women in hiring by federal government contractors.

Discrimination complaints were to be investigated by the newly established Equal Employment Opportunity Commission (EEOC). One of the issues the commission took up in its early years were the sex-based "help wanted" advertisements in newspapers. Under Title VII, it was unlawful for newspapers to have separate classified job advertising sections for whites and blacks, and the commission eventually found sex-segregated classified advertising unlawful in 1968, despite the strong protest of newspaper publishers. However, the ruling was not enforced until several years later, when the National Organization for Women (NOW) took the issue to the Supreme Court.

The proportion of women in the civilian labor force rose from nearly 34 percent in 1950 to 51 percent in 1980, representing an increase of 17 percentage points, while men's role declined from 86 percent to 77 percent in that same period. By 1978, 27 percent of women worked full time and year round. This percentage increased to 42 percent by 1997.[10]

Financial liberation also took place in the 1970s. With the Equal Credit Opportunity Act in 1974, married women were finally allowed to obtain independent credit without their husband's signature. This meant they could open bank accounts and hold credit cards in their own name. Interestingly, Citicorp appointed its first female vice president, Diana K. Mayer, in 1974.

NOW

The National Organization for Women (NOW) was founded by Betty Friedan and 27 other women at the Third National Conference of the Commission on the Status of Women, in Washington, D.C., in 1966. Friedan became its first president. Another founder, the Reverend Pauli Murray (1910–85), the first African-American woman Episcopal priest, coauthored NOW's original Statement of Purpose: "The purpose of NOW is to take action to bring women into full participation in the mainstream of American society now, exercising all privileges and responsibilities thereof in truly equal partnership with men."

Older, middle-class professional women joined the organization in large numbers and helped NOW to grow into an important organization that stood for civil and equal rights. NOW campaigned for changes through legislation in abortion rights, federal support of child care centers, equal access to funding for education, and employment.

EDUCATION

Title IX in the Education Codes of 1972 made equal access to higher education and to professional schools the law and prohibited discrimination based on sex. Women could now become doctors, lawyers, engineers, architects, and other professionals and attend graduate schools. However, perhaps its most visible impact has been on female athletes. An increase in female participation—one in 27 high school girls played sports in 1971 compared with one in three in 2004—affected girls and women from grade school to the Olympic Games.

AFFIRMATIVE ACTION

The EEOC established a commission in 1972 to enforce the establishment of racial and sex quotas, called *affirmative action*, a term first coined in

1964 when the then-president, Lyndon B. Johnson, issued two executive orders, 11246 and 11375, requiring government contractors and educational institutions receiving federal funds "to correct the effects of past and present discrimination." The policy sought to address the problem of unequal representation of women, ethnic, and other disadvantaged groups.

Charges of reverse discrimination challenged affirmative action in the late 1970s. In spite of several court cases, such as the *Regents of the University of California v. Bakke* (1978), and voluntary affirmative-action programs in unions and private businesses, the U.S. Supreme Court let existing programs stand and approved the use of quotas in 1979. In the 1980s, the federal government's role in affirmative action was considerably diluted. In three cases in 1989, the Supreme Court undercut court-approved affirmative action plans by giving greater standing to claims of reverse discrimination, voiding the use of minority set-asides where past discrimination against minority contractors was unproved, and restricting the use of statistics to prove discrimination, since statistics did not prove intent.

The Supreme Court further limited the use of race in awarding of government contracts in 1995 in *Adarand Constructors, Inc. v. Federico Pena, Secretary of Transportation,* when a firm contested being passed over for a contract, in spite of its low bid for a guard-rail highway contract, for another firm with ethnically diverse employees. The decision caused government programs to change their criterion for eligibility from race- or sex-based discrimination to a condition of being "socially disadvantaged." California and other states followed suit by prohibiting race and sex preference in state and local programs. A 2003 Supreme Court decision concerning affirmative action in universities allowed educational institutions to consider race as a factor in admitting students as long as it was not used in a mechanical, formulaic manner.

AFRICAN-AMERICAN WOMEN

The roots of black feminism go back to the late 19th century, when Mary Church Terrell (1863–1954), Josephine St. Pierre Ruffin (1842–1924), and Anna Julia Cooper (1858–1964) formed the National Association of Colored Women (NACW) in 1896, joining more than 100 black women's clubs. By 1935, Mary McLeod Bethune organized the National Council of Negro Women, a coalition of black women's groups that lobbied against job discrimination, racism, and sexism, further carrying out the mission.

It would take several more decades, and the Civil Rights movement in the 1960s, for the women's movement to unite black and white women on issues common to both, namely, rights for all women, regardless of race or creed.

73

Black feminism gained prominence in the 1970s when black women perceived that their concerns about sexism and racism were not being addressed by the women's movement or the black Civil Rights movement. In May 1973, approximately 30 African-American women held an all-day gathering in NOW's donated New York offices. With no specific agenda other than mutual recognition, the women discovered their politics were diverse, causing them to form separate organizations. The National Black Feminist Organization (NBFO) was one of the organizations founded as a result of the meeting. Its first chapter was formed in August 1973 in New York City. Other chapters soon followed suit in other major U.S. cities. In addition to seeking change in the way black women were portrayed in the media, NBFO fought for minimum wage for domestic workers, raised consciousness about rape and sexual abuse, and worked with political candidates on black women's issues. By November, the first Eastern Regional Conference on Black Feminism was held, attracting a few hundred African-American women from around the United States. Among the objectives of the conference organizers was to address politics, racism, and sexism from the perspective of the black community and the larger women's movement. The national organization dissolved in 1977, but independent chapters continued to work at local and regional levels.

Other organizations were Black Women Organized for Action (BWOA) in San Francisco in 1973 and the Combahee River Collective in Boston in 1974, which later protested the murders of 12 black women in Boston in 1979. Black feminist scholarship grew, starting with the publication of *Conditions: Five—The Black Womens Issue* in 1979, and began to identify with women in developing countries. Black feminism became a field of study in the 1990s.

One of the leaders of the black feminist movement was Coretta Scott King (1928–2006), who pursued the goals of equality for minorities long after her husband, Martin Luther King, Jr., died in April 1968. While raising their four children, she was successful in establishing the federal King holiday in February and making it a day of action and service using the slogan "A Day On Not a Day Off." She helped secure social reform legislation, including the 1978 Humphrey-Hawkins Full Employment Act and the Anti-Apartheid Act of 1986, and supported campaigns for national health care and better funding for education. She also supported gay rights with the Employment Non-Discrimination Act (ENDA) of 1994, when she argued that "freedom and justice cannot be parceled out in pieces to suit political convenience."[11]

Dorothy Height (1912-2010)—known as the "godmother" of the women's rights movement in the 1960s—was another African-American proponent of civil rights. She shared the platform at Dr. King's "I have a dream" speech in Washington, D.C. on August 28, 1963, because she felt there should be a female speaker.

BIRTH CONTROL

Although the knowledge of how to make a contraceptive pill had been available since the 1920s, it was not until the 1950s that the "Pill" was developed by a reproductive scientist, Gregory Pincus. Supported financially and morally by Sanger it was put on the market in the 1960s.

In 1965, a Supreme Court decision in *Griswold v. Connecticut* ruled that married couples in all states could obtain contraceptives legally, and in 1972, in *Eisenstadt v. Baird,* the U.S. Supreme Court found that the right of privacy recognized for married couples in *Griswold v. Connecticut* should extend to unmarried couples and their procreative decisions. These two decisions finally overturned the Comstock Law of 1873, which had ruled information about birth control as "obscene."

Opponents to birth control denounced the Pill as a way to control the population and limit births among certain races. Others proclaimed its unnatural effects, manipulative nature, and irreverence for what should occur naturally. Nevertheless, by 1982, about 54 million women of childbearing age (15 to 44) in the United States would use some form of contraception. By 2002, this number grew to 61.5 million.[12]

However, in 1969, the medical journalist Barbara Seaman published *The Doctor's Case against the Pill,* in which she assembled evidence from physicians, medical researchers, and women who had used oral contraceptives that the Pill posed a serious health threat to women. Simultaneously, African Americans became increasingly ambivalent about the motives of the U.S. government in making the Pill available to low-income black communities: In 1969, a violent protest by men in an African-American community of Pittsburgh, Pennsylvania, who opposed contraception as a potential means of population control, led to the closing of a Planned Parenthood Clinic. In response to the controversial closing, feminist writers such as Toni Cade Bambara (1939–95) touted the benefits of the Pill, arguing that it allowed women to make their own decisions about fertility.

Pill hearings in 1970 held pharmaceutical companies accountable for cancer-producing levels of estrogen and consequently led to the lowering of the dosage and a rise in prescriptions. The National Women's Health Network also used the occasion to demand an end to "white-coated" gods and their practice of not informing patients of all potential side effects or risks. This was the beginning of what evolved into a patient/physician partnership in decision making about patients' care.

ROE V. WADE

Soon after the Supreme Court recognized the right to privacy for unmarried couples in *Eisenstadt v. Baird*, it guaranteed in *Roe v. Wade* the right to obtain an abortion during the first trimester of pregnancy. The decision in 1973 represented freedom of choice for millions of couples and single women about terminating an unplanned pregnancy. In 1973, 616,000 legal abortions were performed. This grew to a peak of 1.4 million by 1990 and declined to 820,000 by 2005.[13] Legalized abortion generated a backlash of antiabortion and antifeminist activism. Even though the number of abortions declined after its peak in 1990 as a result of more effective birth control methods, the right to obtain an abortion continued to fuel opposition.

THE EQUAL RIGHTS AMENDMENT

The Equal Rights Amendment (ERA), first introduced by Alice Paul in 1923, was passed by Congress in 1972 and sent on to individual states for ratification with a time limit of 1982. The wording of the ERA was simple: "Equality of rights under the law shall not be denied or abridged by the United States or by any state on account of sex."

Many women's organizations, including NOW and the League of Women Voters, supported the legislation. Others, however, opposed it. Stop ERA, founded by Phyllis Schlafly (1924–   ), was one of the chief opponents of the ERA; the organization was formed to demonstrate how ratifying such a measure would undo the work of protective labor laws. Other anti-ERA organizers, including fundamentalist religious women's groups, warned it would prevent women from being supported by their husbands, overturn privacy rights, obligate women to be drafted into combat, and allow widespread abortion and homosexual marriage.

When the deadline for ratification came and went in 1982, the ERA was just three states short of the 38 needed to amend the U.S. Constitution. Seventy-five percent of the women legislators in those three pivotal states supported the ERA, but only 46 percent of the men voted to ratify it.

Taken up as one of the top priorities of NOW in 2006, constitutional equality is still on the agenda in the 21st century. Its supporters argue that the ERA would serve as a permanent guarantee of women's rights in the United States. Most women's rights, however, rely on the Fourteenth Amendment, which was instrumental for about 100 years. Even so, it did not guarantee equal rights for women.

CURRENT SITUATION

The early work to win the right to vote that culminated in the ratification of the Nineteenth Amendment in 1920 freed subsequent generations of women in the United States to express their political will. Generations of women have since enjoyed this right and others, such as property and educational rights. After a second wave of feminists began in the 1960s and 1970s, a third wave of activists began in the 1990s to address the issues that have stubbornly persisted. They include fair pay, better access to high-level career opportunities, and fair representation of women in government and management—just some of the issues detailed in the U.N. Convention on the Elimination of All Forms of Discrimination Against Women (CEDAW), which the United States helped draft but has not yet ratified.

However, areas of interest to the current generation of the movement go well beyond politics and economics and the borders of the United States. In addition to concerns about violence against women, women are seeking improved conditions for child care and kinship care, gay rights, reproductive rights, racism, and transnationalism. Among the Latina population in the United States, immigration rights are part of the agenda. How women are portrayed in television and film and the small number of meaningful, strong characters in movies are also themes that rally women. Adequate access to health care, health insurance, abortions, and screening for potentially deadly viruses, such as human papilloma virus (HPV), are now also included in the list of concerns. A more recent addition is the demand for additional research into the biological distinctions between women and men and their different reactions to medical treatments.

Political and Legal Rights

In the eight decades since women in the United States won the right to vote, women have gradually become educated about how to use the power of suffrage. Women have consistently been voting at higher rates than men in presidential elections since 1980, and the gap widens with each election as proportionally more women vote. In the 2008 presidential elections, according to the U.S. Census Bureau, women turned up at the polls at a rate of 65.7 percent, compared with 61.4 percent for men, which is consistent with what happened in 2004 (about a 4 percent difference, with 60.1 percent for women and 56.3 percent for men). The 70.4 million women who voted, compared with 60.7 million men, for a difference of 9.7 million, continues the trend of more women than men voting, as seen in the 2000 elections, when 7.8 million more women than men voted. Women, as a group, continue to outvote other racial and ethnic groups—African-American, Latino, or Asian/Pacific Islander. Still, not all women are yet taking advantage of the privilege of voting. During the 2008 election, 27.2 percent of eligible women 18 years and older were not registered to vote.

A balanced gender representation is needed within legislation, especially when it comes to women's issues, and yet the percentage of judicial, executive, and legislative seats held by women in the federal government continues to be limited in the United States. Following the November 2010 elections for the 112th Congress, 16.8 percent (73 seats) were held by women in the House of Representatives and 17 percent (17 seats) in the Senate. Incumbent Senator Lisa Murkowski (R-AK) experienced a hotly contested race for the 100th Senate seat, in which the results were challenged in court by Republican candidate Joe Miller, backed by the recently formed Tea Party.[14] The United States' rank of women's representation in national legislatures or parliaments dropped from 67th in the 2004 elections to 72nd in the 2010 mid-term elections, out of more than 188 directly electing countries.[15] But while this election was the first time in 30 years that the number of women in Congress declined, more women (and from ethnically diverse backgrounds) were elected to governorships—in the states of South Carolina, New Mexico, and Oklahoma.[16]

Critical strides have been made by women in recent presidential administrations and national elections. During Republican George W. Bush's presidency, Representative Nancy Pelosi (1940–) (D-CA) became the first female Speaker of the House of Representatives elected during the mid-term elections of 2006. Then-Senator Hillary Rodham Clinton (1947–) (D-NY) campaigned to be the presidential nominee for the Democratic Party in the 2008 elections, losing to now-President Barack Obama (1961–). The nomination of then–Alaska governor Sarah Palin (1964–) as the Republican running mate to Senator John McCain (1936–) was considered a way to rejuvenate the Republican platform.

Clinton's speech conceding defeat in June 2008 will be remembered for its vision ("If we can blast 50 women into space, we will someday launch a woman into the White House.") and renewed image of the glass ceiling ("Although we weren't able to shatter that highest, hardest glass ceiling this time, thanks to you, it's got about 18 million cracks in it".)[17]

As of 2010, three of the nine Supreme Court justices were women—Elena Kagan (1960–), Ruth Bader Ginsburg (1933–), Sonia Sotomayor (1954–)—the first time ever in the history of the United States.

Organizations such as EMILY's List (EMILY stands for Early Money Is Like Yeast), a grassroots political network of Democratic Party women in Washington, D.C., are attracting and supporting pro-choice women who wish to occupy seats within the government. During the 2010 mid-term primary election, a flurry of young female candidates came forward to run for seats in the House of Representatives and the Senate, all with different backgrounds and experience.[18]

Property and Financial Rights

Early English common law in America dictated that husband and wife formed one union or person, represented by the husband. Legislation from the 1830s to the 1890s helped to protect married women's legal right to property, particularly from husbands' creditors.

Property ownership has been less of an issue in the United States since 1974, when married women won the right to maintain credit cards and bank accounts in their own name with the passage of the Equal Credit Opportunity Act (ECOA).

Until the 1980s, most states opposed premarital agreements, as common law held that both husband and wife equally own property. But since 1983, half of the states have adopted the Uniform Premarital Agreement Act to protect an individual's property owned prior to marriage. The Uniform Marital Property Act of 1983 supports spouses' sharing equally in property acquired during the marriage.

Educational Rights

Since the time women were granted the right to equal access to education in the 1970s, the focus has shifted to fulfilling these rights and using them to influence girl's and women's behavior and life choices, from self-esteem to career choices.

Gender inequality was addressed by the government in the 1970s through a variety of measures. Title IX of the Educational Amendment Act in 1972 revolutionized the way universities and colleges could treat women. Until then, women could be denied access to the best libraries in the university or even the school cafeteria. The act excluded military academies, however. In 1970, of the 8.5 million people enrolled in colleges, women represented only 41 percent. By 1980, women represented 51 percent, surpassing men in higher education enrollment.

The number of students who do not complete high school has declined from 14.1 percent in 1980 to 8.0 percent in 2008. The greatest part of this decline occurred between 2000 and 2008, from 11 to 8 percent, most likely aided by government-driven programs like "No Child Left Behind." The dropout rate is still slightly higher among Latinos.[19]

Of the 77 percent of all teenagers age 17 graduating from high school in 2004, however, women were as likely as, or more likely than, men to graduate, a pattern that has been consistent since data were collected in the late 1800s.[20]

Women high school graduates are also more likely to enroll in college than their male counterparts. As of 2008, 71.6 percent of recent female high school graduates enrolled in higher education, as compared with 65.9 percent of male students. However, of the 3.2 million high school graduates, the proportion of men who enrolled in colleges grew slightly between 2004 and 2008, to 1.08 million, which is the same number as women.[21]

Yet, the increase in the number of young women who enroll in college does not mean women are improving their options of what to train for, and they are largely still destined for female occupations as opposed to the traditionally male-dominated fields of science, mathematics, politics, and law. For example, although more than 50 percent of law students are women, and more women than men graduate from law school today, only 34 percent of lawyers in 2008 were women, and even fewer females were partners in law firms.[22] Nevertheless, law is one of the seven occupations with the highest median weekly earnings among full-time working women, at $1,509 a week.[23]

In spite of their dwindling numbers, private four-year women's colleges confer a larger proportion of women's bachelor's degrees in mathematics, computer sciences, and physical sciences than private four-year coeducational institutions. Since the early 1990s, women have occupied nearly 70 percent of professional staff and faculty positions in women's colleges. The average salaries of full-time faculty members at women's colleges were also higher than those at similar coeducational institutions.

Overall, the number of women who have completed higher education has tripled in one generation, which, in turn, is injecting the workforce with more qualified women. In 2009, of the 1,648,000 bachelor degrees conferred, 946,000 (57 percent) were earned by women, as compared with 702,000 (53 percent) by men.[24] About 36 percent of women in the workforce ages 25 to 64 held a college degree in 2009, compared with about 11 percent in 1970.[25] Since 1981, females have represented more than half of the total number of graduates from college, and in 2006–07, surpassed men in the number of Ph.D. degrees awarded for the first time.[26]

Social, Employment, and Economic Rights

Access to education has meant access to better employment opportunities and overall earnings. In 2009, women who graduated from college earned about 78 percent more than women holding only a high school diploma.[27] Nevertheless, women still faced the challenge of receiving equivalent pay to that of their male counterparts and accessing high-level jobs. On average, women with a four-year college degree earned 26 percent less in weekly wages than men, at $891 and $1,200 respectively.[28]

THE WORKING WOMAN

Women increased their participation in the labor force from 43 percent in 1970 to a peak of 60 percent in 1999, according to the U.S. Census. It has held steady, despite the flailing economy, which started to tumble in December 2007.[29] Beginning with the need in the labor force to replace men who were going off to war, this trend continued in the first half of the 21st century.[30] Men have represented 82 percent of the job losses, which mostly occurred in jobs traditionally held by males—construction and manufacturing. This has led to a 10.3 percent unemployment rate among men, while 6.3 million women, or 8.1 percent, were unemployed in 2009.[31,32]

Whereas one in three women was employed in 1950, three in five were employed in 1998, and by 2009, one in two women were either employed or looking for work. Between 1950 and 1998, the dramatic increase in the number of women in the workforce—especially women ages 25–34—more than compensated for the decline in men's participation, which occurred once disability and pensions became more available to men under the age of 50 (with an amendment of the Social Security Act in 1960) and men became eligible for Social Security benefits at age 62.[33] More women found themselves not leaving the workforce after they married and had children.

Although the employment gap is narrowing, women's pay rate ceiling is still quite low compared to men's, even accounting for factors such as occupation, industry, race, marital status, and job tenure. From 1979 to 2008, women's earnings as a percentage of men's increased by 18 percentage points, from 62 to 80 percent.[34]

One factor contributing to the unequal pay of men and women seems to be the difference in work patterns. On average, women spend fewer years in the workforce and work fewer hours per year. More women than men take on part-time work, and on average, they leave the labor force for longer periods than men do. Industry, occupation, race, marital status, and job tenure are additional factors that account for earning differences.[35]

Although women make up nearly half of the labor force today and have experienced greater job earning growth than men, they still do not receive equal pay. The wage gap between men and women for full-time year-round work held at between 77 and 80 percent in 2008, a trend that received much press coverage in 2011. Women who were full-time wage and salary workers had median annual earnings of $36,278, versus $47,127 for men, in 2009.[36] In 2009, median weekly earnings were highest for older women (age 55 to 64), at $727, while young women 16–24 earned lower weekly wages ($424).

In an effort to close this gap, President Obama signed the Lilly Ledbetter bill in 2009 providing legal recourse for workers who had been underpaid

81

without a statute of limitation. At the same time, Congress considered legislation entitled the Paycheck Fairness Act, which was an expansion of the bill and the Equal Pay Act of 1963, which passed in the House, in January 2009, but not the Senate, in November 2010. Considered by opponents as a jobs killer, it would have increased the amount workers could claim as damages from pay discrimination and limit how employers may fight such claims or penalize employees for obtaining comparative salary information.

Most recent census findings in the United States found that women still earn less than men in all occupational groupings: With median weekly earnings of $907 for women, compared with $1,248 for men, in 2009 in management, professional, and related occupations, women's earnings reflect 72.7 percent of men's earnings in this category.[37]

The gender gap in pay declines with youth. Women 35 years and older had earnings roughly three-fourths that of their male counterparts, while the earnings differences between women and men were not as great among younger workers. Among 25- to 34-year-olds, women earned 89 percent as much as men, and among 16- to 24-year-olds, women earned 93 percent as much as men.[38]

Interestingly, wage parity between men and women is closest in "blue-collar" construction, maintenance, and extraction jobs, which make up the second-highest-paying occupational group for women ($29,000). Women in these professions earn about 90.6 percent of what their male counterparts do.

As of 2009, the top 10 most prevalent occupations for employed women were

1. Secretaries and administrative assistants
2. Registered nurses
3. Elementary and middle school teachers
4. Cashiers
5. Nursing, psychiatric, and home health aides
6. Retail salespersons
7. First-line supervisors/managers of retail sales workers
8. Waiters and waitresses
9. Maids and housekeeping cleaners
10. Customer service representatives
11. Child care workers
12. Bookkeeping, accounting, and auditing clerks
13. Receptionists and information clerks
14. First-line supervisors/managers of office and administrative support workers
15. Managers, all other

The censuses of 1990 and 2000 also observed a new trend: the significant increase in the number of female workers in what were considered traditionally male-dominated occupations, such as police detectives and supervisors, millwrights, civil engineers, automobile mechanics, firefighters, and airplane pilots and navigators.

Another notable trend has been among Asian women, who are better employed than women from other U.S. ethnic or racial groups. Not only did Asian women experience the lowest unemployment rate in 2008, 3.7 percent, but employed Asian women were more likely (46 percent) to work in better-paying management, professional, and related occupations in 2008 than were women from other demographic groups and had higher weekly wages ($753). This may be due to the types of careers Asian women are educated for, namely industrial jobs.

Until the late 20th century, women were denied access to these fields or deterred from studying for them. Trailblazing women such as Sally Ride (1951–   ), who became the first American female astronaut in 1983, have since made an effort to ensure that girls who have mathematical aptitude know their options include careers in science, math, and engineering. The Sally Ride Science Club reaches out to elementary and middle school girls, and Sally Ride Science creates science publications and educational programs for girls, teachers, and parents.

With this outlook, universities are creating special programs to foster the growth of female students interested in studying science and math. In 2006, New York University established a four-year program to attract and retain women for postgraduate and professional work in these fields.

Sports are also experiencing radical reforms with regard to how women are treated and paid. Billy Jean King (1943–   ) was considered highly influential in using her rank within the United States Tennis Association to lobby for equal pay at the U.S. Open in Flushing Meadows, Queens, New York. These measures, however, are less publicized than the famously televised 1973 "Battle of the Sexes" tennis match King played against Bobby Riggs (1918–95).

A current concern is about the employment of female head coaches in women's college teams, which is down to 42 percent from more than 90 percent in 1972, when Title IX outlawed gender discrimination in school sports. This is largely due to the high expectations that go with the job (of meeting a minimum number of wins), with the additional duties of child care.[39]

WORKING MOTHERS

The issue of juggling work and motherhood is as pressing today as it was for women 25 years ago. That women continue to fulfill their traditional roles as caretaker—in effect, doubling up on tasks—and the lack of affordable day care in the United States have become key issues, spawning public debate over the different approaches taken in the United States, in contrast with more successful ones in European countries. American women are increasingly relying on statewide paid-leave measures to compensate for the absence of one at a national level. Women also have recourse through the EEOC to file pregnancy discrimination claims, where the number of claims increased notably from 4,730 in 2005 to 6,196 in 2009. A little over half of all claims are resolved with having "no reasonable cause," but the percentage of claims where settlements were reached grew from 8.6 percent in 1997 to 14.1 percent in 2009.[40]

Proportionately, more adult women today are doing "the balancing act," even though the number of weekly hours of paid work an employed woman must balance with other commitments has not increased substantially beyond what it was in 1980. The exception to this, however, is among married women who have children under the age of three. Their labor force participation increased from 39.4 percent in 1978 to 60.1 percent in 2007.[41]

By the year 2008, 69 percent of married women were in the labor force, compared with 76 percent of unmarried women. Married women with children make up as much as 71.2 percent of the labor force, compared with 47.4 percent in 1975.[42]

Of the married couples in which both earn income, the percentage of women outearning their husbands grew from 17.8 percent in 1987 to 25.9 in 2007.[43]

By the late 1980s, many European nations, especially Scandinavian countries, had systems of public funding of day care for between 50 and 95 percent of all children between the age of three and compulsory school age (ranging from ages five to seven).[44] Women's organizations in the United States lobbied hard to make affordable child care services available to low- and middle-income mothers and families. These efforts finally resulted in the Child Care and Development Fund (CCDF), federal legislation that provides state-level block grants to day care services since 1990. Nevertheless, with 60 percent of working mothers' children under the age of five in some form of day care by 1999, the problem of high-quality and affordable day care has persisted, largely due to the high cost of day care at an average of $85 per week, which represents nearly one-third of a low-income salary. By fiscal year 2004–05, CCDF funded $4.8 billion in block grants for low-income family child care in U.S. states, territories, and tribes.[45]

THE GLASS CEILING

Senator Robert Dole introduced the Glass Ceiling Act in 1991, and the U.S. Department of Labor created a 21-member, bipartisan Federal Glass Ceiling

Commission in the name of Title II of the Civil Rights Act of 1991, with a mandate to study barriers to advancement of minorities and women within corporate hierarchies—a problem that would come to be known as the "glass ceiling."[46] The commission reported its findings and recommendations on ways to dismantle the glass ceiling in 1995:

> *While minorities and women have made strides in the last 30 years, and employers increasingly recognize the value of workforce diversity, the executive suite is still overwhelmingly a white man's world. Over half of all Master's degrees are now awarded to women, yet 95 percent of senior-level managers of the top Fortune 1000 industrial and 500 service companies are men.*[47]

The percentages are the same for Fortune 2000 industrial and service companies. The commission recommended that corporate America use affirmative action as a tool to ensure that all qualified individuals have equal access and opportunity to compete on the basis of ability and merit. The commission also asked that "organizations expand their vision and seek candidates from non-customary sources, backgrounds and experiences, and that the executive recruiting industry work with businesses to explore ways to expand the universe of qualified candidates."[48] Business leaders claimed that they often could not find suitable minority and female candidates because the networks from which they recruited male candidates—with the possible exception of the military—did not include them.

In March 1995, the commission prepared a fact-finding report, *The Environmental Scan,*[49] based on commission hearings, interviews, focus groups, panel discussions, and public and private research. According to this report, there are three kinds of barriers to women who want to make gains in the high-level management world:

- Societal barriers, "which may be outside the direct control of business"
- Internal structural barriers, "within the direct control of business"
- Governmental barriers: lack of monitoring and law enforcement, weak collection of employment-related data, and inadequate reporting on the issue

Improving stature of women in the workplace has made some gains in the United States, with women's share of the labor market steadily holding between 46 and 47 percent between 1995 and 2009. Market research has indicated that 48.8 percent of professional and managerial positions in the private sector were held by women in 1995. By 2009, this rate had grown to 51.4 percent. Still, only 14.4 percent of executive officer seats were held by women in 2010.[50]

The General Accounting Office's 2002 study of 10 major industries revealed that five (communications, public administration, business, entertainment, and diverse professions) had female management in proportion to the number of women employed in the industry. The data also showed that within seven of the 10 industries (entertainment, communications, finance, business, professional services, retail trade, professional medical services), the wage gap between male and female managers had actually worsened between 1995 and 2000, as women earned two to 21 cents less than every dollar earned by male managers.[51]

Some progress has been made by women of color in the labor market between 1990 and 2001. African-American women saw a 75 percent increase in their participation as managers and officials, and Hispanic women 130 percent growth. Asian women also saw a rate change of 130 percent during that period.[52]

Still, much work remains to break past the Fortune 500 ceiling, with only 3 percent of CEOs and 15.7 percent of board seats occupied by women in 2010.[53]

A 2010 study by nonprofit Catalyst Inc. has hypothesized that women— who often expect to be noticed for their good works—might advance to higher-level jobs if they deploy mentors and/or advocates who explicitly champion their candidacy, the way men often do.[54]

SEXUAL HARASSMENT

Sexual harassment in the workplace has always been an issue for women working outside the home, but dealing with its legal liability is a relatively recent issue. Defined by the Equal Employment Opportunity Commission (EEOC) as "unwelcome sexual advances, requests for sexual favors, and other verbal or physical conduct of a sexual nature . . . when submission to or rejection of this conduct explicitly or implicitly affects an individual's employment, unreasonably interferes with an individual's work performance, or creates an intimidating, hostile or offensive work environment," claims of sexual harassment, which violate Title VII of the Civil Rights Act of 1964, are dealt with by the EEOC. The specifics of Title VII apply to employers who have 15 or more employees, including state and local governments, employment agencies, labor organizations, and the federal government.

Sexual harassment was not highly publicized at first. The first case under Title VII was not filed until 1976. Not until 1991—and the law professor Anita Hill's charges that the Supreme Court nominee Clarence Thomas had made unwelcome sexual advances while he was her supervisor at the EEOC in the 1980s—did it receive wide public attention. Thomas's appointment was subsequently confirmed, but Hill's testimony changed relations between men and women in the workplace from that point forward. Hill's testimony led to an increased sensitivity among employers and employees of both genders to all forms of aggressive discrimination against women in the workplace, which in turn accounted for the sudden increase in complaints. The number of claims received by the EEOC has been on a downward trend since 2000, from 15,836 in 2000 to 12,696 in 2009. The EEOC resolved 44 and 47 percent of these sexual harassment charges in these years, respectively, with the settlement of "no reasonable cause."[55]

FINANCIAL FREEDOM

Compared with those in countries in sub-Saharan Africa and South Asia, fewer women live in poverty in the United States. However, women in the United States fare worse when compared to those of western European nations and Japan, Australia, and Canada, with an average of 10 to 15 percent living in poverty. By 2009, 43.6 million people (14.3 percent) were living in poverty in the United States, up from 39 million in 2008 (13.2 percent).[56] Of adult women (age 18–64 years), 13.2 percent were living in poverty, while 10.1 percent of adult men were considered poor.[57] Female heads of households with no husband present accounted for a third (29.9 percent) of those living in poverty in 2009. The poverty rate is proportionally higher for minorities—African Americans, Hispanics, and Native Americans—at about 25 percent.[58] Single mothers are more likely than any other group to file for bankruptcy. One report indicates that nearly half of all single mothers live in or near poverty, and 53 percent are employed in service or administrative fields that tend to offer low earnings, few benefits, and little opportunity for advancement.

Adjacent to this has been the trend of fathers' not fulfilling child support obligations. In the United States, state laws govern child support and vary from state to state. The fourth article of the U.S. Constitution empowers states with the final decision on child support matters, but it was not until the 1910 Uniform Desertion and Non-Support Act that fathers were held punishable by law for deserting and/or not supporting a spouse and/or child under the age of 16. Further measures were taken over the next century to ensure enforcement, resulting in what is known as the Uniform Interstate Family Support Act (UIFSA), especially with the increasing likelihood that a parent will move to a different state. In spite of increased federal and state government resources toward child support enforcement since the 1980s— including the 1984 Child Support Enforcement Amendments to Title IV-D of the Social Security Act enforcing women's ability to collect delinquent child support payments[59]— only 31 percent of single mothers received child-support in 2007.[60]

The Bankruptcy Abuse Prevention and Consumer Protection Act law was passed in April 2005 and put in effect in October 2005. Prior bankruptcy law had protected women whose former husbands filed for bankruptcy. The child support and alimony owed could not be discharged by bankruptcy. Under the 2005 law, both child support and some credit card debts are nondischargeable, thus making it more difficult for the former spouse to collect the child support. When the Senate voted to pass the bankruptcy reform bill, an amendment that would have extended protection to struggling single mothers was voted down.

The reforms being advocated by women's organizations include equal allocation of Social Security benefits between married partners. Less than 40 percent of women currently receive benefits as retired workers compared with 80 percent of men, although 60 percent of women receive some kind of benefit as a spouse of a retired, disabled, divorced (after 10 years of marriage), or deceased worker. Homemakers and working mothers tend to receive less than their working spouses even though they may live longer. Women, 56 percent of all beneficiaries, made up 68 percent of beneficiaries over the age of 65 in 2008.[61] Since the program is intended to provide security to the family, women's organizations—the National Women's Law Center, for one—are guarding women's interests against government reforms that could leave women in poverty at an older age. Privatizing the system and reducing benefits, which were proposed by the George W. Bush administration but never passed by Congress, ran the risk of decreasing the Social Security benefits women receive under the current law for high- and average-income workers.

WOMEN IN THE MILITARY

Since 1973, when the government switched from all-male conscription to a volunteer force, women have been allowed to enlist in the armed forces. Women enlisted in large numbers during the Vietnam War, doubling their presence between 1972 and 1975, although the number of female officers remained virtually unchanged. Women's organizations were divided over the issue: Some were rallying against U.S. troops in Vietnam in the name of world peace, while others were seeing it as an opportunity for honorable employment.

In the late 1970s, the National Organization for Women (NOW) lobbied for women's equal access to the military. Nevertheless, a 1981 Supreme Court decision, *Rostker v. Goldberg*, only required male 18-year-olds to register with the draft board, maintaining that the exclusion of requiring women to register was not a violation of the due process clause (Fifth Amendment) of the U.S. Constitution. The Selective Service law still does not require women to register for the draft because of the Department of Defense's policy of restricting women from direct ground combat.

After a prolonged court battle, a high school student, Shannon Faulkner, became the first woman to enroll in a military academy, the Citadel in South Carolina, in 1995. Although she remained there only for her first year of college, she set a precedent for four other female cadets to enroll in 1996. The 1995 Supreme Court decision in her case ruled that discrimination against women was illegal in state-supported military schools, such as the Citadel and Virginia Military Institute.

As with other hard-won rights, the legal battle proved to be only a first step. The military was slow to adjust to the new requirements, and physical assault and harassment made the first decade of coeducational military school a rocky one for the female cadets. At a 1991 convention of the Tailhook Association, a navy aviators' group, 83 female officers and other women were physically assaulted by 117 naval officers. The resulting lawsuit damaged the careers of 14 admirals and 300 aviators and instigated a zero-tolerance policy of discrimination and harassment within the U.S. Navy. In 2003, the Air Force Academy began investigating what turned out to be a decade-long list of sexual harassment allegations against cadets in the air force and overlooked by senior officers. A report issued in September 2004 highlighted several issues that would need to be addressed in the future, including female cadets' fear to report such incidents, lack of training of personnel to handle this kind of violence, absence of documentation and evidence about allegations, an overly strict application of the Privacy Act preventing follow-up on status of cases, and the added complexity of alcohol and consensual sex factors.

Women account for 35 percent of the general population employed within the U.S. Department of Defense. Within the armed forces, as of 2009, 13.5 percent of active duty troops of the army, 19.5 percent of the air force, and 15.5 percent of the navy were women.[62] The marine corps remains largely a male force, with women forming only 6.4 percent of active-duty troops. Women make up 12.5 percent of the Coast Guard.[63]

Of the 229,301 people employed by the army in 2008, 36.75 percent were women; of the 1,148 senior-level official managers, 16.29 percent were women. The largest group of enrolled women in the permanent workforce were employed in logistics management (31.47 percent) and first-level official/managers (29.57 percent).[64]

The debate continues as to what role women should play in the U.S. military. A Pentagon mandate prohibiting women from serving in ground combat units was loosened in 1994 to allow women to take on "supporting" combat roles. In October 2010, the U.S. Department of the Navy announced a change in its policy that will permit female officers to serve on submarines beginning in December 2011. Women have served on the U.S. Navy's noncombat surface ships since 1973 and combat surface ships since 1993.

Although women have been involved as allied professionals, they are increasingly needed to supplement shortages of men in active militarized zones. Between 2002 and 2005, 33 women were killed in Iraq, five in Afghanistan, and more than 250 were wounded in action.[65] As of 2006, the number of women who died in Iraq grew to 48, representing 2 percent of the total number of U.S. troops killed to that date, and 300 had been wounded, which, although a small number, already exceeds the number of women wounded during the entire Vietnam War.[66] Despite the U.S. Department of Defense combat exclusion policies for women, the toll continues to mount, with 700 wounded and 150 U.S. female troops reported dead in the Iraq and Afghanistan wars by May 2011.[67]

The Department of Defense identifies 17.3 percent of the selected reserves (the highest status of reserves that is considered essential to wartime mission) as women, making up nearly one-quarter of the army and air force reserves, and 4.7 percent of the marines.

Associated with this has been the need for adequate Veterans Administration (VA) health care benefits for women. The VA estimates that by 2020, women will be 10.5 percent of the veteran population and 9.5 of all VA patients.[68] Women veterans are considered at greater risk than men for post-traumatic stress disorder (PTSD), with nearly a quarter of female veterans having experienced some form of sexual harassment or trauma during their service in Iraq and Afghanistan. They also have higher rates of single parenthood and homelessness than their male counterparts.[69]

The Family and Medical Leave Act (FMLA) of 1993 has been another means of support for women (and men) in the armed forces, especially among reservists' and National Guard members who serve during national emergencies. President George W. Bush signed a memorandum in July 2002 that extended rights protected under this bill to include uniformed service members' active duty time in their eligibility to take time off from work under the FMLA.

Still, the handling of family programs and child custody are issues that need to be addressed as more single-parent mothers enlist. In 2007, Lt. Eva Crouch was mobilized with the Kentucky National Guard and arranged to leave her daughter with her ex-husband; she ultimately had to enter into a legal battle to regain custody of her child. In 2009, a single-mother soldier from Georgia was arrested by the army when she did not comply with her orders to deploy to Afghanistan because her family arrangements for her child fell through.

Access to Medical Care

With improved medical screening technologies, it has become obvious that certain diseases afflict American women in a more devastating way than was recognized before the 1990s, paving the way for a field of study now known as women's health. At the turn of the 21st century, heart disease was to be the number one cause of death in both men and women, followed by cancer and stroke.

However, women's symptoms of heart disease—including shortness of breath and weakness in muscles—are less dramatic than those typical in men, such as sharp chest pain. As a result, men and women have received disproportionate treatment. This situation is quickly changing with public awareness campaigns. Other diseases that have a high mortality rate among women in the United States include cancer, stroke, and chronic lower respiratory diseases; Alzheimer's disease; diabetes; accidents (unintentional injuries); influenza/pneumonia; kidney disease, and septicemia.[70]

Adequate female and child representation in clinical trials and more accurate attention to symptoms in women that may indicate serious conditions are among the concerns of women about quality of access to health care.

Sex- or biology-based medicine, as a new field of investigation, garnered interest at the legislative level during the 1990s and was one of the issues lobbying for attention in Washington, D.C., before terrorism became the center of attention after the September 11, 2001, attacks on the United States.

The Society for Women's Health Research called attention to sex-based differences in 2001 by initiating the landmark study "Exploring the Biological Contribution to Human Health: Does Sex Matter?" for the Institute of Medicine. The report underscored the need for better understanding of the importance of sex differences and application of that knowledge in improved medical practices and therapies.[71]

Family and Sexuality

The notion of "family" as a societal unit underwent a radical change in the latter half of the 20th century. A number of factors have led to changes in the expected roles of men and women as husbands and wives, subsequently affecting local, state, and federal policies, and, ultimately, human behavior. What was once assumed to be the woman's domain of caretaking is now extending into policies for either parent. Sexual orientation of the parents is yet another factor to consider in a couple's ability to have or adopt children. A variety of forms of birth control are now sanctioned, no longer making abortion the only option. As in many other countries, sterilization, the birth control pill, and other modern methods of contraception have expanded couples' choices for "family planning."

FORCED STERILIZATION AND LIMITING REPRODUCTIVE FREEDOM

In the early 1900s, the U.S. government founded a eugenics program in an attempt to perfect the gene pool of the population, envisioning a society without crime, mental illness, and homelessness. By the 1970s, an estimated 65,000 males and females had been sterilized, many without their knowledge.[72]

The case of Carrie Buck, a young, "feeble-minded," Virginia woman in the state's care who was forcibly sterilized to prevent her from having more children, set a precedent for the rest of the United States and the Western world, even Nazi Germany, for curbing reproductive freedom. The 1927 decision in *Buck v. Bell*, which upheld a Virginia law permitting the government to order the compulsory sterilization of young women it believed were "unfit to continue their kind," received little public attention compared with the implementation by Germany in 1933 of the Law for the Prevention of Hereditarily Diseased Offspring, a sterilization law that led to more than 400,000 forced sterilizations by the end of World War II. *Buck v. Bell* paved the way for other states to implement sterilization laws in the 1930s and 1940s, and the practice continued well into the 1970s. Although *Buck v. Bell* has yet to be repealed, public attitudes have shifted dramatically against its application, and the practice ended in the 1970s. In 2002, the Commonwealth of Virginia issued an apology for its part in eugenics.

REPRODUCTIVE RIGHTS AND ABORTION DEBATE CONTINUES

Women have exercised their right to abortion since it became legal in 1973 as a result the federal Supreme Court decision in *Roe v. Wade*. The annual number of abortions has fallen steadily to 1.2 million in 2007, down from a high of 1.6 million in 1990.[73] From 1973 through 2007, nearly 50 million legal abortions occurred. The majority of abortions were performed in the first 12 weeks of pregnancy. With half of American women experiencing unintended pregnancies, an estimated one in three women will have had an abortion by the time she is 45 years old.[74]

In a 2003 *Time*/CNN poll, 55 percent of respondents said they support a woman's right to have an abortion in the first three months of pregnancy; however, 60 percent believed abortion had become too easily accessible. A 2004 Zogby Poll found that 56 percent of respondents support legal abortion in only specific circumstances: when the pregnancy results from rape or incest or when it threatens the life of the mother.[75]

The successful constitutional challenge to the statute prohibiting abortion was brought against the district attorney of Dallas County, Henry Wade. The original decision in *Roe v. Wade* was based on two cases: that of an unmarried woman from Texas (anonymously named Roe), where abortion was illegal unless the mother's life was at risk, and that of a poor married mother of three from Georgia, where state law required permission for an abortion from a panel of doctors and hospital officials. The Supreme Court ruled on the legality of abortion from these cases and overrode several state laws preventing it. While establishing the right to an abortion in the first trimester, the decision gave states the right to intervene in the second and third trimesters of pregnancy to protect the woman and the "potential" life of the unborn child.

The National Council of Bishops denounced the Supreme Court decision and soon an antiabortion movement was on the move. In 1976, Congress enacted the Hyde Amendment, which undermined *Roe v. Wade* by barring the use of federal funds to reimburse for the medical expenses involved in abortions for the poor under its Medicaid program, except when the woman's life was endangered by a full-term pregnancy or in the case of rape or incest.

ROE V. WADE

The decision caused pressure on the courts. In a 1989 case, *Webster v. Reproductive Health Services,* the Court limited its application, giving states greater latitude in regulating and restricting abortions. A 1992 case, *Planned Parenthood v. Casey,* reaffirmed the right to have an abortion granted in *Roe v. Wade,* while applying further restrictions. In response to violence against abortion clinics, President Bill Clinton signed the Freedom of Access to Clinic Entrances (FACE) Act in 1994, providing a legal defense against anti-abortion terrorism.

In September 2000, the use of the early abortion pill RU-486, mifepristone, was approved by the U.S. Food and Drug Administration, to be marketed in the United States as an alternative to surgical abortion. About 37,000 medication abortions were performed in the first half of 2001; these procedures involved the use of mifepristone or methotrexate. Although the drug was already available to women in 13 other countries, antiabortion activists prepared for their battle in Congress. The Bush administration imposed restrictions on the drug.

Several rulings in 2003 and 2004 are evidence that the right to abortion is not yet secure. President Bush signed a Congress-approved abortion ban in November 2003 that became the first federal law to make a particular form of abortion—partial-birth abortion—illegal. Planned Parenthood Federation of America (PPFA) and the National Abortion Federation both challenged the constitutionality of the ban in court cases, naming the absence of a health exception for women as one of its faults. In *Planned Parenthood Federation v. Ashcroft*, the judge ruled in favor of PPFA in June 2004, citing its unconstitutionality. The same ruling occurred in *National Abortion Federation v. Ashcroft* in August 2004.

The 2006 appointment of Judge Samuel Anthony Alito, Jr. (1950–   ), as a new Supreme Court justice to replace the retiring justice Sandra Day O'Connor, the first woman on the high court, who was known for her decisive "swing" vote on abortion, has abortion activists concerned. Alito believes the Constitution does not protect abortion rights. Chief Justice John Roberts, appointed in 2006 to replace William Rehnquist after the latter's death, has expressed that he supports limited abortion restrictions, though his views are thus far less clear than Alito's. About 30 states have a predominantly antiabortion legislature and government that could quickly pass laws restricting abortion access in as little as two years. An ongoing concern of women's organizations in the United States is how the Supreme Court might handle abortion cases in the future.

CONTRACEPTIVE OPTIONS

The decline in the number of abortions in the United States may be due to the increase in contraceptive options available to women: the female condom, foam, cervical cap, Today Sponge, suppository or insert, jelly or cream, and both female and male sterilization. By 2009, 38 million women of childbearing age, representing about 73 percent of all women, used some form of contraception. In that same year, while the pill was one of the most common methods of contraception among women age 15 to 49, 21.2 percent used female sterilization and 12.2 percent, condoms.[76] As a result, the fertility rate has held steady at 2.05 children per woman in 2009.[77]

The emergency contraceptive Plan B (levonorgestrel)—also known as the "morning after pill"—approved by the FDA in 1999 by prescription only works essentially the same way the Pill works. Advocates believe it will help to reduce unintended pregnancies and lead to fewer abortions; some even envision a future when pharmacies associated with major retail outlets, such as Wal-Mart, can dispense the drug over the counter. In August 2006, the

FDA, after several years' consideration, agreed to permit the sale of Plan B to women over the age of 18. At least 41 other countries currently allow Plan B to be sold over the counter.

ALTERNATIVE GENDER ROLES: LESBIAN RIGHTS

On a national level, the movement for equal rights for lesbians—or women who have sexual orientation toward other women—has been emerging in the political and legal arenas alongside the gay rights movement in the 1970s. The extent of rights runs a broad gamut, from basic legal rights to sexual freedom, employment, family and adoption, political power, cultural and social rights, as well as means by which to respond to violence and employment discrimination.

Homosexuality in the female population varies according to location within the United States, from 1 to 5 percent in rural areas and possibly as high as 12 percent in urban areas.[78]

At the time the U.S. Supreme Court ruled in *Lawrence v. Texas* in 2003 that laws attempting to criminalize homosexual activity between consenting adults are unconstitutional, 14 states in America had sodomy laws on the book.

Since 1994, the Employment Non-Discrimination Act has given gays and lesbians legal recourse in the workplace and the military. President Clinton reaffirmed the government's policy of nondiscrimination in the hiring and promotion of federal employees in Executive Order 13087, by adding sexual orientation to the list of protected parameters. In the U.S. military service, an informal code of conduct of "don't ask, don't tell" was implemented by the late 1990s. The debate of this code continued right up to a vote by Congress, which repealed the policy in December 2010. Most political and military leaders agree with the repeal of "don't ask, don't tell," which will allow gay men and lesbian women service members to serve openly.

Federal discrimination laws and sexual harassment under Title XIX as well as state laws are supposed to protect gays and lesbians from harassment. Hate crimes against gays and transgender people accounted for 18.5 percent of 6,598 single-bias incidents reported in 2009.[79]

Today, gay-rights activists focus on a wide range of issues, including the recognition of gay marriages and families as legal entities with access to the same tax and social benefits and adoption, parenting, and other legal rights that couples in heterosexual marriages receive. Since 1998, the Defense of Marriage Act (DOMA) passed by Congress in 1996 has challenged attempts to institute same-sex marriage privileges by defining a married couple as a man and a woman and permitting states the right to reject any other definition.

By the end of 2010, more than half of the states have passed language defining marriage between a man and a woman in their state constitutions. Three states already had statutory language defining marriage predating

DOMA: Wyoming (1957), Maryland (1973), and New Hampshire (1987). Thirty-nine states have statutes defining marriage as between one man and one woman.[80]

In the United States, marriages among same-sex couples were first permitted in Massachusetts in May 2004 and in California, from June to November 2008, the same year as it became legal in Connecticut, but not recognized elsewhere in the United States. Californian voters approved Proposition 8 to ban gay marriage in November 2008, which was overturned in August 2010 by U.S. District Court Judge Vaughn Walker. By an appeal, a trial is expected in 2011. In June 2011, the New York State legislature passed a bill permitting same-sex marriage.

Since January 2008, Oregon allows for domestic partnerships, which can receive all the rights, benefits, privileges, and immunities extended to married couples.

In 2010, same-sex marriages became legal in New Hampshire and Washington, D.C., where it also has an official registry for same-sex couples and recognizes gay marriages performed in other states.[81]

Since 2000 in Vermont, 2004 in Connecticut, and 2006 in New Jersey, civil unions of same-sex partners were allowed, but without the rights automatically conferred on married couples or recognition by the federal government. In addition to New Hampshire, Connecticut and Vermont now have replaced civil unions with same-sex marriage legislation.

A landmark decision by the New Jersey Supreme Court on October 25, 2006, gave the state legislature 180 days (April 22, 2007) to provide same-sex couples with equal access to the protection of marriage. Same-sex marriage legislation failed to pass in the state senate, however. The Religious Freedom and Civil Marriage Protection Act, which redefines civil unions to include same-sex couples, was caught in a legislative battle in California in 2004 and 2005. The District of Columbia, Maine, and Hawaii provide rights under domestic partnership laws, which recognize entitlement to various state benefits of gay couples, such as conferring on the partner of a state employee benefits related to entitlements, alimony, divorce, and property division.

Opponents are trying to settle the issue by implementing a constitutional amendment that defines marriage as the union of a man and a woman; to date, that idea has not been accepted.

Violence

Crime-prevention strategies have proliferated as a measure of public safety globally, and the United States is no exception. The efficacy of these programs is, however, put to the test during exceptional circumstances, such as war, economic recession, and political unrest. This, perhaps, is the reason the United States, where citizens can exercise their Second Amendment right to bear arms, has one of the highest estimated rates of civilian-owned firearms in the world.[82] Gender-oriented crime, whether through domestic violence or sexually obscene material, is one aspect of violence that affects all segments of society—women, men, and children.

RAPE AND DOMESTIC VIOLENCE

Domestic violence in the United States is still one of the leading causes of injury to women ages 15 to 44. A woman is more likely to experience violence by a family member than by a stranger, with females knowing their offenders in 70 percent of reported violent crimes, compared with 45 percent of men knowing their attackers. Of the 1,510 deaths reported in 2005 related to intimate violence, 78 percent were of females and 22 percent were of males.[83] Overall, however, the number of reported crimes—including rape and sexual assault—has declined between 2000 and 2010 in the United States. The number of rapes dropped to 125,910 in 2009, compared with 203,830 in 2008—a 38.7 percent change.[84] Still, a woman is five times more likely to be victimized in "intimate partner violence" (IPV) by someone she knows.[85]

In the 1990s, a theoretical correlation was made between violence toward women and its portrayal in the media through television, movies, and magazines. Scientific studies conducted on the relation between pornography—or sexually explicit material—and sexual aggression remain inconclusive, however, in proving that all men who viewed such material were moved to aggression.[86] More recently, economic stress and substance abuse have been recognized as significant risk factors for violence between couples, in addition to having experienced it as a child.

Attempts to turn this tide have been largely legislative. The Violence against Women Act (VAWA) was passed in 1994 to create a means to deal with violence in the home. The landmark legislation set out to improve criminal justice and community-based responses to domestic violence, dating violence, sexual assault, and stalking in the United States. Under the government-sponsored STOP (which stands for "services, training, officers, and prosecutors," or aspects of the criminal justice system) program, grants are issued to train state agencies and educate young women. In 1996, gender was added as a category to hate crimes legislation, providing ammunition to counter the offense in court.

The National Institute of Justice annually tracks IPV, as part of its National Crime Victimization Survey (NCVS), within the context of general crime victimization. Data findings are hampered by the way "behaviorally-oriented questions" are asked, however. The last survey specifically devoted to violence against women was in 2000, when findings from the National Violence Against Women Survey conducted by the U.S. Justice Department and the Centers for Disease Control and Prevention (CDC) from 1995 to 1996 were published. Then, both men and women were surveyed to provide a balanced view of the victimization experience.[87] The high incidence of rape at an early age—over half of the women who have experienced rape in their lifetime said it occurred before they were 17 years of age—suggested measures need to be taken to combat child abuse, which have since attracted much media attention. A pattern of victimization also began to appear when it was discovered that women who reported they were raped, assaulted, or stalked before age 18 were at least twice as likely to report experiencing the same offense as an adult. The results from the 2010 survey will be available in 2011.[88]

Joining the global effort to develop a strategy for preventing domestic violence, the CDC is now more closely tracking trends and offering resources for IPV through its National Center for Injury Prevention and Control.[89] The National Coalition Against Domestic Violence is also campaigning for greater awareness in what will impact not only one in every four women at some point in her life, but men as well.

PORNOGRAPHY

Pornography has been a topic of debate in the United States for nearly half a century, but it has been in existence since the invention of the printing press. Women's concerns about pornography stem from the manipulation of the feminine image and the resulting value that is placed on it by society. With the advent of computer technology in the 1980s, pornography in computer and video games and, more recently, on the Internet has been the focus of legislation and concerned women and parents. The development of child pornography has also raised ethical concerns that are difficult for pornography proponents—in the name of free speech—to counter. As have other countries, America has its own form of antipornography laws, but they have been difficult to enforce. As an industry, pornography has also taken on the characteristics of organized crime, attracting vulnerable populations of girls and women into prostitution and human trafficking.[90]

The significance of pornography as a representation of the feminine gender in popular media and advertising has led to diverse views. To some it represents sexual emancipation and liberation from inhibition, while others see it as reinforcing the perception of women as sexual objects. A survey of literature and research by the Commission of Obscenity and Pornography in

1970 in the United States could find no proven causality between pornography and violence against women. Yet in 1986, in a final report by the Attorney General's Commission on Pornography, clinical and experimental research showed that exposure to sexually violent material increases the likelihood of aggression toward women, or antisocial, even unlawful, acts of sexual violence.[91] On the other hand, the report concluded that erotic material that is nondegrading and nonviolent did not bear a causal relationship to rape and other acts of sexual violence.

Obscenity—defined as that which appeals to an interest in sex, or depicts sexual conduct in an offensive manner, and lacks serious literary, artistic, political, or scientific merit—is a category of sexual material that the courts hold to be unprotected by the First Amendment and subject to regulation by the state. Its distribution is a federal crime and a crime in most states, along with distribution of child pornography. In the United States, the antiporn activist Catherine MacKinnon drafted the Minneapolis, Minnesota, and Indianapolis, Indiana, antiporn ordinances of 1983 stating that all women who worked in porn and were coerced could bring a civil lawsuit against producers and distributors. Coercion was deemed to be present even if the woman was of age, she fully understood the nature of the performance, she signed a contract and release, there were witnesses, she was under no threat, and she was fully paid. This was supported by the notion that women are not able to provide true consent in a male-dominated society. (These ordinances were struck down in legal challenges.) Another ordinance also permitted a woman to sue the creators and sellers of pornography provided she could prove that she, or women as a class, had been injured by the pornography, an act that was struck down by a Supreme Court decision in 1986, in *American Booksellers v. Hudnut,* when it favored the protection of the First Amendment over the harm done to women.

In the absence of conclusive evidence that pornography leads to violence against women—although there was much evidence that children needed to be protected from being used in pornography—the laws remained in favor of adults' choosing whether to view pornographic material or not. However, the legal struggle to outlaw pornography has had some success in proving that free speech is not necessarily applicable to regulating pornography. Several Supreme Court decisions have determined that pornography may be an exception to free speech in its association with adverse conditions for women.[92]

HUMAN TRAFFICKING

Human trafficking is defined as the ongoing exploitation of victims who are forced to work against their will and is considered involuntary servitude under the Thirteenth Amendment of the U.S. Constitution. Its victims do not consent to their situation, or their consent is invalidated by the coercive, deceptive, or abusive actions of the traffickers. In spite of the United States' signing of multilateral treaties declaring trafficking of women and children a crime in 1905 (International Agreement for the Suppression of the White Slave Traffic) and 1908 (Traffic in Women and Children), the lucrative trade persists. Although precise dollar estimates have been difficult to come by, the conclusion of one two-year investigation by the Federal Bureau of Investigation of a single brothel in Atlanta, Georgia, estimated that up to 1,000 women had been rotated through brothels in 16 states, with some brothels grossing over $1.5 million in a 28-month period.[93]

The Victims of Trafficking and Violence Protection Act of 2000 enforces tougher sentences on traffickers inside and outside the United States and documents international activities in country reports.

On October 2, 2002, then-president George W. Bush proclaimed, "Trafficking is nothing less than a modern form of slavery, an unspeakable and unforgivable crime against the most vulnerable members of the global society."[94] Since then, the U.S. Department of Justice has been developing an anti-trafficking strategy that prosecuted 156 trafficking cases, which secured 342 convictions and rescued more than 1,400 victims between 2002 and 2007. In 2008, Congress passed, and the president signed H.R. 3887, the William Wilberforce Trafficking Victims Protection Reauthorization Act of 2008. At the urging of the Justice Department, laws criminalizing prostitution, pimping, pandering, and solicitation would remain primarily the concern of the state, while federal prosecutors would pursue sex and labor trafficking. Thirty-three states passed comprehensive anti-trafficking laws by 2008.

To address trafficking on a global level, the United States signed an international protocol that was entered into force in December 2003 and was ratified in November 2005 by the United States along with 116 other signatory countries, the Protocol to Prevent, Suppress and Punish Trafficking in Persons, Especially Women and Children, which supplements the United Nations Convention against Transnational Organized Crime of September 2003.

The U.S. Department of State believes 12.3 million adults and children worldwide are subject to forced labor, bonded labor, and forced prostitution. It also perceives this country to be a source, transit, and destination country and, as such, is considered a Tier 1 country on the international watch lists.[95] Of the estimated 600,000 to 800,000 people trafficked across international borders each year, women and girls comprise at least 56 percent.[96] The U.S. government estimates that about 18,000 to 20,000 men and women are trafficked annually into the United States. Additionally, 200,000 youths (ages 10 to 17) are believed to be commercially exploited and trafficked within the United States each year.[97]

Sex-trafficking operations often masquerade as viable but often illegal commercial businesses, such as modeling agencies, prostitution, pornography, escort services, or those that exploit labor in sweatshops, construction, and agricultural settings. *Smuggling* is distinct from trafficking in that it involves "the illegal movement of *consenting* people across a national border for financial or material remuneration," in which the relationship between the smuggler and the migrant ends upon arrival at the destination.[98] Additional forms of forced labor and abuse include domestic servitude and forced marriages.

Although sentencing guidelines were issued to produce more effective judgments against offenders, the sentences are still not as strong as they would need to be to deter others from the lucrative business. In one case, *United States v. Quinton Williams*, the defendant was the operator of a prostitution business who transported a 16-year-old juvenile and an adult victim cross-country by car to Indiana, Texas, Arizona, and Nevada, where he supervised their prostitution activities and collected and kept all of their earnings. He was convicted of sex trafficking of children, transporting both a minor and an adult for prostitution, money laundering, and interstate travel in aid of racketeering; was sentenced to 125 months in prison; and was ordered to pay a $2,500 fine.

Religion and Spirituality

Citizens in the United States are entitled to the freedom to choose their religion and the way they practice it or do not. More than 78 percent of the U.S. population is Christian, and the balance adheres to nearly all the world religions, including Judaism (1.7 percent), Buddhism (0.7 percent), and Islam (0.6 percent), as well as about 17 percent unaffiliated with any religion.[99]

Societal pressures based on religious beliefs often have a part in women's not taking advantage of legal rights. In the South, for example, a strong Baptist influence often prevents young teenage women from having abortions.

LEADERSHIP ROLES IN RELIGIOUS WORSHIP

Some religious organizations—such as the Quakers (Society of Friends) and the Unitarian Church—have ordained women in the United States since the early 1800s. Even earlier, the 1660 writing of a Friends's founder, Margaret Fell (1614–1702), justified the equal roles of men and women on the premise of God's spirit in every soul. The Church of God began ordaining women in Cleveland, Tennessee, in 1909. The Unitarian Universalist religion, which has been ordaining women in large numbers since 1963, was the first major faith group to establish a majority of female clergy in 1999. The role of women in the clergy did not significantly increase, however, until the 1980s and 1990s, when the Protestant United Methodists, Anglicans, and Episcopalians began ordaining women. This paralleled an atmosphere of more liberal business practices as a result of the 1985 U.S. Supreme Court decision in *Estate of Thornton v. Calder* to uphold separation of church from state and not enforce business closings on the sabbath or Sunday, a practice that dated from the 1600s but did not take into account other religions in America.

Large numbers of women were being ordained by the United Methodist (one-dozen bishops, 5 percent of Protestant senior pastors), Southern Baptist (1,000 ministers), and Anglican and Episcopal Churches (16 bishops) at the start of the 21st century.[100] Churches of various denominations remain biased, however, against women in offering lower pay and demanding more educational requirements of women than of men. Nevertheless, women are making advances: In June 2006, Katherine Jefferts Schori, bishop of Nevada, was elected to be the first female presiding bishop of the Episcopal Church, the U.S. arm of the Anglican Communion.

Meanwhile, the Roman Catholic Church, Eastern Orthodox churches, provinces within the Anglican Communion, the Mormons—also known as the Church of Jesus Christ of Latter-day Saints—and many fundamentalist and evangelical Protestant denominations still do not have female clergy.

THE THIRD WAVE

The legislative changes pushed through by women's organizations in the 20th century allowed women to gain access to rights and created equal opportunity of the sexes in the United States in all aspects of life, from property ownership to equal pay and sexual reproduction rights. Social change—such as shared responsibilities within the household and equal compensation at work—has been slower. American women have had the right to vote since 1920, but their political power has increased only minimally. It was not until 1984 that a major party chose a woman, Geraldine Ferraro of New York, to run for vice president, and then again in the 2008 election, with Sarah Palin, then-governor of Alaska, as the running mate of Republican presidential nominee John McCain. Despite these defeats, the presence of strong female candidates perhaps reflects at least a partial shift in American political power toward women.

It has been more than 40 years since the Equal Pay Act was enacted, but the task of convincing employers that women are worth their equal pay stubbornly persists, although the situation has improved for professional women. Women in their 50s are now going back to school to train for careers as physicians, nurses, and lawyers, prolonging their participation in the labor market to make up for the shortfall that is beginning to occur between available retirement and Social Security funds and the retiring population of baby boomers.

Taking advantage of the opportunities now provided and monitoring the implementation of laws and compliance with them are taking on new measures of effort. With its membership of 50,000 women, NOW is considered one of the major women's rights organizations in the United States today. The National Women's Political Caucus, which has chapters in 38 states and advocates leadership training for girls and young women, is also essential to pursuing and tracking legislation that provides gender equality.

The current generation of young women has no personal recall of the struggles their predecessors endured in securing the rights they now have: access to the Pill, abortion, higher education, and workplace equality, among others. Yet problems persist. As the *New York Times* columnist Maureen Dowd writes: "Despite the best efforts of philosophers, politicians, historians, novelists, screenwriters, linguists, therapists, anthropologists and facilitators, men and women are still in a muddle in the boardroom, the bedroom and the Situation Room."[101]

However, whereas the first and second generations of feminists were able to rally around the obvious issues of their time, such as the lack of suffrage and property ownership, problems today are often more subtle and extend to all areas of living, from the right to fair representation in clinical trials to protection against enforced collection of debt, leading to a more diffused movement.[102]

Dorothy Height also expressed a position representative of proponents of women's rights: She was not so much disappointed in the apathy of today's women toward civil rights as by their lack of perspective about being in service to progress, not only for themselves, but for others.

Today, only 34 percent of young women ages 13 to 20 identify themselves as "feminists." However, although many will not use the term *feminist,* the overwhelming majority of them agree with or assume traditional feminist values. One study shows that 97 percent of women in this age bracket believe a woman should receive the same pay for the same work as men, and 92 percent agree that a woman's lifestyle choices should not be limited by her gender. Eighty-nine percent say a woman can be successful without either a man or children.[103]

In a 1998 Time/CNN poll, among those who perceived themselves as feminists, education appears to be the common bond. Fifty-three percent of white college-educated women living in cities embrace the label. Fifty percent of white women who have postgraduate training and no children also do.[104]

Efforts by the movement to monitor the implementation of rights—such as the President's Interagency Council on Women (PICW), which was founded by President Clinton's executive order on the eve of the UN Fourth World Conference on Women in Beijing in 1995—although well intended, are short-lived when dependent on political priorities. The council was developed to "make sure that all the effort and good ideas actually get implemented when we get back home."[105] Chaired by Health and Human Services Secretary Donna Shalala and then–first lady Hillary Rodham Clinton as honorary chair, activities supporting the Beijing Platform for Action by this agency were discontinued after President Clinton left office in 2001. On the other hand, the other initiative mentioned by then-First Lady Hillary Clinton during her speech at the 1995 Beijing conference, Vital Voices, has continued its mission to promote the advancement of women as a U.S. foreign policy goal.

The United States now ranks 19th in the world for parity between the sexes, having risen 12 places since 2009 to be among the top 20 countries in 2010.[106] Even so, the UN CEDAW treaty still awaits a vote by the U.S. Senate Foreign Relations Committee, which would then place it before Congress for ratification. Many women's organizations fear that ensuing "Reservations, Declarations and Understandings [RDUs]" would weaken the treaty's platforms for improved access to health care, equal pay, or improved maternity-leave terms, undermining the United States' commitment to women's equality.[107]

The Women's Story—Past, Present, Future

The events in the 1960s and 1970s helped women's history to become a field of higher educational study, which added to the credibility of the cause. During that time, the term *herstory* was coined to characterize the unrecognized contributions of women to history.

A study conducted in the 1990s to measure the effect of women's studies departments on college students showed that the curriculum in women's programs led to intellectual and personal growth and change. Participation in a women's studies program resulted in "a more progressive gender role orientation and an increased sense of personal control over life outcomes." The latter is associated with *empowerment*, a term often seen in feminist literature today. The other effect measured was improved self-esteem.[108]

In the late 1990s and early 2000s, women's studies programs increasingly evolved into gender studies, the theoretical analysis of how gender identities are constructed, making this domain of study more practical for gender-based applications within society. In April 2002, Yale University renamed its Women's Studies Department the Women and Gender Studies Department. The National Women's Studies Association (NWSA) hosts an annual conference that fosters national, cultural, and political dialogue about women and their role in race, class, sexuality, and gender developments.

In 2005, the U.S. Senate approved the National Women's History Museum Act by unanimous consent. The museum has been an official organization since 1996 and needs a site for its exhibits and archives; two bills—S. 2129 and H.R. 1700—passed out of committee on April 21, 2010. If passed into law, the bills will authorize the Administrator of General Services to convey a parcel of real property to the museum.

According to Senator Susan Collins (1952–), who spearheaded the legislation along with a coalition of other women leaders, including Senator Barbara Boxer (1940–): "Such a museum would also showcase the many important social, economic, cultural, and political contributions that women have made to our country."[109]

---

[1] Claudia Goldin and Lawrence F. Katz. "Putting the 'Co' in Education: Timing, Reasons, and Consequences of College Coeducation from 1835 to the Present," Department of Economics, Harvard University, and National Bureau of Economic Research, August 8, 2010. p. 1.

[2] Andrew Sum, Neeta Fogg, Paul Harrington, et al. "The Growing Gender Gaps in College Enrollment and Degree Attainment in the U.S. and Their Potential Economic and Social Consequences." Center for Labor Market Studies, Northeastern University, Boston, Massachusetts, May 2003, p. 13.

[3] Margaret Sanger. "A Public Nuisance." *Birth Control Review*, October 1931, pp. 277–280. The Public Writings and Speeches of Margaret Sanger. Available online. URL: http://www.nyu.edu/projects/sanger/webedition/app/documents/show.php?sangerDoc=225696.xml. Accessed October 20, 2011.

[4] Christopher J. Tassava. "The American Economy during World War II." EH.Net Encyclopedia. Available online. URL: http://eh.net/encyclopedia/article/tassava.WWII. Accessed May 28, 2006.

[5] Robert A. Guisepi, ed. "History of the United States." Part 7. World History Project. Available online. URL: http://history-world.org/history_of_the_united_states7.htm. Accessed May 28, 2006.

[6] Women in Military Service for America Memorial Foundation. "World War II : Women and the War." Available online. URL: http://www.womensmemorial.org/H&C/History/wwii.html. Accessed December 24, 2010.

[7] Women in Military Service for America Memorial Foundation, Inc. "Woman's Place in War." Poster, 1941–44. Available online. URL: http://www.womensmemorial.org/H&C/History/wwii(wac).html. Accessed May 31, 2006.

[8] Jacqueline Cochran. "Jacqueline Cochran's Final Report." WASP Records. Available online. URL: http://www.wasp-wwii.org/wasp/final_report.htm. Accessed May 22, 2006.

[9] "American Association for Affirmative Action Observes the 50th Anniversary of Executive Order 10925. The First Presidential Order Mandating Affirmative Action in Employment." Available online. URL: http://affirmact.blogspot.com/2011/03/aaaa-observes-50th-anniversary-of.html. Accessed on June 19, 2011.

[10] Howard N Fullerton, Jr. "Labor Force Participation: 75 Years of Change, 1950–98 and 1998–2025." *Monthly Labor Review,* Bureau of Labor Statistics, December 1999, p. 4.

[11] Civilrights.org. "Remarks by Coretta Scott King on ENDA" (June 23, 1994). Available online. URL: http://www.civilrights.org/issues/glbt/details.cfm?id=4727. Accessed June 3, 2006.

[12] Centers for Disease Control and Prevention (CDC). "Health, United States, 2009," report, p. 171.

[13] CDC. "Health, United States, 2009," report, p. 169.

[14] Becky Bohrer. "Lisa Murkowski Certified Winner of Alaska Senate Election." Huffington Post. Available online. URL: http://www.huffingtonpost.com/2010/12/30/lisa-murkowski-certified-_n_802823.html. Accessed January 9, 2011.

[15] International Parliamentary Union (IPU). "Women in Parliaments: World Classification, Situation as of 30 November 2010." Available online. URL: http://www.ipu.org/wmn-e/classif.htm. Accessed December 24, 2010.

[16] ABC News. *This Week with Christiane Amanpour.* Show transcript, November 7, 2010. Available online. URL: http://abcnews.go.com/ThisWeek/week-transcript-rand-paul-rep-mike-pence-david/story?id=12078824. Accessed January 9, 2011.

[17] Dana Milbank. "A Thank-You for 18 Million Cracks in the Glass Ceiling." *Washington Post* (June 8, 2008). Available online. URL: http://www.washingtonpost.com/wp-dyn/content/article/2008/06/07/AR2008060701879.html. Accessed January 9, 2011.

[18] "40 Under 40." Special Report.*Time*, October 25, 2010.

[19] U.S. Department of Education. "The Condition of Education 2010." National Center for Education Statistics (NCES), NCES 2010-028, Indicator 19. 2010, p. 68.

[20] NCES. "Digest of Education Statistics 2009." April 2010, Table 103. High School Graduates, by Sex and Control of School: Selected Years, 1869–70 through 2018–19, p. 164.

[21] NCES. "Digest of Education Statistics 2009." April 2010, Table 200. Recent High School Completers and Their Enrollment in College, by Sex: 1960 through 2008, p. 291.

[22] U.S. Department of Labor. *Women in the Labor Force: A Databook.* September 2009, p. 30.

[23] U.S. Department of Labor. *Women in the Labor Force: A Databook.* September 2009, Table 18. Median Usual Weekly Earnings of Full-Time Wage and Salary Workers by Detailed Occupation and Sex, 2008 annual averages, p. 57.

[24] National Center for Education Statistics (NCES). Table 268. Degrees Conferred by Degree-Granting Institutions, by Level of Degree and Sex of Student: Selected Years, 1869–70 through 2018–19. Available online. URL: http://nces.ed.gov/programs/digest/d09/tables/dt09_268.asp. Accessed January 5, 2011.

[25] U.S. Bureau of Labor Statistics. *Women in the Labor Force: A Databook.* September 2010, Report 1026, p. 23.

[26] NCES. Table 268. Degrees Conferred by Degree-Granting Institutions, by Level of Degree and Sex of Student: Selected Years, 1869–70 through 2018–19. Available online. URL: http://nces.ed.gov/programs/digest/d09/tables/dt09_268.asp. Accessed January 5, 2011.

[27] U.S. Bureau of Labor Statistics. *Women in the Labor Force: A Databook.* September 2010, Report 1026, Table 17. Median Usual Weekly Earnings of Full-Time Wage and Salary Workers 25 Years of Age and over by Educational Attainment and Sex, 2009 annual averages, p. 53.

[28] U.S. Bureau of Labor Statistics. *Women in the Labor Force: A Databook.* December 2010, Table 17. Median Usual Weekly Earnings of Full-Time Wage and Salary Workers 25 Years of Age and over by Educational Attainment and Sex, 2010 annual averages, p. 54.

[29] U.S. Bureau of Labor Statistics. *Women in the Labor Force: A Databook.* September 2009, Report 1018.

[30] Howard N. Fullerton, Jr. "Labor Force Participation: 75 Years of Change, 1950–98 and 1998–2025." Bureau of Labor Statistics *Monthly Labor Review* (December 1999), p. 3.

[31] Bonnie Rochman. "Economoms." *Time*, March 29, 2009.

[32] Institute for Women's Policy Research (IWPR). "Women and Men's Employment and Unemployment in the Great Recession." February 2010.

[33] Fullerton. "Labor Force Participation," Table 1, p. 4.

[34] U.S. Department of Labor, Bureau of Labor Statistics. *Women in the Labor Force: A Databook.* September 2009, Report 1018. Available online. URL: http://www.bls.gov/cps/wlf-databook2009.htm. Accessed September 23, 2010.

[35] "Women's Earnings: Work Patterns Partially Explain Difference between Men's and Women's Earnings." Report to Congressional Requesters, United States General Accounting Office, October 2003, p. 2.

[36] IWPR. "Fact Sheet: The Gender Wage Gap, 2009," September 2010.

[37] U.S. Department of Labor, U.S. Bureau of Labor Statistics (BLS). "Highlights of Women's Earnings in 2009." Report 1025, Table 2. Median Usual Weekly Earnings of Full-Time Wage and Salary Workers, by Detailed Occupation and Sex, 2009 annual averages, June 2010.

[38] U.S. Bureau of Labor Statistics. "Highlights of Women's Earnings in 2009," Report 1025, June 2010.

[39] Sean Gregory. "Uneven Playing Field: Where Are the Women Coaches?" *Time*, August 16, 2007, p. 49.

[40] EEOC. Pregnancy Discrimination Charges EEOC & FEPAs Combined: FY 1997–FY 2009. Available online. URL:http://www.eeoc.gov/eeoc/statistics/enforcement/pregnancy.cfm. Accessed September 24, 2010.

[41] U.S. Bureau of Labor Statistics. "Labor Force Participation Rate of Mothers, 1975–2007." January 2009.

[42] U.S. Bureau of Labor Statistics. *Women in the Labor Force: A Databook.* Table 7. Employment Status of Women by Presence and Age of Youngest Child, March 1975–2008, p. 18.

[43] U.S. Bureau of Labor Statistics. *Women in the Labor Force: A Databook.* Table 25. Wives Who Earn More Than Their Husbands, 1987–2007, p. 78.

[44] June Hannan, Mitzi Auchter Ionie, and Katherine Holden, eds. "Child Care." In *International Encyclopedia of Women's Suffrage*. Santa Barbara, Calif.: ABC-CLIO, 2000, p. 159.

[45] National Childcare Information Center. "Child Care and Development Fund Report of State Plans FY 2004–2005." Report, October 2004, p. 1.

[46] Stephen Gaskill. "A Solid Investment: Making Use of the Nation's Human Capital. U.S. Glass Ceiling Commission." U.S. Department of Labor, November 1995.

[47] Gaskill. "A Solid Investment," p. 6.

[48] Gaskill. "A Solid Investment," p. 13.

[49] Federal Glass Ceiling Commission. "Good for Business: Making Full Use of the Nation's Human Capital—the Environmental Scan." Fact-Finding Report, Washington, D.C., March 1995.

[50] Catalyst Inc. "Women in U.S. Management." December 13, 2010. Available online. URL: http://www.catalyst.org/publication/206/. Accessed December 26, 2010.

[51] U.S. General Accounting Office. "A New Look through the Glass Ceiling: Where Are the Women? The Status of Women in Management in Ten Selected Industries" (January 2002), p. 7. Available online. URL: http://www.gao.gov. Accessed May 29, 2006.

[52] Equal Employment Opportunity Commission (EEOC). "Women of Color: Their Employment in the Private Sector," 2003.

[53] Catalyst Inc. "Women in U.S. Management." March 16, 2010. Available online. URL: http://www.catalyst.org/publication/206/. Accessed October 30, 2010.

[54] Catalyst Inc. "New Study Indicates Clue to Reversing Trend." Press release, December 13, 2010. Available online URL: http://www.catalyst.org/press-release/181/11/latest-catalyst-census-shows-women-still-not-scaling-the-corporate-ladder-in-2010-new-study-indicates-clue-to-reversing-trend. Accessed December 26, 2010.

[55] EEOC. Sexual Harassment Charges EEOC & FEPAs. Combined: FY 1997–FY 2009. Available online. URL: http://www.eeoc.gov/eeoc/statistics/enforcement/sexual_harassment.cfm. Accessed September 24, 2010.

[56] US Census Bureau. "Poverty-Highlights." Available online. URL: http://www.census.gov/hhes/www/poverty/about/overview/index.html. Accessed October 26, 2010, p. 15.

[57] IWPR. "Women and Men's Employment and Unemployment in the Great Recession." Publication C373, February 2010, p. 5.

[58] US Census Bureau. "Poverty-Highlights." Table 4. People and Families in Poverty by Selected Characteristics: 2008 and 2009, p. 15. Available online. URL: http://www.census.gov/hhes/www/poverty/about/overview/index.html. Accessed September 19, 2010.

[59] Elaine Sorensen and Ariel Halpern. "Child Support Enforcement: How Well Is It Doing?" Report, Urban Institute, December 1999, p. 19.

[60] Population Reference Bureau. "U.S. Children in Single-Mother Families." May 2010. Available online. URL:http://www.wkkf.org/~/media/39F70A1BE2364C50A610B7E806CC4D02.ashx. Accessed December 19, 2010.

[61] Social Security Administration. Recipients, by Sex and Age, December 2008. Available online. URL: http://www.ssa.gov/policy/docs/chartbooks/fast_facts/2009/fast_facts09.html#oasdi. Accessed December 19, 2010.

[62] U.S. Equal Employment Opportunity Commission. "Workforce Composition of the U.S. Department of the Army, Navy, Marines, Air Force" (May 3, 2005). Available online. URL: http://www.eeoc.gov/federal/fsp2004/profiles. Accessed November 29, 2005.

[63] Women in Military Service for America Memorial Foundation, Inc. "Statistics on Women in the Military." September 2009.

[64] EEOC. Department of the Army. "Workforce Composition, Army. Permanent Workforce." Available online. URL: http://www.eeoc.gov/federal/reports/fsp2008/agencies/Department oftheArmyARMY.html. Accessed October 29, 2010.

[65] Janie Blankenship. "Ever-Changing Roles of Women in the Military: More and More, Women in Uniform Are Thrust into Dangerous Situations Overseas." *VFW Magazine*, March 2005.

[66] Tim McGirk. "Crossing the Line." *Time*, February 27, 2006, p. 38.

[67] Kristina Wong. "Women Fighting and Dying in War, Despite Combat Exclusion Policy" (May 30, 2011). ABC News. Available online. URL: http://abcnews.go.com/US/women-fight-iraq-afghanistan-preclusion-ground-combat/story?id=13716419&page=3. Accessed June 15, 2011.

[68] Donna Lyons. Women Veterans' Health Issues 2010 (November 17, 2010). Defense Media Network. Available online. http://www.defensemedianetwork.com/stories/women-veterans-health-issues-2010/. Accessed November 16, 2011.

[69] PBS NewsHour. "Women Veterans Face Unique Obstacles, Needs." November 30, 2010. Available online. URL: http://www.pbs.org/newshour/bb/military/july-dec10/womenvets_11-30.html?print. Accessed November 30, 2010.

[70] Centers for Disease Control. National Vital Statistics System. "Leading Causes of Death by Race/Ethnicity, All Females-United States, 2006*". Available online. URL:http://www.cdc.gov/women/lcod/06_females_by_race.pdf. Accessed December 4, 2010.

[71] Theresa M. Wizemann and Mary-Lou Pardue, eds. "Exploring the Biological Contributions to Human Health: Does Sex Matter?" Report, Institute of Medicine, 2001.

[72] "State Secret: Thousands Secretly Sterilized" (May 15, 2005). ABC News. Available online. URL: http://abcnews.go.com/WNT/Health/story?id=708780. Accessed January 23, 2006.

[73] National Right to Life. "Abortion in the United States: Statistics and Trends." Available online. URL: http://www.nrlc.org/abortion/facts/abortionstats.html. Accessed September 27, 2010.

[74] Guttmacher Institute, Media Kit, "Overview of Abortion in the United States," 2002.

[75] NRIC. Abortion Facts. Available online. URL: http://www.nrlc.org/abortion/facts/abortionstats2.html. Accessed September 27, 2010.

[76] UN Department of Economic & Social Affairs, Population Division, 2009. Contraceptive Prevalence.

[77] CIA World Factbook. United States country profile. Available online. URL: https://www.cia.gov/library/publications/the-world-factbook/geos/us.html. Accessed September 24, 2010.

[78] James Alm, M. V. Lee Badgett, and Leslie A. Whittington. "Wedding Bell Blues: The Income Tax Consequences of Legalizing Same-Sex Marriage." Center for Economic Analysis, Department of Economics, University of Colorado, Boulder, November 1998, p. 9.

[79] Federal Bureau of Investigation (FBI). Crime in the United States. Available online. URL: http://www2.fbi.gov/ucr/cius2009/index.html. Accessed on December 24, 2010.

[80] National Conference of State Legislatures. Available online. URL: http://www.ncsl.org/default.aspx?tabid=16430. Accessed December 26, 2010.

[81] National Conference of State Legislatures. Available online. URL: http://www.ncsl.org/default.aspx?tabid=16430. Accessed December 26, 2010.

[82] International Centre for the Prevention of Crime. "International Report on Crime Prevention and Community Safety: Trends and Perspectives, 2010," p. 30. Available online. URL: http://www.crime-prevention-intl.org/uploads/media/International_Report_2010.pdf. Accessed October 3, 2010.

[83] CDC. "Understanding IPV," Fact Sheet 2009, p. 1.

[84] U.S. Department of Justice. Bureau of Justice Statistics. October 2010 Bulletin, NCJ 231327. Table 1, Criminal victimization, numbers, rates, and percent change, by type of crime, 2008 and 2009. Available online. URL: http://bjs.ojp.usdoj.gov/content/pub/pdf/cv09.pdf. Accessed December 26, 2010.

[85] U.S. Department of Justice. Bureau of Justice Statistics. October 2010 Bulletin, NCJ 231327, p. 7. Available online. URL: http://bjs.ojp.usdoj.gov/content/pub/pdf/cv09.pdf. Accessed December 26, 2010.

[86] Robert Jensen. "Pornography and Sexual Violence." July 2004. Available online. URL: http://www.oneangrygirl.net/jensenlong.pdf. Accessed December 26, 2010.

[87] Patricia Tjaden and Nancy Thoennes. "Full Report of the Prevalence, Incidence, and Consequences of Violence against Women." U.S. Department of Justice, Office of Justice Programs, National Institute of Justice and Centers for Disease Control, November 2000, p. iii.

[88] National Institute of Justice. "Measuring Intimate Partner (Domestic) Violence." May 2010. Available online. URL: http://www.ojp.usdoj.gov/nij/topics/crime/intimate-partner-violence/measuring.htm. Accessed December 26, 2010.

[89] CDC. "Costs of Intimate Partner Violence Against Women in the United States, 2003." National Centers for Injury Prevention and Control. Atlanta, Georgia.

[90] International Centre for the Prevention of Crime. "International Report Crime Prevention and Community Safety: Trends and Perspectives, 2010," p. 57. Available online. URL: http://www.crime-prevention-intl.org/uploads/media/International_Report_2010.pdf. Accessed October 3, 2010.

[91] Mappes and Zembaty. *Social Ethics.* New York: McGraw-Hill, 1997, p. 215.

[92] Gail Dines, Robert Jensen, and Ann Russo. *Pornography: The Production and Consumption of Inequality.* London: Routledge, 1997, p. 4.

[93] Janice G. Raymond and Donna M. Hughes. "Sex Trafficking of Women in the United States: International and Domestic Trends." Coalition against Trafficking in Women, report sponsored by the National Institute of Justice, March 2001, p. 102.

[94] "Assessment of U.S. Activities to Combat Trafficking in Persons." U.S. Department of State, 2003, p. 1. Available online. URL: http://www.state.gov/g/tip/rls/rpt/23495.htm. Accessed December 19, 2005.

[95] U.S. Department of State. "Trafficking in Persons Report, 2010," p. 338.

[96] U.S. Department of State. "Trafficking in Persons Report, 2010," p. 35.

[97] "Assessment of U.S. Activities to Combat Trafficking in Persons," p. 1.

[98] International Rescue Committee. "Trafficking in the United States" (November 24, 2003). Available online. URL: http://www.theirc.org/media/www/trafficking_in_the_united_states.html#search. Accessed May 11, 2006.

[99] The Pew Forum. "U.S. Religious Landscape Survey; Religious Affiliation: Diverse and Dynamic." February 2008, p. 5.

[100] Ontario Consultants on Religious Tolerance. "When Some Faith Groups Started to Ordain Women." Available online. URL: http://www.religioustolerance.org. Accessed May 30, 2006.

[101] Maureen Dowd. "What's a Modern Girl to Do?" *New York Times Magazine,* October 30, 2005, pp. 50–55.

[102] Jennifer Friedlin. "Second and Third Wave Feminists Clash over the Future" (May 26, 2002). Women's Enews. Available online. URL: http://www.womensenews.org/article.cfm/dyn/aid/920/context/cover. Accessed June 5, 2006.

[103] Rebecca Gardyn. "Granddaughters of Feminism." *American Demographics,* April 2001, p. 42.

[104] Ginia Bellafante. "It's All about Me! Want to Know What Today's Chic Young Feminist Thinkers Care About? Their Bodies! Themselves!" *Time,* June 29, 1998, p. 54.

[105] Feminist.com. Articles and speeches. Available online. URL: http://www.feminist.com/resources/artspeech/wword/ww1.htm. Accessed December 26, 2010.

[106] World Economic Forum. "The Global Gender Gap 2010." October 12, 2010.

[107] NOW. "CEDAW Hearing Encouraging, U.S. Ratification Long Overdue." November 19, 2010. Available online. URL: http://www.now.org/press/11-10/11-19.html. Accessed January 10, 2011.

[108] Karen L. Harris, et al. "The Impact of Women's Studies Courses on College Students of the 1990s." *Sex Roles: A Journal of Research* (June 1999), p. 969.

[109] National Museum of Women's History. "U.S. Senate Approves the National Women's History Museum Act of 2005 (S. 501) by Unanimous Consent" (August 1, 2005). Available online. URL: http://www.nmwh.org/news/museumsite.htm. Accessed November 1, 2005.

3

Global Perspectives

In the following section, the way the women's movement arose and is evolving in the United States is compared with that in four countries that have distinctly different cultural traditions and economic situations: France, China, Afghanistan, and the Democratic Republic of the Congo.

Each country is surveyed for specific characteristics—historical, cultural, religious, national—that make the women's movement in these countries similar to or different from the movement in the United States.

Features of comparison include the following:

1. Issues and events that sparked the women's movement and the timing of the movement
2. The political background of the movement and its challenges
3. The current issues of the movement
4. The connection with the international movement
5. The direction in which the movement is heading

FRANCE

The women's movement in France grew through resistance to the status quo—whether deeply rooted family values, language traditions, socioeconomic trends, or political parties. The political climate that shaped women's rights through legal and political reforms would largely be recognized and mainstreamed by government.

Certain rights for women arrived late in France compared with other countries, such as the right to vote. The delay was due to the fundamental loyalty of the French culture to the institution of family (*familialisation*) and the strength of that social model through World War II and until the end of the 20th century. Even today, family-driven institutions and national dependency on women's labor-market participation continue to reshape the women's movement.

Spurs of the Women's Movement

In the first of two revolutions, women gained momentum when they were finally recognized as citizens (*citoyennes*) after the storming of the Bastille, July 14, 1789. Still, the National Assembly only sanctioned male suffrage. In an atmosphere of disaffection, Olympe de Gouges (1745–93) wrote the *Declaration of the Rights of Women and the Female Citizen* in 1791, based on the 1789 *Declaration of the Rights of Man and of the Citizen*. This set a precedent for American-born Elizabeth Cady Stanton to author the *Declaration of Sentiments* for the Seneca Falls Convention of 1848. Both works mirrored documents that considered only men as citizens of their respective countries.

But it was not until the affront on King Louis-Philippe by the populist National Assembly in 1848 that women would meet an even greater resistance in times ahead. In the early 19th century, France had seen radical suppression of women's rights by a growing monarchy led by Napoléon Bonaparte. His enforcement of a civil code (Code Napoléon) would engrain itself into the psychology of the French culture and that of the countries he invaded. It bestowed such values as husbands having ownership over their wives and their wives' properties.

Dissenting views were popularized in writings by well-known literary figures, such as Victor Hugo (*New York Times*, April 18, 1875, in response to an appeal from the U.S. Society for the Improvement of the Condition of Women) and John Stuart Mill (*On the Subjection of Women*, 1869).

Louise Michel (1830–80), a former schoolteacher turned anarchist, would be remembered as *le communarde* to the Third Republic—*la république bourgeoise*—in 1871. Opposed to Napoléon III during the Second Empire and to the bourgeois republic that followed, her anarchist views clashed with the policies of the early Third Republic (1870–1940), subjecting her to intermittent imprisonment. She moved to Britain, where she persisted until her death in educating women about their rights.

Nineteenth-century child care facilities and waged-work policies introduced a large number of women into the labor market in France well before women entered it in other countries. Because of this, sophisticated labor protections evolved in the latter half of the 19th century. Workdays were limited to 11 hours in 1892, at the height of the Industrial Revolution.

As in the United States and other European countries, women were admitted into French universities in the 1880s. Julie-Victoire Daubie (1824–74) became the first female to pass the *baccalaureat*, in 1861.

Between the two world wars, family programs of President Léon Blum (1872–1950) in the 1930s—including the creation of *allocations familiales*, or family services—added impetus to women's ability to function more fully in society, extending their wartime decision-making responsibilities when their husbands were absent for military service. During the Vichy regime of French collaboration with Nazi Germany, women demonstrated their ability to resist all manners of tyranny—a quality that would not be recognized until much later in French history books.

Women's growing political and social involvement beyond the *foyer* continued after the war. Then-president Charles de Gaulle (1890–1970) spoke before the Provisional Consultative Assembly in March 1944, and his decree persuaded the assembly to grant women suffrage rights that would take effect at the next national election, on October 21, 1945. This was not perceived as a radical reform to the international scene, which required women's suffrage of member nations in the United Nations. That women were allowed to vote, present themselves at elections, and otherwise have a say in public-policy matters led to significant changes in the mighty institution of "family" in French life and its inextricable ties to the Catholic faith. The French constitution was amended in 1946 with a preamble that foresaw the need to highlight equality for the sexes, but true reform would not come for another 20 years.

Simone de Beauvoir (1908–86), like her American counterpart Betty Friedan, guided women through the bewilderingly un-French Mouvement de liberation des femmes. Women's policy agencies began altering the structures sustaining family values in the 1960s. The confluence of marriage reforms in 1965, contraception laws of 1967–74, divorce law changes in 1975, and reformed family-planning laws in 1974, paved the way for change that would break with much of French cultural tradition.

Political opportunities for women also emerged, leading to the appointment between 1974 and 1976 of Françoise Giroud as the first secretary for women's affairs in a ministerial post in the French government, foretelling of what was to come in the 1980s.

Women set about formalizing the changes they fought for through policy making and laws. The creation in 1981 of the Ministry of Women's Rights, during François Mitterrand's reign as a socialist president, was in many ways a landmark occurrence for the spirited movement.

Current Issues

Further reforms in the 2000s—labor laws, family planning, divorce amendments, equal rights, domestic violence, equal pay—emerged with France's growing partnership and identification with the European Union, where gender mainstreaming became a priority in 1998.[1] This shift in mindset—from a single nation to a union—was furthered with the change in currency from

French francs to euros on January 1, 1999. By making women part of the status quo, the question has also evolved: In a highly bureaucratic society, how would government intervention further women's goals and aspirations to do and be more?

With women representing more than half of the estimated 64.8 million people in 2010—32.9 million women versus 31.9 million men—and a life expectancy that well outpaces that of men—certain issues are magnified as the nation heads into the aging of baby-boomers.[2]

EMPLOYMENT

Since the 1970s, women's involvement in the labor force has not stopped rising. Various forms of child-care arrangements in the 1970s would formalize into day-care services, making it easier for women to return to the workforce. Still, inequities persisted, with higher unemployment rates than for men, encouragement to work part time, and less access to professional or management opportunities, which would become the focus of a more formal resistance.

Minister Yvette Roudy (1929–), minister of women's rights (1981–83), addressed equality in employment as her campaign priority, a promise that would eventually lead to affirmative-action programs that she considered key to women's liberation. The Roudy Law of 1983 was the underpinning of equal treatment in the French labor code, to be later companioned by laws that called for equal pay.

Since the 1980s, the disparity in the workplace between men and women has been narrowing. This is due to the measures taken to improve women's participation and skills development within the trades and business sector, as well as a drop in women's unemployment. Women are more educated than men but continue to be underrepresented in the labor market.[3] While 62.4 percent of men 15 years old or older are employed, only 51.9 percent of women of equal age were in the labor force in 2009. The unemployment rate is slightly higher among women than men—9.8 percent compared with 9.2 percent—and women are still more likely to work part time to accommodate domestic duties.[4]

The more often women have children, and the younger they are, the more likely they will limit their professional activity, even if they have the requisite skills and education. The disparity in salary rates between men and women is often justified in terms of seniority, educational levels, as well as the employment industry.

French labor laws are reflective of this determination to hold companies accountable, though enforcement is a challenge. Not since the Ameline law of 2006—for professional equality— in which "Equality Labels for Companies" were issued as a form of affirmative action, has there been such efforts. A special commission delivers the labels to companies that prove that they promote equality between men and women.[5]

Mostly unreported, sexual harassment claims by women who were polled in 1991 and 2000 suggest occurrences were comparatively higher in France than in the European Union. Sixty-two percent of women reported having experienced some form of harassment on the job at some point during their working life, compared with the average 40 to 50 percent of women in the European Union in 1991.[6] A series of legislative measures in 1990 in both the United States and the European Union effectively moderated sexual harassment cases and prevented the subject from being silenced by taboo. In 1992, France's Ministry of Work put in place a sexual harassment law.[7] A more recent poll by the Ministry of the Interior, Overseas France, and Local Authorities, found that the number of reported sexual harassment cases had dropped by 12 percent from 2006 to 2007, but was not gender-specific.[8]

The Council of Ministers of the European Community defined sexual harassment for its member states, and the Equal Employment Opportunities Commission (EEOC) updated its Guidelines on Discrimination Because of Sex, adding regulations on definition and prevention. These guidelines even designated sexual favoritism as a form of sexual harassment. This was further supported by a European Union parliamentary directive, known as Directive 2002/73/EC, which required its member nations to implement legislative agencies similar to the U.S. EEOC to deal with sexual harassment at the legislative level by October 2002. It also amended the previously existing directives on the equality of men and women in the workplace with the definitions of *harassment* and *sexual harassment.*

POLITICAL PARITY

It Is not surprising that among the first women to acquire political stature in France was a lawyer, Simone Veil (1927–), who lost part of her family in the Auschwitz-Birkenau concentration camp during World War II. Her advocacy for access to contraception and legalized abortion—platforms of the emerging Mouvement de libération des femmes since 1968—led to the Veil Act in 1975, despite opposition from conservatives within her own Union for French Democracy (UFD) party. She served as minister of health from 1974 to 1979, until her election as the first female president of the European Parliament, from 1979 to 1982. She would hold several more French ministerial positions between 1993 and 1995.

Édith Cresson (1934–) was elected the first female prime minister in 1991, but political parity in France would not truly be achieved during her tenure, which was rescinded in 1992 because of a drop in opinion polls.

Much hope banked on the passing of laws in 2000. The law of 6 June favored equal access of women and men to *mandats électoraux* and high-level public office. The July 10th law was specific to French *départements* (administrative divisions) electing three or more senators. The benefits of such mandates would be immediately perceptible in the 2001 elections, when more than 10 percent of seats were won by women compared with the 2002 rate of 6 percent.

Although efforts to enforce gender balance have persisted since the 2000 electoral equality legislation, parity is achieved mostly within areas where quotas are enforced by law, such as in municipalities with a population of 3,500 or more. Whatever gains women made in being elected at the department level in administrative divisions (being allowed three or more senatorial seats) were hindered by a 2003 law that required only a majority vote for a candidate to win an election, regardless of gender. Some balance was hoped to be achieved by a January 2007 law mandating that assistant mayorship and executive boards alternate qualifying candidates by gender. Women's local participation at the mayoral level was 13.5 percent in 2008, which compared with their participation as deputies at 18.5 percent and 21.9 percent of senators at a national level.[9]

The presence of women on the political scene has progressed rapidly in the past 10 years, but still within a largely male-dominated leadership. Although women represented more than 53 percent of the electoral vote in 2010, only 20 percent of parliamentary seats are held by women, ranking France at 17th in the world, just ahead of the United States (18th) in gender empowerment rankings in 2009. Sweden and Norway are considered the top-ranking countries.[10] Of legislators, senior officials, and managers, females occupy 38 percent of the total. No woman has, as of yet, presided over the French parliament or one of its houses, unlike its European Union cohorts. Ségolène Royal (1953–   ), several times a minister between 1992 and 2002, was a presidential candidate representing the Socialist Party in the 2007 elections and proof that the tide was turning. Eventually, President Nicolas Sarkozy (1955–   ) created a cabinet that would be populated by 47 percent women in ministerial positions, making France one of the top countries in terms of female representation in the European Parliament.

As the first female minister of finance, Christine Lagarde (1956–   ) reduced the unemployment rate in France from 9.6 percent to 9.3 percent by October 2010, the second consecutive decline that year.[11] Notable qualities are her ties with the international finance community and her mastery of the English language. Lagarde became head of the International Monetary Fund in June 2011, replacing Dominique Strauss-Kahn, the former managing director, who resigned while under imprisonment in New York City on charges of committing sexual assault. The charges were later dropped.

Representing the next generation of women emerging on the political scene is Marine LePen (1968–   ), daughter of former right-wing leader Jean-Marie LePen, who is now upholding the National Front party platform and will be a candidate in the presidential elections in 2012.

FAMILY RIGHTS

Marriage as an institution was initially entrusted to the Catholic Church in France. The swing in post–World War II France to a more secular-based system led to a government-supported formula of three children per family with two parents of both genders. However, with modernization and globalization, family life has come to encompass a complex array of relationships— from the traditional family model to same-sex civil unions, single-parent households, and an unprecedented increase in divorces and remarriages. The increasingly diverse population has also allowed a variety of faiths and practices.

The composition of households has also become more diverse, breaking away from traditional family patterns. The annual number of marriages dropped by 4 percent between 2007 and 2009, from 266,000 to 256,000, respectively.[12] The average age at which men get married (31.6 years old) was about two years older than that of women (29.7) in 2008. Households with no children increased from 38.4 percent in 1999 to 41.7 percent in 2007.[13]

Divorce laws have been shaped by different political regimes. First legal in 1792, then abolished in 1816 by the monarchy, domestic rights to divorce were brought back in 1850, following the Revolution of 1848, and would remain effective until the 21st century. Divorce laws in January 2005 precipitated changes that were immediately perceptible in the 15.3 percent increase (155,000) in divorces that year. By 2008, the annual number of divorces—at its highest among couples who had been married for four years—had since leveled off to what it was prior to 2004, at 129,379 divorces.[14] The average age of couples seeking divorce by mutual consent was 42.9 years for men and 40.4 years for women; fewer but more contentious divorces were occurring among more elderly couples. Since 1990, second marriages have been more common among men.

Certain measures were taken by the French government to promote sharing of domestic duties—the Allocation Parentale d'Éducation (APE) in 1985—but with strict conditions: It only applied to parents of families with three children.[15] The emphasis upon work/family balance continues to be considered a "woman's issue" with domestic chores unequally distributed with men, who also have a disproportionate amount of leisure time, averaging 40 minutes more per day for leisure activities than women.[16]

FAMILY PLANNING

Birth control was legalized in 1967, but it was not until December 4, 1974, when access to the sale of contraceptives (such as the combined oral contraceptive pill) became possible. Despite opposition from the Catholic Church, which discourages contraceptive use, 81.8 percent of French women in 2000 were using some form of contraception, higher than the 72.8 percent rate in the United States.[17]

Abortion, once considered a crime in 1810 and even punished by death in 1942, became an option for women in 1975 with the passing of the Loi Veil, which bore the name of its proponent, minister of health Simone Veil. By 1982, the French Social Security Administration was even paying for abortions.

In an effort to promote contraceptive use as an impediment to abortion, France's minister of employment and health, Justine Aubry, introduced a bill liberalizing access to abortions and emergency contraception. The Aubry bill of 2000 addressed the high number of abortions in France, unwanted teenage pregnancies, and the problem of young women traveling to other countries for abortions if they surpassed the 10-week maximum stipulated by French law. Aubry intended to make abortion more accessible, modifying its requirements for parental consent for minors and lengthening the permitted period authorizing abortions to 12 weeks. In addition to permitting school nurses to administer the morning-after abortion pill, it would allow minors to purchase the pill over the counter.

The paradox is that since the law's implementation, the number of abortions has not declined, holding at a rate of about 14 abortions per year per 1,000 women, aged 15–49, or approximately 200,000 abortions annually.[18] Conservatives among pharmacists and hospitals continue to use means to avoid or dissuade women seeking abortions, such as long waiting lists.

GAY RIGHTS

An alternative to marriage, legal unions—or *le pacte civil de solidarité* (PACS)—continue to grow since legalized in 1999, to 77,400 in 2006, of which 64,271 were between opposite-sex partners. By 2008, a 2:4 ratio of civil unions to marriages was recorded.[19] This alternative has helped to reverse the overall drop in unions that were seen in the 1990s. The advantage of PACS was to offer gay couples legal recourse for their domestic dependencies, but in 2008, 95.9 percent of these unions were with mixed-gender couples.[20]

Gay rights in France have largely evolved from the acceptance of PACs and similar programs in other European countries, unlike in the United

States, where the status of same-sex marriages is being debated on a state-by-state basis, as well as at the federal and constitutional levels.

VIOLENCE AGAINST WOMEN

Following the initial provision of women's shelters and telephone help lines for female victims of crime, in the 1970s, the second wave of the women's movement has been credited with bringing the issue of domestic violence into the spotlight.

In 1987, Fédération Nationale Solidarité Femmes (FNSF) brought together various associations around the country under one national organization to raise public awareness and influence public policy. Using the data culled from the various agencies, they made the public aware that 40 percent of rapists are known by victims—a characteristic that is typical in most countries—and occurrences are dramatically underreported.[21]

A case study of the Departmental Observatory on Violence against Women in Seine-Saint-Denis, France, by the International Center for the Prevention of Crime highlighted the reality of women's safety as a risk. The 2006 survey of young women in this region showed a 68 percent under-reporting of violence, making the rate two to five times higher than earlier reported in 2000. The observatory has countered this trend by action-oriented, widespread training, using role-play and theater techniques to train women how to react to various types of situations encountered in real life.[22]

An estimated 177,750 cases of rape are reported each year by the NGO Observatory of Violence towards Women.[23] Domestic violence has overall experienced a 6 percent decrease from 2007 to 2008 in the number of women killed by their spouses as a consequence of domestic violence (from 166 to 156). This is largely due to the work of 25 associations and NGOs under the tutelage of the "great national cause" promoted by the French government. According to estimates by the French National Institute for Statistics and Economic Studies (INSEE), 675,000 women were victims of domestic assaults between 2008 and 2009.[24]

Prostitution is legal in spite of being on political agendas since the late 1990s. Under the Lionel Jospin government (1997–2002), the issue became polarized as a security issue versus a sex worker's right. Prostitution eventually came under the Domestic Security bill of 2001, which addressed behaviors that were perceived to be a public nuisance or threatened French citizen's safety.

The intention was to also protect women from trafficking within international rings. Then–interior minister Sarkozy claimed that the number of prostitution rings dismantled increased from 39 in 2003 to 47 in 2004.

CULTURAL INTEGRITY AND INTEGRATION

Measures to feminize words that imply masculine dominance in a profession or industry were subject to a language-reform commission in spring 1983. This parallels language use in the United States, where greater care has been taken by editors and policy makers to use words and pronouns that are inclusive of women.

The illustrious Académie française, one of the last all-male assemblies in high French culture, inducted Margeurite Yourcenar (1903–87) as the first female member in 1980. Simone Veil became the sixth women to have been inducted into the Académie in March 2010.[25] There are 40 members in the Académie, which was created in 1635 to set standards and keep surveillance as guardians of the French language.

Diverse cultures settling in France, especially from former French colonies in Africa, have brought with them atypical practices, such as polygamy. In 2002, the Pasque law was introduced as a means of stopping this practice of having multiple wives at a time after decades of leniency and tolerance that was beginning to wreak havoc on the health-care system in France. People living in a polygamous relationship would not be entitled to resident cards. Having married according to a mostly African tribal custom, women from immigrant families found themselves sometimes abandoned, if not formally separated or divorced, in order to comply with the law allowing only one wife in France.

Similarly, laws disallowing female genital mutilation (FGM) have been implemented, after many years of tolerating the practice, a fact that made the French government a target of NGOs and human rights watch groups.[26] The French government's adherence to separating religion from state would now confront additional religious traditions—epitomized by the concern about Islamic female students wearing headscarves in French schools. When French premier Jean-Pierre Raffarin passed a bill banning the headscarf—a symbol of the Muslim faith—in schools in 2003, no one anticipated the public unrest that act would instigate. The ban on headscarves crossed over into other domains—mainly women's religious freedoms, sense of multiculturalism, and migration issues. The future of the headscarf ban remains in debate today, with numerous legal challenges to the ban still in the French courts.

The Future

Women's rights in France saw their achievements of the 1980s deteriorate in the 1990s, only to regain momentum in the 2000s through laws enforcing parity in the workplace and in national life.

For many, the "reconciliation policy"—the work/family balance trend that was the focus of policies in the 1980s and 1990s—has grown to encompass both genders in current challenges, whether it is about the 35-hour work week or change in the retirement age from 60 to 62.

Although resulting policies have legitimized the grievances of women in contemporary France, they may still not have attained their full impact—socioeconomically or politically—because of low political importance, slow implementation, or underfunding—a plight similar to that of women in other countries, regardless of degree of development. This was demonstrated during a November 2010 visit by China's President Hu Jintao to Paris, when President Sarkozy praised the $20 billion in industrial contracts the two countries signed as an "opportunity," in turn distancing the occasion from the human rights issues of both China and France.[27] All policy needs financing, but policy related to human and women's rights has unfortunately failed to be a priority to many world leaders in recent years, on account of the current global economic crisis.

CHINA

Women's rights in mainland China emerged as one of many changes in the transition from imperial and military rule in the early 20th century to the Chinese Communist Party (CCP) in 1949. As in the United States and Europe during the 19th-century Industrial Revolution, the People's Republic of China (PRC) under Mao Zedong (1903–76) and his successors, Deng Xiaoping (1904–97) and Jiang Zemin (1925–   ), gradually moved from being a centrally planned, agriculturally based economy to one that promoted trade liberalization, decentralization, and increased autonomy in state enterprises. Economic reforms that began in the late 1970s transformed the country into a modern, industrialized nation with the second most economically powerful country in the world by 2005. As of 2009, China's gross domestic product (GDP) of $8.8 trillion ranked third behind the United States ($14.1 trillion) and the collective countries in the European Union ($14.4 trillion).[28] In early 2010, China was recognized by OECD—with which it has maintained an enhanced relationship, although it is not yet formally part of the 30-nation cooperation—for leading the world out of recession through its economic activity.[29]

Whereas the women's movement was initially driven by politics and social issues in the United States, in China the impetus has been economics. One of the largest countries in the world, China covers an area only slightly smaller than the United States with a population that is four times that of the United States, at 1.3 billion people and 310.2 million people, respectively.[30] On this scale, all issues tend to be magnified, whether about population control, health care, pollution, or the environment. Furthermore, unlike its relatively young

American counterpart, China is endowed with one of the oldest civilizations and religions (Confucianism and Taoism) in existence, making it fertile ground for the meeting of ancient ways with global change. The persuasive power of aggressive economic growth between 1985 and 2005—often referred to as the reform years—had driven the country into a deep divide between the poor and the wealthy. But overall, much of the country has seen improved living standards and greater personal choice over the past few decades. The number of poor people living on $1.25 or less a day decreased from 1.8 billion persons in 1990 to 1.4 billion globally in 2005, and most of this improvement took place in China."[30]

Women and the New Culture Movement

From about 500 B.C.E. until the early 20th century, Chinese society was heavily influenced by Confucianism, a school of thought founded by Confucius (551–479 B.C.E.) that placed the patriarchal family at the center of society. Confucius maintained that when family relationships are in order—when children respect and obey their father and wives obey their husband—there will be order in society. Footbinding, a practice primarily among elite classes that began during the early Sung (Song) dynasty (960–1279), was known as a mark of beauty that lasted well into the 20th century. Women whose feet had been bound could not walk; thus the custom made women highly dependent on their husbands, whom they could not leave. The home was central to a proper women's life, and her sequestered life was the ideal.

In the early 20th century, men and women began to reevaluate the Confucianism-based institutions and beliefs that had defined the Chinese cultural tradition for two millennia. Scholars who were part of this New Culture movement advocated scientific methods to analyze history and literature. Influenced by revolutionary movements in the West, including the women's movement and socialism, they protested Japan's treatment of China, and many joined the Chinese Communist Party when it was founded in 1921.

PARLAY FOR SUFFRAGE

When China formed a new republic with a constitution, Chinese women demanded the right to participate in political decision making and began working for the right to vote in the early 1900s, at the same time as a fresh wave of the suffrage movement was occurring in the United States. A flux of organizations, including the Chinese Women's Franchise Association, the Chinese Women's Cooperative Association, and the Chinese Suffragette Society, were formed. They felt the militant influences of pre–World War

I activities by American and international feminist groups and participated in the Wuchang Uprising in 1911, which created a separate Republic of China government under Sun Yat-sen (1866–1925) and ultimately overthrew the Manchu (Qing or Ch'ing) dynasty, the last imperial dynasty of China, in 1912.

Women from 18 provinces rallied for equal rights before the national legislature as the Women's Suffragette Alliance in 1912 in Nanking (Nanjing). They used militant and near-violent tactics, imitating their American and British fellow suffragists. This backfired as measures were taken to protect the traditional family model, and as a result, no women were members of the 1913 Permanent Assembly in Canton. A conservative military government took its place under Sun Yat-sen and the women's movement was silenced.

"The women question" resurfaced seven years later, after mass demonstrations by women opposing Japanese persecution of Chinese and expressing their desire to be part of mainstream daily life and the economy. Women were also targeting higher education, professional status, and entrepreneurship, just as their American sisters were honing in on enfranchisement.

Once again Sun Yat-sen's Nationalist Kuomintang (Guomindang) government suppressed activities by the newly formed Women's Suffrage Association and the Women's Rights League in 1921. The National Congress drafted a new constitution that excluded women's voting rights. Meanwhile the newly forming CCP made equality one of its guiding principles, earning the support of many women. By 1923, the Kuomintang and the CCP entered into a short-lived alliance that incorporated the women's movement in a nationalist revolution, although Chiang Kai-shek (1887–1975) led an offensive against women believed to be Communist sympathizers.

Women were not enfranchised at a national level until after the PRC's establishment in 1949, when the Communists had full control of the country. The All-China Democratic Women's Federation was established with representatives from all the provinces and local women's organizations. Renamed the All-China Women's Federation (ACWF), the organization was disbanded briefly during the Cultural Revolution of 1966 to 1976. During the post-Mao reform era in the 1970s, it was reinstated; it continues its work today as an NGO under the close scrutiny of the CCP.

Current Issues

By 1950, the Chinese constitution and other laws recognized equal rights for men and women in many spheres of life, including property ownership, inheritance, land use, and educational opportunities, although their enforcement was modified by custom and reformed laws. Cultural interpretation of the concept of rights differed greatly from its meaning in the United States. Many of the women's issues that arose throughout the 19th and 20th centuries in the United States—inheritance, property ownership, suffrage, and education—as well as the more contemporary ones voiced at the 1995 UN Fourth World Conference on Women in Beijing—equal pay, health care access, and violence—have been under the scrutiny of the ACWF and NGOs in China. When there is a conflict of interest between women's rights and government policy, the latter takes precedence. The CCP limits media coverage of public discussion about unpopular topics: family planning policy, domestic violence and abuse, lesbian rights, and female trafficking.

EDUCATION

Women's ability to receive education and become more skilled is largely perceived as an economic issue and is reflected in government policies that caused the near 90 percent illiteracy rate of 1949 to transmogrify into a 93 percent literacy rate in just under 60 years.[32] In urban areas, women are encouraged to complete higher education, be independent, and enter fields traditionally dominated by men, such as medicine, law, engineering, science, telecommunications, and even sports. They also play a more active part in the community and society compared with women who live in rural areas.

Despite the 1986 Law on Nine-Year Compulsory Education that made primary school compulsory for both girls and boys, many girls living in rural areas do not attend school since their families do not want to lose the income the child might produce by working in the fields, a pattern that also prevailed in the United States until the late 1800s.

Until recently, the proportion of women to men declined at each educational tier for the general population. However, by 2007, the combined gross enrollment ratio in education was nearly even between boys and girls, at 68.9 percent and 68.5 percent respectively.[33] And, as in the United States and other countries, the percentage of female college undergraduates has grown, from 38 percent in 1998 to 44 percent in 2003, and the number of women in colleges and universities has nearly tripled in that same period. Of master's and doctoral students, an estimated 46.4 percent and 34.6 percent were female, respectively, in 2007.[34]

However, institutions of higher education that have a large proportion of female applicants, such as polytechnical schools and foreign language institutes, have been known to require higher entrance exam grades of women.[35]

FAMILY LIFE

In China, the strong patriarchal society still expects women to marry—although government policies encourage them to marry later than the legal age, as a measure of austerity—and have children, a pattern that also persists in the United States, but with greater tolerance for other lifestyle choices. As in other Asian nations, arranged marriages are commonplace. Regions still influenced by Chinese traditions expect the new wife to relocate to the husband's community and to handle the domestic and child care chores, but gender roles are starting to modify as couples find themselves needing to be more flexible, with men often traveling to the city for work and women balancing decision-making tasks at home with working in rural industry. After decades of low divorce and remarriage rates, the number of divorces increased 73 percent between 2000 and 2007, an increase that may be attributable to revised marriage laws that recognize domestic violence, drug and substance abuse, and extramarital affairs as grounds for divorce. The rate has since slowed down to 8.1 percent between 2007 and 2009.[36]

Although state and village governments own the land, families are given land usage rights. Divorced and widowed women usually lose their usage rights and are forced to relocate to an urban location where rentals are scarce, unless the widow has parents or children who require care. Their land is often then passed into the hands of a son or male relative of the deceased husband.

EMPLOYMENT

According to data collected by the United Nations Statistics Division, Chinese women's salaries in manufacturing averaged 60 percent of men's salaries in 2008.[37] This is 10 percentage points lower than the United States' 70.8 percent for women employed in manufacturing.[38] Open sexual discrimination in hiring practices, which was prevalent well into the 1970s in the United States, still plagues Chinese women, as employers advertise positions for men only and university campus recruiters often state that they will not hire women. Employers justify such discrimination by saying they cannot afford the benefits required for pregnant women, nursing mothers, and infants. As of 2007, Chinese women received 90 days of maternity leave, paid by their employer.[39]

Nevertheless, the government's efforts to curb overt employment discrimination have been documented since 1995, when it stated its intention to "develop energetically vocational education, professional training and practical technical training at all levels and in all categories to raise women's competence in job hunting" in its program for the development of women at the Beijing conference.[40] Women have since been encouraged to enter technical fields to help maintain a competitive edge with other countries. Nearly one-third of teachers at the associate-professor level or above in China's colleges and universities were women in 2001.[41]

In 2008–09, of the 813.5 million workers in the country, agricultural workers led by 39.5 percent, followed by services (33.2 percent) and industry (27.3 percent).[42] Estimates by occupation in 2005 demonstrated that women made up 16 percent of legislators, senior officials, and managers; 30 percent of clerks; and about half of service (including shop and market sales workers) and skilled agricultural and fishery workers.[43]

Women in China have not been as affected by the global economic downturn, with their labor force participation growing by more than 25 percentage points between 1980 and 2008, placing China among the top 10 countries in the world for the number of women in the labor force.[44] Within China, women account for about 50 percent of the 8.86 million registered unemployed people in cities and towns, at a national unemployment rate of 4.2 percent in 2010.[45] This is significantly lower than in the United States, where women's unemployment nearly doubled from 4.1 percent in 2000 to 8.1 percent in 2009. Of note, Asian women in the United States had the lowest rate (6.6 percent) of unemployment among racial groups of women.[46]

Use of microcredit funds to help rural women emerge from poverty through self-employment in the past decade is a strategy that has been gradually implemented around the world. The Asian Development Bank has been involved with distributing $100 million between 2006 and 2010 to capacity-building and sustainable farm practices (e.g., water-saving/irrigation techniques) and microfinance to poor women.[47] Other microcredit funds have helped urban women become reemployed. At present, the initiative has been launched in 23 provinces, autonomous regions, and municipalities. The Chinese Women Entrepreneurs' Association reported that by 2010, 20 percent of all entrepreneurs in China were women.[48] Thus far, China has not been included in the reports of profiteering that have hindered the strategy in other countries.

FAMILY PLANNING

Unlike in the United States, where family planning is left to individual choice, in China it is a constitutional duty. Since 1979, the one-child policy has been used to control the Chinese population rate, enforced through various measures of fines and benefits, from property confiscation and salary cuts to medical, educational, and housing quotas. Residence cards may be denied to "out of plan" children, thus denying them access to education and other state benefits.

Compliance has also been achieved through easy access to contraceptives, abortion for women who already have one child, and sterilization. Until the mid-1990s, forced sterilization was mandatory in certain provinces of China for men (for whom the procedure is referred to as a vasectomy) and for women who had mental illness, retardation, and communicable or hereditary diseases. Even under the 1994 Maternal and Infant Health Care Law and 2002 Population and Family Planning Law, certain categories of people still may be prevented from bearing children, or one member of a couple may be pressured into sterilization if a couple has more than one child. In 2009, 33.1 percent of women and 6.9 percent of men were sterilized.[49] As of 2009, the United Nations Department of Economic and Social Affairs (UN DESA) reported that 87 percent of Chinese women used some form of contraception, among the highest rates in the world, alongside the United States at 72.8 percent.[50]

The one-child policy has taken its toll on the population. The sex ratio increased from 111 males to 100 females in 1989 to 118 males to 100 females in 2000, although there are signs that this ratio had declined to 114 males to 100 females in 2010.[51] This was much higher than the 105 males to 100 females in the United States in 2010.[52] This has also made it difficult for men to find wives and for the active population in the labor market to support the survival of aged persons. On this course, it is estimated that about 40 million Chinese males may have to live as bachelors in 2020.[53] The resulting imbalance of females to males has caused the Chinese government to relax the one-child policy for couples who have only a girl, especially in rural areas.[54] By the same reasoning, it has reduced the number of approved U.S. adoptions of Chinese children by nearly 50 percent since 2005.[55]

Traditional preference for male children has led to the concealment of female births and female infanticide, as well as prenatal sex identification, in spite of a governmental ban on the use of ultrasound machines for this purpose. Unregistered female children cannot attend school or receive medical care or other state services. Female and mentally or physically challenged children populate Chinese orphanages. The Population and Family Planning Law of the PRC went into effect in September 2003 to exert population control yet put an end to coerced abortions and other practices in China: "to bring population into balance with social economic development, resources, and the environment; to promote family planning; to protect citizens' legitimate rights and interests; to enhance family happiness; and to contribute to the nation's prosperity and social progress."[56]

China's high rate of abortion—28 percent of pregnancies were terminated in 2005—was originally thought to be largely due to the one-child policy, but recent research shows that the procedure is mostly performed on young unwed women. Although the country does not have a high rate of maternal mortality or unsafe abortions, with 97 percent of births and abortions attended to by skilled personnel, induced abortions along with female infanticide are influencing the sex ratio.[57]

Proponents opine that women have benefited from the controversial one-child policy by families having to invest in girls' education and the public's increased awareness of gender inequality from the workplace to professional sports. Such proactive measures could translate long-term into greater self-esteem for women, measurable by their participation in the workforce, as well as by their career and lifestyle choices.[58]

SEXUAL FREEDOM

The transition to a global economy in which citizens make their own personal decisions—if not political ones—has challenged the Chinese government's control over daily life. American and European music, lifestyle, and fashion are influencing the younger generation through television and the Internet, causing a sort of sexual revolution. The average young woman today has her first sexual experience at 17 in urban areas, much sooner than the 24 years of age reported by women who are now in the 31- to 40-year-old range. In the capital of Beijing, in 2005, 70 percent of residents claimed they had had sexual relations before marriage, compared with 15.5 percent in 1989.[59] With economic growth and the persuasion of liberal attitudes, requests for abortions by single women in Chinese cities rose sharply at the beginning of the new millennium, from 25 percent in 1999 to 65 percent in 2004. The government estimates the number of abortions performed has grown from 7.6 million in 2007 to 9.2 million in 2008 and could be actually as high as 13 million, when including abortions that are not performed in hospitals or clinics.[60]

Although homosexuality is no longer illegal, as it was during the Cultural Revolution of 1966 to 1976, protective laws for lesbians and gays are nonexistent. Same-sex marriages were not included in marriage law revisions. The media minimize coverage of gays, even with advocacy for controlling the burgeoning HIV/AIDs problem. Authorities are quick to close down public events that involve gays or lesbians. The government is dealing with these issues in the same way they were treated for many years in the United States: with no acknowledgment.

VIOLENCE

China does not deny the global attention to the issue of violence against women and acknowledges infanticide, female trafficking, prostitution, and domestic violence as major problems. In many parts of the country, spousal abuse is common and still socially acceptable, affecting an estimated one-third of marriages. Comprehensive statistics about the extent of domestic violence are unavailable, according to the ACWF and the Women's Federation, since few women report abuse in rural areas. A revised Marriage Law in 2001 provided legislation to protect women but is not regularly enforced.

There appears to be a causal relationship between domestic violence and child abuse, a trend that has also been documented in the United States since 2001 and addressed through the federally funded Children's Justice Act, which is administered through states.[61] In a landmark study on violence and health by WHO in 2002, the use of harsh physical punishment has been self-reported by parents in China, with a frequency of 461 per 1,000 children.[62] Advocates of the one-child policy claim that the system reduces the number of child-abuse cases, but opponents say the system has led to an increase in female infanticide and abandonment. A 2004 survey by the China Legal Studies Association found that 95 percent of domestic abuse incidences involved girls.[63] To address the situation, the Chinese government modified the platform of the National Programme of Action for Child Development in China, developed in the 1990s, to ensure adequate protections for children in a long-term plan for 2001–2010.[64]

Another area of violence that is emerging into public light is elder abuse, also a recently noted trend in the United States. Chinese senior citizens were traditionally respected, so mere neglect of an elder can constitute abuse. The higher than average rate of suicide among people over 60 years of age in China, especially among married women and widows, may be due to domestic violence and social isolation.[65]

Because shelters and other resources are not available, it is difficult for battered women to escape abuse. Women are under considerable social pressure to keep families together regardless of the circumstances. Legal action is not taken against batterers unless the victim initiates it, and if she withdraws her testimony, the proceedings end. This may be somewhat alleviated by the presence of mobile courts, which are increasingly being used to improve access to the formal justice system in rural areas.[66]

Trafficking and sale of women as brides or into prostitution are large-scale problems both within China, where women have been sold into brothels in Southeast Asia, and outside of East Asia. Like the United States, China is one of the principal origins and destinations for female trafficking. In 2007, 41 percent of certified victims of female trafficking found in the United States originated from Asia.[67] Until recently, men were not prosecuted for purchasing women as wives. Unless a woman or her family complains, local officials do not follow up on evidence that women are sold into marriage. The Chinese Ministry of Public Security cracked down on trafficking as a crime, beginning in April 2009, which led to freeing 10,621 women and 5,896 children, apprehending 2,398 gangs, and prosecuting 13,500 cases by September 2010.[68]

Possible Progress

The PRC ratified the UN Convention on the Elimination of All Forms of Discrimination against Women in 1980 and enacted the Law on the Protection of Women's Rights and Interests in 1992. After hosting the 1995 UN-sponsored Global Women's Conference, where the Beijing Platform for Action was created, China formed a five-year plan that established programs for the development of Chinese women, with oversight by the ACWF and the East Asia office of the United Nations Development Fund for Women (UNI-FEM). To marry the ideals of equality, development, and peace with actions, the program has targeted integrating women into legal and political systems so that they can play a more active role in the "open-and-reform" modernization efforts, those the Chinese government began in 1978 to establish a market economy system.

In a 2007 report published by the World Economic Forum, the regions of sub-Saharan Africa and Asia closed approximately 63 percent of their gender gap between 2006 and 2007. China now ranks 73rd of 128 countries. Improved access to all levels of education and an increase in the literacy rate to 87 percent are indicators of this improvement, along with stronger labor force participation and wage equality and discrete improvements in health, which are mostly hindered by the "missing women" factor (disproportionate sex ratio at birth).[69] More data are needed to assess their access to medical care, free choice for marriage, limiting of violence against women, and establishment of a system of accountability. Although many female-run NGOs have established themselves in China, the movement continues to identify with organizational efforts rather than those of individuals, underscoring its socialist nature.

The Future

Before the Beijing+10 conference in New York in March 2005, the PRC passed a comprehensive law protecting women's rights and interests on a variety of issues, allocating funds to women's education and health and loans to poor women. They then issued a White Paper that outlined progress made in areas of economic rights and security, political participation, law, health, education, family and marriage, and the environment. An interesting parallel were President Bill Clinton's similar efforts before the World Conference on Women in 1995 in Beijing, when he established the Presidential Interagency

Council on Women (PICW) by executive order on the eve of the UN Fourth World Conference on Women to track results of CEDAW-inspired efforts.

Although Chinese women's participation in the economy and political decision making has improved according to the White Paper, the report and the law showed that women are still underrepresented in high-level politics and commerce, where gaps in income between men and women also persist.

In 2005, through UNIFEM, other UN agencies, and NGOs, the China Gender Facility for Research and Advocacy was launched to initiate programs for gender mainstreaming and development. As an initiative inspired by CEDAW, the facility funds proposals that address issues of domestic violence, employment, gender mainstreaming, aging, and disability, highlighting 12 areas as priorities for research and advocacy, including the revision of women's law and the collection and use of data about gender, sex ratios, and girl children.

On a global scale, a 2007 World Economic Forum report noted "a correlation between the gender gap and national competitiveness, providing an added impetus for countries to incorporate gender equality into their national priorities."[70]

AFGHANISTAN

Although Afghanistan is considered an Asian country, the role of women in society is more similar to that of countries in the Middle East, which share Afghanistan's Islamic tradition. Unlike those of their American counterparts, women's rights in Afghanistan did not include suffrage until late in the 20th century. Women were conferred rights that were compatible with the Muslim culture when Afghanistan declared national independence of Britain in 1921. The first constitution recognized equal rights of men and women in 1923, but not the right to vote for women.

Since the early 20th century, various Afghan rulers have tried to introduce reforms favorable to women's rights, which often provoked anger among religious and tribal leaders. King Amanullah (1892–1960), who reigned from 1919 to 1929, encouraged women to remove their veils and established girls' schools.

In the 1950s, under Prime Minister Muhammad Daoud (1909–78), and as part of a secularization campaign, attempts were made to institute marriage registration, promote female literacy and women's suffrage, ban the exchange of girls for bride prices, and ban the chadri, or burqa, a head-to-toe garment that women were forced to wear. Under King Mohammad Zahir Shah (1914–   ), the reformed constitution, which women were involved in writing, gave women the right to vote and stand for election in 1963, to go to school, and to earn the same wages as men, generating in Afghanistan "women's liberation" similar to that in the United States at that time.

Political Potential and Challenges

The 1970s Saur Revolution led to the empowerment of a social democracy under the People's Democratic Party of Afghanistan, which also favored a secular lifestyle. By then, there were three women in the parliament. Women's causes were furthered in the 1980s with the socialist government of Nur Mohammed Taraki (1913–79), who favored women's access to political appointments, employment, equal protection, a minimal age for marriage, a ban on forced marriages, and a growing educational system. The implementation of these rights was subject to regional and tribal influence, however.

The civil war that followed the 1979 invasion of Afghanistan by the Soviet Union and the Taliban rule from 1994 to 2001 dramatically curbed, even eliminated, these gains for women. When the country entered into extremist Islamic rule, even pleasurable aspects of life such as kite flying, bright colors, and women's laughter were forbidden, according to one activist, Zoya (1978–   ), who describes the life of a teenager during this time in her book *Zoya's Story: An Afghan Woman's Battle for Freedom*.[71]

By 2001, unsanitary conditions and lack of shelter, food, and medical care posed a serious risk to pregnant women and their infant children, regardless of economic background. The United Nations Population Fund (UNFPA) mounted an unprecedented humanitarian operation in September 2001 as a response to health emergencies facing thousands of people, including pregnant Afghan women, who were fleeing their homes for the border countries of Pakistan, Iran, Tajikistan, Turkmenistan, and Uzbekistan in fear of a United States–backed invasion after the September 11 terrorist attacks. UNFPA prepositioned emergency relief supplies and lifesaving reproductive health-care services, with a plan to distribute them within Afghanistan.

In November 2001, after the fall of the Taliban, the UN Security Council, through Resolution 1378, supported efforts of the Afghan people to establish a new transitional administration leading to the formation of a new government. The goal was to establish a government that would be broad-based, multiethnic, and fully representative of all the Afghan people and respectful of human rights, regardless of gender, ethnicity, or religion. What subsequently evolved has been a decade of civil war from ethnic insurgency and the Taliban, whose base has been in an agriculturally rich area west of Afghanistan's second-largest city, Kandahar. This has further been complicated by elements within the Taliban providing refuge for al-Qaeda terrorists, also the target of NATO and U.S. troops.

Rebuilding women's rights after more than 30 years of warfare has emerged as an integral part of reconstructing the country under the terms of the 2001 Bonn Agreement, but not without a constant struggle, as the nation seeks to achieve self-governance. What role Islam should play in the new nation—integrated into the new democratic government or as a belief system guiding a secular state—was, and is still, being decided.

Hamid Karzai (1957–), the president of the Afghan government, showed support for women's rights by signing the Declaration of the Essential Rights of Afghan Women, which was adopted at a meeting in Dushanbe, Tajikistan, in January 2002. The document conferred the right of women to equality with men. The Ministry of Women's Affairs (MOWA) was established with a focus on developing gender-based policy and strategic development, improving women's participation in all levels of government, and capacity-building.[72]

A *loya jirga* (grand council) convened in June 2002 for the first time since 1964 to discuss the terms of the interim government. Rahima Jami (1961–) and Nasrine Gross (1945–), two female educators, were invited to attend as consultants to the process, supporting women's issues and questioning of the role of Islam. Jami wore a head scarf knotted under her chin and a long coat, while Gross wore a black pantsuit and tied her hair in a ponytail. Gross's Paris-based organization, NEGAR, an international NGO that supports Afghan women's rights, was successful in having an equal-rights law signed and moved the *loya jirga*'s attention to its implementation.

At the *loya jirga* convention, an Afghan woman, Dr. Massouda Jalal (1962–), became the first female presidential candidate in Afghanistan's history. Two women secured seats as ministers: General Dr. Suhaila Siddiq (1941–), a female surgeon who practiced in the capital city of Kabul throughout the Taliban regime and served in the Afghan National Army, became minister of public health, and Dr. Sima Samar (1957–), a physician and founder of the Shuhada Organization network of clinics, hospitals, and schools in Pakistan and central Afghanistan, was elected minister of women's affairs.

Dr. Samar resigned from her post in early 2002 because of bomb threats instigated by her secular views. She took a position within the Human Rights Commission and was replaced in the ministry of women's affairs by Dr. Habiba Surabi (1956–), a hematologist, who offered more moderate views and served from 2003 to 2004. She was followed by Dr. Massoda Jalal, from 2004 to 2006, and Dr. Husn Banu Ghazanfar (1957–), in 2006.

A new constitution enacted in January 2004 asserted specific rights for women, including the right to vote in democratic elections and with legal protection. Article 22 guaranteed men and women equal rights and duties before the law. Article 44 provided that the state must promote education for women. Approximately 27 percent (68 out of 249 seats) of the seats in the lower house (Wolesi Jirga, or House of the People) was the constitutional quota reserved for women, and the president would be required to appoint women as 50 percent of the 34 presidential appointees to the Meshrano Jirga (House of the Elders).[73]

The presidential election took place in October 2004 and was won by Karzai, and the first free parliamentary and provincial council elections in 30 years were delayed until September 18, 2005, fulfilling the terms of the Bonn Agreement. More than 600 women candidates competed for the 68 (27 percent of the total 249 seats) lower parliamentary seats reserved for women by the 2004 constitution, just shy of the internationally recommended 30 percent quota of the Wolesi Jirga. The long-term national goal for the *loya jirga* is said to be 50 percent female representation.[74]

Despite confusion that surrounded the voting process because of the many terrorist threats from Taliban and al-Qaeda insurgents, the registered voter turnout of between 35 percent and 50 percent ushered into office several women during the 2005 landmark election: Fauzia Gailani (1971–   ) in Herat, Malai Joya (1979–   ) in Farah, and Shukria Barekzai (1972–   ) of Kabul. Barekzai, editor of *Women Mirror,* a weekly magazine, finished 24th out of 33 candidates. Their victories showed that, given the chance, women of Afghanistan could be part of the political process. Surabi went on to become the first female provincial governor of Bamiyan in 2005.

Karzai's presidency was renewed for a second term following the elections in December 2009. With the quota system in place, women were given 28 out of the 102 lower house seats (27.5 percent) in February 2010.[75] The share of women in parliament grew to 22 percent in the upper house.[76] Jami, Gailani and Barekzai, as former and current fellow members of parliament (MPs), are regularly threatened for their criticism of warlords.

Still, political progress for women remains elusive. In December 2005, the first session of the parliament convened with a higher percentage of women representatives, 27.3 percent, than in the national legislatures of many established democracies, including the U.S. Congress (15.2 percent) and British parliament (19.7 percent) at that time.[77] This rate subsequently declined to 26 percent by 2010. During the parliamentary elections of September 2010, Afghan electoral observers requested that an independent investigation be conducted into reports of widespread fraud, intimidation of voters, and interference by warlords and Taliban.

Current Issues

The news in fall 2010 of a possible peace settlement between President Karzai and the Taliban to end the civil war has left some women's groups wary. They expressed concern about faltering promises to include them in the peace process with Taliban insurgents who are disassociating themselves from al-Qaeda. In an August interview with journalist Christiane Amanpour (1958–   ), President Karzai stated his "roadmap" for peace with the Taliban includes women as part of the high council for peace negotiations. He also assured Amanpour that "their representation will be solid, meaningful, and substantive."

Afghan women—who constitute 47 percent of the country's 29 million people—may have regained their right to work and go to school, but recent statistics demonstrate they are hard pressed to exercise them.[78,79] In essence, women are still paying the price for national instability.

THE ROLE OF VIOLENCE IN TRIGGERING THE WOMEN'S MOVEMENT

As in the United States, violence has acted as a catalyst for the resurrection of the women's movement in Afghanistan, although rooted in different causes. One of the main causes of violence in Afghanistan is the opium drug trade, wherein 95 percent of the world's supply is controlled by warlords. Women in villages are easily victimized in the cross fire between warlords and used as pawns in their settling of disputes or attempts to increase their market share.[80]

In addition to that, the high level of violence caused by civil and tribal warfare has taken its toll on women in Afghanistan in the form of rape and other sexual violence, with relatively few cases officially reported for fear of the woman's or her family's safety and the associated stigma. Violence has caused conditions that put both Afghan women and men at risk of having a low life expectancy, 43.5 years of age, which has declined in the past five years, although that level is still an improvement over the Taliban era.[81] This life expectancy level is among the lowest in the world, along with those of several sub-Saharan African countries, including the Democratic Republic of the Congo.

Repressive customs and 30 years of war have made wife beating commonplace. One highly publicized case is that of 18-year-old Aisha, who was punished for running away from her abusive in-laws' and husband's house. Her picture with a cut-off nose on the cover of *Time* magazine in August

2010 rekindled international awareness. Still, paradoxically, only 500 cases a year of abuse of women, usually wife beatings, are reported in Afghanistan, and few arrests are made.[82] Although victims could seek legal support for divorce, such action is taboo and socially detrimental to women, as no one will care for the victim after divorce. In the entire year of 2004, within Kabul, a city of about 4 million people, only 10 to 15 divorces were granted by the family court.[83] In 2006, a survey of 4,700 households across 16 provinces revealed that 87 percent of women had experienced some form of physical, psychological, or sexual violence—including forced marriage—and at least 62 percent experienced several forms of violence.[84]

FAMILY LIFE AND SEXUALITY

Suppression of women's femininity by the Taliban regime and by extremist Islamic edicts has had consequences upon Afghan society. In Afghanistan, women continue to wear the burqa for various reasons. Many women are only permitted to leave their home wearing a burqa and accompanied by a male. Some women still do not feel safe unless they are covered; others wish to respect Muslim customs or the Qur'an, which is subject to different interpretations, although it seems clear that the holy text of Islam acknowledges the economic role of women in public life: "Men shall have a benefit from what they earn, and women shall have a benefit from what they earn. [Verse 4:32]."[85,86] These customs were introduced one century after the prophet Muhammad's death in the seventh century and were symbolic of chastity after puberty and life close to home. The traditions persisted until the 20th century and were respected by Christian, Jewish, and Muslim women. In contemporary times, the customs have been enforced in the name of Islam, however. Foreigners' opinions about the tradition of burqa wearing are often perceived as racist by Muslim women, especially those who are loyal to the tenets of traditional Islam.

FORCED MARRIAGES

In spite of the reemergence of democracy and women's rights in Afghanistan in the post-Taliban era, an estimated 60 to 80 percent of marriages in the country are forced on women, especially in rural areas where tradition is powerful. Girls and women are often married off for economic gain—as much as 352,100 Afghanistan afghanis (U.S. $7,000, which is significantly more than the estimated 2009 per capita income of $1,000)[87] can be earned from a marriage—or for settling of scores between feuding families, even though both practices run counter to civil and Islamic law.[88] Between 2000 and 2008, 43 percent of girls were married before the age of 16.[89] While arranged marriages are normal in this conservative Muslim country, they

137

are meant to have the consent of both the bride and groom. This is further complicated by polygamy being supported by the Afghan Constitution and sharia (religious law), which permits men to have up to four wives at a time.

PROPERTY RIGHTS

As in other Asian countries, legal rights in Afghanistan often are not implemented, particularly property rights. Further, inheritance and property rights differ according to the Muslim population: They are passed entirely through the males of the family among the Sunni Pashtuns, while the Shiite Hazaras allow a daughter half and a wife one-fourth of a father's landholdings.

ACCESS TO HEALTH CARE

As are women in sub-Saharan countries, Afghan women are being called to service and trained by national public health programs to make up for a deficient health care system taxed by war, a poor economy, and lack of professional care. NGOs and organizations such as the International Organization for Migration (IOM) are helping to rebuild the health-care system by training women as community health workers and midwives.[90] With the departure of many physicians from the country, the ratio of physicians to patients was about two to 10,000 people, and fewer than 14 percent of births were attended by skilled health personnel.[91] Only 35 percent of the nation had some kind of access to care by 2001. Common preventable diseases such as measles, malaria, and cholera escalated as a result of shortages of clean water, inadequate sanitation, and malnourishment.

War between factional governments and tribal warlords directly affected women's quality of life and ability to access health care and contraception. In 2008, the population in rural areas significantly lacked clean water and sanitation more than in urban areas, bringing the national percentage down to 48 and 37 percent of the population accessing improved services, respectively.[92]

Contraceptive use was extremely low, at about 5 percent of women between 1995 and 2002, and was attributed to ignorance, illiteracy, and poor access by the general population of women.[93] As of 2006, overall contraceptive use has grown to 18.6 percent, between the pill as one of the modern methods (along with implants, IUDs, condoms, vaginal barriers, and sterilization) and other traditional methods (rhythm, withdrawal, etc.), offering an encouraging trend of growth by 1.4 percentage points annually between 1997 and 2007.[94] This is still significantly lower than the average use rate of 62 percent attributed to less developed nations.[95]

Of married women under age 50 in 2004 72 percent were unaware of contraceptives or methods to delay pregnancy.[96] The fertility rate was one of the highest in the world, at 7.8 births per woman in 2005.[97] The rate declined to 6.6 births per woman between 2005 and 2010.[98] Early marriages, however, continue to contribute to this high fertility rate, and to the likelihood of girls not being aware of contraceptive options, as well as a high maternal mortality rate. Under the Taliban, the rate was 1,900 maternal deaths per 100,000 births. In 2004, the rate decreased but was still considered high: 1,600 maternal deaths per 100,000 births, where it has held until 2009. One province, Badakhshan, had a rate of 6,500 maternal deaths per 100,000 live births, the highest recorded rate ever in the world.[99] Currently, midwives are being trained as alternatives to physicians to provide skilled attendance at birth, helping to decrease complications of early maternity, such as obstetric fistula or death.

Afghanistan is noted for having one of the highest rates of discriminatory, sex-selective abortions in the world, which accounts for the "missing women" in the population.[100] One in 10 pregnancies results in unsafe abortion, an approximate figure based on that of countries in Asia, Africa, and Latin America, where the maternal mortality rates are highest.[101]

EDUCATION

Like women in the United States, where education and suffrage were important early targets of the women's rights movement, women in Afghanistan continue to focus on these issues. Until 1979, even though channels of education existed within urban and rural areas in Afghanistan, Islamic practices determined whether daughters would receive an education. Of the main ethnic groupings, Shiite Hazaras and Tajiks in the north usually educated their daughters, while Sunni Pashtuns in the south usually kept their daughters home.

During the Taliban's fundamentalist regime, girls' schools were completely shut down, female teachers dismissed, and girls were either kept home or found their way to secretly established schools. An estimated 3 percent of girls were educated in primary schools during this time.[102] The Taliban policy on female teachers also affected boys' education, as the majority of teachers had formerly been women. By the time the Taliban's extremist rule ended in December 2001, the estimated literacy rate among women had dropped to 7 percent.

In the past decade, schools reopened, and slowly, girls are making their way back, especially in the north, where 40 percent of girls attend school, compared with 20 percent in the south. Conditions are slightly more conducive to girls' education in the capital of Kabul, where more than 162 schools have reopened, employing 20,000 teachers, of whom 17,000 are women. Still, rates of educational enrollment and literacy remain among the lowest in the world.

As of 2007, about 35 percent of girls were enrolled in schools, compared with 67 percent of boys. The literacy rate between 1999 and 2007 has been estimated at 12.6 percent among women and 43.1 percent among men.[103]

EMPLOYMENT

Afghan women are burdened with one of the highest pay gaps in the world, in 2008 at 24 percent of what men earned. Whether educated career women or day laborers, their pay is not equitable to the task nor equal to what men earn for the same performance, a plight shared by women from around the globe. Prior to the civil war and Taliban rule, employment opportunities for urban middle-class women were similar to those in the United States. Women had been allowed to work in civil service jobs and in a variety of professions, as teachers, doctors, professors, lawyers, judges, journalists, writers, and artists, and were even provided with 90 days of maternity leave paid by the employer.[104] Some women have regained their jobs, but few are empowered as before. Of government employees, 22 percent are women, and only 9 percent of these hold jobs at the decision-making level. Some are also finding jobs as television and radio announcers and even as performers.[105] Through activities by the Ministry of Women's Affairs, the government intends to increase women's civil service participation to 30 percent by 2013.[106]

What remains different, however, is the trend in rural areas. Even though the seclusion code of the Taliban had been lifted in 2001, tribal customs in the provinces continue to challenge women, considering those who work outside the home as dishonoring the men and the tribe. Mostly, women are expected to serve the family and maintain the land. Data on female agricultural activities remain underreported because women are not considered part of the national labor effort and are often unpaid. Those considered laborers receive about 30 cents a day, compared with one dollar per day earned by soldiers, which is higher than the national pay gap of women earning 24 cents to every dollar earned by men.[107]

International Assistance

With the help of international organizations and NGOs, Afghan women participated in high-level negotiations to set up a transitional government for Afghanistan. At the UN talks in Bonn, Germany, on November 27, 2001, four Afghan groups attended: representatives of the Rome process, associated with the former king; the United Front, also known as the Northern Alliance; the Cyprus Group; and the Peshawar Group. About 40 Afghan women leaders of different ethnic, linguistic, and religious backgrounds also met at the Afghan Women's Summit for Democracy in Brussels, Belgium, on December 4 and 5, 2001. They consulted with members of the European

Parliament, the U.S. Congress, the UN Security Council, then UN secretary-general Kofi Annan, and female ambassadors to the United Nations with requests to increase security in Afghanistan and assist in disarming warring tribal factions. After demands for assistance with education, media and culture, health, human rights, refugees, and internally displaced women were voiced, the Brussels Proclamation was adopted. A UNIFEM-sponsored roundtable drew together Afghan women and UN agencies, the World Bank, and donors, in Brussels December 10–11; their program, Building Women's Leadership in Afghanistan, focused on an action plan of specific strategies to support the role and leadership of Afghan women in shaping the future of their country.

Despite the measurable effects of these high-level meetings in women's and girls' daily lives, circumstances remain difficult. Women's advocacy invites intimidation by hard-line Islamic fundamentalists. Zoya, a spokesperson for the Revolutionary Association of the Women of Afghanistan (RAWA), needed the protection of a bodyguard when she spoke at the 2004 Women and Power Conference in New York City. The murder of Safia Amajan (1943–2006), the head of the Department of Women's Affairs in Kandahar, on September 25, 2006, is another example of how insurgency is creating setbacks for women in Afghanistan. Amajan promoted girls' right to an education and women's right to work.

UNIFEM facilitated the first public forum of its kind on women's rights, with activists, journalists, and presidential candidates, before the 2005 national elections. As part of the effort, the United Nations Population Fund (UNFPA) trained women leaders on gender issues. In addition, other international agencies, such as USAID, funded income-generating training programs—in craft making, beekeeping, poultry farming, kitchen gardening, and home-based dairy production—with local NGOs in 2006 for the large population of women widowed during the decades of war in rural areas.

In February 2010, Dr. Samar, now head of Afghanistan's Independent Human Rights Commission, and Rachel Reid of Human Rights Watch, urged the U.S. Senate Foreign Relations Committee to include Afghan women in the reconciliation and reintegration process that is expected to take place while the United States transfers security duties to the Afghan government and begins to move its troops out of the country between 2011 and 2014.

The Future

Ending the civil war, and promoting reconstruction and development are Afghanistan's principal focuses, given its status as one of the 50 least-developed countries in the world. A conscious effort to include women in the decision-making process continues, although women still face challenges from Islamic fundamentalists, the Taliban, and other conservative elements of the population in daily life.

By 2010, Afghanistan had started to report statistics, but they are erratic. War conditions still prevailing in parts of the country make it difficult to hold programs accountable for progress.[108] UNIFEM has been working to build the skills of women leaders and encourage women voters to involve themselves in the political process. Advocates continue to inform the public through writings, public appearances, and fund raisers, about the condition of women. Afghan American Nasrine Gross writes in 2008: "I do believe that we must develop a new paradigm of dealing with countries. The old concept of divide and rule, or the newer one of confuse and conquer no longer create results that promote correct and enduring success. We must develop relationships that deal with peoples and cultures and countries on an equal footing and with the same standards of caring and dignity."[109]

DEMOCRATIC REPUBLIC OF THE CONGO (DRC)

Controversy has plagued the Democratic Republic of the Congo (DRC) since its emergence from Belgian colonial rule in 1960. Within a week of then–Republic of the Congo's independence, tribal disputes in the eastern region erupted—backed by neighboring countries encumbered by famine and drought—over fertile soil and natural resources of gold, copper, and tin ore (cassiterite). In the 50 years of intertribal power struggles and extreme violence, the women's movement has shaped itself as a humanitarian force.

Governance in a country as large as DRC is complex. As the third-largest African country—905,564 square miles—located in the middle of the African continent, it is home to roughly 250 ethnolinguistic groups.[110] The majority tribe is Bantu, with the four largest groups being the Mongo, Luba, Kongo (all Bantu), and the Mangbetu-Azande (Hamitic), which make up about 45 percent of the population.[111] The primary native languages are Lingala (a trade language), Kingwana (a dialect of Kiswahili or Swahili), Kikongo, and Tshiluba, although French is the official language used for governance.

Violence and war have caused the country's population of nearly 62.5 to 70.9 million people to receive international attention on every conceivable social issue—from HIV/AIDS, displaced population, poverty, and malnutrition to lack of education and an attendant low adult literacy rate of 67.2 percent.[112]

While other African countries have evolved from diverse cultures, they have been able to follow the precedents set by women's struggles in other parts of the world: using women's rights as an economic incentive to develop a nation. In war-torn DRC, infrastructure and political rule repeatedly disintegrate following periodic attempts at a peace process. Congolese women have in earnest attempted to envision a culture of peace through which they could be safe, aided by grassroots organizations and NGOs, ever since the peace pact was introduced in 2002.[113] Now, basic safety is needed for both genders, requiring attention in all areas of national development, from equal access to education and health to economic resources and political oversight.

Political Background

Like the 57 countries of sub-Saharan Africa, DRC made the transition to independence comparatively late in the 20th century, leaving it unprepared for the war, drought, famine, and ethnic animosity that would beset the country for the next 50 years as it sought to establish its identity in the modern world.

When Colonel Joseph Mobutu (1930–97) took over as president in 1965, he changed his name to Mobutu Sese Seko and the country's name to Zaire. The constitution was revised in 1978, and Mobutu was officially elected to a seven-year term. He instituted totalitarianism and single-party rule, centralizing authority around his own political party, the Popular Movement of the Revolution.

The First Congo War (1996–97) was triggered by a Tutsi-led insurgency from neighboring Rwanda and Uganda wishing to end Mobutu's 32-year reign. The Alliance des Forces Démocratiques pour la Liberation du Congo-Zaire (AFDL)—a coalition of the neighboring states—overthrew Mobutu in May 1997, bringing Laurent Désiré Kabila (1939–2001) to power. The takeover by Kabila, coupled with yet-another name change to the Democratic Republic of the Congo in May 1997 began the long transition of the country's systems of governance, formerly based on the Napoleonic Civil Code, into the modern world.

As political unrest continued to destabilize DRC, women become a means by which war would be waged. Referred to as "weapons of war,"[114] they suffered mass atrocities, especially in the eastern provinces of North and South Kivu, which border Rwanda and Uganda, creating what would be termed a "security dilemma" involving several militant groups.

Despite the Lusaka Cease-fire Agreement of July 1999, territorial and ethnic conflict between rebel groups—the Ugandan-backed Mouvement de Libération du Congo (MLC), the Rwandan-backed Rassemblement Congolais pour la Démocratie (RCD), and the Hutu-backed Forces Démocratique pour la Libération de Rwanda (FDLR)—and the government's Forces Armées de la République Démocratique du Congo (FARDC) would further destabilize the country, leading to poor infrastructure, high taxes, and extortion.[115] Kabila's break with Rwanda and Uganda led to the Second Congo War from 1998 to 2003, when Angola, Namibia, and Zimbabwe joined DRC's defense.

Largely because of the extreme sexual violence, DRC was one of many sub-Saharan countries that would come under the scrutiny of the United Nations Population Fund (UNFP), and thus within the purview of the Millennium Development Goals in 2000 and later again in 2010.

Joseph Kabila (1971–   ), son of Laurent Kabila, took over after his father's assassination in 2001, overseeing the withdrawal of Rwandan troops from eastern Congo and bringing all the parties to the table for the December 2002 Pretoria Agreement to end the war. He was part of the transitional government from 2003 to 2005, until the runoff elections in October 2006, when he won a tight race over Vice President Jean-Pierre Bemba (1962–   ), a wealthy, Western-educated rebel leader of the MLC.

Women's Part in the Political Process

Although Congolese women were granted suffrage in 1967 and the right to stand for election in 1970, violence and traditional attitudes inhibited their ability to participate in most political processes. Not before the adoption in 2000 of UN Security Council Resolution 1325 on Women, Peace, and Security did the government receive pressure to make women a part of the peace process—both at the negotiating table and in the implementation of peace.[116]

At the 2004 International Conference on Peace, Security, Democracy and Development in November in Tanzania, female parliamentarians from the Great Lakes region addressed specific issues and announced their intentions to take a prominent role in talks to end fighting.[117]

Preparations by the transitional government for national elections—from voter registration to installing the first bicameral government consisting of a 500-seat National Assembly and 108-seat Senate—was hailed as a major achievement, given that there had not been a census in more than four decades. During the 2006 national elections, of an initial estimate of 28 million potential voters (suffrage being permitted at the age of 18 years), a total of 25,021,703 citizens registered to participate in the referendum and the general elections.[118] Details, such as what percentage of voters was female, were hard to come by. The International Parliamentary Union (IPU) did observe that women lost gains made from the earlier transition government, however.[119] In spite of systematic efforts to prepare women for the peace process and subsequent follow-up action plans, the number of DRC women in politics remains modest. As of July 2010, 8.4 percent of lower house seats in parliament, 4.6 percent of upper house seats (equivalent to the U.S. Senate), and 12 percent of ministerial positions were held by women, ranking DRC at 109 out of 186 countries.[120]

The Issues

Women's conditions are challenged on several fronts in DRC. They live in one of the 50 poorest countries in the world, although surrounded by rich natural resources. Nearly half of the population is under the age of 14 and, at a median age of 16.5 years, lacks the experience needed to cope with the conflict. Low life expectancy is matched by high infant mortality, thus yielding high death rates. Normally, this would lead to a low population growth, which is not the case because of the above-average maternity age of 16 and the adolescent fertility rate of 12.4 percent (124 per 1,000 girls, age 15 to 19), among the highest in the world.[121]

In addition, an already high adult mortality rate of 40.7 percent[122] of persons likely to die between 15 and 60 years per 1,000 people, is compounded by a high AIDS rate, with 4.2 percent of adults living with AIDS. Yet women are giving birth at a rate of 42.6 births per 1,000, ranking the country eighth in the world, with a fertility rate of 6.11 children per woman.[123] The economic and social systems left over from the colonial era were no match for the dissonance that exists among rival ethnic groups, leaving the country wide open for transnational concerns, such as human trafficking.

SEXUAL VIOLENCE AND SAFETY

Often referred to as "the war within a war," the extreme cruelty that has been leveled against girls and women in exchange for control by rebel forces has devastated more than 5.4 million lives and all but dissolved traditional and contemporary systems of governance.[124]

The UNFPA estimated from reported cases of girls and women seeking aid that 10,658 cases of sexual violence took place between 2004 and 2006 in South Kivu.[125] One hospital reported performing 10 surgeries per week for obstetric and traumatic fistula.[126]

The inability of the government—allied with Zimbabwe, Angola, and Namibia—to take control over armed groups, particularly in the Kivu provinces, has led to an increase in violent acts perpetrated on women and children in 2009. Both the MLC and the RCD are also responsible for these insurgencies. An attempt in December 2008 by the governments of DRC and Rwanda to confront extremist Rwandan Hutus resulted in more civilian casualties. The 20,509 peacekeeping troops installed in the DRC in 2009 were not able to prevent the April 2010 killings of 50 civilians and July–August 2010 attacks on 242 civilians who were raped in 13 villages.[127]

POVERTY

Perpetual violence has exposed a large population of Congolese to poverty. DRC rankied in the top 50 of poorest countries in the world. Of the rural population, the majority of Congolese, 75.7 percent, subsist below the national rural poverty line as of 2005, according to World Bank estimates.[128] About 59.2 percent of the country's entire population was living on less than a dollar a day between 2000 and 2007.[129]

HUMAN MOVEMENT AND TRAFFICKING

Of the 26 million people involved in global conflict-induced trafficking and human movement in 2009, DRC accounted for 1.4 million.[130] Populations of internally displaced and refugee children and women are coerced into forced labor and sexual exploitation, making DRC a Tier 2 country on the Watch List by the CIA "for its failure to provide evidence of increasing efforts to combat trafficking in persons in 2007."[131] Combined with the rebel fighting, this is severely affecting the quality of life of women, who are used as bargaining chips by rebel forces.

Although both a destination and source country for human trafficking, DRC waited until 2005 to sign the Protocol to Prevent, Suppress and Punish Trafficking in Persons, Especially Women and Children, supplementing the UN Convention against Transnational Organized Crime (2000). As with other African nations, data about human trafficking can only be estimated, exacerbated by poor reporting mechanisms. As of 2005, 89 percent of African countries were affected by intra-African trafficking, 34 percent with trafficking to Europe, and 26 percent to the Middle East.[132] The law in DRC does not specifically prohibit trafficking in persons, but traffickers can be prosecuted under laws that prohibit child labor, the transportation of children for sale, the commercial exploitation of children, and the detention of females against their will for the purposes of prostitution. About 7 percent of trafficking victims who were later sheltered in South Africa in 2005–06 were from DRC.[133]

Though data on human trafficking continue to be hampered by underreporting or lack of self-reporting, measures are nevertheless being taken by awareness campaigns—local, national, and global.[134] A reproductive health assessment survey by the CDC in 2009 of women living in a camp for internally displaced persons (IDP) found a strong association between HIV and sexual violence, which had been used against 10 percent of the women.[135] Successful treatment of HIV with antiretroviral drugs through organizations like Médecins sans Frontières has proven that it is possible to achieve treatment adherence rates comparable to those reported in nonconflict settings.[136]

Without recourse within the criminal justice system, other than for constitutionally forbidden child soldiering, the DRC government has been accepting aid from NGOs and international organizations to provide legal protection and medical assistance to trafficking victims. That and a mass door-to-door campaign are part of the anti-trafficking initiatives within the country that appear to be working.[137]

FAMILY LIFE

With half of the population Roman Catholic and the other half a mix of Protestant (20 percent), Muslim (10 percent), and indigenous religions (20 percent Kimbanguist/animist beliefs, syncretic sects), women have roles as healers and counselors, in addition to being responsible for child-rearing and agricultural labor.

The once respectful family tradition of betrothing a daughter has been severely challenged by the two civil wars. Rather than the traditional exchange of gifts, as a mark of respect between families, young couples are eloping. Without having to produce the *mali*, or dowry, the groom's ability to support his wife goes unproven.

An increase in early marriages by younger women and in informal unions, juxtaposed with the higher maternity rate of 12.4 percent of girls age 15 to 19, has led to an increase in marital rape, early maternity, obstetric fistula, and domestic violence that mostly goes unchallenged by the lack of legislation in place.[138,139]

THE SPREAD OF HIV/AIDS

In DRC, HIV/AIDS had already made its impact felt during the First Congo War of 1996–97.[140] Afterward, the disease further put women at risk, not only by exposing them to the virus, but also leaving them vulnerable to violence when family members abandoned them or when they leave home alone. As 1 million refugees, mostly Rwandan Hutus, made their way into eastern DRC in a matter of days, they brought with them disease and violence.

By 2008, women were 58 percent of people age 15 to 49 living with HIV in sub-Saharan Africa, making this the largest majority of women living with the disease in all developing regions.[141] The UNAIDS estimates that between 400,000 and 500,000 adults and children were living with HIV as of 2008 in DRC. Of the 1.1 million Congolese living with HIV/AIDS in 2008, between 24,000 and 34,000 deaths in adults and children were noted in 2007. The impact on women and children has made news headlines, especially with the staggering 270,000 to 380,000 children orphaned by the disease in DRC alone. The sub-Saharan continent was host to 75 percent of the world's children orphaned by AIDS—between 10.6 million and 15.3 million in 2007.[142]

FAMILY PLANNING

By 1970, DRC was one of nine African countries that adopted legislation supporting family planning, meaning it would need to break from pronatalist policies of colonial days. With encouragement to governments to intervene with couples and plan family size and childbirth timing, 1984 was a pivotal year for population politics and programs in Africa. Following the Second African Population Conference and the subsequent Arusha conference preceding the World Population Conference in Mexico City, a program of action encouraged the connection between family planning and socioeconomic development, a call that many African governments would slowly begin to heed. As a result, the fertility rate decreased from 7.1 to 6.0 children per woman between 1990 and 2008.[143]

Family planning has played a critical role in preventing HIV/AIDS, assisted by a growing installed base of cell phones in the country, which is used to deliver information about family planning to both parents—to men who would otherwise be reticent to practice safe methods and to mothers who would otherwise miss important information and appointment reminders.

Contraceptive use in DRC is one of many proposed strategies that still need advocacy and public education to be effective. Condom use by adults age 15–49 years—with only 16 percent of men and 8 percent of women using condoms—is low compared with other nations—in spite of the open distribution of condoms through NGOs and government facilities.[144]

ACCESS TO HEALTH CARE

The 1994 Rwandan crisis evolved into a public health crisis in DRC, exposing the need for international emergency preparedness as well as the willingness of countries to weigh the consequences of not intervening versus economic benefits. Population surveys at the time of the flight in August 1994 found women's households to have the highest rate of malnutrition and the highest incidence of diarrheal disease.[145]

Repercussions of the public health crisis in DRC are readily seen in the poor quality of life experienced by most of the population:

- The maternal mortality rate was 549 per 100,000 live births between 2000 and 2009 (although 2005 interagency reports actually estimated it to be higher, at 1,100 per 100,000 births).[146]
- The ratio of births attended by skilled medical personnel is 40 percent lower in rural areas than in urban areas.[147]
- There are 30 percent fewer children being immunized in rural settings.[148]

148

To cope with the surge in population with HIV/AIDS, international and NGO agencies are pursuing strategies that take into account the Congolese people's strong spiritual and religious foundation.[149] The development of "City of Joy" safe centers is a result of this collaboration. A developing network of health-care zones—a combination of one hospital and about 20 health clinics—typically serve 100,000 to 150,000 people and are often run by nurses.[150]

The large-scale disruption of infrastructure has also led to what is commonly referred to as "brain drain," when physicians who are trained at the expense of the government immigrate to other countries to practice.

The MDG platform is to "improve maternal and child health as a means to increasing economic development."[151] As a result, several health issues have been of concern, from the aftereffects of nutrition deficiency to secondhand smoke. Congolese women experience higher rates of zinc deficiency (77.6 percent) than the typical population of the sub-Sahara. Many blame the deficiency on diet, but in the case of the Congolese, a diet rich in phytates from eating vegetables, legumes (beans, peas, tubers), and their staple food cassava, defy that explanation, leaving the one possibility of "limited bioavailability" due to inflammation.[152] It also may be caused by frequent pregnancies or trauma, when zinc levels are typically lower.[153] Secondhand smoke is also considered a health risk to women and children in developing countries, particularly in the sub-Saharan countries.[157]

EMPLOYMENT

Unlike the United States' industry-based economy, DRC's economy largely depends on agriculture, which accounted for 55 percent of the gross domestic product by 2000.[155] Despite rich crop potential, only 3 percent of the landmass is actually cultivated, hindered by poor transportation and infrastructure.

War, poverty, and an unstable economy have contributed to a drop in per capita income, from $400 in 1990 to $210 in 2000, but it saw some rebound by 2008, at $290.[156] Congolese women constitute the majority of the agriculture workforce—about 43 percent—and do the difficult work in the fields. Carrying drinking water to the home is a burden usually left to women in rural households, 95 percent of which are without piped water.[157] Of the gross domestic product, 55 percent is agricultural, followed by 11 percent industrial, and 34 percent services-oriented. Women still tend to be underrepresented in other industries.[158]

As families break up, women and girls resort to other means to earn a living. Male heads of households have become increasingly removed from their former roles and identities as patriarchs and farmers, causing women to take more of a lead in decision making on behalf of the family and turning to other means of income. Even in the midst of war camps, women display an aptitude for enterprise—selling charcoal, spinach, mangos, beans, and salt in the camps.[159]

Prostitution has been a less attractive option, particularly for adolescent girls from poor families, if they are not abandoned altogether. Amnesty International recorded frequent cases of sexual exploitation near coltan mines (coltan is the mineral source of the elements niobium and tantalum used to manufacture electronics, among other products) as early as 2001, where young girls were offered shelter and food in exchange for sexual services for the "coltan men."[160]

EDUCATION-LITERACY CONNECTION

Despite gains made in girls' enrollment between 1985 and 1995, gender gaps persist at the beginning of the 21st century. Educating girls and women is a long-standing battle, as girls are not expected to stay as long in schools as boys. Partly the result of cultural attitudes, partly owing to risks of exposure to violence, the low enrollment of girls in all levels of education—40.5 percent of girls, compared with 55.99 percent of boys, in 2009—feeds directly into a lower adult literacy rate, particularly noted among women between 1999 and 2007 (54.1 percent) as compared with men (80.9 percent).[161,162] Although MDG-inspired efforts anticipate a reversal of this trend, with women's literacy growing to 58 percent, to compensate for the drop in literacy among men to 76.3 percent, it is still woefully short of the MDG universal goal of 97 percent literacy by 2015.[163]

Children fortunate enough to be schooled experience a challenge similar to that of children in other parts of the sub-Sahara: Their opportunity has been hampered by poor conditions—no classrooms, not enough textbooks, overcrowded classrooms, teacher shortages—leading to overall poor learning achievement. In addition, fewer than 60 percent of teachers in the DRC in 2002 were actually trained there.[164] This underscores DRC's inability to train its own teachers and reliance on international agencies and governments for educational resources and funding.

ECONOMIC INCENTIVE FOR WAR

DRC is in the very early stages of establishing gender equality as a developing country, but these efforts have been constantly upstaged by more immediate needs. This paradigm of resource-rich countries, such as Afghanistan, Kuwait, and DRC, plagued by "poor governance, clientelism, and the abuse of a social contract between ruler and ruled" is the price that is being paid in human blood for rich natural resources the rest of the world needs, according to a United States Institute of Peace report.[165] Multinational corporations pursue their interests in resources for cell phone and laptop manufacturing. As poppy and opium are to Afghanistan, so are cobalt, copper, coltan, tin ore (cassiterite), diamonds, gold, and radium to DRC—all precious commodities in international trading, which ultimately push women's issues to the background. Thus, rebel factions continue to vie for political and economic control.

CHALLENGES TO WOMEN'S COALITIONS

Women's groups have been relentless and ambitious in their efforts toward achieving peace for their country, despite consistent setbacks. The year 2002 was one of extreme highs and lows and ultimately resulted in a weakening in women's solidarity.

Femmes Afrique Solidarité (FAS) joined with Women as Partners for Peace in Africa–DRC (WOPPA-DRC) in a UNIFEM-supported event in February 2002 in Kenya. The Inter-Congolese Dialogues (ICD) brought to the table representatives of the different warring parties, government, and civil entities to develop a common position. Here, the "Nairobi Declaration" and cease-fire were declared, along with the formation of the Women's Caucus to participate in the peace process, and the requirement to implement a 30-percent quota for women at all government levels in the final settlement.

Preparations toward a peace negotiation gave momentum and wide representation to women through several hundred women's groups, including La Dynamique des Femmes Politiques au Congo Démocratique (DYNAFEP), Synergy Africa, and the Réseau des Femmes pour la Défense des Droits et la Paix (RFDP). But women encountered resistance: from status-quo attitudes, suspicions about the Women's Caucus as a political party, threats on delegates' lives, intimidation by rebel armies, and lack of donor funding for travel to the negotiations and follow-up meetings.[166]

At the preparatory meetings of the ICD in Sun City, South Africa, only one woman was permitted to participate. Despite UNIFEM's proactive support, only 40 of the 340 delegates were allowed to participate in the March–April 2002 diplomatic negotiation in Sun City, proof that gender balance remained a notion for the future.[167]

What resulted from the Sun City negotiations—Article 51 of the transitional government's constitution—was promising, but not solid. Though it included women's concerns and acknowledged their role in decision making and representation, it lacked specific language from CEDAW regarding quotas and from the Beijing Platform for Action on accountability. Mostly undocumented was the loss in momentum felt by women's groups.[168]

Intervention and Advocacy

At the G8 summit in Canada in July 2002, numerous countries (Japan, Russia, France, Germany, Canada, Italy, Britain, and the United States) showed support for the DRC by pledging to increase donations by $12 billion per annum by 2006 through an African nation initiative called the New Partnership for Africa's Development (NEPAD).[169] Women Waging Peace hosted a conference that November with 11 African women leaders and representatives from governments and NEPAD to address the impact on women of this support.[170] Though respectful of the opportunity, they were critical of the proposed framework and process, noting, once again, it was short on "gender perspective."

This message was reaffirmed when only 10 women were able to attend the ICD Sun City follow-up meetings in Pretoria, South Africa, in November and December 2002, thus unable to participate fully in drafting the agreement in the Amani Program of disarmament, demobilization, and integration.[171]

UNIFEM persisted with a joint-sponsored UNIFEM/UNDEF initiative in 2004. During the two-day Great Lakes Parliamentary Forum on Peace (also referred to as the Amani Forum), 100 legislators convened to address women's roles in the peace process.[172,173] Here, they coalesced around Resolution 1325 on Women, Peace, and Security, endorsing its ratification and application at a national level. One outcome was the agreement by Burundi, DRC, and Rwanda to create gender-specific departments and budgets. Still, the sponsors noted the lack of a long-term strategy for sustaining these intentions.

The notable absence of a women's coalition at the Goma Peace Conference in January 2008 reflected the lack of cohesion now felt by women's groups, added to which were the difficulties they faced from the beginning—security risks, intimidation, and lack of donor financing.[174] The absence of input from women in the peace agreements—the Act of Engagement and the Amani Program—was considered a setback for gender equality and women's rights.

Foreign governments and international agencies have made efforts to intervene and address the human dilemma, but progress has been slow or thwarted by rebels. Resolution 1820 introduced by the United States and adopted by the UN Security Council in June 2008 has made sexual violence a security issue. U.S. Secretary of State Hillary Clinton's trip to the DRC in August 2009 was accompanied by a pledge of $17 million in aid.

An investigation in June 2010 by the International Criminal Court (ICC) into cases of crimes against humanity, war crimes, and genocide were hampered by fear instilled by rebel armies in communities.[175]

U.S. Senator Barbara Boxer (D-CA), who addressed the use of rape and sexual violence during a 2009 hearing by the U.S. Senate Foreign Relations Subcommittee, restated the U.S. position when the UN Security Council convened in September 2010.[176]

Theater plays, documentaries, and photography exhibits have played a role in keeping the issues in DRC within public view. Celebrities, such as the activist/playwright Eve Ensler, with worldwide local productions of her play *The Vagina Monologues*, and documentarian Lisa F. Jackson have also used their skills to keep the issue up front. African-American playwright Lynn Nottage won a 2009 Pulitzer Prize for *Ruined*, a play about the sexual violence in DRC.

Congo Sabbath—a specific day at the end of April created by the Religious Institute on Sexual Morality, Justice and Healing—has been set aside by several U.S. congregations to recognize the violence against women in the DRC and to conduct fund-raising events.[177]

The Future

Gender balance through quota is considered to be one of the remaining strategies that stand a chance of making a difference for the civilian population of DRC, which continues to be displaced by armed groups. This will need to be applied in many areas of civilian life—military service, police force, land rights for widows—alongside the participation of women's groups in social, political, and civil decision-making processes. Data collection to track efforts—prevention programs, access to justice for victims, and rehabilitation services for the displaced populations—is also perceived as an essential part of the solution, as has been the case in other developing countries.

Despite the inherent difficulties experienced by women's groups, strategic coalitions and partnerships are still key to their development and survival. The continued reports of human rights abuse suggest that local and regional advocacy and networking are the most effective recourse for women to achieve literacy and societal empowerment, such as the alliance with South African women that provides training in lobbying techniques. Through faith, reconciliation, self-help, community advocacy, and entrepreneurial skill building, women can use their ingenuity and intrinsic sense of entrepreneurship not only to build a culture of peace for the country but a culture that will give them confidence to face the difficult road to development and implementing gender balance.

---

[1] EUROPA. "Gender mainstreaming in EU policies: European Commission reports significant progress." March 4, 1998. Available online. URL: http://europa.eu/rapid/pressReleasesAction.do?reference=IP/98/210&format=HTML&aged=0&language=EN&guiLanguage=en. Accessed November 12, 2010.

[2] CIA. The World Factbook. France. 2009.

[3] Institut national de la statistique et des études économiques (INSEE). "Regards sur la parité. De l'emploi à la représentativité politique . . ." p. 1–2.

[4] ILO. "Selected labour statistics: by country." France, September 2010, p. 78.

[5] Pascale Bloch "Diversity and Labor Law in France." *Vermont Law Review* 30, no. 3 (Spring 2006): 717–747.

[6] Confederation Federale Democratique du Travail (CFDT). "Respectées—Contre les violences sexuelles et sexistes faites aux femmes au travail." Available online. URL: http://respectees.cfdtparis.com/Les-chiffres-a-propos-des. Accessed November 10, 2010.

[7] INSEE. "Femmes et Hommes—Regards sur la parité." Édition 2008. Available online. URL: http://www.insee.fr/fr/ffc/docs_ffc/ref/fhparit08i.pdf. Accessed August 23, 2010.

[8] U.S. Department of State. "2009 Human Rights Report: France." March 11, 2010. Available online. URL: http://www.state.gov/g/drl/rls/hrrpt/2009/eur/136031.htm. Accessed October 16, 2010.

[9] INSEE. "Regards sur la parité de l'emploi à la représentativité politique." No. 1226, March 2009, p. 3.

[10] United Nations Development Programme (UNDP). Human Development Report 2009, Table K, Gender empowerment measure and its components, p. 186.

[11] ABC News. *This Week with Christiane Amanpour*, October 10, 2010.

[12] Solveig Vanovermeir. INSEE. "Vue d'Ensemble," 2008, p. 12.

[13] INSEE. Online database, RP1999 and RP2007 exploitations complémentaires. Available online. URL: http://www.insee.fr/fr/themes/tableau.asp?reg_id=0&ref_id=NATTEF02332. Accessed November 8, 2010.

[14] INSEE. "Regards sur la parité de l'emploi à la représentativité politique." No. 1226, March 2009, p. 26.

[15] Anne Revillard. "Work/Family Policy In France: From State Familialism to State Feminism?" *International Journal of Law, Policy and the Family*. 20, no. 2 (May 24, 2006): 141.

[16] INSEE. "Regards sur la parité, édition 2008," p. 28.

[17] UN DESA. Online database. Population Division, 2009. Accessed October 15, 2010.

[18] Nathalie Bajos, Caroline Moreau, Henri Leridon and Michèle Ferrand. *Bulletin Mensuel d'Information de l'Institut National d'Études Démographiques. Population & Societies.* "Why has the number of abortions not declined in France over the past 30 years?" No. 407. December 2004. Available online. URL: http://www.ined.fr/fichier/t_publication/69/publi_pdf2_pop.and.soc.english.407.pdf. Accessed 10/16/10.

[19] INSEE. "Tableaux de L'Économie Française." Edition 2010, p. 26.

[20] INSEE. Online database search. "Unions conclues entre partenaires de sexes opposés." 2000-2009. Available online. URL: http://www.insee.fr/fr/themes/tableau.asp?reg_id=0&ref_id=NATTEF02327. Accessed November 25, 2010.

[21] Gill Allwood and Khursheed Wadia. "Gender and Policy in France," p. 129.

[22] L'Observatoire departmental des violence envers des femmes. Compendium of Practices and Policies—Background Information for 2008 Colloquium, p. 21.

[23] U.S. Department of State. France Human Rights Report. Available online. URL:http://www.state.gov/g/drl/rls/hrrpt/2009/eur/136031.htm. Accessed October 16, 2010.

[24] INSEE. Online database search. Available online. URL: http://www.insee.fr/en/bases-de-donnees/.

[25] Jacqueline de Romilly (1988), Hélène Carrère d'Encausse (1990), Florence Delay (2000), Assia Djebar (2005), and Simone Veil (2008).

[26] Women's International News. "Reports from around the world: Europe." Summer 2002, p. 57.

[27] France24. "Rights activists protest against Chinese leader's visit." November 5, 2010.

[28] CIA. *The World Factbook.* Country Comparison: GDP (purchasing power parity). 2009.

[29] IDN-InDepthNews. "OECD Has Good News For China." Available online. URL: http://www.indepthnews.net/news/news.php?key1=2010-02-03%2000:59:30&key2=1. Accessed November 5, 2010.

[30] CIA. *The World Factbook.* Country profiles for the United States and China (July 2010). Available online. URL: http://www.cia.gov/cia/publications/factbook/geos/. Accessed November 3, 2010.

[31] UN DESA. "World Economic and Social Survey," 2010, p. v.

[32] UNDP. Human Development Report 2009, Table J, 2007, Gender-related development index and its components, p. 182.

[33] UNDP. Human Development Report 2009, Table J, 2007, Gender-related development index and its components, p. 182.

[34] All-China Women Federation (ACWF). "Chinese Women Statistics." Women of China. Source: acwf.people.com.cn. Translated by ACWF. September 16, 2010. Available online. URL:http://www.WomenofChina.cn. Accessed October 17, 2010.

[35] ACWF. Chinese Women. "Women and Education." Available online. URL: http://www.women.org.cn/english/duomeiti/english/ssysj/ssysj05.htm. Accessed February 6, 2006.

[36] National Bureau of Statistics of China. Yearly data. General survey, 2009. *China Statistical Yearbook 2009.* Available online. URL: http://www.stats.gov.cn/english/statisticaldata/yearlydata/. Accessed November 3, 2010.

[37] UN Statistics Division. Table 5e. Women's wages relative to men's. Available online. URL: http://unstats.un.org/unsd/demographic/products/indwm/tab5e.htm. Accessed November 3, 2010.

[38] U.S. Census Bureau. "Income, Earnings, and Poverty Data from the 2007 American Community Survey. Table 7. Median Earnings in the Past 12 Months of Workers by Sex and Women's Earnings as a Percentage of Men's Earnings by Selected Characteristics for the United States: 2007." August 2008, p. 15.

[39] World Economic Forum. "Global Gender Gap Report 2007." Collaboration with faculty at Harvard University and University of California, Berkeley. 2007, p. 57.

[40] UNESCAP. The Program for the Development of Chinese Women (1995–2000). Available online. URL: http://www.unescap.org/esid/psis/population/database/poplaws/law_china/ch_record016.htm. Accessed February 6, 2006.

[41] ACWF. Chinese Women. "Women and Science." Available online. URL: http://www.women.org.cn/english/duomeiti/english/ssysj/ssysj04.htm. Accessed February 6, 2006.

[42] CIA. *The World Factbook*. China country profile. October 28, 2010.

[43] International Labour Organisation (ILO). LaborSTA database online search. Employment - 2C Total employment, by occupation (Thousands). Accessed October 17, 2010.

[44] ILO. "Women in labour markets: Measuring progress and identifying challenges." March 2010, p. 16.

[45] ILO. LaborSTA database online search. Unemployment—3A Unemployment, general level (Thousands). Accessed October 17, 2010.

[46] U.S. Department of Labor. *Women in the Labor Force: A Databook*. U.S. Bureau of Labor Statistics, December 2010, p.1.

[47] Asian Development Bank. "Proposed Loan and Administration of Grants People's Republic of China: Shanxi Integrated Agricultural Development Project," November 2009, p. ii.

[48] National Working Committee for Children and Women under the State Council. Available online. URL: http://www.nwccw.gov.cn/html/65/n-141665.html. Accessed December 31, 2010.

[49] UN DESA. Online database. Population Division, 2009. Accessed September 15, 2010.

[50] UN DESA. Online database. Population Division, 2009. Accessed September 15, 2010.

[51] CIA. *The World Factbook*. China country indicators (October 28, 2010). Available online. URL: https://www.cia.gov/library/publications/the-world-factbook/geos/countrytemplate_ch.html. Accessed November 3, 2010.

[52] CIA. *The World Factbook*. United States indicators (October 28, 2010). Available online. URL: https://www.cia.gov/library/publications/the-world-factbook/geos/countrytemplate_us.html. Accessed November 3, 2010, .

[53] World Socialist Web Site. "Protests in China over the one child policy." Available online. URL: http://www.wsws.org/tools/index.php?page=print&url=http%3A%2F%2Fwww.wsws.org%2Farticles%2F2007%2Fjun2007%2Fchin-j01.shtml. Accessed November 5, 2010.

[54] "Serious Birth Gender Imbalance Inflicts 9 Chinese Regions" (August 25, 2004). *People's Daily Online*. Available online. URL: http://english.people.com.cn/200408/25/eng20040825_154752.html. Accessed April 27, 2006.

[55] Kayla Webley. "Behind the Drop in Chinese Adoptions." *Time*, June 15, 2009, p. 55.

[56] "Population and Family Planning Law of the People's Republic of China." Beijing: China Population Publishing House, 2002. Available online. URL: http://www.unescap.org/esid/psis/population/database/poplaws/law_china/china%20pop%20and%20family%20planning.pdf. Accessed January 1, 2006.

[57] Van Lerberghe, Manuel, Matthews, and Wolfheim. "The World Health Report 2005: Make Every Mother and Child Count." Report, World Health Organization, 2005, p. 212.

[58] Marianne Barriaux. "Developing World Cracks Glass Ceiling: Stereotypes a Greater Bar to Western Women: China's One-Child Policy Brings Benefits to Girls." *The Guardian*. London, October 15, 2007. p. 24.

[59] Hannah Beech. "Sex, Please—We're Young and Chinese." *Time*, December 12, 2005, p. 61.

[60] Associated Press/Fox News.com. "Rise in abortions in China, young women targeted." Available online. URL: http://www.foxnews.com/world/2011/01/08/rise-abortions-china-young-women-targeted/. Accessed January 9, 2011.

[61] U.S. Department of Health and Human Services. "Children's Justice Act." Available online. URL: http://www.childwelfare.gov/management/reform/court/cja.cfm. Accessed January 9, 2011.

[62] Etienne G. Krug, Linda L. Dahlberg, James A. Mercy, Anthony B. Zwi, and Rafael Lozano, eds. "World Report on Violence and Health." Report, World Health Organization, 2002, p. 62.

[63] The China Daily. "60% of Chinese children suffer corporal punishment." December 7, 2004. Available online. URL: http://www.chinadaily.com.cn/english/doc/2004-12/07/content_397964.htm. Accessed on January 1, 2011.

[64] ACWF. "National Program of Action for Child Development in China (2001-2010)." June 13,2007. Available online. URL: http://www.womenofchina.cn/Policies_Laws/Policies/17088.jsp. Accessed October 17, 2010.

[65] WHO. "World Report on Violence and Health," 2002, p. 195.

[66] UNIFEM. "Progress of the World's Women 2008/2009." 2010, p. 80.

[67] UNODC. "Global Report on Trafficking in Persons." Global Initiative to Fight Human Trafficking (GIFT). February 2009, p. 137.

[68] ACWF. "16,517 Women, Children Rescued in Anti-Trafficking Drive." September 20, 2010. Available online. URL: http://www.womenofchina.cn/news/Spotlight/223945.jsp. Accessed October 17, 2010.

[69] World Economic Forum (WEF). "Global Gender Gap Report 2007." Collaboration with faculty at Harvard University and University of California, Berkeley. 2007, p. 57.

[70] WEF. "Global Gender Gap Report 2007." p. 20

[71] Zoya, James R. Follain, John Follain, and Rita Cristofari. *Zoya's Story: An Afghan Woman's Battle for Freedom*. New York: HarperCollins Publishers, 2002.

[72] Abdul Razaq Asmar. "Islamic Republic of Afghanistan, Ministry of Women's Affairs, Four-Year period, Main Achievements of MoWA." January 2007.

[73] UNIFEM. "Women and Men in Afghanistan: BASELINE STATISTICS ON GENDER." 2008, p. 24.

[74] UNIFEM. "Women and Men in Afghanistan: BASELINE STATISTICS ON GENDER." 2008, p. 24.

[75] Inter-Parliamentary Union (IPU). Women in Parliaments: World Classifications. Situation as of July 31, 2010. Available online. URL:http://www.ipu.org. Accessed September 24, 2010.

[76] UN DESA. "The World's Women 2010," p. 219.

[77] M. Ashraf Haidari. "Civil Society—Afghanistan's Parliamentary Election Results Confirm Stunning Gains for Women" (October 28, 2005). Eurasianet.org. Available online. URL: http://www.eurasianet.org/departments/civilsociety/articles/eav102805b.shtml. Accessed February 3, 2006.

[78] CIA. *World Factbook*. Afghanistan country profile. October 27, 2010.

[79] Aryn Baker. "The Girl Gap." *Time*, January 28, 2008, p. 41.

[80] WHO. "World Report on Violence and Health," 2002, p. 245.

[81] United Nations Development Programme (UNDP). "Human Development Report: Overcoming Barriers: Human Mobility and Development," 2009, p. 184.

[82] Aryn Baker. "What Happens if We Leave Afghanistan." *Time*, August 9, 2010, p. 20.

[83] Matthew Pennington. "Forced Marriage Still Rife in Afghanistan." Associated Press, March 14, 2005.

[84] Diya Nijhowne; Lauryn Oates. "Violence Against Women in Afghanistan," *PeaceWork* December 2008–January 2009 no. 391 (391).

[85] IslamicWorld.net. "Hijab in the Al-Quran and Sunnah." Available online. URL: http://islamic-world.net/sister/hijab_in_quran.htm. Accessed January 9, 2011.

[86] Muslim Women's League. "Women in Society: Economic Rights" Available online. URL: http://www.mwlusa.org/topics/rights/econrights.html. Accessed January 9, 2011.

[87] CIA. *The World Factbook*. Afghanistan country indicators (October 27, 2010). Available online. URL: https://www.cia.gov/library/publications/the-world-factbook/geos/country-template_af.html. Accessed November 3, 2010.

[88] Pennington. "Forced Marriage." Associated Press, March 14, 2005.

[89] UNData. Online database search for child marriages. Source: "The State of the World's Children." Updated July 14, 2010. United Nations Children's Fund. Searched on November 7, 2010.

[90] United Nations Population Fund (UNFPA). State of World Population, 2010. Report, 2010, p. 68.

[91] WHO. "World Health Statistics 2010." Part 2-Global Health Indicators. Health service coverage, p. 88.

[92] WHO. "World Health Statistics 2010." Part 2-Global Health Indicators. Health service coverage, p. 102.

[93] United Nations Department of Economic and Social Affairs (UN DESA). The World's Women, 2005: Progress in Statistics, 2006, p. 132.

[94] UN DESA. Online database. Population Division, "Contraceptive prevalence," 2009. Accessed October 15, 2010.

[95] UN DESA. "The World's Women, 2010—Trends and Statistics." Report, p. 37.

[96] Human Rights Watch. "Asia: The Status of Women in Afghanistan, October 2004." Available online. URL: http://hrw.org/campaigns/afghanistan/facts.htm. Accessed December 19, 2005.

[97] UN DESA. The World's Women, 2010, p. 178.

[98] CIA. *The World Factbook.* Afghanistan country profile. October 27, 2010.

[99] Van Lerberghe, Manuel, Matthews, and Wolfheim. "The World Health Report 2005: Make Every Mother and Child Count," p. 213.

[100] OECD. Selected GID Indicators, 2007. Available online. URL:http://www.oecd.org/dev/gender. Accessed September 23, 2010.

[101] Alcalá. State of World Population, 2005, p. 35.

[102] United Nations International Women's Day, 2002. "Afghan Women Today: Realities and Opportunities." Available online. URL: http://www.un.org.pk/iwd/index.htm. Accessed June 15, 2006.

[103] UNDP. Human Development Report 2009, Table J, 2007, Gender-Related Development Index and Its Components, p. 182.

[104] The World Women's 2005, p. 150.

[105] UN Development Fund for Women (UNIFEM), Women and Men in Afghanistan: Baseline Statistics on Gender, 2008. Available online. URL: http://www.unhcr.org/refworld/docid/4a7959272.html. Accessed September 19, 2010.

[106] UNIFEM. "Progress of the World's Women 2008/2009." 2010, p. 29.

[107] UNDP. Human Development Report 2009, Table K. Gender Empowerment Measure and Its Components. p. 188.

[108] The World Women's 2005, p. 120.

[109] Email dated February 14, 2009 from Nasrine Gross containing text from article presented on February 6, 2008 at a conference organized by the American University of Paris entitled "Afghanistan: Strategies for the Future."

[110] ACE Electoral Knowledge Network. "Post-Transitional elections in the DRC," 2006. Available online. URL:http://aceproject.org/regions-en/search?SearchableText=women+DRC+vote. Accessed October 3, 2010.

[111] CIA. *The World Factbook.* Democratic Republic of the Congo country profile. August 3, 2010.

[112] UNDP. Human Development Report 2009, Table H, 2007, Human development index 2007 and its components, p. 173.

[113] Marithe Kapnga. "Women in Congo Form Common Front for Peace." *Ms. News,* p. 27, Spring 2003.

[114] U.S. Department of State. "2009 Human Rights Report: Democratic Republic of the Congo." Bureau of Democracy, Human Rights, and Labor. 2009 Country Reports on Human Rights Practices. March 11, 2010. Available online. URL: http://www.state.gov/g/drl/rls/hrrpt/2009/af/135947.htm. Accessed October 3, 2010.

[115] Dominic Burbidge. Training for Peace Programme. "The Security Dilemma in North Kivu, the Democratic Republic of the Congo." *Conflict Trends,* no. 3 (2009): 45.

[116] Also referred to as the Peace and Security Pact with its protocol on the Prevention and Suppression for Sexual Violence.

[117] The Great Lakes region encompasses Kenya, Uganda, Tanzania, the Democratic Republic of the Congo (DRC), Burundi, Rwanda and Zambia.

[118] ACE Electoral Knowledge Network. "Post-Transitional Elections in the Democratic Republic of Congo." 2007. Available online. URL: http://aceproject.org/today/feature-articles/post-transitional-elections-in-the-democratic-republic-of-congo. Accessed October 3, 2010.

[119] IPU. Women in Parliament in 2006.The Year in Perspective. 2007.

[120] UNDP. Human Development Report 2009, Table K. Gender Empowerment measure and its components. p. 188.

[121] WHO. "World Health Statistics 2010."

[122] WHO. "World Health Statistics 2010." 1. Mortality and Burden of Disease. 2010, p. 49.

[123] CIA. *The World Factbook*. Democratic Republic of the Congo country profile. August 3, 2010.

[124] U.S. Department of State. "2009 Human Rights Report: Democratic Republic of the Congo." Bureau of Democracy, Human Rights, and Labor. 2009 Country Reports on Human Rights Practices. March 11, 2010. Available online. URL: http://www.state.gov/g/drl/rls/hrrpt/2009/af/135947.htm. Accessed October 3, 2010.

[125] Giulia d'Odorico and Nathalie Holvoet. "Combating Violence against Women (VAW) in South Kivu: A Critical Analysis." *Journal of International Women's Studies* 11, no. 2 (November 2009): 49 and 53.

[126] Amanda Truscott. "Congo ceasefire brings little relief for women." *Canadian Medical Association Journal* (July 15, 2008): 134.

[127] Alexis Arieff. "Sexual Violence in African Conflicts." *Congressional Research Service*, November 30, 2010, p. 1.

[128] World Bank. Online database search. "Poverty gap at rural poverty line (%)." Accessed October 3, 2010.

[129] WHO. "World Health Statistics 2010."

[130] UNDP. Human Development Report 2009, p. 26.

[131] CIA. *The World Factbook*. Democratic Republic of the Congo country profile. Accessed August 3, 2010.

[132] Ademola Kazeem Fayemi. "The Challenges of Prostitution and Female Trafficking in Africa: An African Ethico-Feminist Perspective." *Journal of Pan African Studies* 3, no. 1 (September 2009): 200.

[133] UNODC. Global Report on Trafficking in Persons. February 2009, p. 64.

[134] UNDP. Human Development Report 2009, p. 66.

[135] Andrea A Kim, Faustin Malele, Reinhard Kaiser, Nicaise Mama, et al. "HIV Infection among Internally Displaced Women and Women Residing in River Populations Along the Congo River, Democratic Republic of Congo." *AIDS and Behavior* 13, no. 5 (October 2009): 914.

[136] UNAIDS. "2008 Report on the Global Aids Epidemic," p. 136.

[137] UNDP. Human Development Report 2009, p. 66.

[138] WHO. "World Health Statistics 2010." 9. Demographics and socioeconomic statistics. 2010, p. 159.

Global Perspectives

[139] UNIFEM. "Progress of the World's Women 2008/2009." 2010, p. 76.

[140] Victoria Brittain. "A Nation That Hates Its Women." *New Statesman*, June 24, 2002, p. 14.

[141] UN DESA. "Millennium Development Goals: Gender Equality and Women's Empowerment. Progress Chart 2010," July 2010.

[142] UNAIDS. "2008 Report on the Global Aids Epidemic," pp. 214–218.

[143] WHO. "World Health Statistics 2010." Table 1. Mortality and burden of disease.

[144] WHO. "World Health Statistics 2010." 5 Risk Factors, 2006–2007, p. 103.

[145] Michael J. Toole. "Public Health Impact of Rwandan Refugee Crisis: What Happened in Goma, Zaire, in July 1994?" *The Lancet*. February 11, 1995, p. 339.

[146] WHO. "World Health Statistics 2010." 8. Health inequities, 2007, p. 144.

[147] WHO. "World Health Statistics 2010." 8. Health inequities, 2007, p. 144.

[148] WHO. "World Health Statistics 2010." 8. Health inequities, 2007, p. 144.

[149] Suzanne Maman, Rebecca Cathcart, Gillian Burkhardt, Serge Omba. "The role of religion in HIV-positive women's disclosure experiences and coping strategies in Kinshasa, Democratic Republic of Congo." *Social Science and Medicine*, 68, no. 5 (March 2009): 965.

[150] Christine Gorman. "Country Doctor." *Time*, October 31, 2005.

[151] Michele Bloch, M.D., Ph.D., et al. "Tobacco Use and Secondhand Smoke Exposure during Pregnancy: An Investigative Survey of Women in 9 Developing Nations." *American Journal of Public Health* 98 no. 10 (October 2008): 1833.

[152] Bioavailability: extent and rate at which a drug or metabolite enters systemic circulation, thereby accessing the site of action. Also, absorption potential determined by amount of time for absorption in GI tract.

[153] Solo Kuvibidila and Mbele Vuvu. "Unusual low plasma levels of zinc in non-pregnant Congolese women." *British Journal of Nutrition* 101 (2009): 1783–1786.

[154] Michele Bloch, MD, PhD, et al. "Tobacco Use and Secondhand Smoke Exposure During Pregnancy: An Investigative Survey of Women in 9 Developing Nations." *American Journal of Public Health* 98, no. 10 (October 2008): 1833.

[155] CIA. *The World Factbook.* Democratic Republic of the Congo country profile. August 3, 2010.

[156] WHO. "World Health Statistics 2010."

[157] UN DESA. "Millennium Development Goals: Gender Equality and Women's Empowerment. Progress Chart 2010," July 2010.

[158] UN DESA. "Millennium Development Goals: Gender Equality and Women's Empowerment. Progress Chart 2010," July 2010.

[159] National Public Radio. *Future for Women in DRC,* July 7, 2003.

[160] Amnesty International. "Democratic Republic of Congo: Our Brothers Who Help Kill Us: Economic Exploitation And Human Rights Abuses in The East. Section 4—The Destructive Social Impact." 2003.

[161] Women's International Network. "Africa: Women Are Losing the Battle for Education." *WIN News* 27, no. 2 (Spring 2001): p. 75.

[162] UNDP. Human Development Report 2009. Table J, 2007, Gender-related development index and its components, p. 182.

[163] EFA Global Monitoring Report, 2006.

[164] EFA Global Monitoring Report, 2006.

[165] USIP. "Conflict-Business Dynamics in the Democratic Republic of Congo." October 2009, p. 2.

[166] Doris Mpoumou. IDEA. "Women's Participation in Peace Negotiations: Discourse in the Democratic Republic of the Congo." November 2004.

[167] UNIFEM provided training in negotiation techniques and leadership coaching to women participating from the DRC, facilitated women's transport to the meeting, and invited 40 additional "experts" to improve women's participation at the Sun City meeting.

[168] Surendrini Wijeyaratne. Training for Peace Programme. "Women in Peace Processes: Lessons from the Democratic Republic of the Congo and Uganda." *Conflict Trends* 3 (2009): 34.

[169] NEPAD was designed by African leaders to bring the continent out of poverty through rebuilding and attracting investment capital.

[170] Women and Environments. "African Women Respond: Summary Report on G8 and NEPAD Plans and the Impact on Women in Africa." Spring 2003, p. 51.

[171] Moyiga Nduru. "Development-Southern Africa NEPAD Highlights Infrastructure Needs Doubts about NEPAD." IPS. July 10, 2004.

[172] Joyce Mulama. "Politics-Africa: Great Lakes Women Legislators Press for Peace." Global Information Network. July 19, 2004, p. 1.

[173] UNIFEM/UNDEF. "Democracy with Women, for Women—Seven Grants That Helped Change the Face of Governance. Great Lakes Region: New Room for Gender Advances in Peace Processes," 2008, p. 15.

[174] The Goma Peace Conference, January 6–17, 2008, involved the government, armed groups in North and South Kivu Provinces in eastern DRC, and church and civilian groups.

[175] Evelyn Matsamura Kiapi. Global information Network, June 1, 2010.

[176] Congressional Documents and Publications. "Boxer, Brownback, Feingold, Shaheen Call on United Nations to Better Prevent and Respond to Sexual Violence in the Democratic Republic of Congo," September 9, 2010.

[177] Toya Richards Hill. "Our Sisters' Anguish." *Sojourners Magazine*, April 2009, p. 8.

PART II

Primary Sources

4

United States Documents

This section draws together excerpts of significant U.S. primary source documents. Please note that all the documents are in their original grammatical style and spelling, with respect to different international and European systems, and any changes to the original text are indicated in brackets. For source notes indicated within documents, consult the original documents. The documents are organized into the following sections:

Historical Documents

Newspaper Articles

Magazine Articles

Studies

Speeches

Legal Documents

Court Cases

HISTORICAL DOCUMENTS

Declaration of Sentiments, Elizabeth Cady Stanton (1848) (excerpt)

A landmark document in the women's movement in the United States, written by Elizabeth Cady Stanton on the occasion of the first major conference in Seneca Falls, New York, on July 19, 1848. It was adopted at a meeting of 300 people who focused on the "social, civil, and religious condition and rights of woman," in the Wesleyan Chapel. Modeled on the Declaration of Independence, the declaration spells out the "injuries" sustained by women from men's tyranny over them. It also outlines resolutions to change this condition through efforts of both genders to secure fair and equal participation of both women and men "in the various trades, professions, and commerce."

When, in the course of human events, it becomes necessary for one portion of the family of man to assume among the people of the earth a position different from that which they have hitherto occupied, but one to which the laws of nature and of nature's God entitle them, a decent respect to the opinions of mankind requires that they should declare the causes that impel them to such a course.

We hold these truths to be self-evident: that all men and women are created equal; that they are endowed by their Creator with certain inalienable rights; that among these are life, liberty, and the pursuit of happiness; that to secure these rights governments are instituted, deriving their just powers from the consent of the governed. Whenever any form of government becomes destructive of these ends, it is the right of those who suffer from it to refuse allegiance to it, and to insist upon the institution of a new government, laying its foundation on such principles, and organizing its powers in such form, as to them shall seem most likely to effect their safety and happiness. Prudence, indeed, will dictate that governments long established should not be changed for light and transient causes; and accordingly all experience hath shown that mankind are more disposed to suffer, while evils are sufferable, than to right themselves by abolishing the forms to which they were accustomed. But when a long train of abuses and usurpations, pursuing invariably the same object evinces a design to reduce them under absolute despotism, it is their duty to throw off such government, and to provide new guards for their future security. Such has been the patient sufferance of the women under this government, and such is now the necessity which constrains them to demand the equal station to which they are entitled. . . .

Source: Excerpted from Elizabeth Cady Stanton, Susan B. Anthony, and Matilda Joslyn Gage, eds., *History of Women's Suffrage.* Vol. 1. Rochester, N.Y.: Susan B. Anthony; Charles Mann Printing Co., 1887, p. 70.

Glass Ceiling Commission, U.S. Department of Labor (1991–1996) (excerpt)

In 1991, the U.S. Department of Labor defined glass ceiling as "those artificial barriers based on attitudinal or organizational bias that prevent qualified individuals from advancing upward in their organization into management-level positions." The department's Glass Ceiling Commission (1991–96) studied these barriers as they apply not only to women but also to minorities.

While minorities and women have made strides in the last 30 years, and employers increasingly recognize the value of workforce diversity, the executive suite is still overwhelmingly a white man's world. Over half of all Master's degrees are now awarded to women, yet 95 percent of senior-level managers of the top Fortune 1000 industrial and 500 service companies are men. Of them, 97 percent are white. African Americans, Hispanics, Asian and Pacific Islander Americans and American Indians also remain woefully under-represented in the upper echelons of American business.

The Commission's recommendations emphasize that government must lead by example, followed by strong commitment and leadership from corporate America. Yet, action by government and business are not enough. For real change to occur, bias and discrimination must be banished from the boardrooms and executive suites of corporate America.

These recommendations build upon strategies that companies and government are already using to end discrimination. The recommendations must be seen as a beginning, not the end. We as a nation, and in particular corporate leaders, must continue to strive to overcome the barriers that keep minorities and women from advancing. We also must encourage the development of business organizations that reflect our population.

The Commission's work clearly shows that breaking the glass ceiling opens avenues to the American Dream, and gives all Americans the opportunity to benefit from and contribute to economic growth. Economic gains must, and can, be shared by all.

Source: Excerpted from "Glass Ceiling Commission—A Solid Investment: Making Full Use of the Nation's Human Capital," by the Glass Ceiling Commission, November 1995, p. 6. Available online. URL: http://digitalcommons.ilr.cornell.edu/glassceiling. Accessed December 30, 2010.

NEWSPAPER ARTICLES

"Suffrage Wins in Senate; Now Goes to States" (June 5, 1919) (excerpt)

Just eight months after the Eighteenth Amendment to the U.S. Constitution, which prohibited the manufacture, sale, or transportation of alcohol, went into effect in January 1920—and heavily relied on the few women who could vote in 16 U.S. states for passage, women's suffrage was ratified by Congress in the Nineteenth Amendment in August 1920.

WASHINGTON, June 4—After a long and persistent fight advocates of woman suffrage won a victory in the Senate today when that body, by a vote of 56 to 25, adopted the Susan Anthony amendment to the Constitution. The suffrage supporters had two more than the necessary two-thirds vote of Senators present. Had all the Senators known to be in favor of suffrage been present the amendment would have had 66 votes, or two more than a two-thirds vote of the entire Senate.

The amendment, having already been passed by the House, where the vote was 304 to 89, now goes to the States for ratification, where it will be passed upon in the form in which it has been adopted by Congress, as follows:

"Article—, Section 1.—The right of citizens of the United States to vote shall not be denied or abridged by the United States or by any State on account of sex.

"Section 2.—Congress shall have power, by appropriate legislation, to enforce the provisions of this article."

Leaders of the National Woman's Party announced tonight that they would at once embark upon a campaign to obtain ratification of the amendment by the necessary three-fourths of the States so that women might have the vote in the next Presidential election. To achieve this ratification it will be necessary to hold special sessions of some Legislatures which otherwise would not convene until after the Presidential election in 1920. Miss Alice Paul, Chairman of the Woman's Party, predicted that the campaign for ratification would succeed and that women would vote for the next President.

Source: Excerpted from "Suffrage Wins in Senate; Now Goes to States," *New York Times*, June 5, 1919, p. 1. Available online. URL: http://www.nytimes.com/gst/abstract.html?res=F70617FC345D147A93C79178DD85F4D8185F9. Accessed May 24, 2011.

"Second and Third Wave Feminists Clash over the Future" (May 26, 2002) (excerpt)

Organizations like the Third Wave Foundation lend their vision and voice to young women from all walks of life, ages 15 to 30, for gender, racial, social, and economic issues. They advocate on their behalf through strategic grant making, leadership development, and philanthropy.

A growing conflict between two generations of feminists comes to light at a recent Veteran Feminists of America conference. Do women in their 20s appreciate what was done 30 years ago? Do women in their 50s understand what women young now still cope with?

NEW YORK (WOMEN'S E-NEWS)—Feminists have never been known for their uniformity of opinions, so it should come as no surprise that the transition from the second to the third wave of feminists has left a clear rift between the generations.

Feminist revolutionaries from the 1960s and 1970s gathered at a recent conference at Barnard College in New York to share their thoughts on the effects their words and actions have had on the history of the United States. Although the conference, sponsored by the Veteran Feminists of America, was designed as a celebration of feminist nonfiction and fiction literature and not as a forum to discuss the problems with the women's movement today, the theme of "us versus them" emerged time and again.

Source: Excerpted from "Second and Third Wave Feminists Clash over the Future," by Jennifer Friedlin, *Women's E-News,* May 26, 2002. Available online. URL:http://www.womensenews.org/story/cultural-trendspopular-culture/020526/second-and-third-wave-feminists-clash-over-the-future. Accessed December 30, 2010.

Forced Sterilization: "State Secret: Thousands Secretly Sterilized" (May 15, 2005) (excerpt)

Female sterilization, or tubal ligation ("tying tubes"), can be done in a hospital setting or as an outpatient procedure. About 17 percent of women, age 15 to 44—roughly 10.3 million women—were sterilized in the United States between 2006 and 2008. More than one-third of women who were sterilized were between 40 and 44 years of age. In addition to this, however, has been the use of sterilization as a means of population control.

WINDFALL, N.C.—Beneath the surface of this Southern town, with its lush evergreens and winding riverbanks, is a largely forgotten legacy of pain, secrecy and human indignity.

"My heart still bleeds, and it will forever bleed, because of what had happened to me," local resident Elaine Riddick said.

Riddick was one of thousands of people secretly sterilized by the state between 1929 and 1974.

From the early 1900s to the 1970s, some 65,000 men and women were sterilized in this country, many without their knowledge, as part of a government eugenics program to keep so-called undesirables from reproducing.

Source: Excerpted from "State Secret: Thousands Secretly Sterilized: N.C. Woman among 65,000 Sterilized by Gov't., Often without Their Knowledge, in 20th Century," by ABC News, May 15, 2005. Available online. URL: http://abc news.go.com/WNT/Health/story?id=708780. Accessed December 30, 2010.

EEOC Issues New Guide on Workplace Bias
(April 19, 2006) (excerpt)

Charge receipts filed by individuals for race-based claims jumped from 26,740 in 2005 to 35,890 in 2010, representing a 34 percent increase in claims, according to the Equal Employment Opportunity Commission. This proves the theory that with new guidelines, more people would be inclined to report incidences, as long as they felt protected in doing so, and that "systemic" discrimination would be considered.

WASHINGTON—The U.S. Equal Employment Opportunity Commission issued new guidelines Wednesday aimed at combating subtle forms of race discrimination, a persistent problem in the workplace. . . .

The manual also addresses harassment and retaliation, "glass ceilings" for groups based on stereotypes, as well as cases in which discrimination may involve a multiple set of categories—such as race, gender and disability—and thus involve bias laws with varying standards to win in court.

"Issuing this chapter reaffirms the EEOC's commitment to the vigorous enforcement of Title VII's prohibitions against race and color discrimination in the workplace," EEOC commissioner Stuart J. Ishimaru said at the agency's meeting Wednesday.

"We want to educate people so they know to complain, go to the EEOC and vindicate their rights," he said.

EEOC staff said at the meeting that the guidelines also encourage people to look beyond an employer's explanation for a job decision to see if bias is actually at work, as well as to determine whether there is a pattern of behavior that might point to systemic discrimination.

The guidelines come as workplace bias suits have been in the forefront.

Source: Excerpted from "EEOC Issues New Guide on Workplace Bias," by Hope Yen, Associated Press *(*April 19, 2006). Available online. URL: http://www.highbeam.com/doc/1P1-122143531.html. Accessed on June 15, 2011.

"Puberty Comes Earlier For Today's Girls"
(August 9, 2010) (excerpt)

A 2004–2006 study in the United States found breast development occurring in females as young as seven years of age. Opinions vary as to causal factors, but exposure to estrogen-mimicking chemicals in food may play a role.

The rates of early puberty for girls have doubled in a little more than a decade, a new study of girls between 6 and 8 years old finds. Some 10 percent of 7-year-old white girls were developing breasts compared to 5 percent more than 10 years ago, researchers found. For young black girls, early maturation was seen in 25 percent of 7 year olds, also an increase from previous studies. The results come from a study of more than a thousand girls in three American cities. Researchers at the Cincinnati Children's Hospital who led the work say the rise in early puberty is linked to the rise in obesity in U.S. children, but they also say environment and genetics may be factors.

The results were just published online by the journal *Pediatrics*. Previous studies have shown a link between an earlier age for the start of menstruation and an increased risk of breast cancer. Researchers also noted that earlier maturation of girls is associated with lower self-esteem, and greater rates of depression, eating problems and suicide attempts. Dr. Marcia E. Herman-Giddens, a researcher at the University of North Carolina, Chapel Hill, told the New York Times that if there is an ideal age when girls should reach puberty, no one knows what it is. And that's been the case all the while that the age of puberty has been declining. Thirteen years ago, Herman-Giddens remarked that no adequate studies on norms for the age of puberty had been done. A study she led at the time found that by age 8, 48 percent of black girls and 15 percent of white girls showed signs of puberty.

Source: Excerpted from "Puberty Comes Earlier for Today's Girls," by Scott Hensley. National Public Radio, August 9, 2010.

MAGAZINE ARTICLES

The Modern Feminist Movement: "It's All about Me!" (June 29, 1998) (excerpt)

Regardless of what young feminists may think, a "quiet revolution" continues in the form of attention to gender issues, quotas, and conscious female empowerment by individuals, organizations, and educational institutions.

If women were able to make their case in the '60s and '70s, it was largely because, as the slogan went, they turned the personal into the political. They used their daily experience as the basis for a critique, often a scholarly one, of larger institutions and social arrangements. From Simone de Beauvoir's *Second Sex* to Betty Friedan's *Feminine Mystique* to Kate Millett's *Sexual Politics*—a doctoral dissertation that became a national best seller—feminists made big, unambiguous demands of the world. They sought absolute equal rights and opportunities for women, a constitutional amendment to

New Orleans native, handles medical logistics for the U.S. 10th Mountain Division—the kind of deskbound job often assigned to women G.I.s. Now she found herself wearing a first-aid kit on her belt, gripping an M-4 rifle and crawling on her stomach as enemy fire rained down. "I could hear the rounds pinging all around me," she says. "It was surreal." The scene was horrific. Flies were everywhere, and so was blood. "I'd dealt with people dying in the hospital, but it was nothing like this," she says. Makwakwa and another soldier kicked in the bullet-shattered windshield of the lead vehicle, but the driver was already dead. The driver of the second vehicle was screaming in agony from his wounds; he later died. Makwakwa and the patrol were able to save three other wounded drivers, but the memories of Checkpoint 50 are hard to erase—a constant reminder that while the military officially bars women from combat, the insurgency makes no such distinctions. "In Iraq, female soldiers are in combat," she says. "We're out there.". . .

It is also the first time they are suffering substantial casualties. Women troops make up nearly 15% of active-duty service members. Since 2003, 48 women have died in Iraq—just 2% of the total number of U.S. troops killed but far more than the 8 nurses killed out of 7,500 servicewomen in the Vietnam War. Three hundred have been wounded in Iraq. Few female troops are out of the line of fire. While military police patrol Baghdad with Iraqi cops who skirmish almost daily with insurgents, women clerks and cooks inside U.S. camps are vulnerable to rocket and mortar attacks by militants. Such hazards underscore the threats to life and limb that still confront all U.S. troops in Iraq, even as the military attempts to turn over more combat responsibility to Iraqi forces. First Sergeant Michelle Collins, 38, who waits anxiously every day for "her kids" to come back to Camp Liberty from patrol, says, "An IED [improvised explosive device] or a bullet doesn't have the gender marked on it."

Source: Excerpted from "Crossing the Lines: Though Barred from Combat, Female Troops in Iraq Often Find Themselves in Full-Fledged Battle. An Intimate Look at the Lives of the Real G.I. Janes," by Tim McGirk, *Time*, February 19, 2006, p. 36.

Women in the Workplace: "Why Your Boss May Start Sweating the Small Stuff" (March 15, 2006) (excerpt)

Employment lawyers are familiar with the signs of "microinequities," which can range from absence of informal mentoring, perceived underperformance, and aggressive communication to isolation and being ignored.

As corporate America struggles to promote more women and minorities up the ladder, a new workplace buzzword is moving from executive suite to lowly cubicle. Part pop psychology, part human-resources jargon, the term microinequities puts a name on all the indirect offenses that can demoralize a talented employee. Equipped with this handy label, scores of companies, including IBM and Wells Fargo, are starting to hold training seminars that don't so much teach office etiquette as hold up a mirror showing how such minor, often nonverbal unpleasantries affect everyone.

This growing awareness is due largely to the efforts of globetrotting consultant Stephen Young, a former chief diversity officer at JP Morgan Chase who has addressed audiences as varied as rocket scientists at Raytheon and readers of *Seventeen Magazine* on the power of small signals. "It's not so much what I say, but what you hear," he says. One of his most effective demonstrations—the one that has left even mighty CEOs stammering—has him role-playing a guy who is less and less interested in what a speaker is saying. "When you do this," Young says of the exercise, "you see performance change right on the spot."

Here's why: many of the companies that already spend big bucks to recruit and train talented employees are bracing for even stiffer competition as baby boomers start to retire amid a shortage of skilled labor. Teaching execs to be on the lookout for microinequities—a term that has bounced around academia since a professor at M.I.T. coined it in 1973—is a cheap way to hold on to hard-won recruits. After all, says Andrea Bernstein, diversity chair at the New York City–based white-shoe law firm Weil Gotshal, "you never know, when somebody leaves, if she would have been the next rainmaker." And no company wants even a single good idea to fall through the cracks because a manager has subconsciously written off the employee making the suggestion.

Source: Excerpted from "Why Your Boss May Start Sweating the Small Stuff," by Julie Rawe, *Time*, March 15, 2006, p. 80.

Ongoing Inequality: "What Women Want Now" (October 14, 2009) (excerpt)

Unequal pay, lack of child-care policies in the workplace, biased tax code and credit ratings, sexual violence, disproportionate health-care attention, and poverty among lesbian couples and elderly women are the issues of today.

Progress is seldom simple; it comes with costs and casualties, even challenges about whether a change represents an advance or a retreat. The *Time* survey provides evidence of both. At the most basic level, the argument over where women belong is over; the battle of the sexes becomes a costume drama, like *Middlemarch* or *Mad Men.*

Large majorities, across ages and incomes and ideologies, view women's growing role in the workforce as good for both the economy and society in general. More than 8 in 10 say mothers are just as productive at work as fathers or childless workers are. Even more, some 84% affirm that husbands and wives negotiate the rules, relationships and responsibilities more than those of earlier generations did; roughly 7 in 10 men say they are more comfortable than their fathers were with women working outside the home, while women say they are less financially dependent on their spouse than their mother was.

This is not to say there's nothing left to argue about. More than two-thirds of women still think men resent powerful women, yet women are more likely than men to say female bosses are harder to work for than male ones. Men are much more likely to say there are no longer any barriers to female advancement, while a majority of women say men still have it better in life. People are evenly split over whether the "mommy wars" between working and nonworking mothers are finally over.

Source: Excerpted from "What Women Want Now," by Nancy Gibbs, *Time*, October 14, 2009, p. 24.

"Women Will Rule the World" (July 6, 2010) (excerpt)

According to a Time magazine poll published in October 2009, 70 percent of American women stated they are less financially dependent on their spouses than their mothers were, and 3.3 million couples reported the wife as the sole earner.

When historians write about the great recession of 2007–08, they may very well have a new name for it: the Mancession. It's a term already being bandied about in the popular media as business writers chronicle the sad tales of the main victims of the recession: men. They were disproportionately represented in the industries hit hardest during the downturn, including financial services, manufacturing, and construction, and their higher salaries often put them first in the line of fire. Men are the victims of two thirds of the 11 million jobs lost since the recession began in 2007; in August 2009, when U.S. male unemployment stood at 11 percent (versus 8.3 for women), it was the largest unemployment gender gap in the postwar era. Those numbers have improved, a bit—new unemployment figures show men at

9.9 percent and women at 7.8—but not enough to stop Larry Summers, the president's top economic adviser, from speculating recently that "when the economy recovers, five years from now, one in six men who are 25 to 54 will not be working."

If they are lucky, they'll have wives who can take care of them. American women are already the breadwinners or co-breadwinners in two thirds of American households; in the European Union, women filled 75 percent of the 8 million new jobs created since 2000. Even with the pay gap factored into the equation, economists predict that by 2024, the average woman in the U.S. and a number of rich European countries will outearn the average man. And she'll be spending that money: as a new book on female economic power, Influence, points out, American women are responsible for 83 percent of all consumer purchases; they hold 89 percent of U.S. bank accounts, 51 percent of all personal wealth, and are worth more than $5 trillion in consumer spending power—larger than the entire Japanese economy. On a global level, women are the biggest emerging market in the history of the planet—more than twice the size of India and China combined. It's a seismic change, and by all indications it will continue: of the 15 job categories expected to grow the most in the next decade, all but two are filled primarily by women.

Source: Excerpted from "Women Will Rule the World: Men Were the Main Victims of the Recession. The Recovery Will Be Female," by Jessica Bennett and Jesse Ellison, *Newsweek,* July 6, 2010, p. 38.

STUDIES

"The Impact of Women's Studies Courses on College Students of the 1990s—Statistical Data Included" (June 1999) (excerpt)

This research considers the benefits of studying women's history and gender issues and how this knowledge can empower women. As modern living becomes more complex and technologically driven, gender studies cross over into many socioeconomic areas, from women's online habits to their shopping choices—metrics for which are captured and data warehoused.

In response to many of the challenges facing women, women's studies courses emerged among universities in the 1970s (Berkovitz, 1993). Over 600 programs exist today offering a major or minor in women's studies (Sandler, Silverberg, & Hall, 1996). A flurry of research activity examining the usefulness of women's studies courses was conducted in the mid- to

make the voyage of life alone, and for safety in an emergency, they must know something of the laws of navigation. To guide our own craft, we must be captain, pilot, engineer; with chart and compass to stand at the wheel; to watch the winds and waves, and know when to take in the sail, and to read the signs in the firmament over all. It matters not whether the solitary voyager is man or woman; nature, having endowed them equally, leaves them to their own skill and judgment in the hour of danger, and, if not equal to the occasion, alike they perish. . . .

Source: Excerpted from "The Solitude of Self," by Elizabeth Cady Stanton, *The Woman's Journal*, January 23, 1892. Available online. URL: http://www.lclark.edu/~ria/stanton.solitude.html. Accessed December 22, 2010.

Shirley Chisholm's Speech to the House of Representatives (May 21, 1969) (excerpt)

The Honorable Shirley Chisholm of New York, the first black woman to serve in the U.S. House of Representatives, was an advocate for the urban poor and for civil and women's rights. Subsequent to President Lyndon B. Johnson's 1965 affirmative-action policy, which addressed gender and racial discrimination in the workplace, Chisolm presented this speech on May 21, 1969, to the U.S. House of Representatives.

Mr. Speaker, when a young woman graduates from college and starts looking for a job, she is likely to have a frustrating and even demeaning experience ahead of her. If she walks into an office for an interview, the first question she will be asked is, "Do you type?"

There is a calculated system of prejudice that lies unspoken behind that question. Why is it acceptable for women to be secretaries, librarians, and teachers, but totally unacceptable for them to be managers, administrators, doctors, lawyers, and Members of Congress.

The unspoken assumption is that women are different. They do not have executive ability orderly minds, stability, leadership skills, and they are too emotional.

It has been observed before, that society for a long time, discriminated against another minority, the blacks, on the same basis—that they were different and inferior. The happy little homemaker and the contented "old darkey" on the plantation were both produced by prejudice.

As a black person, I am no stranger to race prejudice. But the truth is that in the political world I have been far oftener discriminated against because I am a woman than because I am black.

Prejudice against blacks is becoming unacceptable although it will take years to eliminate it. But it is doomed because, slowly, white America is beginning to admit that it exists. Prejudice against women is still acceptable. There is very little understanding yet of the immorality involved in double pay scales and the classification of most of the better jobs as "for men only."

More than half of the population of the United States is female. But women occupy only 2 percent of the managerial positions. They have not even reached the level of tokenism yet. No women sit on the AFL-CIO council or Supreme Court. There have been only two women who have held Cabinet rank, and at present there are none. Only two women now hold ambassadorial rank in the diplomatic corps. In Congress, we are down to one Senator and 10 Representatives.

Considering that there are about 3 1/2 million more women in the United States than men, this situation is outrageous.

It is true that part of the problem has been that women have not been aggressive in demanding their rights. This was also true of the black population for many years. They submitted to oppression and even cooperated with it. Women have done the same thing. But now there is an awareness of this situation particularly among the younger segment of the population.

As in the field of equal rights for blacks, Spanish-Americans, the Indians, and other groups, laws will not change such deep-seated problems overnight. But they can be used to provide protection for those who are most abused, and to begin the process of evolutionary change by compelling the insensitive majority to reexamine it's unconscious attitudes.

It is for this reason that I wish to introduce today a proposal that has been before every Congress for the last 40 years and that sooner or later must become part of the basic law of the land—the equal rights amendment.

Let me note and try to refute two of the commonest arguments that are offered against this amendment. One is that women are already protected under the law and do not need legislation. Existing laws are not adequate to secure equal rights for women. Sufficient proof of this is the concentration of women in lower paying, menial, unrewarding jobs and their incredible scarcity in the upper level jobs. If women are already equal, why is it such an event whenever one happens to be elected to Congress?

It is obvious that discrimination exists. Women do not have the opportunities that men do. And women that do not conform to the system, who try to break with the accepted patterns, are stigmatized as "odd" and "unfeminine." The fact is that a woman who aspires to be chairman of the board, or a Member of the House, does so for exactly the same reasons as any man. Basically, these are that she thinks she can do the job and she wants to try.

A second argument often heard against the equal rights amendment is that is would eliminate legislation that many States and the Federal Government have enacted giving special protection to women and that it would throw the marriage and divorce laws into chaos.

As for the marriage laws, they are due for a sweeping reform, and an excellent beginning would be to wipe the existing ones off the books. Regarding special protection for working women, I cannot understand why it should be needed. Women need no protection that men do not need. What we need are laws to protect working people, to guarantee them fair pay, safe working conditions, protection against sickness and layoffs, and provision for dignified, comfortable retirement. Men and women need these things equally. That one sex needs protection more than the other is a male supremacist myth as ridiculous and unworthy of respect as the white supremacist myths that society is trying to cure itself of at this time.

Source: Excerpted from "Equal Rights for Women," by Shirley Chisholm, "Documents from the Women's Liberation Movement. An On-line Archival Collection," Special Collections Library, Duke University. Available online. URL: http://scriptorium.lib.duke.edu/wlm/equal. Accessed December 22, 2010.

Gloria Steinem's Speech at the Third Annual Women & Power Conference (September 2004) (excerpt)

The following excerpt is from a transcript of the keynote speech delivered by Gloria Steinem at the Third Annual Women & Power Conference organized by Omega Institute and V-Day in September 2004 in New York City.

But a friend asked me—a friend who had been going to some women's meetings and the subject of those meetings was what is the future? What's next? What is new? What are the leaps of consciousness? And she said to me what would you say? And in that way the questions are precious because they help us to understand what we ourselves have been thinking and not said.

I said well, I guess in a very general way I would say first we had dependence. And that was women's classical role. And then we understood and celebrated and are still exploring independence. Absolutely crucial. It cannot be—we can't do, we can't progress without that. But probably when we're ready the next step is interdependence.

Bella Abzug always used to say about nations and this country especially, we've had our Declaration of Independence. Now this country needs a declaration of interdependence.

Source: Excerpted from "Leaps of Consciousness," by Gloria Steinem. Available online. URL: http://www.feminist.com/resources/artspeech/genwom/ leaps.html. Accessed December 22, 2010.

Statement by Nicole Kidman to the Congressional Hearing on International Violence Against Women: Stories and Solutions (October 21, 2009) (excerpt)

Despite efforts made by international organizations on behalf of women in conflict zones, absence of accountability, donor funding, and opportunity to implement agreements remain issues. One other course of action is to find mentors or champions—people who use their notoriety or good offices—to represent individuals or causes seeking assistance. An example is actor Nicole Kidman, who testified on the floor of the U.S. House of Representatives on October 21, 2009, as a goodwill ambassador for the United Nations Development Fund for Women about the continuing sexual violence against women in the DRC—despite the laws and acts of recent years.

Ms. KIDMAN. Thank you, Chairman Delahunt, Congressman Rohrabacher, Chairman Berman and members of the committee, for granting me this opportunity to speak in my role of Goodwill Ambassador for the United Nations Development Fund for Women. Violence against women and girls is perhaps the most systematic, widespread human rights violation in the world. It recognizes no borders, no race or class. I became UNIFEM's Goodwill Ambassador in 2006 to amplify the voices of women and shine a light on solutions that work and make a lasting difference. Until recently violence against women and the instability it causes hid in the shadows. I think the attention today underscores a new recognition that the issue is urgent and really deserves to be center stage. And while I have learned a lot by working with UNIFEM, I am far from an expert. I am here just to be a voice. I rely on people I have met to make the case. A year ago I was honored to talk with Marie Zaina from the Democratic Republic of the Congo. Like the speaker who just spoke, Mallika Dutt, Marie's work on the ground merited a grant from the UNIFEM-managed United Nations Trust Fund to End Violence Against Women. Through contributions, including essential funding from the United States for which UNIFEM is very, very grateful, the Fund promotes the implementation of existing commitments. There are laws in many countries to end discrimination against women, to punish rape, to outlaw spousal abuse, child marriage and more. But in the real world the laws go unenforced, and impunity is the norm. I learned from Marie that she was a survivor of violence. Forced by her father into an abusive marriage as a young adult, she fled after her first pregnancy, found support to further her education through a religious organization, and confronted with the cruel impact on women and girls from the continuing conflict in the DRC—where rape is systematically used as a tactic of war—Marie took action.

She started an organization to help victims of violence, mostly widows and orphans, many affected by HIV/AIDS. Over the years she built a national network of NGOs to care for survivors and empower women. And with the Trust Fund grant, her group expanded services to include medical care, counseling, legal and economic support. Marie fully understands the need for a comprehensive approach. Another time when I visited Kosovo, I met and listened to women sharing experiences. One of them told me how she was raped repeatedly and abused by soldiers, leaving her with lasting physical and psychological scars, and also leaving her pregnant. Yet she did not remain silent. Together with other women's rights advocates, she bravely took her testimony on how mass rape shatters lives and communities to the International Tribunal for Yugoslavia, a legal landmark for prosecuting rape in wartime as a crime against humanity. Now, these champions need and deserve our support not with a box of Band-Aids, but with a comprehensive and well-funded approach that acknowledges that women's rights are human rights. It is time for policies that intentionally involve society's key communities, from health and education departments to the police and judiciary, to deliver on that commitment. The plan must build strong alliances with men and collaborate with faith-based and traditional leaders. To succeed, it requires political will at the highest levels. Violence against women deprives countries of a critical resource in the struggle to end poverty and attain sustainability. Economists confirm that women's empowerment is an essential engine for development. If they cannot participate, the targets governments and the U.N. set will continue to be unmet.

Source: Excerpted from "International Violence Against Women: Stories and Solutions." Hearing before the Subcommittee on International Organizations, Human Rights and Oversight of the Committee on Foreign Affairs, U.S. House of Representatives. Available online. URL: http://www.internationalrelations.house.gov/hearing_notice.asp?id=1124. Accessed December 22, 2010.

LEGAL DOCUMENTS

New York Married Women's Property Act (1848) (excerpt)

During the 19th century, states began enacting laws affecting the property rights of married women, which otherwise automatically transferred to their husbands. Connecticut was one of the first states to pass a law (1809) that would permit women to write wills. New York's 1848 Married Women's Property Act was used by other states as a model, as they began to pass similar statutes in the 1850s. Paulina Wright Davis, Ernestine Rose, and Elizabeth Cady Stanton were among the women who worked for the passage of the New York law.

AN ACT for the effectual protection of the property of married women.
Passed April 7, 1848.

The People of the State of New York, represented in Senate and Assembly do enact as follows:

Sec. 1. The real and personal property of any female who may hereafter marry, and which she shall own at the time of marriage, and the rents issues and profits thereof shall not be subject to the disposal of her husband, nor be liable for his debts, and shall continue her sole and separate property, as if she were a single female.

Sec. 2. The real and personal property, and the rents issues and profits thereof of any female now married shall not be subject to the disposal of her husband; but shall be her sole and separate property as if she were a single female except so far as the same may be liable for the debts of her husband heretofore contracted.

Sec. 3. It shall be lawful for any married female to receive, by gift, grant devise or bequest, from any person other than her husband and hold to her sole and separate use, as if she were a single female, real and personal property, and the rents, issues and profits thereof, and the same shall not be subject to the disposal of her husband, nor be liable for his debts.

Source: Excerpted from the New York Married Women's Property Act. Available online. URL: http://memory.loc.gov/ammem/awhhtml/awlaw3/ property_law.html. Accessed December 30, 2010.

The Fourteenth Amendment to the U.S. Constitution (1868) (excerpt)

The Fourteenth Amendment, ratified on July 9, 1868, gave all males, age 21 and over, who were residents of the United States, the right to vote. Susan B. Anthony, testing the interpretation of this amendment as a citizen of the United States, voted in the 1872 presidential elections and was arrested.

1. All persons born or naturalized in the United States, and subject to the jurisdiction thereof, are citizens of the United States and of the State wherein they reside. No State shall make or enforce any law which shall abridge the privileges or immunities of citizens of the United States; nor shall any State deprive any person of life, liberty, or property, without due process of law; nor deny to any person within its jurisdiction the equal protection of the laws.

2. Representatives shall be apportioned among the several States according to their respective numbers, counting the whole number of per-

sons in each State, excluding Indians not taxed. But when the right to vote at any election for the choice of electors for President and Vice-President of the United States, Representatives in Congress, the Executive and Judicial officers of a State, or the members of the Legislature thereof, is denied to any of the male inhabitants of such State, being twenty-one years of age, and citizens of the United States, or in any way abridged, except for participation in rebellion, or other crime, the basis of representation therein shall be reduced in the proportion which the number of such male citizens shall bear to the whole number of male citizens twenty-one years of age in such State.

3. No person shall be a Senator or Representative in Congress, or elector of President and Vice-President, or hold any office, civil or military, under the United States, or under any State, who, having previously taken an oath, as a member of Congress, or as an officer of the United States, or as a member of any State legislature, or as an executive or judicial officer of any State, to support the Constitution of the United States, shall have engaged in insurrection or rebellion against the same, or given aid or comfort to the enemies thereof. But Congress may by a vote of two-thirds of each House, remove such disability.

4. The validity of the public debt of the United States, authorized by law, including debts incurred for payment of pensions and bounties for services in suppressing insurrection or rebellion, shall not be questioned. But neither the United States nor any State shall assume or pay any debt or obligation incurred in aid of insurrection or rebellion against the United States, or any claim for the loss or emancipation of any slave; but all such debts, obligations and claims shall be held illegal and void.

5. The Congress shall have power to enforce, by appropriate legislation, the provisions of this article.

Source: Excerpted from the U.S. Constitution. Available online. URL: http://www.usconstitution.net/const.html Am14. Accessed December 22, 2010.

The Nineteenth Amendment to the U.S. Constitution (1920) (excerpt)

The Nineteenth Amendment guaranteed all American women the right to vote and was considered a radical change of the Constitution. After being passed by Congress on June 4, 1919, the amendment needed three-fourths of the 48 states to be ratified. The momentous event occurred on August 18, 1920, when Harry T. Burn, from Niota, Tennessee, after receiving a persuasive note from his mother, cast the deciding vote that made Tennessee the

36th state required for the amendment to pass, changing the way Americans voted from that point forward.

Sixty-sixth Congress of the United States of America; At the First Session, Begun and held at the City of Washington on Monday, the nineteenth day of May, one thousand nine hundred and nineteen.

JOINT RESOLUTION

Proposing an amendment to the Constitution extending the right of suffrage to women.

Resolved by the Senate and House of Representatives of the United States of America in Congress assembled (two-thirds of each House concurring therein), That the following article is proposed as an amendment to the Constitution, which shall be valid to all intents and purposes as part of the Constitution when ratified by the legislature of three-fourths of the several States.

"ARTICLE ——.

"The right of citizens of the United States to vote shall not be denied or abridged by the United States or by any State on account of sex.

Congress shall have power to enforce this article by appropriate legislation."

[endorsements]

Source: Excerpted from the 19th Amendment to the U.S. Constitution. Available online. URL: http://ourdocuments. gov/ doc.php?flash=true&doc=63. Accessed December 22, 2010.

Equal Rights Amendment (1929) (excerpt)

The ERA was first drafted in 1923 by Alice Paul, suffragist leader and founder of the National Woman's Party, who considered it the next step after enacting the Nineteenth Amendment (woman suffrage) to guarantee "equal justice under law" to all citizens. The ERA asserted the equal application of the U.S. Constitution to both females and males. It was introduced into every session of Congress between 1923 and 1972, when it was passed and sent to the states for ratification. The seven-year time limit in the ERA's proposing clause was extended by Congress to June 30, 1982, but at the deadline, the ERA had been ratified by 35 states, leaving it three states short of the 38 required for ratification. It has been reintroduced into every Congress since that time.

Section 1. Equality of rights under the law shall not be denied or abridged by the United States or by any state on account of sex.

Section 2. The Congress shall have the power to enforce, by appropriate legislation, the provisions of this article.

Section 3. This amendment shall take effect two years after the date of ratification.

Source: Excerpted from the Equal Rights Amendment, by Alice Paul, 1923. Available online. URL: http://www. equalrightsamendment.org. Accessed December 22, 2010

Title VII of the 1964 Civil Rights Act (excerpt)

This act signed into law by President Lyndon Johnson on July 2, 1964, prohibited discrimination on the basis of sex as well as race, religion, and national origin in public places and employment. It also provided for the integration of schools and other public facilities. The specifics of Title VII applied to employers with 15 or more employees and included state and local governments, employment agencies, labor organizations, and the federal government.

DISCRIMINATION BECAUSE OF RACE, COLOR, RELIGION, SEX, OR NATIONAL ORIGIN

SEC. 703. (a) It shall be an unlawful employment practice for an employer—

(1) to fail or refuse to hire or to discharge any individual, or otherwise to discriminate against any individual with respect to his compensation, terms, conditions, or privileges of employment, because of such individual's race, color, religion, sex, or national origin; or

(2) to limit, segregate, or classify his employees in any way which would deprive or tend to deprive any individual of employment opportunities or otherwise adversely affect his status as an employee, because of such individual's race, color, religion, sex, or national origin.

(b) It shall be an unlawful employment practice for an employment agency to fail or refuse to refer for employment, or otherwise to discriminate against, any individual because of his race, color, religion, sex, or national origin, or to classify or refer for employment any individual on the basis of his race, color, religion, sex, or national origin.

(c) It shall be an unlawful employment practice for a labor organization—

(1) to exclude or to expel from its membership, or otherwise to discriminate against, any individual because of his race, color, religion, sex, or national origin;

(2) to limit, segregate, or classify its membership, or to classify or fail or refuse to refer for employment any individual, in any way which would

deprive or tend to deprive any individual of employment opportunities, or would limit such employment opportunities or otherwise adversely affect his status as an employee or as an applicant for employment, because of such individual's race, color, religion, sex, or national origin; or

(3) to cause or attempt to cause an employer to discriminate against an individual in violation of this section.

(d) It shall be an unlawful employment practice for any employer, labor organization, or joint labor-management committee controlling apprenticeship or other training or retraining, including on-the-job training programs to discriminate against any individual because of his race, color, religion, sex, or national origin in admission to, or employment in, any program established to provide apprenticeship or other training.

(e) Notwithstanding any other provision of this title, (1) it shall not be an unlawful employment practice for an employer to hire and employ employees, for an employment agency to classify, or refer for employment any individual, for a labor organization to classify its membership or to classify or refer for employment any individual, or for an employer, labor organization, or joint labor-management committee controlling apprenticeship or other training or retraining programs to admit or employ any individual in any such program, on the basis of his religion, sex, or national origin in those certain instances where religion, sex, or national origin is a bona fide occupational qualification reasonably necessary to the normal operation of that particular business or enterprise, and (2) it shall not be an unlawful employment practice for a school, college, university, or other educational institution or institution of learning to hire and employ employees of a particular religion if such school, college, university, or other educational institution or institution of learning is, in whole or in substantial part, owned, supported, controlled, or managed by a particular religion or by a particular religious corporation, association, or society, or if the curriculum of such school, college, university, or other educational institution or institution of learning is directed toward the propagation of a particular religion.

(f) As used in this title, the phrase "unlawful employment practice" shall not be deemed to include any action or measure taken by an employer, labor organization, joint labor-management committee, or employment agency with respect to an individual who is a member of the Communist Party of the United States or of any other organization required to register as a Communist-action or Communist-front organization by final order of the Subversive Activities Control Board pursuant to the Subversive Activities Control Act of 1950.

(g) Notwithstanding any other provision of this title, it shall not be an unlawful employment practice for an employer to fail or refuse to hire and employ any individual for any position, for an employer to discharge any individual from any position, or for an employment agency to fail or refuse to refer any individual for employment in any position, or for a labor organization to fail or refuse to refer any individual for employment in any position, if—

(1) the occupancy of such position, or access to the premises in or upon which any part of the duties of such position is performed or is to be performed, is subject to any requirement imposed in the interest of the national security of the United States under any security program in effect pursuant to or administered under any statute of the United States or any Executive order of the President; and

(2) such individual has not fulfilled or has ceased to fulfill that requirement.

(h) Notwithstanding any other provision of this title, it shall not be an unlawful employment practice for an employer to apply different standards of compensation, or different terms, conditions, or privileges of employment pursuant to a bona fide seniority or merit system, or a system which measures earnings by quantity or quality of production or to employees who work in different locations, provided that such differences are not the result of an intention to discriminate because of race, color, religion, sex, or national origin, nor shall it be an unlawful employment practice for an employer to give and to act upon the results of any professionally developed ability test provided that such test, its administration or action upon the results is not designed, intended or used to discriminate because of race, color, religion, sex or national origin. It shall not be an unlawful employment practice under this title for any employer to differentiate upon the basis of sex in determining the amount of the wages or compensation paid or to be paid to employees of such employer if such differentiation is authorized by the provisions of section 6(d) of the Fair Labor Standards Act of 1938, as amended (29 U.S.C. 206(d)).

(i) Nothing contained in this title shall apply to any business or enterprise on or near an Indian reservation with respect to any publicly announced employment practice of such business or enterprise under which a preferential treatment is given to any individual because he is an Indian living on or near a reservation.

(j) Nothing contained in this title shall be interpreted to require any employer, employment agency, labor organization, or joint labor-management committee subject to this title to grant preferential treatment to any individual or to any group because of the race, color, religion, sex, or national origin of such individual or group on account of an imbalance which may exist with respect to the total number or percentage of persons of any race, color, religion, sex, or national origin employed by any employer, referred or classified for employment by any employment agency or labor organization, admitted to membership or classified by any labor organization, or admitted to, or employed in, any apprenticeship or other training program, in comparison with the total number or percentage of persons of such race, color, religion, sex, or national origin in any community, State, section, or other area, or in the available work force in any community, State, section, or other area.

Source: Excerpted from Title VII of the 1964 Civil Rights Act, July 2, 1964. Available online. URL: http://ourdocuments. gov/doc.php?doc=97. Accessed December 22, 2010.

Title IX in the Education Codes of 1972 (excerpt)

The purpose of Title IX of the Education Amendments of 1972 was to eliminate discrimination on the basis of sex in any education program or activity receiving federal financial assistance. In addition, the Women's Educational Equity Act of 1974, which provided for federal financing and technical support to local efforts to remove barriers for females in all areas of education, and Title IV of the Civil Rights Act of 1964, which ensured funding for regional Desegregation Assistance Centers and grants to state education departments, helped make higher education more available to women.

Sec. 1681. Sex
   (a) Prohibition against discrimination; exceptions
   No person in the United States shall, on the basis of sex, be excluded from participation in, be denied the benefits of, or be subjected to discrimination under any education program or activity receiving Federal financial assistance, except that:
   (1) Classes of educational institutions subject to prohibition
   in regard to admissions to educational institutions, this section shall apply only to institutions of vocational education, professional education, and graduate higher education, and to public institutions of undergraduate higher education;
   (2) Educational institutions commencing planned change in admissions
   in regard to admissions to educational institutions, this section shall not apply

193

(A) for one year from June 23, 1972, nor for six years after June 23, 1972, in the case of an educational institution which has begun the process of changing from being an institution which admits only students of one sex to being an institution which admits students of both sexes, but only if it is carrying out a plan for such a change which is approved by the Secretary of Education or

(B) for seven years from the date an educational institution begins the process of changing from being an institution which admits only students of only one sex to being an institution which admits students of both sexes, but only if it is carrying out a plan for such a change which is approved by the Secretary of Education, whichever is the later;

(3) Educational institutions of religious organizations with contrary religious tenets

this section shall not apply to an educational institution which is controlled by a religious organization if the application of this subsection would not be consistent with the religious tenets of such organization;

(4) Educational institutions training individuals for military services or merchant marine

this section shall not apply to an educational institution whose primary purpose is the training of individuals for the military services of the United States, or the merchant marine;

(5) Public educational institutions with traditional and continuing admissions policy

in regard to admissions this section shall not apply to any public institution of undergraduate higher education which is an institution that traditionally and continually from its establishment has had a policy of admitting only students of one sex;

(6) Social fraternities or sororities; voluntary youth service organizations

this section shall not apply to membership practices—

(A) of a social fraternity or social sorority which is exempt from taxation under section 501 (a) of title 26, the active membership of which consists primarily of students in attendance at an institution of higher education, or

(B) of the Young Men's Christian Association, Young Women's Christian Association, Girl Scouts, Boy Scouts, Camp Fire Girls, and voluntary youth service organizations which are so exempt, the membership of which has traditionally been limited to persons of one sex and principally to persons of less than nineteen years of age;

(7) Boy or Girl conferences

this section shall not apply to—

(A) any program or activity of the American Legion undertaken in connection with the organization or operation of any Boys State conference, Boys Nation conference, Girls State conference, or Girls Nation conference; or

(B) any program or activity of any secondary school or educational institution specifically for—

(i) the promotion of any Boys State conference, Boys Nation conference, Girls State conference, or Girls Nation conference; or

(ii) the selection of students to attend any such conference;

(8) Father-son or mother-daughter activities at educational institutions

this section shall not preclude father-son or mother-daughter activities at an educational institution, but if such activities are provided for students of one sex, opportunities for reasonably comparable activities shall be provided for students of the other sex; and

(9) Institution of higher education scholarship awards in "beauty" pageants

this section shall not apply with respect to any scholarship or other financial assistance awarded by an institution of higher education to any individual because such individual has received such award in any pageant in which the attainment of such award is based upon a combination of factors related to the personal appearance, poise, and talent of such individual and in which participation is limited to individuals of one sex only, so long as such pageant is in compliance with other nondiscrimination provisions of Federal law.

(b) Preferential or disparate treatment because of imbalance in participation or receipt of Federal benefits; statistical evidence of imbalance

Nothing contained in subsection (a) of this section shall be interpreted to require any educational institution to grant preferential or disparate treatment to the members of one sex on account of an imbalance which may exist with respect to the total number or percentage of persons of that sex participating in or receiving the benefits of any federally supported program or activity, in comparison with the total number or percentage of persons of that sex in any community, State, section, or other area: Provided, That this subsection shall not be construed to prevent the consideration in any hearing or proceeding under this chapter of statistical evidence tending to show that such an imbalance exists with respect to the participation in, or receipt of the benefits of, any such program or activity by the members of one sex.

(c) "Educational institution" defined

For purposes of this chapter an educational institution means any public or private preschool, elementary, or secondary school, or any institution of vocational, professional, or higher education, except that in the case of an educational institution composed of more than one school, college, or department which are administratively separate units, such term means each such school, college, or department.

Source: Excerpted from Title IX of the Education Amendments of 1972, 20 U.S.C., 1681–1688. Available online. URL: http://www.usdoj.gov/crt/cor/coord/titleixstat.htm. Accessed December 22, 2010.

The Family and Medical Leave Act of 1993 (excerpt)

The Family and Medical Leave Act of 1993 took effect in the United States as a result of finding an equitable arrangement for employers and employees to accommodate these needs. In addition, President George W. Bush signed an order in 2002 to preserve reservists' and armed forces members' rights to accrued time during their leave of absence from the workplace.

(a) The Family and Medical Leave Act of 1993 (FMLA or Act) allows "eligible" employees of a covered employer to take job-protected, unpaid leave, or to substitute appropriate paid leave if the employee has earned or accrued it, for up to a total of 12 workweeks in any 12 months because of the birth of a child and to care for the newborn child, because of the placement of a child with the employee for adoption or foster care, because the employee is needed to care for a family member (child, spouse, or parent) with a serious health condition, or because the employee's own serious health condition makes the employee unable to perform the functions of his or her job (see Sec. 825.306(b)(4)). In certain cases, this leave may be taken on an intermittent basis rather than all at once, or the employee may work a part-time schedule.

(b) An employee on FMLA leave is also entitled to have health benefits maintained while on leave as if the employee had continued to work instead of taking the leave. If an employee was paying all or part of the premium payments prior to leave, the employee would continue to pay his or her share during the leave period. The employer may recover its share only if the employee does not return to work for a reason other than the serious health condition of the employee or the employee's immediate family member, or another reason beyond the employee's control . . . .

(c) An employee generally has a right to return to the same position or an equivalent position with equivalent pay, benefits and working conditions at the conclusion of the leave. The taking of FMLA leave cannot result in the loss of any benefit that accrued prior to the start of the leave.

Source: Excerpted from The Family and Medical Leave Act of 1993. Available online. URL: http://www.bna.com/ bnabooks/ababna/annual/99/annual09.pdf Accessed January 12, 2011.

Victims of Trafficking and Violence Protection Act of 2000 (excerpt)

In October 2000, Congress passed the Victims of Trafficking and Violence Protection Act (VTVPA) of 2000 to extend to victims of trafficking the ability to remain in the United States (temporarily and in some cases longer) and receive federal and state assistance. The law offers protections to victims of certain crimes, such as those specific to women. The law also offers law enforcement agencies a comprehensive law that will enable them to pursue the prosecution and conviction of traffickers.

SEC. 102. PURPOSES AND FINDINGS.

(a) PURPOSES.—The purposes of this division are to combat trafficking in persons, a contemporary manifestation of slavery whose victims are predominantly women and children, to ensure just and effective punishment of traffickers, and to protect their victims.

(b) FINDINGS.—Congress finds that:

(1) As the 21st century begins, the degrading institution of slavery continues throughout the world. Trafficking in persons is a modern form of slavery, and it is the largest manifestation of slavery today. At least 700,000 persons annually, primarily women and children, are trafficked within or across international borders. Approximately 50,000 women and children are trafficked into the United States each year.

(2) Many of these persons are trafficked into the international sex trade, often by force, fraud, or coercion. The sex industry has rapidly expanded over the past several decades. It involves sexual exploitation of persons, predominantly women and girls, involving activities related to prostitution, pornography, sex tourism, and other commercial sexual services. The low status of women in many parts of the world has contributed to a burgeoning of the trafficking industry.

(3) Trafficking in persons is not limited to the sex industry. This growing transnational crime also includes forced labor and involves significant violations of labor, public health, and human rights standards worldwide.

(4) Traffickers primarily target women and girls, who are disproportionately affected by poverty, the lack of access to education, chronic unemployment, discrimination, and the lack of economic opportunities in countries of origin. Traffickers lure women and girls into their networks through false promises of decent working conditions at relatively good pay as nannies, maids, dancers, factory workers, restaurant workers, sales clerks, or models. Traffickers also buy children from poor families and sell them into prostitution or into various types of forced or bonded labor.

(5) Traffickers often transport victims from their home communities to unfamiliar destinations, including foreign countries away from family and friends, religious institutions, and other sources of protection and support, leaving the victims defenseless and vulnerable.

(6) Victims are often forced through physical violence to engage in sex acts or perform slaverylike labor. Such force includes rape and other forms of sexual abuse, torture, starvation, imprisonment, threats, psychological abuse, and coercion.

(7) Traffickers often make representations to their victims that physical harm may occur to them or others should the victim escape or attempt to escape. Such representations can have the same coercive effects on victims as direct threats to inflict such harm.

(8) Trafficking in persons is increasingly perpetrated by organized, sophisticated criminal enterprises. Such trafficking is the fastest growing source of profits for organized criminal enterprises worldwide. Profits from the trafficking industry contribute to the expansion of organized crime in the United States and worldwide. Trafficking in persons is often aided by official corruption in countries of origin, transit, and destination, thereby threatening the rule of law.

(9) Trafficking includes all the elements of the crime of forcible rape when it involves the involuntary participation of another person in sex acts by means of fraud, force, or coercion.

(10) Trafficking also involves violations of other laws, including labor and immigration codes and laws against kidnapping, slavery, false imprisonment, assault, battery, pandering, fraud, and extortion.

(11) Trafficking exposes victims to serious health risks. Women and children trafficked in the sex industry are exposed to deadly diseases, including HIV and AIDS. Trafficking victims are sometimes worked or physically brutalized to death.

(12) Trafficking in persons substantially affects interstate and foreign commerce. Trafficking for such purposes as involuntary servitude, peonage, and other forms of forced labor has an impact on the nationwide employment network and labor market. Within the context of slavery, servitude, and labor or services which are obtained or maintained through coercive conduct that amounts to a condition of servitude, victims are subjected to a range of violations.

(13) Involuntary servitude statutes are intended to reach cases in which persons are held in a condition of servitude through nonviolent coercion. In United States v. Kozminski, 487 U.S. 931 (1988), the Supreme Court found that section 1584 of title 18, United States Code, should be narrowly interpreted, absent a definition of involuntary servitude by Congress. As a result,

that section was interpreted to criminalize only servitude that is brought about through use or threatened use of physical or legal coercion, and to exclude other conduct that can have the same purpose and effect.

(14) Existing legislation and law enforcement in the United States and other countries are inadequate to deter trafficking and bring traffickers to justice, failing to reflect the gravity of the offenses involved. No comprehensive law exists in the United States that penalizes the range of offenses involved in the trafficking scheme. Instead, even the most brutal instances of trafficking in the sex industry are often punished under laws that also apply to lesser offenses, so that traffickers typically escape deserved punishment.

(15) In the United States, the seriousness of this crime and its components is not reflected in current sentencing guidelines, resulting in weak penalties for convicted traffickers.

(16) In some countries, enforcement against traffickers is also hindered by official indifference, by corruption, and sometimes even by official participation in trafficking.

Source: Excerpted from Trafficking Victims Protection Act of 2000, October 28, 2000. Available online. URL: http://www.state.gov/documents/organization/10492.pdf . Accessed January 12, 2011.

William Wilberforce Trafficking Victims Protection Reauthorization Act of 2008 (excerpt)

This bill was sponsored by then-senator Joseph Biden (D-DE) on May 22, 2008, to authorize appropriations for fiscal years 2008 through 2011 for the Trafficking Victims Protection Act of 2000, to enhance measures to combat trafficking in persons, and for other purposes. It directs the secretary of state to establish within the U.S. Department of State an office to monitor and combat human trafficking, making it a federal crime to recruit or use child soldiers.

SEC. 102. PURPOSES AND FINDINGS.

(a) PURPOSES.—The purposes of this division are to combat trafficking in persons, a contemporary manifestation of slavery whose victims are predominantly women and children, to ensure just and effective punishment of traffickers, and to protect their victims.

(b) FINDINGS.—Congress finds that:

(1) As the 21st century begins, the degrading institution of slavery continues throughout the world. Trafficking in persons is a modern form of slavery, and it is the largest manifestation of slavery today. At least 700,000

persons annually, primarily women and children, are trafficked within or across international borders. Approximately 50,000 women and children are trafficked into the United States each year.

(2) Many of these persons are trafficked into the international sex trade, often by force, fraud, or coercion. The sex industry has rapidly expanded over the past several decades. It involves sexual exploitation of persons, predominantly women and girls, involving activities related to prostitution, pornography, sex tourism, and other commercial sexual services. The low status of women in many parts of the world has contributed to a burgeoning of the trafficking industry.

(3) Trafficking in persons is not limited to the sex industry. This growing transnational crime also includes forced labor and involves significant violations of labor, public health, and human rights standards worldwide.

(15) In the United States, the seriousness of this crime and its components is not reflected in current sentencing guidelines, resulting in weak penalties for convicted traffickers.

(16) In some countries, enforcement against traffickers is also hindered by official indifference, by corruption, and sometimes even by official participation in trafficking.

Source: Excerpted from Senate Bill S. 3061, May 22, 2008. Available online. URL: http://www.govtrack.us/congress/ bill.xpd?bill=s110-3061. Accessed December 23, 2010.

COURT CASES

Buck v. Bell (1927) (excerpt)

Carrie Buck was deemed a weak-minded (a term then applied to the mentally disabled and abnormal) daughter of a mother who was institutionalized by the state of Virginia. Her condition had been present in her family for the last three generations. A Virginia law allowed for the sexual sterilization of inmates of institutions to promote the "health of the patient and the welfare of society." Before the procedure could be performed, however, a hearing was required to determine whether or not performing the operation would be wise. This 1927 Virginia Supreme Court case decision legalized forced sterilization in the United States.

ERROR TO THE SUPREME COURT OF APPEALS
OF THE STATE OF VIRGINIA
No. 292 Argued: April 22, 1927—Decided: May 2, 1927
Mr. JUSTICE HOLMES delivered the opinion of the Court.

Carrie Buck is a feeble minded white woman who was committed to the State Colony above mentioned in due form. She is the daughter of a feeble minded mother in the same institution, and the mother of an illegitimate feeble minded child. She was eighteen years old at the time of the trial of her case in the Circuit Court, in the latter part of 1924. An Act of Virginia, approved March 20, 1924, recites that the health of the patient and the welfare of society may be promoted in certain cases by the sterilization of mental defectives, under careful safeguard, &c.; that the sterilization may be effected in males by vasectomy and in females by salpingectomy, without serious pain or substantial danger to life; that the Commonwealth is supporting in various institutions many defective persons who, if now discharged, would become a menace, but, if incapable of procreating, might be discharged with safety and become self-supporting with benefit to themselves and to society, and that experience has shown that heredity plays an important part in the transmission of insanity, imbecility, &c. The statute then enacts that, whenever the superintendent of certain institutions, including the above-named State Colony, shall be of opinion that it is for the best interests of the patients and of society that an inmate under his care should be sexually sterilized, he may have the operation performed upon any patient afflicted with hereditary forms of insanity, imbecility, &c., on complying with the very careful provisions by which the act protects the patients from possible abuse.

The superintendent first presents a petition to the special board of directors of his hospital or colony, stating the facts and the grounds for his opinion, verified by affidavit. Notice of the petition and of the time and place of the hearing in the institution is to be served upon the inmate, and also upon his guardian, and if there is no guardian, the superintendent is to apply to the Circuit Court of the County to appoint one. If the inmate is a minor, notice also is to be given to his parents, if any, with a copy of the petition. The board is to see to it that the inmate may attend the hearings if desired by him or his guardian. The evidence is all to be reduced to writing, and, after the board has made its order for or against the operation, the superintendent, or the inmate, or his guardian, may appeal to the Circuit Court of the County. The Circuit Court may consider the record of the board and the evidence before it and such other admissible evidence as may be offered, and may affirm, revise, or reverse the order of the board and enter such order as it deems just. Finally any party may apply to the Supreme Court of Appeals, which, if it grants the appeal, is to hear the case upon the record of the trial in the Circuit Court, and may enter such order as it thinks the Circuit Court should have entered. There can be no doubt that, so far as procedure is concerned, the rights of the patient are most carefully considered, and, as every step in this case was taken in scrupulous compliance with the statute and after months of observation, there is no doubt that, in that respect, the plaintiff in error has had due process of law.

The attack is not upon the procedure, but upon the substantive law. It seems to be contended that in no circumstances could such an order be justified. It certainly is contended that the order cannot be justified upon the existing grounds. The judgment finds the facts that have been recited, and that Carrie Buck is the probable potential parent of socially inadequate offspring, likewise afflicted, that she may be sexually sterilized without detriment to her general health, and that her welfare and that of society will be promoted by her sterilization, and thereupon makes the order. In view of the general declarations of the legislature and the specific findings of the Court, obviously we cannot say as matter of law that the grounds do not exist, and, if they exist, they justify the result. We have seen more than once that the public welfare may call upon the best citizens for their lives. It would be strange if it could not call upon those who already sap the strength of the State for these lesser sacrifices, often not felt to be such by those concerned, in order to prevent our being swamped with incompetence. It is better for all the world if, instead of waiting to execute degenerate offspring for crime or to let them starve for their imbecility, society can prevent those who are manifestly unfit from continuing their kind. The principle that sustains compulsory vaccination is broad enough to cover cutting the Fallopian tubes. Jacobson v. Massachusetts, 197 U.S. 11. Three generations of imbeciles are enough.

But, it is said, however it might be if this reasoning were applied generally, it fails when it is confined to the small number who are in the institutions named and is not applied to the multitudes outside. It is the usual last resort of constitutional arguments to point out shortcomings of this sort. But the answer is that the law does all that is needed when it does all that it can, indicates a policy, applies it to all within the lines, and seeks to bring within the lines all similarly situated so far and so fast as its means allow. Of course, so far as the operations enable those who otherwise must be kept confined to be returned to the world, and thus open the asylum to others, the equality aimed at will be more nearly reached.

Judgment affirmed.

MR. JUSTICE BUTLER dissents.

Source: Excerpted from *Buck v. Bell,* 274 U.S. 200 (1927). Available online. URL: http://caselaw.lp.findlaw.com/cgi-bin/getcase.pl?court=us&vol=274&invol=200. Accessed January 12, 2011.

Griswold v. Connecticut (1965) (excerpt)

In 1965, the Supreme Court decision in Griswold v. Connecticut *allowed married couples in all states to obtain contraceptives legally. In 1972, in* Eisenstadt v. Baird, *the U.S. Supreme Court found that the right of privacy recognized for married couples in* Griswold v. Connecticut *should extend to unmarried couples and their procreative decisions. These two decisions finally overturned the Comstock Law of 1873, which had ruled information about birth control "obscene."*

MR. JUSTICE DOUGLAS delivered the opinion of the Court.

Appellant Griswold is Executive Director of the Planned Parenthood League of Connecticut. Appellant Buxton is a licensed physician and a professor at the Yale Medical School who served as Medical Director for the League at its Center in New Haven—a center open and operating from November 1 to November 10, 1961, when appellants were arrested.

They gave information, instruction, and medical advice to married persons as to the means of preventing conception. They examined the wife and prescribed the best contraceptive device or material for her use. Fees were usually charged, although some couples were serviced free.

The statutes whose constitutionality is involved in this appeal are 53-32 and 54-196 of the General Statutes of Connecticut (1958 rev.). The former provides:

"Any person who uses any drug, medicinal article or instrument for the purpose of preventing conception shall be fined not less than fifty dollars or imprisoned not less than sixty days nor more than one year or be both fined and imprisoned."

Section 54-196 provides:

"Any person who assists, abets, counsels, causes, hires or commands another to commit any offense may be prosecuted and punished as if he were the principal offender."

The appellants were found guilty as accessories and fined $100 each, against the claim that the accessory statute as so applied violated the Fourteenth Amendment. The Appellate Division of the Circuit Court affirmed. The Supreme Court of Errors affirmed that judgment. 151 Conn. 544, 200 A. 2d 479. We noted probable jurisdiction. 379 U.S. 926.

Page 381 U.S. 479, 481

We think that appellants have standing to raise the constitutional rights of the married people with whom they had a professional relationship. Tileston v. Ullman, 318 U.S. 44, is different, for there the plaintiff seeking to represent others asked for a declaratory judgment. In that situation we thought that the requirements of standing should be strict, lest the standards of "case or controversy" in Article III of the Constitution become blurred. Here those doubts are removed by reason of a criminal conviction for serving married couples in violation of an aiding-and-abetting statute. Certainly the accessory should have standing to assert that the offense which he is charged with assisting is not, or cannot constitutionally be, a crime.

Source: Excerpted from *Griswold v. Connecticut,* 381 U.S. 479 (1965). Justia.com. Supreme Court Center. Available online. URL: http://supreme.justia.com/us/381/479/case.html. Accessed December 28, 2010.

Reed v. Reed (1971) (excerpt)

Argued on October 19, 1971, and decided on November 22, 1971, this U.S. Supreme Court case resulted in a decision that found a mandatory provision of the Idaho probate code that gave preference to men over women for appointment as estate administrators to be a violation of the equal protection clause of the Fourteenth Amendment.

Allen R. Derr argued the cause for appellant. With him on the briefs were Melvin L. Wulf, Ruth Bader Ginsburg, Pauli Murray, and Dorothy Kenyon.

Charles S. Stout argued the cause for appellee. With him on the brief was Myron E. Anderson.

Briefs of amici curiae urging reversal were filed by J. Lee Rankin and Norman Redlich for the City of New York; by Martha W. Griffiths, Phineas Indritz, Leo Kanowitz, Marguerite Rawalt, Sylvia Roberts, and Faith Seidenberg for American Veterans Committee, Inc., et al.; and by Birch Bayh for the National Federation of Business and Professional Women's Clubs, Inc.

MR. CHIEF JUSTICE BURGER delivered the opinion of the Court.

Richard Lynn Reed, a minor, died intestate in Ada County, Idaho, on March 29, 1967. His adoptive parents, who had separated sometime prior to his death, are the parties to this appeal. Approximately seven months after Richard's death, his mother, appellant Sally Reed, filed a petition in the Probate Court of Ada County, [404 U.S. 71, 72] seeking appointment as administratrix of her son's estate. Prior to the date set for a hearing on the mother's petition, appellee Cecil Reed, the father of the decedent, filed a competing petition seeking to have himself appointed administrator of the son's estate. The probate court held a joint hearing on the two petitions and thereafter ordered that letters of administration be issued to appellee Cecil

Reed upon his taking the oath and filing the bond required by law. The court treated 15-312 and 15-314 of the Idaho Code as the controlling statutes and read those sections as compelling a preference for Cecil Reed because he was a male.

Section 15-312 designates the persons who are entitled to administer the estate of one who dies intestate. In making these designations, that section lists 11 classes of persons who are so entitled and provides, in substance, [404 U.S. 71, 73] that the order in which those classes are listed in the section shall be determinative of the relative rights of competing applicants for letters of administration. One of the 11 classes so enumerated is "[t]he father or mother" of the person dying intestate. Under this section, then, appellant and appellee, being members of the same entitlement class, would seem to have been equally entitled to administer their son's estate. Section 15-314 provides, however, that

> "[o]f several persons claiming and equally entitled [under 15-3121 to administer, males must be preferred to females, and relatives of the whole to those of the half blood."

In issuing its order, the probate court implicitly recognized the equality of entitlement of the two applicants under 15-312 and noted that neither of the applicants was under any legal disability; the court ruled, however, that appellee, being a male, was to be preferred to the female appellant "by reason of Section 15-314 of the Idaho Code." In stating this conclusion, the probate judge gave no indication that he had attempted to determine the relative capabilities of the competing applicants to perform the functions incident to the administration of an estate. It seems clear the probate judge considered himself bound by statute to give preference to the male candidate over the female, each being otherwise "equally entitled."

Sally Reed appealed from the probate court order, and her appeal was treated by the District Court of the Fourth Judicial District of Idaho as a constitutional attack on 15-314. In dealing with the attack, that court held that the challenged section violated the Equal Protection Clause of the Fourteenth Amendment and was, therefore, [404 U.S. 71, 74] void; the matter was ordered "returned to the Probate Court for its determination of which of the two parties" was better qualified to administer the estate.

This order was never carried out, however, for Cecil Reed took a further appeal to the Idaho Supreme Court, which reversed the District Court and reinstated the original order naming the father administrator of the estate. In reaching this result, the Idaho Supreme Court first dealt with the governing statutory law and held that under 15-312 "a father and mother are 'equally entitled' to letters of administration," but the preference given to males by 15-314 is "mandatory" and leaves no room for the exercise of a probate court's discretion in the appointment of administrators. Having thus definitively and authoritatively interpreted the statutory provisions involved, the Idaho Supreme Court then proceeded to examine, and reject, Sally Reed's contention that 15-314 violates the Equal Protection Clause by gaining a mandatory preference to males over females, without regard to their individual qualifications as potential estate administrators. 93 Idaho 511, 465 P.2d 635.

Source: Excerpted from *Reed v. Reed*, 404 U.S. 71 (1971). Available online. URL: http://caselaw.lp.findlaw.com/cgi-bin/getcase.pl?court=us&vol=404&invol=71. Accessed January 12, 2011.

Eisenstadt v. Baird (1972) (excerpt)

In 1972, Massachusetts law did not allow unmarried couples or single persons to purchase or use contraceptives, which could only be obtained through a physician or distributor. Professor William Baird was accused of giving away vaginal cream following his Boston University lecture on birth and population control.

Appellee attacks his conviction of violating Massachusetts law for giving a woman a contraceptive foam at the close of his lecture to students on contraception. That law makes it a felony for anyone to give away a drug, medicine, instrument, or article for the prevention of conception except in the case of (1) a registered physician administering or prescribing it for a married person or (2) an active registered pharmacist furnishing it to a married person presenting a registered physician's prescription. The District Court dismissed appellee's petition for a writ of habeas corpus. The Court of Appeals vacated the dismissal, holding that the statute is a prohibition on contraception per se and conflicts "with fundamental human rights" under Griswold v. Connecticut, 381 U.S. 479. Appellant, inter alia, argues that appellee lacks standing to assert the rights of unmarried persons denied access to contraceptives because he was neither an authorized distributor under the statute nor a single person unable to obtain contraceptives. Held:

1. If, as the Court of Appeals held, the statute under which appellee was convicted is not a health measure, appellee may not be prevented, because he was not an authorized distributor, from attacking the statute in its alleged discriminatory application to potential distributees. Appellee, furthermore, has standing to assert the rights of unmarried persons denied

United States Documents

access to contraceptives because their ability to obtain them will be materially impaired by enforcement of the statute. Cf. Griswold, supra; Barrows v. Jackson, 346 U.S. 249. Pp. 443–446.

2. By providing dissimilar treatment for married and unmarried persons who are similarly situated, the statute violates the Equal Protection Clause of the Fourteenth Amendment. Pp. 446–455.

(a) The deterrence of fornication, a 90-day misdemeanor under Massachusetts law, cannot reasonably be regarded as the purpose of the statute, since the statute is riddled with exceptions making contraceptives freely available for use in premarital sexual relations and its scope and penalty structure are inconsistent with that purpose. Pp. 447–450.

(b) Similarly, the protection of public health through the regulation of the distribution of potentially harmful articles cannot reasonably be regarded as the purpose of the law, since, if health were the rationale, the statute would be both discriminatory and overbroad, and federal and state laws already regulate the distribution of drugs unsafe for use except under the supervision of a licensed physician. Pp. 450–452.

(c) Nor can the statute be sustained simply as a prohibition on contraception per se, for whatever the rights of the individual to access to contraceptives may be, the rights must be the same for the unmarried and the married alike. If under Griswold, supra, the distribution of contraceptives to married persons cannot be prohibited, a ban on distribution to unmarried persons would be equally impermissible, since the constitutionally protected right of privacy inheres in the individual, not the marital couple. If, on the other hand, Griswold is no bar to a prohibition on the distribution of contraceptives, a prohibition limited to unmarried persons would be underinclusive and invidiously discriminatory. Pp. 452–455.

Source: Excerpted from *Eisenstadt v. Baird*, 405 U.S. 438 (1972). Justia.com. Supreme Court Center. Available online. URL: http://supreme.justia.com/us/405/438/case.html. Accessed December 28, 2010.

Roe v. Wade (1973) (excerpt)

The original 1973 decision in Roe v. Wade *(410 U.S. 113) from which the Supreme Court then ruled on the legality of abortions, overriding several state laws preventing them, was based on two cases, that of an unmarried woman from Texas, where abortion was illegal unless the mother's life was at risk, and that of a poor married mother of three from Georgia, where state law required permission for an abortion from a panel of doctors and hospital officials. While establishing the right to an abortion in the first trimester, the decision gave states the right to intervene in the second and third trimesters of pregnancy to protect the woman and the "potential" life of the unborn child.*

U.S. Supreme Court

ROE ET AL. v. WADE, DISTRICT ATTORNEY OF DALLAS COUNTY APPEAL FROM THE UNITED STATES DISTRICT COURT FOR THE NORTHERN DISTRICT OF TEXAS No. 70-18.

Argued December 13, 1971. Reargued October 11, 1972. Decided January 22, 1973

A pregnant single woman (Roe) brought a class action challenging the constitutionality of the Texas criminal abortion laws, which proscribe procuring or attempting an abortion except on medical advice for the purpose of saving the mother's life. A licensed physician (Hallford), who had two state abortion prosecutions pending against him, was permitted to intervene. A childless married couple (the Does), the wife not being pregnant, separately attacked the laws, basing alleged injury on the future possibilities of contraceptive failure, pregnancy, unpreparedness for parenthood, and impairment of the wife's health. A three-judge District Court, which consolidated the actions, held that Roe and Hallford, and members of their classes, had standing to sue and presented justiciable controversies. Ruling that declaratory, though not injunctive, relief was warranted, the court declared the abortion statutes void as vague and overbroadly infringing those plaintiffs' Ninth and Fourteenth Amendment rights. The court ruled the Does' complaint not justiciable. Appellants directly appealed to this Court on the injunctive rulings, and appellee cross-appealed from the District Court's grant of declaratory relief to Roe and Hallford.

Source: Excerpted from *Roe et al. v. Wade,* 410 U.S. 113 (1973). Justia.com. U.S. Supreme Court Center. Available online. URL: http://supreme.justia.com/us/410/113/case.html. Accessed December 28, 2010.

Rostker v. Goldberg (1981) (excerpt)

Opponents of the proposed Equal Rights Amendment are concerned that its exact interpretation could lead to a requirement that women register for military service. In spite of the National Organization for Women's (NOW's) lobbying efforts for women's equal access to the military, this 1981 Supreme Court decision only required male 18-year-olds to register with the draft board. The Selective Service law still does not require women to register for the draft because of the U.S. Department of Defense's policy of restricting women from direct ground combat.

United States Documents

453 U.S. 57 (1981)
ROSTKER, DIRECTOR OF SELECTIVE SERVICE v. GOLDBERG ET AL.
APPEAL FROM THE UNITED STATES DISTRICT COURT FOR THE EAST-
ERN DISTRICT OF PENNSYLVANIA.
No. 80-251.
Argued March 24, 1981. Decided June 25, 1981.

The Military Selective Service Act (Act) authorizes the President to require the registration for possible military service of males but not females, the purpose of registration being to facilitate any eventual conscription under the Act. Registration for the draft was discontinued by Presidential Proclamation in 1975 (the Act was amended in 1973 to preclude conscription), but as the result of a crisis in Southwestern Asia, President Carter decided in 1980 that it was necessary to reactivate the registration process, and sought Congress' allocation of funds for that purpose. He also recommended that Congress amend the Act to permit the registration and conscription of women as well as men. Although agreeing that it was necessary to reactivate the registration process, Congress allocated only those funds necessary to register males and declined to amend the Act to permit the registration of women. Thereafter, the President ordered the registration of specified groups of young men. In a lawsuit brought by several men challenging the Act's constitutionality, a three-judge District Court ultimately held that the Act's gender-based discrimination violated the Due Process Clause of the Fifth Amendment and enjoined registration under the Act.

Held:

The Act's registration provisions do not violate the Fifth Amendment. Congress acted well within its constitutional authority to raise and regulate armies and navies when it authorized the registration of men and not women. Pp. 64–83.

(a) The customary deference accorded Congress' judgments is particularly appropriate when, as here, Congress specifically considered the question of the Act's constitutionality, and perhaps in no area has the Court accorded Congress greater deference than in the area of national defense and military affairs. While Congress is not free to disregard the Constitution when it acts in the area of military affairs, this Court must be particularly careful not to substitute its judgment of what is desirable for that of Congress, or its own evaluation of evidence for a reasonable evaluation by the Legislative Branch. Congress carefully considered whether to register only males for potential conscription or whether to register both sexes, and its broad constitutional authority

209

Page 453 U.S. 57, 58

cannot be ignored in considering the constitutionality of its studied choice of one alternative in preference to the other. Pp. 64–72.

(b) The question of registering women was extensively considered by Congress in hearings held in response to the President's request for authorization to register women, and its decision to exempt women was not the accidental byproduct of a traditional way of thinking about women. Since Congress thoroughly reconsidered the question of exempting women from the Act in 1980, the Act's constitutionality need not be considered solely on the basis of the views expressed by Congress in 1948, when the Act was first enacted in its modern form. Congress' determination that any future draft would be characterized by a need for combat troops was sufficiently supported by testimony adduced at the hearings so that the courts are not free to make their own judgment on the question. And since women are excluded from combat service by statute or military policy, men and women are simply not similarly situated for purposes of a draft or registration for a draft, and Congress' decision to authorize the registration of only men, therefore, does not violate the Due Process Clause. The testimony of executive and military officials before Congress showed that the argument for registering women was based on considerations of equity, but Congress was entitled, in the exercise of its constitutional powers, to focus on the question of military need rather than "equity." The District Court, undertaking an independent evaluation of the evidence, exceeded its authority in ignoring Congress' conclusions that whatever the need for women for noncombat roles during mobilization, it could be met by volunteers, and that staffing noncombat positions with women during a mobilization would be positively detrimental to the important goal of military flexibility. Pp. 72–83.

Source: Excerpted from *Rostker, Director of Selective Service v. Goldberg et al.*, Justia.com. Supreme Court Center. Available online. URL: http://supreme.justia.com/us/448/1306/case.html. Accessed December 28, 2010.

Surrogate Pregnancy Custody Rights: Baby M (1988) (excerpt)

A 1985 surrogacy contract between Mary Beth Whitehead and William and Elizabeth Stern stated their agreement for Whitehead to carry the Sterns' baby, conceived from William's sperm. Within 24 hours of giving birth in March 1986, Whitehead reclaimed the baby and left the state. After freezing her assets and issuing a warrant for her arrest, the Sterns took her to court in 1987, where the superior court justice awarded custody of the baby to the couple—a decision that would be challenged by the New Jersey Supreme Court in 1988.

First Surrogacy Case—In re Baby M, 537 A.2d 1227, 109 N.J. 396 (N.J. 02/03/1988)

New Jersey Supreme Court

Decided: February 3, 1988.

IN THE MATTER OF BABY M, A PSEUDONYM FOR AN ACTUAL PERSON

In this matter the Court is asked to determine the validity of a contract that purports to provide a new way of bringing children into a family. For a fee of $10,000, a woman agrees to be artificially inseminated with the semen of another woman's husband; she is to conceive a child, carry it to term, and after its birth surrender it to the natural father and his wife. The intent of the contract is that the child's natural mother will thereafter be forever separated from her child. The wife is to adopt the child, and she and the natural father are to be regarded as its parents for all purposes. The contract providing for this is called a "surrogacy contract," the natural mother inappropriately called the "surrogate mother."

We invalidate the surrogacy contract because it conflicts with the law and public policy of this State. While we recognize the depth of the yearning of infertile couples to have their own children, we find the payment of money to a "surrogate" mother illegal, perhaps criminal, and potentially degrading to women. Although in this case we grant custody to the natural father, the evidence having clearly proved such custody to be in the best interests of the infant, we void both the termination of the surrogate mother's parental rights and the adoption of the child by the wife/stepparent. We thus restore the "surrogate" as the mother of the child. We remand the issue of the natural mother's visitation rights to the trial court, since that issue was not reached below and the record before us is not sufficient to permit us to decide it de novo. . . .

We find no offense to our present laws where a woman voluntarily and without payment agrees to act as a "surrogate" mother, provided that she is not subject to a binding agreement to surrender her child. Moreover, our holding today does not preclude the Legislature from altering the current statutory scheme, within constitutional limits, so as to permit surrogacy contracts. Under current law, however, the surrogacy agreement before us is illegal and invalid.

Source: Excerpted from "First Surrogacy Case—*In re Baby M*, 537 A.2d 1227, 109 N.J. 396 (N.J. 02/03/1988)." Available online. URL: http://biotech.law.lsu.edu/cases/cloning/baby_m.htm. Accessed January 17. 2011.

HOUSE JOINT RESOLUTION NO. 299
Offered January 25, 2002
Honoring the memory of Carrie Buck (excerpt)

After Buck's sterilization, she was freed from the State Colony for Epileptics and Feebleminded and later married. A formal apology from the state of Virginia was extended to Ms. Buck in 2002.

WHEREAS, in 1924 Virginia passed two eugenics-related laws, the second of which permitted involuntary sterilization, the most egregious outcome of the lamentable eugenics movement in the Commonwealth; and WHEREAS, under this act, those labeled "feebleminded," including the "insane, idiotic, imbecile, feebleminded or epileptic" could be involuntarily sterilized, so that they would not produce similarly disabled offspring; and

WHEREAS, May 2, 2002, is the 75th anniversary of the United States Supreme Court decision in the case of *Buck v. Bell,* in which Virginia's 1924 Eugenical Sterilization Act was allowed to stand; and

WHEREAS, following the *Buck* decision, an estimated 60,000 Americans, including about 8,000 in Virginia, were sterilized under similar state laws, and the decision was applauded by German eugenicists who supported comparable legislation early in the Nazi regime; and

WHEREAS, in 1927 Carrie Buck, a poor and unwed teenage mother from Charlottesville, was the first person sterilized under the provision of the 1924 law; and

WHEREAS, subsequent scholarship has demonstrated that the Sterilization Act was based on the now-discredited and false science of eugenics; and

WHEREAS, legal and historical scholarship analyzing the *Buck* decision has condemned it as an embodiment of bigotry against the disabled and an example of the use of faulty science in support of public policy; and

WHEREAS, that scholarship has also pointed out the fallacies contained in the *Buck* opinion, noting, among other points, that Carrie Buck's daughter, Vivian, the supposed third-generation "imbecile," later won a place on her school's honor roll; and

WHEREAS, the General Assembly in 2001 expressed its "profound regret" over the Commonwealth's role in the eugenics movement in this country and over the damage done in the name of eugenics; now, therefore, be it

RESOLVED by the House of Delegates, the Senate concurring, That the General Assembly honor the memory of Carrie Buck on the occasion of the 75th anniversary of the *Buck v. Bell* Supreme Court decision.

United States Documents

Source: Excerpted from "2002 Session." University of Virginia Center for Biomedical Ethics. Available online. URL: http://leg1.state.va.us/cgi-bin/legp504.exe?021+ful+HJ299. Accessed January 12, 2011.

Partial-Birth Abortion Ban Act of 2003 (excerpt)

In November 2003, President George W. Bush signed a partial-birth abortion ban—legislation that was first introduced in 1995 and subsequently passed by Congress. Partial-birth abortions are performed in the second and third trimesters, when babies are in their 20th to 24th week. The bill proposed to ban "partial-birth abortion," legally defined as any abortion in which the baby is delivered "past the [baby's] navel . . . outside the body of the mother," or "in the case of head-first presentation, the entire fetal head is outside the body of the mother," before being killed. The bill would allow the method if it was necessary to save a mother's life. The following is an excerpt from the ban (as agreed to by the House and Senate).

The Congress finds and declares the following:

(1) A moral, medical, and ethical consensus exists that the practice of performing a partial-birth abortion—an abortion in which a physician deliberately and intentionally vaginally delivers a living, unborn child's body until either the entire baby's head is outside the body of the mother, or any part of the baby's trunk past the navel is outside the body of the mother and only the head remains inside the womb, for the purpose of performing an overt act (usually the puncturing of the back of the child's skull and removing the baby's brains) that the person knows will kill the partially delivered infant, performs this act, and then completes delivery of the dead infant—is a gruesome and inhumane procedure that is never medically necessary and should be prohibited.

(2) Rather than being an abortion procedure that is embraced by the medical community, particularly among physicians who routinely perform other abortion procedures, partial-birth abortion remains a disfavored procedure that is not only unnecessary to preserve the health of the mother, but in fact poses serious risks to the long-term health of women and in some circumstances, their lives. As a result, at least 27 States banned the procedure as did the United States Congress which voted to ban the procedure during the 104th, 105th, and 106th Congresses.

Source: Excerpted from the Partial-Birth Abortion Act of 2003. Available online. URL:http://www.gpo.gov/fdsys/pkg/PLAW-108publ105/pdf/PLAW-108publ105.pdf. Accessed February 7, 2011.

Carhart v. Ashcroft (2004) (excerpt)

Family planning organizations and physicians challenged the constitutionality of the partial-birth abortion ban, which among other things lacked a health exception for the mother. Between June and September 2004, three cases— Planned Parenthood Federation of America v. Ashcroft; National Abortion Federation v. Ashcroft, *and* Carhart v. Ashcroft—*concluded that the ban was unconstitutional and could not be enforced. Below is the summary of evidence that was presented in April 2005 during* Carhart v. Ashcroft. *John Ashcroft was the attorney general at the time.*

The procedures in question in this case are used during late-term abortions and we therefore must, for context, present some basic information regarding these procedures. There are three primary methods of late-term abortions: medical induction; dilation and evacuation (D&E); and dilation and extraction (D&X). In a medical induction, formerly the most common method of second-trimester abortion, a physician uses medication to induce premature labor. Stenberg, 530 U.S. at 924.

In a D&E, now the most common procedure, the physician causes dilation of the woman's cervix and then "the physician reaches into the woman's uterus with an instrument, grasps an extremity of the fetus, and pulls." Women's Med. Prof'l Corp. v. Taft, 353 F.3d 436, 439 (6th Cir. 2003). "When the fetus lodges in the cervix, the traction between the grasping instrument and the cervix causes dismemberment and eventual death, although death may occur prior to dismemberment." Id. This process is repeated until the entire fetus has been removed. D&X and a process called intact D&E are what are "now widely known as partial birth abortion." Id. In these procedures, the fetus is removed "intact" in a single pass. If the fetus presents head first, the physician collapses the skull of the fetus and then removes the "intact" fetus. Stenberg, 530 U.S. at 927. This is what is known as an intact D&E. If the fetus presents feet first, the physician "pulls the fetal body through the cervix, collapses the skull, and extracts the fetus through the cervix." Id. This is the D&X procedure. "Despite the technical differences" between an intact D&E and a D&X, they are "sufficiently similar for us to use the terms interchangeably." Id. at 928. . . .

. . .

There is some evidence in the present record indicating each of the advantages discussed in Stenberg are incorrect and the banned procedures are never medically necessary. See Carhart, 331 F. Supp. 2d at 822–51. There were, however, such assertions in Stenberg as well. See Stenberg, 530 U.S.

at 933–34; id. at 964–66 (Kennedy, J., dissenting). Though the contrary evidence now comes from (some) different doctors, the substance of this evidence does not distinguish this case from Stenberg in any meaningful way. . . .

We need not belabor the point. The record in this case and the record in Stenberg are similar in all significant respects. See Nat'l Abortion Fed'n, 330 F. Supp. 2d at 492 (explaining that the government's arguments "all fail to meaningfully distinguish the evidentiary circumstances present here from those that Stenberg held required a health exception to a ban on partial-birth abortion"). There remains no consensus in the medical community as to the safety and medical necessity of the banned procedures. There is a dearth of studies on the medical necessity of the banned procedures. In the absence of new evidence which would serve to distinguish this record from the record reviewed by the Supreme Court in Stenberg, we are bound by the Supreme Court's conclusion that "substantial medical authority" supports the medical necessity of a health exception. "As a court of law, [our responsibility] is neither to devise ways in which to circumvent the opinion of the Supreme Court nor to indulge delay in the full implementation of the Court's opinions. Rather, our responsibility is to faithfully follow its opinions, because that court is, by constitutional design, vested with the ultimate authority to interpret the Constitution." Richmond Med. Ctr. for Women v. Gilmore, 219 F.3d 376, 378 (4th Cir. 2000) (Luttig, J., concurring). Because the Act does not contain a health exception exception, it is unconstitutional. We therefore do not reach the district court's conclusion of the Act imposing an undue burden on a woman's right to have an abortion.

Source: Excerpted from U.S. Court of Appeals for the Eighth Circuit. Available online. URL: http://www.ca8.uscourts. gov/opndir/05/07/043379P.pdf. Accessed January 12, 2011.

Supreme Court Decision on Partial-Birth Abortion Ban (*Gonzales v. Carhart* Review) (2006) (excerpt)

The ruling banning partial-birth abortion was appealed by the Bush administration in September 2005 and petitioned to the U.S. Supreme Court. On February 21, 2006, the Court agreed to review the case, this time with then-attorney general Alberto Gonzales representing the government as plaintiff. Gonzales v. Carhart was argued before the Court on November 8, 2006, and decided on April 18, 2007. In a 5-4 decision, the Supreme Court overturned the lower court's ruling, thus banning partial-birth abortion and upholding the constitutionality of the ban. Below is an excerpt from that decision.

. . .

2. The Act, on its face, is not void for vagueness and does not impose an undue burden from any overbreadth. Pp. 16-26.

(a) The Act's text demonstrates that it regulates and proscribes performing the intact D&E procedure. First, since the doctor must "vaginally delive[r] a living fetus," §1531(b)(1)(A), the Act does not restrict abortions involving delivery of an expired fetus or those not involving vaginal delivery, *e.g.*, hysterotomy or hysterectomy. And it applies both previability and postviability because, by common understanding and scientific terminology, a fetus is a living organism within the womb, whether or not it is viable outside the womb. Second, because the Act requires the living fetus to be delivered to a specific anatomical landmark depending on the fetus' presentation, *ibid.*, an abortion not involving such partial delivery is permitted. Third, because the doctor must perform an "overt act, other than completion of delivery, that kills the partially delivered fetus," §1531(b)(1)(B), the "overt act" must be separate from delivery. It must also occur after delivery to an anatomical landmark, since killing "the partially delivered" fetus, when read in context, refers to a fetus that has been so delivered, *ibid.* Fourth, given the Act's scienter requirements, delivery of a living fetus past an anatomical landmark by accident or inadvertence is not a crime because it is not "deliberat[e] and intentiona[l], §1531(b)(1)(A). Nor is such a delivery prohibited if the fetus [has not] been delivered "for the purpose of performing an overt act that the [doctor] knows will kill [it]." *Ibid.* Pp. 16-18.

(b) The Act is not unconstitutionally vague on its face. It satisfies both requirements of the void-for-vagueness doctrine. First, it provides doctors "of ordinary intelligence a reasonable opportunity to know what is prohibited," *Grayned v. City of Rockford,* 408 U. S. 104, 108, setting forth "relatively clear guidelines as to prohibited conduct" and providing "objective criteria" to evaluate whether a doctor has performed a prohibited procedure, *Posters 'N' Things, Ltd. v. United States,* 511 U. S. 513, 525-526. Second, it does not encourage arbitrary or discriminatory enforcement. *Kolender v. Lawson,* 461 U. S. 352, 357. Its anatomical landmarks "establish minimal guidelines to govern law enforcement," *Smith v. Goguen,* 415 U. S. 566, 574, and its scienter requirements narrow the scope of its prohibition and limit prosecutorial discretion, see *Kolender, supra,* at 358. Respondents' arbitrary enforcement arguments, furthermore, are somewhat speculative, since this is a preenforcement challenge. Pp. 18-20.

(c) The Court rejects respondents' argument that the Act imposes an undue burden, as a facial matter, because its restrictions on second-trimester abortions are too broad. Pp. 20-26.

(i) The Act's text discloses that it prohibits a doctor from intentionally performing an intact D&E. Its dual prohibitions correspond with the steps generally undertaken in this procedure: The doctor (1) delivers the fetus until its head lodges in the cervix, usually past the anatomical landmark for a breech presentation, see §1531(b)(1)(A), and (2) proceeds to the overt act of piercing or crushing the fetal skull after the partial delivery, see §1531(b)(1)(B). The Act's scienter requirements limit its reach to those physicians who carry out the intact D&E, with the intent to undertake both steps at the outset. The Act excludes most D&Es in which the doctor intends to remove the fetus in pieces from the outset. This interpretation is confirmed by comparing the Act with the Nebraska statute in *Stenberg*. There, the Court concluded that the statute encompassed D&E, which "often involve[s] a physician pulling a 'substantial portion' of a still living fetus . . . , say, an arm or leg, into the vagina prior to the death of the fetus," 530 U. S., at 939, and rejected the Nebraska Attorney General's limiting interpretation that the statute's reference to a "procedure" that "kill[s] the unborn child" was to a distinct procedure, not to the abortion procedure as a whole, *id.*, at 943. It is apparent Congress responded to these concerns because the Act adopts the phrase "delivers a living fetus," 18 U. S. C. §1531(b)(1)(A), instead of "'delivering . . . a living unborn child, or a substantial portion thereof,'" 530 U. S., at 938, thereby targeting extraction of an entire fetus rather than removal of fetal pieces; identifies specific anatomical landmarks to which the fetus must be partially delivered, §1531(b)(1)(A), thereby clarifying that the removal of a small portion of the fetus is not prohibited; requires the fetus to be delivered so that it is partially "outside the [mother's] body," §1531(b)(1)(A), thereby establishing that delivering a substantial portion of the fetus into the vagina would not subject a doctor to criminal sanctions; and adds the overt-act requirement, §1531(b)(1), thereby making the distinction the Nebraska statute failed to draw (but the Nebraska Attorney General advanced). Finally, the canon of constitutional avoidance, see, e.g., *Edward J. DeBartolo Corp. v. Florida Gulf Coast Building & Constr. Trades Council*, 485 U. S. 568, 575, extinguishes any lingering doubt. Interpreting the Act not to prohibit standard D&E is the most reasonable reading and understanding of its terms. Pp. 20-24.

(ii) Respondents' contrary arguments are unavailing. The contention that any D&E may result in the delivery of a living fetus beyond the Act's anatomical landmarks because doctors cannot predict the amount the cervix will dilate before the procedure does not take account of the Act's intent requirements, which preclude liability for an accidental intact D&E. The evidence supports the legislative determination that an intact delivery is almost always a conscious choice rather than a happenstance, belying any claim that a standard D&E cannot be performed without intending or foreseeing an intact D&E. That many doctors begin every D&E with the objective of removing the fetus as intact as possible based on their belief that this is safer does not prove, as respondents suggest, that every D&E might violate the Act, thereby imposing an undue burden. It demonstrates only that those doctors must adjust their conduct to the law by not attempting to deliver the fetus to an anatomical landmark. Respondents have not shown that requiring doctors to intend dismemberment before such a delivery will prohibit the vast majority of D&E abortions. Pp. 24-26.

3. The Act, measured by its text in this facial attack, does not impose a "substantial obstacle" to late-term, but previability, abortions, as prohibited by the *Casey* plurality, 505 U. S., at 878. Pp. 26-37.

(a) The contention that the Act's congressional purpose was to create such an obstacle is rejected. The Act's stated purposes are protecting innocent human life from a brutal and inhumane procedure and protecting the medical community's ethics and reputation. The government undoubtedly "has an interest in protecting the integrity and ethics of the medical profession." *Washington v. Glucksberg,* 521 U. S. 702, 731. Moreover, Casey reaffirmed that the government may use its voice and its regulatory authority to show its profound respect for the life within the woman. See, *e.g.,* 505 U. S., at 873. The Act's ban on abortions involving partial delivery of a living fetus furthers the Government's objectives. Congress determined that such abortions are similar to the killing of a newborn infant. This Court has confirmed the validity of drawing boundaries to prevent practices that extinguish life and are close to actions that are condemned. *Glucksberg, supra,* at 732-735, and n. 23. The Act also recognizes that respect for human life finds an ultimate expression in a mother's love for her child. Whether to have an abortion requires a difficult and painful moral decision, *Casey,* 505 U. S., at 852-853, which some women come to regret. In a decision so fraught with emotional consequence, some doctors may prefer not to disclose precise details of the abortion procedure to be used. It is, however, precisely this lack of information that is of legitimate concern to the State. *Id.,* at 873. The State's interest in respect for life is advanced by the dialogue that better informs the political and legal systems, the medical profession, expectant mothers, and society as a whole of the consequences that follow from a decision to elect a late-term abortion. The objection that the Act accomplishes little because the standard D&E is in some respects as brutal, if not more, than intact D&E, is unpersuasive. It was reasonable for Congress to think that partial-birth abortion, more than standard D&E, undermines the public's perception of the doctor's appropriate role during delivery, and perverts the birth process. Pp. 26-30.

(b) The Act's failure to allow the banned procedure's use where "'necessary, in appropriate medical judgment, for preservation of the [mother's] health,'" *Ayotte v. Planned Parenthood of Northern New Eng.,* 546 U. S. 320, 327-328, does not have the effect of imposing an unconstitutional burden on the abortion right. The Court assumes the Act's prohibition would be unconstitutional, under controlling precedents, if it "subject[ed] [women] to significant health risks." *Id.,* at 328. Whether the Act creates such risks was, however, a contested factual question below: The evidence presented in the trial courts and before Congress demonstrates both sides have medical support for their positions. The Court's precedents instruct that the Act can survive facial attack when this medical uncertainty persists. See, *e.g., Kansas v. Hendricks,* 521 U. S. 346, 360, n. 3. This traditional rule is consistent with Casey, which confirms both that the State has an interest in promoting respect for human life at all stages in the pregnancy, and that abortion doctors should be treated the same as other doctors. Medical uncertainty does not foreclose the exercise of legislative power in the abortion context any more than it does in other contexts. Other considerations also support the Court's conclusion, including the fact that safe alternatives to the prohibited procedure, such as D&E, are available. In addition, if intact D&E is truly necessary in some circumstances, a prior injection to kill the fetus allows a doctor to perform the procedure, given that the Act's prohibition only applies to the delivery of "a living fetus," 18 U. S. C. §1531(b)(1)(A). *Planned Parenthood of Central Mo. v. Danforth,* 428 U. S. 52, 77-79, distinguished. The Court rejects certain of the parties' arguments. On the one hand, the Attorney General's contention that the Act should be upheld based on the congressional findings alone fails because some of the Act's recitations are factually incorrect and some of the important findings have been superseded. Also unavailing, however, is respondents' contention that an abortion regulation must contain a health exception if "substantial medical authority supports the proposition that banning a particular procedure could endanger women's health, " *Stenberg,* 530 U. S., at 938. Interpreting *Stenberg* as leaving no margin for legislative error in the face of medical uncertainty is too exacting a standard. Marginal safety considerations, including the balance of risks, are within the legislative competence where, as here, the regulation is rational and pursues legitimate ends, and standard, safe medical options are available. Pp. 31-37.

4. These facial attacks should not have been entertained in the first instance. In these circumstances the proper means to consider exceptions is by

as-applied challenge. *Cf. Wisconsin Right to Life, Inc. v. Federal Election Comm'n*, 546 U. S. ___, ___. This is the proper manner to protect the woman's health if it can be shown that in discrete and well-defined instances a condition has or is likely to occur in which the procedure prohibited by the Act must be used. No as-applied challenge need be brought if the Act's prohibition threatens a woman's life, because the Act already contains a life exception. 18 U. S. C. §1531(a). Pp. 37-39. No. 05-380, 413 F. 3d 791; 05-1382, 435 F. 3d 1163, reversed.

Kennedy, J., delivered the opinion of the Court, in which Roberts, C. J., and Scalia, Thomas, and Alito, JJ., joined. Thomas, J., filed a concurring opinion, in which Scalia, J., joined. Ginsburg, J., filed a dissenting opinion, in which Stevens, Souter, and Breyer, JJ., joined.

Source: Excerpted from *Gonzales, Attorney General v. Carhart et al.* Available online. URL: http://caselaw.lp.findlaw. com/scripts/getcase.pl?court=US&vol=000&invol=05-380. Accessed July 20, 2011.

Velez et al. v. Novartis Pharmaceuticals Corporation (2010) (excerpt)

On March 6, 2006, a complaint was filed by Amy Velez and 18 other sales representatives under Title VII of the Civil Rights Act of 1964 against Novartis Pharmaceuticals Corporation for exercising gender discrimination in the company's pay, promotions, and pregnancy policies. They also claimed interference with their Family and Medical Leave Act (FMLA) rights. In August 2007, a judge granted class certification of the case, making it representative of about 5,600 potential female claimants employed since July 2002. However, the court also granted a motion of summary judgment to Novartis, protecting it from any Title VII violations as an enterprise—most of the complaints being attributed to individuals in the company. Following a five-week jury trial from April 7 to May 19, 2010, 12 plaintiffs were awarded $3.4 million in compensatory damages in a settlement with the Swiss pharmaceutical company. This proceeded into negotiations, in which Novartis agreed on July 14, 2010, to pay $175 million to the other female employees for individual damages and to address discrimination within the company. As of this printing the case is ongoing.

Novartis to ordered to pay $250 million in punitives in bias case involving female sales reps. On May 19, a federal jury in Manhattan found that the Swiss company's U.S. division, Novartis Pharmaceuticals Corp., engaged in a pattern of discrimination against thousands of female sales representatives over pay, promotions and pregnancy from 2002 through 2007. The punitive damages award represents 2.6 percent of the company's $9.5 billion revenues last year. Novartis said it will appeal.

The award came two days after the same jury ordered the company to pay nearly $3.4 million in compensatory damages to the 12 named plaintiffs in the case. U.S. District Judge Colleen McMahon also will determine a lump sum for back pay, lost benefits and adjusted wages that will be distributed to the plaintiffs.

The award paves the way for 5,588 other women who can also apply for compensatory damages. According to plaintiffs' counsel, the damages likely will be determined on an individual basis by a court-appointed special master.

The suit claimed that the company discouraged pregnancies and ignored complaints of sexual harassment. In addition, it accused Novartis of paying women less and passing them over for promotions in favor of less-qualified men. During the month-long trial, the plaintiffs portrayed one male district manager as particularly abusive, noting that he allegedly showed pornography to women sales representatives and invited them to sit on his lap.

Velez v. Novartis, AG, No. 04-cv-9194 (S.D.N.Y. May 17, 2010) (jury verdict and compensatory damages); (May 19, 2010 jury award of punitive damages).

DISCRIMINATION — GENDER • FAILURE TO HIRE/PROMOTE • CIVIL RIGHTS • CLASS ACTIONS • DAMAGES
Civil Rights Act, 42 U.S.C. §§ 2000e et seq. (Title VII). Equal Pay Act, 29 U.S.C. § 206(d). Pregnancy Discrimination Act (PDA), 42 U.S.C. § 2000e(k) (amending Title VII's definition of discrimination "because of sex" to include discrimination "because of or on the basis of pregnancy, childbirth, or related medical conditions."). *Dukes v. Wal-Mart Stores*, Nos. 04-16688, 04-16720 (9th Cir. April 26, 2010) (en banc), as reported in "Enbanc Ninth Cir. certifies largest-ever class action in Wal-Mart gender bias case," Employment & Labor LAWCAST®, May 3, 2010, Headline Report Pt. I.

Source: Excerpted from "Novartis to Ordered to Pay $250 Million in Punitives in Bias Case Involving Female Sales Reps.." Lawcast Employment and Labor Report Outline 16, no. 10. (May 31, 2010). Available online. URL: http://www.lawcast.com/Outlines/Archive/EL%205_31_10.pdf. Accessed January 15, 2010.

5

International Documents

This section draws together excerpts of significant international primary-source documents and articles. The documents are organized into the following sections:

International Women's Movement

International Treaties

France

China

Afghanistan

Democratic Republic of the Congo (DRC)

INTERNATIONAL WOMEN'S MOVEMENT

A Vindication of the Rights of Woman (1792) (excerpt)

In 1792, Mary Wollstonecraft responded critically with A Vindication of the Rights of Woman *to Charles-Maurice de Talleyrand-Perigord, the late bishop of Autun in France, and a coauthor of the Declaration of the Rights of Man, after she read a pamphlet he had authored that recommended girls education be geared to subservient activities. Her entreaties stirred the hearts of the public with her cry for women "to acquire strength, both of mind and body." She introduced the novel concept of education for women and ventured "to predict that virtue will never prevail in society till the virtues of both sexes are founded on reason; and, till the affections common to both are allowed to gain their due strength by the discharge of mutual duties." She emphasized her principle that if women were not prepared by education to become the companions of men, they had the power to "stop the progress of knowledge and virtue" in the world.*

PART I.

Chap. I. The Rights and Involved Duties of Mankind Considered.

In the present state of society it appears necessary to go back to first principles in search of the most simple truths, and to dispute with some prevailing prejudice every inch of ground. To clear my way, I must be allowed to ask some plain questions, and the answers will probably appear as unequivocal as the axioms on which reasoning is built; though, when entangled with various motives of action, they are formally contradicted, either by the words or conduct of men.

In what does man's pre-eminence over the brute creation consist? The answer is as clear as that a half is less than the whole; in Reason.

What acquirement exalts one being above another? Virtue; we spontaneously reply.

For what purpose were the passions implanted? That man by struggling with them might attain a degree of knowledge denied to the brutes; whispers Experience.

Consequently the perfection of our nature and capability of happiness, must be estimated by the degree of reason, virtue, and knowledge, that distinguish the individual, and direct the laws which bind society: and that from the exercise of reason, knowledge and virtue naturally flow, is equally undeniable, if mankind be viewed collectively.

The rights and duties of man thus simplified, it seems almost impertinent to attempt to illustrate truths that appear so incontrovertible; yet such deeply rooted prejudices have clouded reason, and such spurious qualities have assumed the name of virtues, that it is necessary to pursue the course of reason as it has been perplexed and involved in error, by various adventitious circumstances, comparing the simple axiom with casual deviations. . . .

Chap. II. The Prevailing Opinion of a Sexual Character Discussed.

Women ought to endeavour to purify their heart; but can they do so when their uncultivated understandings make them entirely dependent on their senses for employment and amusement, when no noble pursuit sets them above the little vanities of the day, or enables them to curb the wild emotions that agitate a reed over which every passing breeze has power? To gain the affections of a virtuous man is affectation necessary? Nature has given woman a weaker frame than man; but, to ensure her husband's affections, must a wife, who by the exercise of her mind and body whilst she was discharging the duties of a daughter, wife, and mother, has allowed her constitution to retain its natural strength, and her nerves a healthy tone, is she, I say, to condescend to use art and feign a sickly delicacy in order to secure her husband's affection? Weakness may excite tenderness, and gratify the arrogant pride of man; but the lordly caresses of a protector will not gratify a noble mind that pants for, and deserves to be respected. Fondness is a poor substitute for friendship!

In a seraglio, I grant, that all these arts are necessary; the epicure must have his palate tickled, or he will sink into apathy; but have women so little ambition as to be satisfied with such a condition? Can they supinely dream life away in the lap of pleasure, or the languor of weariness, rather than assert their claim to pursue reasonable pleasures and render themselves conspicuous by practising the virtues which dignify mankind? Surely she has not an immortal soul who can loiter life away merely employed to adorn her person, that she may amuse the languid hours, and soften the cares of a fellow-creature who is willing to be enlivened by her smiles and tricks, when the serious business of life is over.

Besides, the woman who strengthens her body and exercises her mind will, by managing her family and practising various virtues, become the friend, and not the humble dependent of her husband, and if she deserves his regard by possessing such substantial qualities, she will not find it necessary to conceal her affection, nor to pretend to an unnatural coldness of constitution to excite her husband's passions. In fact, if we revert to history, we shall find that the women who have distinguished themselves have neither been the most beautiful nor the most gentle of their sex.

Nature, or, to speak with strict propriety, God, has made all things right; but man has sought him out many inventions to mar the work. I now allude to that part of Dr. Gregory's treatise, where he advises a wife never to let her husband know the extent of her sensibility or affection. Voluptuous precaution, and as ineffectual as absurd.—Love, from its very nature, must be transitory. To seek for a secret that would render it constant, would be as wild a search as for the philosopher's stone, or the grand panacea; and the discovery would be equally useless, or rather pernicious, to mankind. The most holy band of society is friendship. It has been well said, by a shrewd satirist, "that rare as true love is, true friendship is still rarer."

Source: Excerpted from *A Vindication of the Rights of Woman,* by Mary Wollstonecraft, 1792. Available online. URL: http://www.sacred-texts.com/wmn/vind.txt. Accessed December 28, 2010.

First Lady Hillary Rodham Clinton Remarks at Women 2000—Beijing + Five, the United Nations (June 5, 2000) (excerpt)

Five years after the Beijing Conference, the then-first lady, Hillary Clinton, delivered these remarks, commending the recent efforts of international agencies but recognizing what still needed to be achieved.

Beijing was important—because women broke centuries of silence and spoke out on issues that matter most to us, to our families to our societies. Women put our hopes and fears, our concerns and challenges on the world's agenda.

Beijing was important because countries agreed to a Platform for Action to meet goals in 12 different areas. The platform provided a blueprint for achieving economic, social and political equality and progress for women. So that, in the future, inaction and regression on women's rights would be viewed, not simply as the way things are and always have been, but rather as a violation of promises agreed to.

After the delegates went home, we used the Platform as a roadmap for elected officials and as a rallying cry for NGOs and citizens who began forming partnerships to fulfill the commitments that were entered into.

And since we spoke out in Beijing, look what has happened. Countries have passed laws raising the legal age for marriage, banning female genital mutilation, and criminalizing domestic violence.

Since we spoke out in Beijing, rape is now recognized as a crime by international war tribunals. More women are getting microcredit, running their own businesses, and owning property in their own names. . . .

These women and countless others like them who started in Beijing are now part of a movement. Where before women too often worked in isolation, now we are increasingly working together, blending our voices in a chorus for change. . . .

We come here to honor those voices and to speak for all those women who still do not have a voice.

We come here today because, for all our progress we can point to, our work is far from done.

When girls are doused with gasoline, set on fire, and burned to death because their marriage dowries are deemed too small—and when honor killings continue to be tolerated—our work is far from done. When millions of girls are still kept out of school, often by their own families, our work is far from done.

When babies are still denied food, drowned, suffocated, and abandoned simply because they are born girls, our work is far from done.

When women are still denied the right to plan their families, when they are still forced to have abortions, or are circumcised or sterilized against their will, our work is far from done.

When women and girls are increasingly victims of war, and turned into refugees by the millions, our work is far from done.

When girls are abducted, and used as child soldiers, human shields, and sexual slaves, our work is far from done.

225

When UNICEF tells us, as they did this week, that violence against women and girls is a global epidemic that kills, tortures and maims—and yet still it is viewed in too many places as acceptable, cultural or trivial, our work is far from done.

When women in some countries are still denied the right to vote, our work is far from done.

And when women's work is still not valued, by economists, by governments, and by employers who pay them less and treat them worse, our work is far from done.

So we must continue to stand up and speak out and keep working—not only to eliminate the inequities that have confronted women for millennia, but also to confront the new dangers that threaten to derail the progress we have already made.

We must speak out for the women who are still dying in childbirth or from unsafe abortions, for the women who cannot get health care, for the women suffering from cancer, malaria, TB and HIV/AIDS.

You know, the face of AIDS today is increasingly female in the world today. And it is tragically cutting short young women's lives, leaving behind AIDS orphans, who too often are left on dangerous streets to fend for themselves.

Source: Excerpted from "First Lady Hillary Rodham Clinton Remarks at Women 2000—Beijing + Five the United Nations June 5, 2000," unofficial transcript by the U.S. Mission to the United Nations.

"Whatever Happened to Family Planning and, for That Matter, Reproductive Health?" (March 2004) (excerpt)

In 2000, the United Nations included improving maternal health and combating HIV/AIDS, malaria, and other diseases as two of the eight Millennium Development Goals. Some public health-care experts felt these would automatically extend to family planning and reproductive health initiatives, while others felt family planning should have been scrutinized more carefully, either as a means of totalitarian population control or as a way to improve quality of life.

In 1994, the nations of the world gathered in Cairo for the International Conference on Population and Development (ICPD) and hammered out the comprehensive Programme of Action to improve women's sexual and reproductive health.

Just six years later, the nations of the world agreed on eight Millennium Development Goals (MDGs), and reproductive health was excluded.

This exclusion is emblematic of the declining priority placed on reproductive health and is a needed wake-up call. The time has come to reflect on the poor standing of reproductive health as a development issue and to mount efforts to get it back on the agenda. Like reproductive health more generally, family planning has received declining attention as a development priority and is at a disadvantage in the competition for scarce resources. Steps that would sharpen its competitive edge would also result in significant health benefits. . . .

A Tumultuous History

Family planning has always been a contentious issue. In the early 1900s, the debate about "birth control" encompassed a volatile mixture of religion, feminism, eugenics, social reform, and neo-Malthusian and pronatalist philosophies. In the United States, debate over abortion has always been a feature of discussion about family planning.

The legalization of abortion in the 1973 Roe v. Wade decision intensified that debate. In 1984, the Reagan administration unveiled its Mexico City policy, which exported the domestic debate to the rest of the world. The policy prohibits the U.S. Agency for International Development (USAID) from funding foreign nongovernmental organizations that provide abortion services, legal or illegal, or that promote the legalization of abortion, even if those organizations use their own funds for these activities.

The U.S. contribution represents 53% of all donor funds for reproductive health; additionally, the United States devotes 8% of its official development assistance to reproductive health, while the average for all donor countries (including the United States) is 3%.

The ascendancy of the United States over international and reproductive health resources helps explain the policy's success, and also suggests that we must look elsewhere to understand fully the de-emphasis on family planning in the donor community. It is unproductive to unduly focus on the U.S. government as the major cause of family planning's decline when the U.S. government is the sector's paramount donor. Other factors worth examining take us back to the 1990s, when two forces converged to lower the priority of family planning: its marginalization at Cairo and the wide acceptance of the view that family planning was unnecessary because of the drop in the global rate of population growth.

Family Planning at Cairo

Women's groups—many of which have long been uncomfortable with organized family planning—were a powerful force at Cairo. They called for a more complete range of health services for women, correctly pointing out that family planning programs did not serve all of women's reproductive needs. They also proposed major political, social and economic changes to improve women's general wellbeing. Their efforts paid off, and reproductive health became the core of the Programme of Action.

Unfortunately, the new approach not only developed an expanded agenda, it also downgraded and, in the eyes of some, demonized family planning programs. An undercurrent at Cairo was that family planning programs were an instrument of demographic imperialism used by the rich North to control the behavior of women in the developing world as a means of stemming population growth. This criticism was not directed at family planning per se, but at programs that were considered ill conceived and poorly implemented. For many, the message coming out of Cairo was not that we needed to do more than provide family planning, but that we needed to provide less family planning.

Source: Excerpted from Duff G. Gillespie, "Whatever Happened to Family Planning and, for That Matter, Reproductive Health?" International Family Planning Perspectives 30, no. 1 (March 2004): 35–38.

"Women Taking Charge of Retirement Purse Strings, Sort of" (July 2005) (excerpt)

Developed economies, such as in Europe and the United States, are looking for ways to balance the effects of an aging population on global labor markets—still fragile from the recession that started in December 2007. A discouraging economy not only withholds jobs from younger women but causes older ones to postpone their exit from the labor market.

After decades of feminist rhetoric about the need for women to take charge of their money, they are doing it, sort of. Today, most women no longer have a choice about whether to manage their money. They have money, and almost all of them will have to handle that money without a man at some point in their lives.

Women have long worked on a grassroots level to help their peers become financially competent, but lately global aging and the frailty of social safety nets have given the issue of women's financial security a new—some say dire—gravitas. In addition to ongoing activism by women for women, financial services companies have awakened to the fact that women, who control an increasing share of the world's wealth, are an appealing emerging market. Nonetheless, so far, there seems mostly to have been a revolution of ideas, not of action.

"Women are aware of the need to secure a comfortable retirement, invest properly, look at their finances and take responsibility," said Maria Umbach, vice president for life product marketing at Prudential Financial, "but their actions are not matching where they think they need to be. There's a gap."

Globally, the means to ensure a secure retirement and health care are shifting, which is one reason women—and men—around the world report with alarming consistency that they feel ill-equipped to manage their financial futures.

It is not clear that people have been able to adjust adequately to the changing circumstances, whether it is the shift in U.S. and British pension benefit programs, the strain on public retirement plans wrought by aging populations in Europe and Japan, or the declining percentage of children who care for their elderly parents in Asia.

While such insecurity is gender neutral, the failure to prepare for the changing future hits women harder than men. Women have fewer retirement resources than men because they tend to move in and out of the work force more often. This trend is not about to disappear, as evidenced by the rising number of young, professional stay-at-home moms who have "opted out" of the very game their mothers once scrambled to join. In addition, despite rising levels of education and professional attainment, women as a group still have lower wages and lower-level jobs than men have.

At the same time, women live longer than men, which means they have a longer retirement to prepare for with fewer resources.

"While women have entered the labor force in record numbers, their ability to retire is simply not based on access to a pension," said Teresa Heinz Kerry, chairwoman of the Heinz Family Philanthropies and founder of the Women's Institute for a Secure Retirement. "For too many women today, the costs of caring for aging parents, as well as grandparents, adult children and grandchildren, are making retirement a myth, not a reality."

The signs are not good: 83 percent of U.S. women postponed retirement to save more money, compared with 48 percent of men. And women, more than two to one over men, postponed retirement to maximize Social Security benefits, according to a new survey on retirement by Prudential.

At the same time, women control a growing share of the world's wealth—a fact that financial services companies have begun to exploit.

Source: Excerpted from "Women Taking Charge of Retirement Purse Strings, Sort of," by Erika Kinetz, International Herald Tribune, July 2, 2005. Available online. URL: http://www.nytimes.com/2005/07/01/your-money/01iht-mwomen.html. Accessed January 12, 2011.

"UN Links Poverty, Violence against Women" (October 2005) (excerpt)

Improving social and cultural attitudes toward women has emerged as a common gateway through which to eradicate poverty, the first of the eight Millenium Development Goals (MDGs). These attitudes influence to what degree social and economic growth can positively influence literacy, education, employment, and public health and mediate violence.

LONDON (AP)—The world will never eliminate poverty until it confronts social, economic and physical discrimination against women, the United Nations said Wednesday.

"Gender apartheid" could scuttle the global body's goal of halving extreme poverty by 2015, the U.N. Population Fund's annual State of World Population report said.

"We cannot make poverty history until we stop violence against women and girls," the fund's executive director, Thoraya Ahmed Obaid, said at the report's launch in London. "We cannot make poverty history until women enjoy their full social, cultural, economic and political rights."

The report said gender equality and better reproductive health could save the lives of 2 million women and 30 million children over the next decade—and help lift millions around the world out of poverty.

In 2000, the U.N. agreed to eight Millennium Development Goals, which include halving extreme poverty, achieving universal primary education and stemming the AIDS pandemic, all by 2015.

The report said one of the targets—promoting gender equality and empowering women—is "critical to the success of the other seven."

Improving women's political, economic and educational opportunities would lead to "improved economic prospects, smaller families, healthier and more literate children, lower HIV prevalence rates and reduced incidence of harmful traditional practices."

"Inequality is economically inefficient, it is a violation of human rights and it is a hazard to health," Obaid said.

But for many women around the world, the U.N. agency said, the picture remains grim.

It said 250 million years of productive life are lost annually because of reproductive health problems including HIV/AIDS, the leading cause of death among women between 15 and 44. Half the 40 million people infected with HIV around the world are women, and in sub-Saharan Africa, women make up a majority of those infected.

Lack of contraception leads to 76 million unintended pregnancies in the developing world and 19 million unsafe abortions worldwide each year, the agency said. More than half a million women die annually from preventable pregnancy-related causes—a figure that has changed little in a decade.

One woman in three around the world is likely to experience physical, psychological or sexual abuse in her lifetime. Many still lack the educational opportunities available to men: 600 million women around the world are illiterate, compared with 320 million men. . . .

"I think since the world summit, it's the first time world leaders have committed themselves to universal access to reproductive health by 2015. The issue has gone up the scale of importance. I am much more hopeful this time than before."

Source: Excerpted from "U.N. Links Poverty, Violence against Women," by Jill Lawless, Associated Press, October 12, 2005. Available online. URL: http://www.religiousconsultation.org/News_Tracker/UN_links_poverty_violence_against_women.htm. Accessed January 12, 2011.

Presentation to the Third Committee of the Secretary-General's In-depth Study on Violence against Women (October 9, 2006) (excerpt)

The then-secretary-general, Kofi Annan, addressed all forms of violence against women at the United Nations.

The first point I wish to underscore is that violence against women is both a cause and a consequence of **discrimination against women.** In many countries, discriminatory customs and traditions that perpetuate or condone violence against women are allowed to persist, sometimes despite legislation outlawing such practices. And discriminatory attitudes and stereotypes that view violence against women, particularly domestic violence, as a private matter that is acceptable, remain common.

Efforts to prevent and ultimately end violence against women must therefore be systematically grounded in the work of all States and other actors to eliminate discrimination against women and promote women's enjoyment of all their human rights and fundamental freedoms. Let me stress here the particularly important role of local communities—and families—in awareness-raising and education. Men have a role, especially in preventing violence, and this role needs to be further explored and strengthened. And our youth need to learn from their elders—from what we say and especially from what we do; from men as well as women; at home, at school, through our communications networks, and in the wider public domain—that women and men are equal and that violence against women is fundamentally wrong.

The most common of the **forms of violence** against women is intimate partner violence, sometimes leading to death. Certain harmful traditional practices are also widespread, including early and forced marriage and female genital mutilation. Gender-based murder of women, sexual violence, sexual harassment, and trafficking in women are receiving increasing attention. Violence perpetrated by States, through their agents, through omission or through the implications of public policies, spans physical, sexual, and psychological violence. And the high incidence of violence against women in armed conflict, particularly sexual violence including rape, has been clearly documented in several cases.

It is one of the great successes of grass-roots women's organizations and movements around the world that the challenge of violence against women was drawn out of the private domain into public attention and the arena of State accountability. And these advocates continue to push for more "visibility" of the effects of policies and socio-economic practices on women.

The study shows that international attention to violence against women has grown significantly in the last twenty years—and particularly since 1995, when the Beijing Platform for Action called for improved **research and data collection** on different forms of violence against women. In some areas, notable progress has been made in this regard. Intimate partner violence is an example. We now have 71 countries in which at least one survey has been conducted on the subject. And a national survey has been conducted in at least 41 countries. These are complemented by research studies on specific issues or aspects that provide evidence on the scope of particular forms of violence, as well as its consequences and costs, for women, their families, communities, and countries. In general, occurrences of acts of violence against women are well documented, including by advocacy organizations and service providers.

Nonetheless, the available evidence remains uneven and, in many cases, non-existent. As also underscored by our report, The World's Women 2005: Progress in Statistics, we continue to face serious research and data gaps, particularly on forms other than intimate partner violence, including trafficking in women and girls and violence against women by agents of the State. As the Secretary-General's study before you shows, information to assess and evaluate what policies and practices are most effective in addressing violence against women is particularly scarce. The study presents a range of information on specific countries, but this is not to suggest that countries going unmentioned are free from violence against women. It simply means that the information is not available, which should itself be seen as a major cause for concern. Ensuring adequate data collection is part of every State's obligation to address violence against women, yet inadequate data does not diminish that responsibility.

Now is the time to strengthen the knowledge base about the scope and extent of violence against women, as well as the impact of policies and practices that are in place so that resources to address this scourge can be used most effectively. This must include efforts to collect data systematically on the most common forms of violence. We also need to strengthen data collection and knowledge on forms that affect relatively few women overall but have a devastating effect on those concerned, or on new or emerging forms of violence, including economic violence and abuse, stalking, and violence through use of the Internet or cell phones.

The study makes a number of recommendations for action in this area, including developing a set of international indicators for assessing the prevalence of violence against women and the impact of different interventions. As in many other areas of work, this will not be possible unless the international community seriously steps up its support—technical, material, and financial—for strengthening national statistical systems in developing countries, as part of their broader capacity to monitor and evaluate progress in meeting their development goals.

The global attention to violence against women has also resulted in a comprehensive **international legal and policy framework** for addressing violence against women. Yet, States are failing in their responsibility to implement this framework fully at the national level. An example is the field of legislation. Only about half of Member States have some legislative provisions that specifically address domestic violence. Fewer than half have legislation on sexual harassment or on trafficking. And even where such legislation exists, there are often inadequacies in scope and coverage, such as definitions of domestic violence limited to physical violence or penal laws that discriminate against women. Or there are serious gaps in implementation, shown, for example, in the lack of regulations to implement legislation, the lack of clear procedures for law enforcement and health-care professionals, or the lack of legal aid, especially for indigent women.

Source: Excerpted from "Presentation to the Third Committee of the Secretary-General's In-depth Study on Violence Against Women." Available online. URL: http://www.un.org/esa/desa/ousg/statements/2006/20061009_ga61_3rd.html. Accessed December 28, 2010.

Global Strategy for Women's and Children's Health (September 22, 2010) (excerpt)

Following the three-day annual UN Summit, September 20–22, 2010, to review the progress of the Millennium Development Goals (MDGs), United Nations Secretary-General Ban Ki-moon launched a new program. The "Global Strategy for Women's and Children's Health" emphasizes attaining the goals through the lens of women's and children's health (Goals 4 and 5). The strategy targets 16 million women and children, using $40 million pledged by governments and private aid organizations.

- Eradicate extreme poverty and hunger (Mdg 1). Poverty contributes to unintended pregnancies and pregnancy-related mortality and morbidity in adolescent girls and women, and under-nutrition and other nutrition-related factors contribute to 35% of deaths of children under five each year, while also affecting women's health. Charging people less for health services reduces poverty and makes women and children more willing to seek care. Further efforts at the community level must make nutritional interventions (such as exclusive breastfeeding for six months, use of micronutrient supplements and deworming) a routine part of care.

- Achieve universal primary education (Mdg 2). Gender parity in education is still to be achieved. It is essential because educated girls and women improve prospects for the whole family, helping to break the cycle of poverty. In Africa, for example, children whose mothers have been educated for at least five years are 40% more likely to live beyond the age of five. Schools can serve as a point of contact for women and children, allowing health-related information to be shared, services offered and health literacy promoted.

- Promote gender equality and empower women (Mdg 3). Empowerment and gender equality improve the health of women and children by increasing reproductive choices, reducing child marriages and tackling discrimination and gender-based violence. Partners should look for opportunities to coordinate their advocacy and educational programs (including those for men and boys) with organizations focusing on gender equality. Shared programs might include family-planning services, health education services, and systems to identify women at risk of domestic violence.

- Combat HIV/AIDS, malaria and other diseases (Mdg 6). Many women and children die needlessly from diseases that we have the tools to prevent and treat. In Africa, reductions in maternal and childhood mortality have been achieved by effectively treating HIV/AIDS, preventing mother-to-child transmission (PMTCT) of HIV and preventing and treating malaria. We should coordinate efforts on such interventions by, for example, integrating PMTCT into maternal and child health services and ensuring that mothers who bring children for immunization are offered other essential interventions.

* Ensure environmental sustainability – safe drinking water and sanitation (Mdg 7). Dirty water and inadequate sanitation cause diseases such as diarrhea, typhoid, cholera and dysentery, especially among pregnant women, so sustainable access to safe drinking water and adequate sanitation is critical. Community-based health efforts must educate women and children about sanitation and must improve access to safe drinking water.

* Develop a global partnership for development (Mdg 8). Global partnership and the sufficient and effective provision of aid and financing are essential. In addition, collaboration with pharmaceutical companies and the private sector must continue to provide access to affordable, essential drugs as well as to bring the benefits of new technologies and knowledge to those who need them most.

Source: Excerpted from press release and Web site, The Global Strategy for Women's and Children's Health, New York, 22 September 2010. Available online. URL: http://www.un.org/sg/globalstrategy.shtml. Accessed December 28, 2010.

INTERNATIONAL TREATIES

International Agreement for the Suppression of the "White Slave Traffic" (May 18, 1904) (excerpt)

The following international agreement signed on May 18, 1904, in Paris, France, and entered into force July 18, 1905, with oversight by the French Republic, is one of the first documented attempts by an international body to deal with human trafficking, specifically of women and children. A protocol later amended the agreement at Lake Success, New York, in May 1949, when responsibilities were shifted to the newly founded United Nations and its attorney-general.

Being desirous of securing to women of full age who have suffered abuse or compulsion, as also to women and girls under age, effective protection against the criminal traffic known as the "White Slave Traffic," have decided to conclude an Agreement with a view to concerting measures calculated to attain this object, and have appointed as their Plenipotentiaries, that is to say:

Who, having exchanged their full powers, found in good and due form, have agreed upon the following provisions:

Article 1

Each of the Contracting Governments undertakes to establish or name some authority charged with the coordination of all information relative to the procuring of women or girls for immoral purposes abroad; this authority shall be empowered to correspond direct with the similar department established in each of the other Contracting States.

Article 2

Each of the Governments undertakes to have a watch kept, especially in railway stations, ports of embarkation, and en route, for persons in charge of women and girls destined for an immoral life. With this object instructions shall be given to the officials, and all other qualified persons, to obtain, within legal limits, all information likely to lead to the detection of criminal traffic.

The arrival of persons who clearly appear to be the principals, accomplices in, or victims of, such traffic shall be notified, when it occurs, either to the authorities of the place of destination, or to the diplomatic or consular agents interested, or to any other competent authorities.

Article 3

The Governments undertake, when the case arises, and within legal limits, to have the declarations taken of women or girls of foreign nationality who are prostitutes, in order to establish their identity and civil status, and to discover who has caused them to leave their country. The information obtained shall be communicated to the authorities of the country of origin of the said women and girls, with a view to their eventual repatriation.

The Governments undertake, within legal limits, and as far as can be done, to entrust temporarily, and with a view to their eventual repatriation, the victims of a criminal traffic when destitute to public or private charitable institutions, or to private individuals offering the necessary security.

The Governments also undertake, within legal limits, and as far as possible, to send back to their country of origin those women and girls who desire it, or who may be claimed by persons exercising authority over them. Repatriation shall only take place after agreement as to identity and nationality, as well as place and date of arrival at the frontiers. Each of the Contracting Countries shall facilitate transit through its territory.

Correspondence relative to repatriation shall be direct as far as possible.
Article 4

Where the woman or girl to be repatriated cannot herself repay the
cost of transfer, and has neither husband, relations, nor guardian to pay
for her, the cost of repatriation shall be borne by the country where she
is in residence as far as the nearest frontier or port of embarkation in the
direction of the country of origin, and by the country of origin as regards
the rest.

Source: Excerpted from the International Agreement for the Suppression of the White Slave Traffic. Available online.
URL: http://www1.umn.edu/humanrts/instree/whiteslavetraffic1904.html. Accessed December 28, 2010.

The Universal Declaration of Human Rights (1948) (excerpt)

*After World War II and the founding of the United Nations as a mediator for
world peace, the U.S. delegate, Eleanor Roosevelt, chaired the newly formed
UN Commission on Human Rights in June 1946. The horrors of the Nuremberg
trials of Nazi war criminals and recent war experiences fueled the involvement
of several countries and international nongovernmental organizations in the
process of defining human rights and championing human dignity. Adopted
by the General Assembly on December 10, 1948, without dissent upon presentation by Eleanor Roosevelt, the declaration established human rights standards and norms. Although the declaration was intended to be nonbinding,
through time its various provisions have become so respected by states that it
can now be said to be customary international law. Eleanor Roosevelt's words
resounded: "The destiny of human rights is in the hands of all our citizens in
all our communities."*

Whereas the peoples of the United Nations have in the Charter reaffirmed
their faith in fundamental human rights, in the dignity and worth of the human
person and in the equal rights of men and women and have determined to
promote social progress and better standards of life in larger freedom,

Whereas Member States have pledged themselves to achieve, in cooperation with the United Nations, the promotion of universal respect for and
observance of human rights and fundamental freedoms,

Whereas a common understanding of these rights and freedoms is of
the greatest importance for the full realization of this pledge,

Now, therefore,

The General Assembly proclaims

This Universal Declaration of Human Rights

as a common standard of achievement for all peoples and all nations, to the end that every individual and every organ of society, keeping this Declaration constantly in mind, shall strive by teaching and education to promote respect for these rights and freedoms and by progressive measures, national and international, to secure their universal and effective recognition and observance, both among the peoples of Member States themselves and among the peoples of territories under their jurisdiction.

Article 2

Everyone is entitled to all the rights and freedoms set forth in this Declaration, without distinction of any kind, such as race, colour, sex, language, religion, political or other opinion, national or social origin, property, birth or other status.

Furthermore, no distinction shall be made on the basis of the political, jurisdictional or international status of the country or territory to which a person belongs, whether it be independent, trust, non-self-governing or under any other limitation of sovereignty.

Article 3

Everyone has the right to life, liberty and security of person.

Article 4

No one shall be held in slavery or servitude; slavery and the slave trade shall be prohibited in all their forms.

Article 5

No one shall be subjected to torture or to cruel, inhuman or degrading treatment or punishment.

Article 6

Everyone has the right to recognition everywhere as a person before the law.

Article 7

All are equal before the law and are entitled without any discrimination to equal protection of the law. All are entitled to equal protection against any discrimination in violation of this Declaration and against any incitement to such discrimination. . . .

Article 16

(1) Men and women of full age, without any limitation due to race, nationality or religion, have the right to marry and to found a family. They are entitled to equal rights as to marriage, during marriage and at its dissolution.

(2) Marriage shall be entered into only with the free and full consent of the intending spouses.

(3) The family is the natural and fundamental group unit of society and is entitled to protection by society and the State.

Article 17

(1) Everyone has the right to own property alone as well as in association with others.

(2) No one shall be arbitrarily deprived of his property.

Source: Excerpted from The Universal Declaration of Human Rights. Available online. URL: http://www.udhr.org/ UDHR/default.htm. Accessed December 28, 2010.

UN Convention on the Elimination of All Forms of Discrimination against Women (CEDAW) (1981) (excerpt)

CEDAW was adopted in 1979 and entered into force September 3, 1981. It became the first legally binding international document prohibiting discrimination against women and obligating governments to take affirmative steps to advance the equality of women. A group of over 190 national nongovernmental organizations engaged in outreach and education in December 1979 to eliminate discrimination against women. Often referred to as "The Treaty for the Rights of Women" or as an international "Bill of Rights" for women, the treaty in its preamble and 30 articles defines what constitutes discrimination against women in the form of sex trafficking, illiteracy, maternal mortality, HIV/AIDS exposure, domestic violence, political and legal rights, and FGM. It also includes in it provisions that set up an agenda for national action to end such discrimination. The treaty required regular progress reports from ratifying countries, but it did not impose any changes in existing laws or require new laws of countries ratifying the treaty. It laid out models for achieving equality but contained no enforcement authority. As of October 2010, the treaty still awaits ratification by the United States, although it has been ratified by 179 other nations, including Afghanistan and China. The treaty is awaiting approval by a two-thirds vote in the U.S. Senate (67 votes of 100). Ratification does not require consideration by the House of Representatives. The treaty is in the U.S. Senate Foreign Relations Committee, where it has been awaiting review by the presidential administration and Justice Department, the State Department having already concurred that it is "generally desirable and should be ratified." More than 190 U.S. religious, civic, and community organizations have shown support, including the American Association of Retired Persons (AARP), American Nurses Association, National Education Association, National Coalition of Catholic Nuns, American Bar Association, United Methodist Church, Young Women's Christian Association (YWCA), and Amnesty International.

WOMEN'S RIGHTS

The States Parties to the present Convention,

Noting that the Charter of the United Nations reaffirms faith in fundamental human rights, in the dignity and worth of the human person and in the equal rights of men and women,

Noting that the Universal Declaration of Human Rights affirms the principle of the inadmissibility of discrimination and proclaims that all human beings are born free and equal in dignity and rights and that everyone is entitled to all the rights and freedoms set forth therein, without distinction of any kind, including distinction based on sex,

Noting that the States Parties to the International Covenants on Human Rights have the obligation to ensure the equal rights of men and women to enjoy all economic, social, cultural, civil and political rights,

Considering the international conventions concluded under the auspices of the United Nations and the specialized agencies promoting equality of rights of men and women,

Noting also the resolutions, declarations and recommendations adopted by the United Nations and the specialized agencies promoting equality of rights of men and women,

Concerned, however, that despite these various instruments extensive discrimination against women continues to exist,

Recalling that discrimination against women violates the principles of equality of rights and respect for human dignity, is an obstacle to the participation of women, on equal terms with men, in the political, social, economic and cultural life of their countries, hampers the growth of the prosperity of society and the family and makes more difficult the full development of the potentialities of women in the service of their countries and of humanity,

Concerned that in situations of poverty women have the least access to food, health, education, training and opportunities for employment and other needs,

Convinced that the establishment of the new international economic order based on equity and justice will contribute significantly towards the promotion of equality between men and women,

Emphasizing that the eradication of apartheid, all forms of racism, racial discrimination, colonialism, neo-colonialism, aggression, foreign occupation and domination and interference in the internal affairs of States is essential to the full enjoyment of the rights of men and women,

Affirming that the strengthening of international peace and security, the relaxation of international tension, mutual co-operation among all States irrespective of their social and economic systems, general and complete disarmament, in particular nuclear disarmament under strict and effective international control, the affirmation of the principles of justice, equality and mutual benefit in relations among countries and the realization of the right of peoples under alien and colonial domination and foreign occupation to self-determination and independence, as well as respect for national sovereignty and territorial integrity, will promote social progress and development and as a consequence will contribute to the attainment of full equality between men and women,

Convinced that the full and complete development of a country, the welfare of the world and the cause of peace require the maximum participation of women on equal terms with men in all fields,

Bearing in mind the great contribution of women to the welfare of the family and to the development of society, so far not fully recognized, the social significance of maternity and the role of both parents in the family and in the upbringing of children, and aware that the role of women in procreation should not be a basis for discrimination but that the upbringing of children requires a sharing of responsibility between men and women and society as a whole,

Aware that a change in the traditional role of men as well as the role of women in society and in the family is needed to achieve full equality between men and women,

Determined to implement the principles set forth in the Declaration on the Elimination of Discrimination against Women and, for that purpose, to adopt the measures required for the elimination of such discrimination in all its forms and manifestations, . . .

Source: Excerpted from the Convention on the Elimination of All Forms of Discrimination against Women. Available online. URL: http://www.un.org/womenwatch/daw/cedaw. Accessed December 28, 2010.

Achieving Women's Rights: Beijing Declaration and Platform for Action (1995) (excerpt)

Presented and agreed to at the United Nations's fourth world conference on women in Beijing, China, in 1995, the Beijing Declaration and Platform for Action symbolized an international plan for the 189 participating governments who adopted the statement for achieving women's rights and empowerment and served as an agenda for the next 20 years. The declaration identified 12 specific directives for international organizations, national organizations and institutions, and governments to achieve the commitments of the Beijing Declaration, with poverty, education and training, health, and violence against women top priorities. The countries acknowledged that dealing with the issues of violence against women, reproductive control, and poverty was key to progress. The Platform for Action made the public aware of the important economic role that women workers play, including domestic workers, who contribute their remittance to the economy of their countries of origin and participate in the labor force of the country of destination. The participating governments are now held accountable for their follow-up actions by submitting yearly reports to the United Nations and providing international cooperation among agencies.

Chapter III
CRITICAL AREAS OF CONCERN

43. The advancement of women and the achievement of equality between women and men are a matter of human rights and a condition for social justice and should not be seen in isolation as a women's issue. They are the only way to build a sustainable, just and developed society. Empowerment of women and equality between women and men are prerequisites for achieving political, social, economic, cultural and environmental security among all peoples.

44. Most of the goals set out in the Nairobi Forward-looking Strategies for the Advancement of Women have not been achieved. Barriers to women's empowerment remain, despite the efforts of Governments, as well as non-governmental organizations and women and men everywhere. Vast political, economic and ecological crises persist in many parts of the world. Among them are wars of aggression, armed conflicts, colonial or other forms of alien domination or foreign occupation, civil wars and terrorism. These situations, combined with systematic or de facto discrimination, violations of and failure to protect all human rights and fundamental freedoms of all women, and their civil, cultural, economic, political and social rights, including the right to development and ingrained prejudicial attitudes towards women and girls are but a few of the impediments encountered since the World Conference to Review and Appraise the Achievements of the United Nations Decade for Women: Equality, Development and Peace, in 1985.

45. A review of progress since the Nairobi Conference highlights special concerns—areas of particular urgency that stand out as priorities for action. All actors should focus action and resources on the strategic objectives relating to the critical areas of concern which are, necessarily, interrelated, interdependent and of high priority. There is a need for these actors to develop and implement mechanisms of accountability for all the areas of concern.

46. To this end, Governments, the international community and civil society, including non-governmental organizations and the private sector, are called upon to take strategic action in the following critical areas of concern:

—The persistent and increasing burden of poverty on women

—Inequalities and inadequacies in and unequal access to education and training

—Inequalities and inadequacies in and unequal access to health care and related services

—Violence against women

—The effects of armed or other kinds of conflict on women, including those living under foreign occupation

—Inequality in economic structures and policies, in all forms of productive activities and in access to resources

—Inequality between men and women in the sharing of power and decision-making at all levels

—Insufficient mechanisms at all levels to promote the advancement of women

—Lack of respect for and inadequate promotion and protection of the human rights of women

—Stereotyping of women and inequality in women's access to and participation in all communication systems, especially in the media

—Gender inequalities in the management of natural resources and in the safeguarding of the environment

—Persistent discrimination against and violation of the rights of the girl child

Source: Excerpted from the Beijing Declaration and Platform for Action. Available online. URL: http://www.un.org/geninfo/ bp/women.html. Accessed December 28, 2010.

UN Resolution 1325 on Women, Peace and Security (October 2000) (excerpt)

On October 31, 2000, the United Nations Security Council unanimously adopted Resolution 1325 on women, peace, and security. Resolution 1325 represented the first time the Security Council addressed the disproportionate and unique impact of armed conflict on women; recognized the undervalued and underutilized contributions women make to conflict prevention, peace-keeping, conflict resolution, and peace building; and stressed the importance of their equal and full participation as active agents in peace and security.

WOMEN'S RIGHTS

The Security Council,

Recalling its resolutions 1261 (1999) of 25 August 1999, 1265 (1999) of 17 September 1999, 1296 (2000) of 19 April 2000 and 1314 (2000) of 11 August 2000,

as well as relevant statements of its President, and recalling also the statement of its President to the press on the occasion of the United Nations Day for Women's Rights and International Peace (International Women's Day) of 8 March 2000 (SC/6816),

Recalling also the commitments of the Beijing Declaration and Platform for Action (A/52/231) as well as those contained in the outcome document of the twenty-third Special Session of the United Nations General Assembly entitled "Women 2000: Gender Equality, Development and Peace for the Twenty-First Century" (A/S-23/10/Rev.1), in particular those concerning women and armed conflict,

Bearing in mind the purposes and principles of the Charter of the United Nations and the primary responsibility of the Security Council under the Charter for the maintenance of international peace and security,

Expressing concern that civilians, particularly women and children, account for the vast majority of those adversely affected by armed conflict, including as refugees and internally displaced persons, and increasingly are targeted by combatants and armed elements, and recognizing the consequent impact this has on durable peace and reconciliation,

Reaffirming the important role of women in the prevention and resolution of conflicts and in peace-building, and stressing the importance of their equal participation and full involvement in all efforts for the maintenance and promotion of peace and security, and the need to increase their role in decision-making with regard to conflict prevention and resolution,

Reaffirming also the need to implement fully international humanitarian and human rights law that protects the rights of women and girls during and after conflicts,

Emphasizing the need for all parties to ensure that mine clearance and mine awareness programmes take into account the special needs of women and girls,

Recognizing the urgent need to mainstream a gender perspective into peacekeeping operations, and in this regard noting the Windhoek Declaration and the Namibia Plan of Action on Mainstreaming a Gender Perspective in Multidimensional Peace Support Operations

Recognizing also the importance of the recommendation contained in the statement of its President to the press of 8 March 2000 for specialized training for all peacekeeping personnel on the protection, special needs and human rights of women and children in conflict situations,

Recognizing that an understanding of the impact of armed conflict on women and girls, effective institutional arrangements to guarantee their protection and full participation in the peace process can significantly contribute to the maintenance and promotion of international peace and security,

Noting the need to consolidate data on the impact of armed conflict on women and girls,

1. Urges Member States to ensure increased representation of women at all decision-making levels in national, regional and international institutions and mechanisms for the prevention, management, and resolution of conflict;

2. Encourages the Secretary-General to implement his strategic plan of action (A/49/587) calling for an increase in the participation of women at decision making levels in conflict resolution and peace processes;

3. Urges the Secretary-General to appoint more women as special representatives and envoys to pursue good offices on his behalf, and in this regard calls on Member States to provide candidates to the Secretary-General, for inclusion in a regularly updated centralized roster;

4. Further urges the Secretary-General to seek to expand the role and contribution of women in United Nations field-based operations, and especially among military observers, civilian police, human rights and humanitarian personnel;

5. Expresses its willingness to incorporate a gender perspective into peacekeeping operations, and urges the Secretary-General to ensure that, where appropriate, field operations include a gender component;

6. Requests the Secretary-General to provide to Member States training guidelines and materials on the protection, rights and the particular needs of women, as well as on the importance of involving women in all peacekeeping and peacebuilding measures, invites Member States to incorporate these elements as well as HIV/AIDS awareness training into their national training programmes for military and civilian police personnel in preparation for deployment, and further requests the Secretary-General to ensure that civilian personnel of peacekeeping operations receive similar training;

7. Urges Member States to increase their voluntary financial, technical and logistical support for gender-sensitive training efforts, including those undertaken by relevant funds and programmes, inter alia, the United Nations Fund for Women and United Nations Children's Fund, and by the Office of the United Nations High Commissioner for Refugees and other relevant bodies;

8. Calls on all actors involved, when negotiating and implementing peace agreements, to adopt a gender perspective, including, inter alia:

(a) The special needs of women and girls during repatriation and resettlement and for rehabilitation, reintegration and post-conflict reconstruction;

(b) Measures that support local women's peace initiatives and indigenous processes for conflict resolution, and that involve women in all of the implementation mechanisms of the peace agreements;

(c) Measures that ensure the protection of and respect for human rights of women and girls, particularly as they relate to the constitution, the electoral system, the police and the judiciary;

9. Calls upon all parties to armed conflict to respect fully international law applicable to the rights and protection of women and girls, especially as civilians, in particular the obligations applicable to them under the Geneva Conventions of 1949 and the Additional Protocols thereto of 1977, the Refugee Convention of 1951 and the Protocol thereto of 1967, the Convention on the Elimination of All Forms of Discrimination against Women of 1979 and the Optional Protocol thereto of 1999 and the United Nations Convention on the Rights of the Child of 1989 and the two Optional Protocols thereto of 25 May 2000, and to bear in mind the relevant provisions of the Rome Statute of the International Criminal Court;

10. Calls on all parties to armed conflict to take special measures to protect women and girls from gender-based violence, particularly rape and other forms of sexual abuse, and all other forms of violence in situations of armed conflict;

11. Emphasizes the responsibility of all States to put an end to impunity and to prosecute those responsible for genocide, crimes against humanity, and war crimes including those relating to sexual and other violence against women and girls, and in this regard stresses the need to exclude these crimes, where feasible from amnesty provisions;

12. Calls upon all parties to armed conflict to respect the civilian and humanitarian character of refugee camps and settlements, and to take into account the particular needs of women and girls, including in their design, and recalls its resolutions 1208 (1998) of 19 November 1998 and 1296 (2000) of 19 April 2000;

13. Encourages all those involved in the planning for disarmament, demobilization and reintegration to consider the different needs of female and male ex-combatants and to take into account the needs of their dependants;

14. Reaffirms its readiness, whenever measures are adopted under Article 41 of the Charter of the United Nations, to give consideration to their potential impact on the civilian population, bearing in mind the special

needs of women and girls, in order to consider appropriate humanitarian exemptions;

15. Expresses its willingness to ensure that Security Council missions take into account gender considerations and the rights of women, including through consultation with local and international women's groups;

16. Invites the Secretary-General to carry out a study on the impact of armed conflict on women and girls, the role of women in peace-building and the gender dimensions of peace processes and conflict resolution, and further invites him to submit a report to the Security Council on the results of this study and to make this available to all Member States of the United Nations;

17. Requests the Secretary-General, where appropriate, to include in his reporting to the Security Council progress on gender mainstreaming throughout peacekeeping missions and all other aspects relating to women and girls;

18. Decides to remain actively seized of the matter.

Source: Excerpted from the United Nations Security Council Resolution 1325 on Women, Peace and Security. Available online. URL: http://www.un.org/events/res_1325e.pdf. Accessed January 12, 2011.

2006 Political Declaration on HIV/AIDS (excerpt)

In pursuit of Millennium Development Goal 6, Combat HIV/AIDS, malaria & other diseases, member states agreed to the United Nations 2001 Declaration of Commitment, calling for them to file country progress reports to the General Assembly every two years through the UNAIDS Secretariat. By June 2006, UN member states unanimously adopted "Political Declaration on HIV/AIDS" at the close of the United Nations General Assembly high-level meeting on AIDS, in response to the need to escalate response efforts toward universal access to HIV prevention, treatment, care, and support.

1. We, Heads of State and Government and representatives of States and Governments participating in the comprehensive review of the progress achieved in realizing the targets set out in the Declaration of Commitment on HIV/AIDS, held on 31 May and 1 June 2006, and the High-Level Meeting, held on 2 June 2006;

2. Note with alarm that we are facing an unprecedented human catastrophe; that a quarter of a century into the pandemic, AIDS has inflicted immense suffering on countries and communities throughout the world; and that more than 65 million people have been infected with HIV, more than 25 million people have died of AIDS, 15 million children have been orphaned by AIDS

and millions more made vulnerable, and 40 million people are currently living with HIV, more than 95 per cent of whom live in developing countries;

3. Recognize that HIV/AIDS constitutes a global emergency and poses one of the most formidable challenges to the development, progress and stability of our respective societies and the world at large, and requires an exceptional and comprehensive global response;

4. Acknowledge that national and international efforts have resulted in important progress since 2001 in the areas of funding, expanding access to HIV prevention, treatment, care and support and in mitigating the impact of AIDS, and in reducing HIV prevalence in a small but growing number of countries, and also acknowledge that many targets contained in the Declaration of Commitment on HIV/AIDS have not yet been met;

5. Commend the Secretariat and the Co-sponsors of the Joint United Nations Programme on HIV/AIDS for their leadership role on HIV/AIDS policy and coordination, and for the support they provide to countries through the Joint Programme;

6. Recognize the contribution of, and the role played by, various donors in combating HIV/AIDS, as well as the fact that one third of resources spent on HIV/AIDS responses in 2005 came from the domestic sources of low- and middle income countries, and therefore emphasize the importance of enhanced international cooperation and partnership in our responses to HIV/AIDS worldwide;

7. Remain deeply concerned, however, by the overall expansion and feminization of the pandemic and the fact that women now represent 50 per cent of people living with HIV worldwide and nearly 60 per cent of people living with HIV in Africa, and in this regard recognize that gender inequalities and all forms of violence against women and girls increase their vulnerability to HIV/AIDS;

8. Express grave concern that half of all new HIV infections occur among children and young people under the age of 25, and that there is a lack of information, skills and knowledge regarding HIV/AIDS among young people;

9. Remain gravely concerned that 2.3 million children are living with HIV/AIDS today, and recognize that the lack of paediatric drugs in many countries significantly hinders efforts to protect the health of children;

10. Reiterate with profound concern that the pandemic affects every region, that Africa, in particular sub-Saharan Africa, remains the worst-affected region, and that urgent and exceptional action is required at all levels to curb the devastating effects of this pandemic, and recognize the renewed commitment by African Governments and regional institutions to scale up their own HIV/AIDS responses; . . .

Source: Excerpted from Resolution 60/262. Political Declaration on HIV/AIDS. June 15, 2006. Available online. URL: http://data.unaids.org/pub/Report/2006/20060615_hlm_politicaldeclaration_ares60262_en.pdf. Accessed December 28, 2010.

Links between Poverty and Gender Inequality: 2010 World Summit Outcome (September 17, 2010) (excerpt)

The Millennium Declaration adopted by the General Assembly in 2000 was proof that world leaders recognized the link between poverty and gender inequality and acknowledged the central role of gender equality in combating poverty and hunger and stimulating sustainable development. By 2010, it had become clear that unless women's economic security is strengthened, progress toward the Millennium Development Goals would be limited. The following was excerpted from a presentation in September 2010 at the convening of the General Assembly's 65th session.

12. We recognize that gender equality, the empowerment of women, women's full enjoyment of all human rights and the eradication of poverty are essential to economic and social development, including the achievement of all the Millennium Development Goals. We reaffirm the need for the full and effective implementation of the Beijing Declaration and Platform for Action. Achieving gender equality and empowerment of women is both a key development goal and an important means for achieving all of the Millennium Development Goals. We welcome the establishment of the United Nations Entity for Gender Equality and the Empowerment of Women (UN Women), and pledge our full support for its operationalization. . . .

20. We acknowledge that much more needs to be done in achieving the Millennium Development Goals as progress has been uneven among regions and between and within countries. Hunger and malnutrition rose again from 2007 through 2009, partially reversing prior gains. There has been slow progress in reaching full and productive employment and decent work for all advancing gender equality and the empowerment of women, achieving environmental sustainability and providing basic sanitation, and new HIV

infections still outpace the number of people starting treatment. In particular, we express grave concern over the slow progress being made on reducing maternal mortality and improving maternal and reproductive health. Progress on other Millennium Development Goals is fragile and must be sustained to avoid reversal.

Source: Excerpted from "Keeping the Promise: United to Achieve the Millennium Development Goals." Available online. URL: http://www.un.org/en/mdg/summit2010/pdf/ZeroDraftOutcomeDocument_31May2010rev2.pdf. Accessed December 28, 2010.

FRANCE

"Departmental Observatory on Violence against Women" (2008) (excerpt)

This French case study was presented in 2008 at the International Centre for the Prevention of Crime's (ICPC's) 8th Annual Collequium on Crime Prevention, in Querétaro, Mexico, at which countries shared strategies and acknowledged women's safety as a global concern. The study was presented by the Departmental Observatory on Violence against Women in Seine-Saint-Denis, France, an agency created in 2002—the first of its kind—charged with the mission of coordinationg existing services and programs among the many French women's organizaitons. Ultimately, the agency's goal was to more effectively respond to the problem of violence against women through concrete actions and solutions.

In 2006, the Conseil Général de la Seine-Saint-Denis conducted a survey on sexist behaviours and violence against young girls (CSVF). A total of 1566 young women aged 18 to 21 years participated in the survey. Results showed that the rate of violence against young women was two to five times higher than the rate revealed in 2000 by a previous survey (ENVEFF). In addition, while the 2000 survey revealed that 68% of women surveyed reported never having spoken of the violence beforehand, the 2006 CSVF survey demonstrated that 68% of young girls had talked about the violence with other people. This was the first quantitative survey in France to look at sexist behaviours and violence against young women.

Objectives:

- Support collective efforts for putting an end to violence against women;

- Raise public awareness about violence against women.

In Seine-Saint-Denis, 1500 youths participated in an information and awareness-raising campaign to voice their ideas and to help reduce sexist and violent behaviours. The Observatoire des violences envers les femmes called upon the Mouvement français pour le planning familial 93 (the French movement for family planning 93) and its theatrical tool "Y = Y?". On stage is a person who is facing a problem but who cannot find help. The public participates by going on stage to replace the actor in need of help and to propose alternative actions or behaviours to overcome the dangerous situation. The other people on stage then react to the propositions made. This activity trains people how to react to this type of situation should they be faced with it in real life. 50 classes participated in the theatre exercise and each was asked to choose a representative to present their proposed alternative solutions to the vice-president of the Conseil général and to the conseillère régionale (regional counsellor) of Île-de-France. The campaign helped raise awareness of the problem and helped to adapt actions and find innovative solutions to violence against women.

Source: Excerpted from "Women's Safety: A Shared Global Concern—Compendium of Practices and Policies." International Centre for the Prevention of Crime, 2008, pp. 21–22 (footnotes deleted).

"Europe: No Cover Up; France Ponders a Burqa Ban" (2009)

The French government's 2004 decision to ban the Muslim head scarf in state schools, institutions, and other public buildings precipitated debates that have lasted several years. Another contest with French citizens over religious expression and women's rights in a secular state was spurred when a group of deputies called for a parliamentary inquiry into the wearing of the burqa (also called hijabs), with a view to a possible ban in all public places, referring to the burqas as "veritable walking prisons." In July 2010, the French National Assembly approved a bill to implement this law, sending it to a vote in the French Senate in September 2010, where it was passed. This article represents opposing views.

France's strict secularism, entrenched by law since 1905, keeps religion firmly out of the state sphere. There are no religious studies (let alone Nativity plays) in state schools, nor may public workers sport the headscarf. The government denies that such policies constrain religious freedom or are especially aimed at Islam. France welcomes private Muslim schools. Mosque-building is widespread. The 2004 headscarf ban outlawed "conspicuous" religious symbols of all faiths. Yet there are growing worries about the spread of hard-line Islamism in the heavily Muslim banlieues.

Now that Mr. Sarkozy has publicly condemned the burqa, the chances of a ban have risen sharply. Parliament has launched a cross-party mission to report back in six months. In fact, few women wear the full garment in France. But mayors of cities with big Muslim populations report a steady increase in numbers, due not to immigration but to its adoption by French-born women—often from North African countries where the burqa is not traditionally worn.

Mohammed Moussaoui, head of the official French Council of the Muslim Faith, has suggested that the inquiry would itself stigmatise Islam. A ban might be misunderstood abroad, and not only in the Muslim world. In his recent speech in Cairo, Barack Obama said that "it is important for Western countries to avoid impeding Muslim citizens from practising religion as they see fit—for instance, by dictating what clothes a Muslim woman should wear."

Not so, say many French politicians—including such prominent Muslims as Fadela Amara, the cities minister. The founder of a women's rights group, Ms Amara has called the burqa "a coffin that kills individual liberties," and a sign of the "political exploitation of Islam" . . .

Source: "Europe: No Cover Up; France Ponders a Burqa Ban," *Economist* (London), 391 no. 8,637 (June 27, 2009): 58.

CHINA

China's Population and Family Planning Law (2002) (excerpt)

This law was adopted at the 25th Session of the Standing Committee of the Ninth National People's Congress on December 29, 2001.

Chapter I. General provisions
    Article 1. This law is enacted, in accordance with the Constitution, so as to bring population into balance with social economic development, resources, and the environment: to promote family planning; to protect

citizens' legitimate rights and interests; to enhance family happiness, and to contribute to the nation's prosperity and social progress.

Article 2. China is a populous country. Family planning is a fundamental state policy.

The State shall adopt a comprehensive approach to controlling population size and improving socio-economical and public health characteristics of population.

The State shall rely on publicity and education, advances in science and technology, comprehensive services and the establishment and improvement of the incentive and social security systems to carry out the family planning program.

Article 3. Population and family planning programs shall act in concert with programs that expand women's educational and employment opportunities, enhance their health, and elevate their status.

Article 4. The People's Governments and staff at all levels implementing the family planning program shall act strictly within the law, enforcing it in a civil manner, and must not infringe on citizens' legitimate rights and interest.

The family planning administrative departments and their staff acting within the law are protected by law.

Article 5. The State Council shall exercise authority over the national population and family planning program. Local people's governments at all levels shall exercise authority over the population and family planning programs in their respective jurisdictions.

Article 6. The family planning administrative department of the State Council shall be in charge of the national family planning program and population programs related to family planning.

Family planning administrative departments of people's governments at county level and above shall be in charge of family planning programs and population programs related to family planning in their respective jurisdictions.

Other government administrative departments at county level and above shall be in charge of aspects of the population and family planning programs falling within their mandates.

Article 7. Social organizations such as Trade Unions, Communist Youth Leagues, Women's Federations, and Family Planning Associations; enterprises; institutions; and individual citizens shall assist the people's government in carrying out population and family planning programs.

Article 8. Organizations and individuals making outstanding achievements in the population and family planning programs shall be recognized and rewarded by the State.

Source: Excerpted from the Population and Family Planning Law of the People's Republic of China. China Population Publishing House, 2002. Available online. URL: http://www.unescap.org/esid/psis/population/database/poplaws/law_china/china%20pop%20and%20family%20planning.pdf. Accessed December 28, 2010.

Differing Viewpoints of Marriage: "Marry Me, Marry My Customs" (November 1, 2010) (excerpt)

With economic growth in China, new norms in social structures have established themselves, often colliding with deeply rooted values and traditions. Divorce in China has risen nearly tenfold in 30 years, from 28.5 per 10,000 couples in 1978, to 226.9 in 2008.

The last time Tan Xinya, native of Changde, Hunan Province, asked her newly-wed husband, a Wuhan resident, if he was prepared to buy their new home, his angry response was, "I don't care what the custom is in your ancestral home, if we're going to live in a house in Wuhan we should both pay for it."

To Tan's mind, buying the marital home is the responsibility of the groom's family. "I know it's a huge expense these days, but according to the customs I grew up with, my husband's family should buy our house and my family should furnish it," she explained. Tan has since asked her parents to share the cost of buying a house, but they are reluctant because it would mean loss of face. "If I'd married a man from my home city this would not have been a problem. But most of the husbands and wives we know of our age also come from different places," Tan said.

Marriages like Tan's, where husband and wife are registered residents of different cities or areas, are indeed becoming commonplace.

Almost 40% of the total marriages registered in 2009 were of spouses from different regions, according to the latest Shanghai Bureau of Civil Affairs (SBCA) statistics.

But cultural differences like those arising between Tan and her husband often make for hard matrimonial going. Having seen one marriage founder over housing, Tan is keen to make peace with her husband. "My friend is from Wuhan and her now ex-husband is from Tianjin. Her mother-in-law wanted them to move back to Tianjin but she refused. After months of terrible fights they couldn't agree, so they divorced." Tan said. In efforts to avoid a similar fate, Tan is trying to convince her parents to contribute to the cost of her new home. She admits that maintaining a marriage with a spouse from a different province is not easy.

Where to spend the National Day golden week caused a serious difference of opinion between Xiaoning, from northeastern Anshan, Liaoning Province and her husband Yi Bing, from southern Hunan Province. "We fought over whose parents we should visit for the holiday," Xiaoning said. Having lost, she spent the week in Hunan.

"Before we married, the idea of two people from different backgrounds living together seemed romantic. I know now that it's plain inconvenient," Xiaoning said.

Coming from either side of the broad north/south divide creates differences as fundamental as which staple food the happy couple should eat with their stir fry. "I grew up on wheaten foods, but Yi's staple food has always been rice," Xiaoning said. Such culinary preferences can eat away at the very foundations of a marriage. . . .

Source: News.xinhuanet.com. Translated and edited by womenofchina.cn. Available online. URL:http://www. womenofchina.cn/html/report/113727-1.htm. Accessed January 12, 2011.

AFGHANISTAN

"Afghan Women Debate the Terms of Their Future" (June 2002) (excerpt)

As in other developing countries, Afghan women are often the actors in a theater of conflict between past traditions and new roles for participating in the political life of their country.

KABUL, Afghanistan (WOMEN'S E-NEWS)—When at last she was welcomed under the tent of the loya jirga, the grand council convened to determine the future of Afghanistan's government, Rahima Jami decided to wear a headscarf knotted under her chin. A long coat hid the curves of her body.

Nasrine Gross had waited a long time to help determine the next two years of her country's government, too. She wore a black pants suit and tied her soft black hair in a ponytail.

"If you're wearing this because you really believe in it, I respect you, but if you feel you have to wear it, you should take it off," Gross told Jami. "I've chosen to keep my hair visible and I'm sure you respect that too."

The veiled Jami nodded but said, "If you just put on a small headscarf, it would be much better."

This significant discussion took place during the nine-day loya jirga that ended June 19. It was the first meeting of its kind since 1964, when then-king Mohammad Zahir Shah reformed the constitution to give women the right to vote, go to school and earn the same wages as men.

Source: Excerpted from "Afghan Women Debate the Terms of Their Future," by Fariba Nawa, Women's E-News, June 30, 2002. Available online. URL: http://www.womensenews.org/article.cfm/dyn/aid/956. Accessed December 28, 2010.

"New Rights, but Afghan Women Still May Face Forced Marriages" (March 2005) (excerpt)

Improving Afghanistan's vital statistics recordkeeping and updating the population census have been part of the achievements of the Women's Ministry. Still, resistance to new ways and challenges to being accountable for measured change is strongest where tradition continues.

KABUL—Fourteen-year-old Bibi has never seen the father who wants to sell her into marriage with a stranger.

She hid when he sent the police to her village home in northern Afghanistan a month ago. Her elder brother Kareem refused to hand her over and was dragged off to jail.

But Bibi found sanctuary with a sympathetic relative in Kabul, where she now lives in fear her father, divorced from her mother, will one day catch up with her.

The relative, Shahnoz, said the girl's father was not interested in finding a suitable mate for his daughter and only wanted to get his hands on the dowry she could command.

"She's like a check," said Shahnoz, whose husband is a first cousin of Bibi's mother. "She's beautiful and he wants to sell the girl for marriage,"

Bibi's story is far from unique. Despite the re-emergence of democracy and women's rights in Afghanistan, human rights officials say that between 60 percent and 80 percent of marriages in the country are forced on women.

In rural areas, "tradition is so powerful women feel they really are the property of male relatives. Whatever they are told, they obey," said Sima Samar, chairwoman of the Afghan Independent Human Rights Commission, the country's leading rights watchdog.

Girls and women are often wedded off for economic gain or to settle scores between feuding families, even though both practices run counter to civil and Islamic law.

While arranged marriages are normal in this conservative Muslim country, they are meant to have the consent of the bride and groom.

In Bibi's case the groom is a wealthy, older man looking for a second wife. Her relatives reckon he is willing to pay about $7,000 for her—a small fortune in one of the world's poorest countries. . . .

Fawzia Amini, deputy director of the law and rights department at the Ministry of Women's Affairs, said the department investigated about 500 cases a year of abuse against women, usually of husbands beating their wives.

She said victims could seek legal support for divorce, but such a step is so socially detrimental to the woman that it is usually better to try to force the husband to cooperate with the authorities and rescue the marriage. She said there were only 10 to 15 divorces last year in the family court in Kabul, a city of around 4 million people. "Our culture does not tolerate divorce. Divorced women will have a painful life. No one will care for them," Amini said. "There's no legal support for divorced women. Mostly they can't get a share of their dowry and they lose their children."

Source: Excerpted from "New Rights, but Afghan Women Still May Face Forced Marriages," *The International Herald Tribune/Associated Press,* March 15, 2005.

"New Gas Attack on Afghan Girls' School" (August 2010)

In Afghanistan's 35 years of war, a pattern emerges: Where achievements have been made, destruction soon follows. After a decade since the fall of the Taliban in December 2001, women and girls still need their rights to education and employment protected. Under threat of beatings by the Taliban's religious police for trying to receive an education, girls risk their lives going to school.

A girls' school in Kabul, Afghanistan was the target of a gas attack yesterday. The attack sickened 59 students and 14 teachers, reports CNN. Ruqia, a fifteen year old student at the school, said, "I smelled something very, very foul as I was sitting in my classroom. I saw my classmates falling down, my vision got blurred and I heard everyone screaming before I became unconscious," according to Agence France Presse. Doctors report that all of the victims should recover.

"This is not an accident. Similar incidents have happened in girls' schools before. We think there are groups who do not tolerate development and progress—their aim is to prevent girls from going to school," Afghan education ministry spokesman Asef Nang told Agence France Presse. He also said that this is the ninth such gas attack on a girls' school.

The Taliban are suspected to be behind the gas attacks, but the government has not confirmed or identified the perpetrator in the latest attack, according to Reuters.

In May 2010, there were two suspected gas attacks on girls schools in the northern Kunduz Province and in Kabul, Afghanistan's capital. Similarly, in April 2010, at least 88 schoolgirls and teachers became ill after suspected poison gas attacks at schools in Kunduz Province. In May 2009, more than 150 students were also hospitalized in similar attacks.

In Taliban-controlled areas of Afghanistan and Pakistan, violence against schools that educate girls has been a key part of campaigns against the education of women. In Pakistan's Swat Valley, more than 130 primarily all girl schools have been destroyed, probably by the Taliban. In total, hundreds of schools have been destroyed in Pakistan's northwest region over the past several years. During the Taliban regime in Afghanistan, which lasted until 2001, Afghan girls were forbidden to attend school. To date, more than 1,000 girls' or co-educational schools have been bombed or burned in Afghanistan.

Source: "New Gas Attack on Afghan Girls' School," CNN and Agence France Presse, August 25, 2010.

"Mother, Daughter Defy Violence to Run in Afghan Elections" (September 2010)

Living with the possibility of the Taliban regaining some form of control over their lives—whether over the country or as part of an integrated government—women are threatened at all levels of public service by different forms of gender-based violence, from rape to intimidation.

JALALABAD, Afghanistan—When Hawa Alam Nuristani ran for a seat in the Afghan parliament five years ago, gunmen ambushed her on a campaign visit to remote mountain villages and she survived a five-hour rescue on donkeys and her supporters' shoulders with blood oozing from a leg wound.

Last year, she escaped with minor injuries from a car bomb that exploded outside NATO's Kabul headquarters seconds after she'd dropped off her eldest daughter, Rana, who worked for the U.S.-led force's radio service. Rana was among the 91 people who were wounded; seven died.

Yet not only is Hawa Nuristani seeking re-election from Nuristan province in parliamentary elections Saturday, but Rana Nuristani also has followed her mother into the cutthroat arena of Afghan politics, running for one of 33 seats in Kabul province. If they prevail, the pair will make Afghan history as the first mother and daughter to enter the lower house of parliament together.

Many Afghans, however, fear that a repeat of the massive official vote-rigging and insurgent attacks that stained last year's presidential poll will mar Saturday's voting. Campaigning officially ended at midnight Thursday.

Mayhem reportedly flared Friday across Afghanistan. It included the death of a NATO soldier, insurgent attacks in two provincial capitals and the abductions of one candidate and 18 campaign staffers and election workers.

"Yes, I'm very concerned about Rana," said Hawa Nuristani, whose husband, a former army general with whom she had four daughters and a son, died two years ago. "This was her decision. When she told me that she was running for parliament, I didn't oppose it."

Hawa Nuristani decided not to risk campaigning this time in insurgency-racked Nuristan, one of the poorest, most rugged and least developed of Afghanistan's 34 provinces. Instead, she's relying on the efforts of surrogates who traveled to meet her in her home in the eastern city of Jalalabad, in Nangarhar province.

"It's impossible to go to Nuristan. If you campaign, you have to take off your burqa to speak," she said, referring to the body-covering shroud that Afghan women wear. "On the way back, it would be very risky because of the threat of bomb or rocket attack."

Rana Nuristani has had it easier in the relative safety of Kabul , distributing fliers and greeting people in downtown markets and on street corners, drawing gaggles of admiring young men in her wake. It was too dangerous to visit outlying areas, though—she canceled stops in two of them this week—and she's received numerous threatening telephone calls.

"They say, 'You are not a real Muslim girl. Your posters are all over the place. What gave you the right to do that?' " she recounted in the borrowed office that serves as her headquarters. She was referring to a belief among conservative Afghans that a woman should never show her unveiled face in public.

"God gave voting rights to females as well as males. If men can do something, why can't women? We have the same knowledge. We have the same ability," she recalled telling one threatening caller. "After a long discussion, he said he was so sorry, and he agreed to work for me." . . .

Source: "Mother, Daughter Defy Violence to Run in Afghan Elections," by Jonathan S. Landay, McClatchy Newspapers, Friday, September, 17, 2010.

DEMOCRATIC REPUBLIC OF THE CONGO

"Marriage Falls Victim to Congo's War" (Spring 2003) (excerpt)

War has put both genders at risk for forced marriages, breaks with traditional marriage customs, rape, and sexual violence—all of which shame families and whole villages, sometimes leading to the outcast of family members and suicide.

When businessman Etienne Ucoun Bralani counts the costs of Congo's civil war, it's not his looted stores or stolen cars that weigh most heavily on his heart.

His greatest loss, he says, are the two daughters who ran off with their boyfriends. They left without permission and without the traditional exchange of a dowry. In purely financial terms, their elopement cost him only 10 cows and 14 goats. But it is the blow to family and tradition, Mr. Bralani says, that hurts most.

"It's because of this war that boys and girls are marrying in such ways," he says. "In normal times, those boys would be punished for their disrespect. Just because we are at war doesn't mean we should tolerate such behavior."

The Congo's four-year civil war has killed some 3.3 million people. But the conflict has also destroyed families in subtler ways, tearing the fabric of culture and tradition that binds communities together. The most telling sign, people here say, is the wave of young couples who have eloped, violating centuries-old marriage customs.

"Most girls are just running away with the boys," says Marie-Therese Kavira, who has seen three sons leave with their girlfriends since the war began in 1998. "To find those who are respecting the traditional ways is very difficult."

As in other African countries, a marriage in Congo is cemented by the exchange of gifts. When a boy wants to marry a girl, their families negotiate a bride price—usually cows and goats, but sometimes money or cell phones.

The tradition, say women here, is not about selling the bride. Rather, it's a sign of respect showing that a husband values his new wife and can support his new family. The word for dowry in Swahili is *mali,* or "the worth."

These days, however, few families can afford to pay the mali. And young people, surrounded by war, see no reason to wait the months or years it may take to save for one. Nor is there much a family can do to stop lovers from eloping—the war has diminished the authority of traditional chiefs who once mediated such disputes. Other traditions, such as *umoja,* or "oneness," the belief that people should help their neighbors, is falling by the wayside as people struggle simply to survive.

Last month, when instability in Bunia closed schools and forced residents to flee, 18-year-old Anuarite Batolanza ran away with her boyfriend. Her parents wanted her to finish her studies, but she didn't see the point of waiting for schools that might never reopen.

"Because of the war, I thought we wouldn't study anymore—so many teachers and pupils had fled," she explains. "I love my husband and wanted to live with him."

Anuarite's mother warned her that she would be disowned over a man who would probably leave her for another woman. Such marriages, her mother said, were not blessed by God, and such wives were easily discarded. But Anuarite refused to return home.

Source: Excerpted from "Marriage Falls Victim to Congo's War," by Nicole Itano. *The Christian Science Monitor* (June 26, 2003). Available online. URL: http://www.csmonitor.com/2003/0626/p07s01-woaf.html. Accessed December 28, 2010.

"Africa: Women in Congo form common front for peace" (June 26, 2003) (excerpt)

From the Pretoria Peace Accord in December 2002 to the establishment of a new government in 2006, a transitional government was supposed to provide a path of political compromise between the warring groups in the DRC. Despite assistance by NGOs, integration of women into the peacemaking process was challenged by social imparities, ethnic attitudes, and inadequate donor funding.

... At the grassroots, women organizers of NGOs have poured efforts into familiarizing women with the peace process and informing them about electoral basics. Roughly half of all Congolese women are illiterate and do not participate in any decision affecting their society. Women hold an insignificant number of decision-making positions. ...

... That said, the priority today is building a culture of peace. Clashes in the northeastern Ituri region between three armed factions call into question cease-fire accords and hold back implementation of the Pretoria political accord. Women's organizations are actively engaged in keeping the DRC moving toward peace. In February a diverse group of 300 women, representing women's groups that had united to pressure warring parties to abide by the power-sharing pact, blocked traffic in the center of Kinshasa as they held a prayer vigil to protest reports of cannibalism in Ituri. "We condemn all crimes, no matter who committed them," said one of the demonstrators.

Source: Excerpted from "Africa: Women in Congo Form Common Front for Peace," by Marithe Kapinga. *Ms.* Spring 2003; p. 25.

Opening Statement of Henrietta Fore, USAID, at Fiscal Year 2009 Budget Hearing for Foreign Assistance (March 2008)

Excerpt from testimony by the U.S. director of foreign assistance and administrator of USAID, Henrietta H. Fore, before the Subcommittee on State, Foreign Operations, and Related Agencies Committee on Appropriations, United States Senate, on March 4, 2008. Fore was making an appeal for how aid funds are distributed to countries like the DRC.

Thank you for this opportunity to appear before the Committee today in support of the President's Fiscal Year (FY) 2009 Foreign Operations budget request and to discuss our nation's foreign assistance priorities. The degree of turmoil and poverty in the world right now poses both challenges and opportunities for our assistance programs and underscores the vital role of development in achieving our objectives. The dramatic election in Pakistan. The transfer of power in Cuba. Kosovo's declaration of independence. The safety concerns that so many of our staff and the staff of our partners face on a daily basis. The humanitarian crises in Darfur, Chad, West Bank Gaza, Iraq, Burma and Democratic Republic of Congo . . . to name a few. Never has foreign assistance been more critical to our national security, and to the citizens of the developing world.

The path from poverty to prosperity is a long one. Success can't be realized in a matter of months, by a single Administration, or by any one generation of development leadership. But already we have made progress this century. In 1981, 40 percent of the population of developing countries was in poverty. In 2004, that percentage had decreased to 18 percent and is projected to decline further, to 10 percent in 2015. According to Freedom House, by the end of 2007, the number of not free countries dropped from 59 in 1980 to 43, the number of partly free countries increased from 52 to 60, and the number of free countries increased from 51 to 90.

We are here today to talk about the FY 2009 Budget for Foreign Operations. As we discuss these numbers—which can often seem dry and abstract—it is important, as I know you are very aware, to remember what this funding will mean to our partners and recipients all around the world. The surest, truest compass point I know to remember the why of what we do is to see firsthand the people we serve. The Peruvian farmer in the highlands, the Malian girl who just attended her first day at school, the Sudanese family who found safety in a refugee camp, a youth activist in Ukraine, a young trafficking victim from Vietnam, a landmine victim in Lebanon, a Kyrgyz business woman looking to expand her business. These are the people we serve—those who have the least means and opportunity yet still yearn to build their lives, their nations and their futures. With that backdrop, I would like to describe some highlights of the President's Fiscal Year 2009 Foreign Operations request.

. . .

In Africa, we are committed to supporting peace keeping and counterterrorism efforts. The FY 2009 request includes $50 million in Peacekeeping Operations to complete the effort to transform the Liberian military, invest in building and transforming Southern Sudanese guerrilla forces into a conventional army, support peace in the Horn of Africa, and provide technical assistance and training to the Democratic Republic of the Congo to stabilize this volatile region. The $61 million total request in several accounts for the Trans Sahara Counterterrorism Partnership will facilitate coordination in countering terrorism between countries in West and North Africa.

The President's request also includes the Civilian Stabilization Initiative (CSI), designed to strengthen the U.S. Government's response to stabilization and reconstruction crises. While it is funded from the Department of State Operations budget, I would note that CSI provides for the creation of a 250-member interagency Active and 2,000 member Standby Response Corps, of which almost half will be based at USAID. Likewise, the U.S. Civilian Reserve Corps will allow the Secretary of State, and USAID as the development agency, to draw on expertise from citizens across the United States in municipal and local government, the private sector and non-governmental partners. Working closely with our Active and Standby Response Corps, these city managers, community police advisors, municipal utility engineers and other experts will allow us to put the right people in the right place at the right time when we need them most.

Finally, I would like to note that there have been concerns expressed among our partners in the NGO community that humanitarian funding has been reduced in the FY 2009 request. I want to assure the committee that this Administration supports America's proud tradition of helping those most in need when natural or man-made disaster strikes. As always with regard to humanitarian assistance accounts, additional requests for resources will be made during the course of the year, as the level of requirements becomes clearer. While I know that the PL 480 Title II appropriation is handled by a separate subcommittee, the funds requested for emergency food aid have a direct link to our overall development goals and other humanitarian assistance programs funded by this subcommittee. I look forward to engaging with this Committee to ensure that America continues its humanitarian leadership. . . .

Source:. Excerpted from Testimony of Henrietta H. Fore, U.S. Director of Foreign Assistance and Administrator of USAID, FY 2009 Budget Hearing for Foreign Assistance, Senate Appropriations Committee Subcommittee on State, Foreign Operations, and Related Agencies. Available online URL: http://appropriations.senate.gov/customcf/ uploads/4beca12b-f9b0-4165-aaa5-60d1ff50301b/2008_03_04_-State-_Opening_Statement_of_Henretta_ Fore_at_March_4_Hearing_on_USAID_Budget.pdf. Accessed January 12, 2011.

PART III

Research Tools

6

How to Research the Women's Rights Movement

TO BEGIN

Whether you are a student or professional researcher, a similar approach to investigating the U.S. and global women's movement can be used.

Start by consulting a variety of resources, using the following techniques and research suggestions:

- Get a general feeling for the topic by reading part I of this book, then review part II for primary documents and research resources referred to in part I.
- The chronology and glossary can make sense of events and issues encountered in part I.
- Browse through the many Web sites provided by organizations involved in women's issues, including both neutral ones and advocacy groups that support or criticize particular women's legislation. Their pages have current news, articles, and related links to other organizations that describe particular cases and discuss the pros and cons of various aspects.
- Use the relevant sections of the annotated bibliography to find more books, articles, online publications, and multimedia sources about specific topics.
- Find more current materials by using the Internet and bibliographic tools, such as the library, online catalogs, and periodical indexes.

WEB SITES AND ONLINE RESOURCES

The World Wide Web, or the Internet as it is commonly called, provides a vast network of resources at the fingertips of the researcher, where some basic keywords can gain access to significant, historical documents. On the other hand, anyone can publish on the Internet now, especially with the development of blogs, which are online diaries in which one can speak with authority on any subject. The one caution about the Web is always to check sources for validity and accuracy. Good questions to ask include the following:

- Who is responsible for this Web site?
- What is the background or reputation of the person or group?
- Does the person or group have a stated objective or agenda?
- What biases might this person or group have?
- Do a number of high-quality sites link to this one?
- What is the source given for a particular fact?
- Does that source actually say what is quoted?
- Where did they get their information?
- What is the date of the information?

WEB SITES

The following Web sites are recommended as good starting places for research. They offer well-organized overviews of issues, provide numerous resources and links, and answer frequently asked questions. Most are educational institution sites, government sites, or large intergovernmental organizations sites, often with areas focused specifically on gender balance or women's issues.

- U.S. CIA: https://www.cia.gov/library/publications/the-world-factbook

- U.S. Department of State: http://www.state.gov

- U.S. Census Bureau: http://factfinder.census.gov/home/saff/main.html?_lang=en
- U.S. government information through about.com: http://usgovinfo.about.com/od/censusandstatistics/index_a.htm
- The National Archives and Records Administration: http://ourdocuments.gov
- International Labour Organization: http://www.ilo.org/global/lang--en/index.htm
- World Health Organization: http://www.who.int/en
- Organisation for Economic Co-operation and Development (OECD): http://www.oecd.org

- Nongovernmental organizations at the United Nations: http://habitat.igc.org/ngo-rev/index.html
- United Nations Dag Hammarskjöld Library: http://www.un.org/Depts/dhl/resguide/r53.htm
- Interparliamentary Union: http://www.ipu.org
- UNICEF: http://www.unicef.org
- Institut National d'Études Démographiques (INED) is a French-based research institute that specializes in population studies: http://www.ined.fr/en/homepage_of_ined_website/

Educational Web sites host document archives and professional studies that are a useful source of statistical information on women's status in various domains:

- Center for American Woman and Politics: http://www.cawp.rutgers.edu/index.php
- The School of Industrial and Labor Relations (ILR) at Cornell University has an extensive collection of key workplace federal documents: http://digitalcommons.ilr.cornell.edu/key_workplace
- Michigan State University Documentary Library: http://www.lib.msu.edu

The following advocacy Web sites deal with and take positions on specific issues:

- PeaceWomen.org: http://www.peacewomen.org
- ReligiousTolerance.org: http://www.religioustolerance.org/fem_newf.htm
- Feminist Majority: http://www.feministmajority.org
- Human Rights Watch: http://www.hrw.org
- Amnesty International's extensive online document archive on human rights: http://www.amnesty.org

Media Web sites of national magazines, special-interest journals, and metropolitan newspapers can provide the most current information on activities, events, and legislation in the women's movement. Some may require a print subscription—or a less expensive online subscription—to access their archives:

- *U.S. News & World Report:* http://www.usnews.com
- *Time:* http://www.time.com/time

- *Wall Street Journal:* http://online.wsj.com/home-page
- *Washington Post:* http://www.washingtonpost.com
- *New York Times:* http://www.nytimes.com
- *International Herald Tribune:* http://global.nytimes.com/?iht
- *CNN:* http://www.cnn.com
- *USA TODAY:* http://www.usatoday.com
- *BBC NEWS:* http://www.bbc.com

With the United Nation's Millennium Development Goals of the past 10 years has come a much greater capacity for data collection and statistical research. Original submissions of country reports, which provide the data reported by the United Nations in its reports, are also becoming more available—making it possible to construe perceptions from primary research. Many organizations now offer direct access to their databases, providing tutorials and instructions on how to conduct searches ("query"). With this are often simple ways of saving one's search results to a variety of file formats (i.e., Excel, text, PDF) and even to generate graphs and tables. Here follows a sample:

- *OECD:* http://stats.oecd.org/Index.aspx?DatasetCode=CSP2010#
- *ILO:* http://laborsta.ilo.org
- *ILO:* Key Indicators of the Labour Market (KILM) http://kilm.ilo.org/KILMnetBeta/default2.asp
- *UNDESA:* http://unstats.un.org/unsd/databases.htm
- *UNData:* http://data.un.org/Default.aspx
- *IPU:* http://www.ipu.org/parline-e/parlinesearch.asp

SEARCH ENGINES

A search engine index offers a different type of searching, usually scanning through Web documents and indexing them by relevance to the keywords used. There are many search engines; the following are among the most widely used:

- AltaVista: http://www.altavista.com
- Bing: http://www.bing.com
- Dogpile: http://www.dogpile.com
- Excite: http://www.excite.com

- Google: http://www.google.com
- Hotbot: http://www.hotbot.com
- Lycos: http://www.lycos.com
- WebCrawler: http://www.webcrawler.com

When looking for a general topic that might be expressed with several different words or phrases, try using several descriptive words. The following search techniques may help:

- Use AND to narrow a search.
- Use OR to broaden a search.
- Use NOT to exclude unwanted results.
- Use quotes to search for a specific set of words.

Metasearch engines automate the process of submitting a keyword query to many search engines at the same time. There are new engines added frequently; the following are some of the well-known search tools:

- Answer: http://www.answers.com searches authoritative sites such as Columbia University Press and Merriam-Webster.
- Ask: http://www.ask.com (formerly Ask Jeeves) sorts by topic.
- Yippy: http://search.yippy.com sorts by topic and also searches news sources including Reuters.
- Info: http://www.info.com searches 14 different search engines and directories and integrates news feeds from Topix.net.
- IPL2: http://www.ipl.org is a consortium of librarian-selected Internet resources from around the United States.
- Teoma: http://www.teoma.com focuses on relevance and filters the topic findings.
- Metacrawler: http://www.metacrawler.com.
- SurfWax: http://www.surfwax.com.
- Copernic: http://www.copernic.com is a search utility that is downloaded and operated from the user's personal computer (PC) to gather Web references from the Internet.

The one drawback is that the many results can be overwhelming and generate an enormous list of unrelated references.

KEYWORDS

To search with a search engine, use keywords that include specific phrases, names, dates, and proper nouns. For example:

- Women's movement
- Women's history
- Women
- Working women
- Feminists
- Women clergy
- Feminism today
- Women voter statistics U.S. Census Bureau
- 1972 ERA
- Affirmative action China
- Denmark Equal Pay Act
- Afghanistan women
- Violence Against Women Congressional Hearing
- Female cutting
- ICCPR

These words should be accompanied by qualifiers such as *in the United States* or the name of the country to which the search pertains.

ORGANIZATIONS AND PEOPLE

Although much of what an organization has to offer can now be found on its Web site, it may also be useful to follow up with an in-person visit or phone call for further information.

Chapter 9 provides a list of organizations and agencies, and chapter 8 lists key players involved with research or advocacy concerning women's issues. News organizations also supply up-to-date information. The resource sites and Web portals mentioned earlier are good places to look for information and links to organizations or individuals.

When reading materials by an unfamiliar author, it is often useful to learn about that person's affiliation, credentials, and other achievements. There are several ways to find a person on the Internet:

- Try typing *contact information* and the person's name in a search engine, which may lead you to a paper he or she authored, his or her home page, or a biographical sketch put out by the institution for which the person works.

- Contact the person's employer (such as a university for an academic, or a corporation for a technical professional). Most such organizations have Web pages that include a searchable faculty or employee directory.

- A people-finder service, such as Yahoo! People Search (http://www. people. yahoo.com) may yield contact information, including an e-mail address, mail address, and/or phone number.

ONLINE DATABASES AND PERIODICAL INDEXES

Likewise, you may also be able to access abstracts and bibliographies through a library where you hold a card. IngentaConnect (http://www. ingentaconnect.com) is an index that contains brief descriptions about documents from journals in all disciplines. The complete documents can then be ordered with a credit card or obtained free at a local library.

Most public libraries subscribe to database services such as InfoTrac or EBSCO Host, which index articles from thousands of general-interest and specialized periodicals. This kind of database can be searched by author or by words in the title, subject headings, and sometimes words found anywhere in the article text. Depending on the database used, *hits* can produce a bibliographical citation (author, title, pages, periodical name, issue date, etc.), a citation and abstract, or the full text of the article. With InfoTrac, it is useful to view the list of newspapers and magazines covered, decide whether the search will cover all or a selection of them, and determine which years to include in the search.

Libraries often provide password-protected Internet or telnet access to their periodical databases from their public Web pages with the user's library card bar code number as the password. Ask your public or school librarian about databases and electronic resources with which they are affiliated.

The International Parliamentary Union allows users to conduct free bibliographic searches in their Women in Politics Bibliographic Database (http://www.ipu.org/bdf-e/BDFsearch.asp), complete with abstracts and Internet links to articles.

PRINT SOURCES

Although the Web sites are useful for quickly becoming acquainted with a topic, in-depth research can still require trips to the library or bookstore. Getting the most out of the library, in turn, requires the use of reference tools.

Magazines

Many articles can now be retrieved via online databases, such as findarticle. com, or in a library online consortium subscribing to InfoTrac or other online catalogs.

Articles about women's issues can be found in many kinds of publications, not just political or feminist sources. *Marie Claire,* a women's magazine known mostly for its fashion and grooming tips, published several articles on female genital mutilation that helped to draw attention to the dilemma in 2003. The November 2005 issue of *Elle* has a lengthy interview about women and the U.S. Army.

Library Catalogs

Most libraries maintain their holdings on computer. Many have adapted their systems to the Internet, making it possible for people who are not cardholders to survey their system from any location. The Library of Congress, the largest library in the United States, has a catalog that can be accessed at http://catalog.loc.gov. Yahoo! offers a categorized listing of libraries at http:// dir.yahoo.com/Reference/Libraries. Searches often depend on the system and whether it offers word searches that are "fuzzy" (editing words you may have entered and providing alternate findings) or exact.

A typical way to search catalogs is by category:

- Author—Try cross-referencing the first and last name, or just the last name.
- Title—Generally you need only use the first few words of the title, excluding initial articles (*a, an, the*).
- Keyword—Although it is more flexible than a title search, the search may fail if all keywords are not present.
- Subject—Search by subject headings assigned by the library with words that are not necessarily in the book's title.

Often systems list additional subject, title, and author headings that might be of interest to someone searching that item. If not, consider using some of the keywords or subject headings assigned to that book in a subsequent search.

Newspapers

Major metropolitan area newspapers, such as the *Washington Post, New York Times, Boston Globe,* and *Los Angeles Times,* often are a ready resource for articles with current perspectives on the topic. Most newspapers have Web sites with current news and features, offering recent articles from the past 15 to 30 days free, with earlier material found in the archives. It is common to have to pay for older articles, but it is worth checking with your local library about free online access to nationwide databases for cardholders. Also, if you know the e-mail address of the author, a request for the article might encourage him or her to send you a PDF file of the article.

If your library does not provide you access to one of the databases in which such articles can be obtained free, you can pay a fee of a few dollars to the publisher of the information for the complete article, or even buy access to articles at a discount within a specified time limit on the Web. Of course, back issues of newspapers and magazines can also be found in hard copy, bound, or on microfilm in local libraries.

Textbooks

Certain texts used in secondary education can be useful. Check with a reference librarian and consult the annotated bibliography in chapter 10.

Books

Library catalogs and online directories will direct you to books that complement your research into the subject.

For instance, *Desert Flower,* by Waris Dirie, although an autobiography, holds a tremendous amount of information about trafficking and prostitution of women as well as a detailed description of female genital mutilation.

Digital books are a relatively recent development in technology that can put books at the fingertips of readers. The search engine Google now has a partnership with a consortium of universities to make some of their holdings available in digital format at http://books.google.com/. Also, ask your librarian about other digital book projects within your state.

Many people have discovered that online bookstores such as Amazon (http://www.amazon.com) and Barnes & Noble (http://www.barnesand noble.com) provide convenient ways to shop for books. A less-known benefit of online bookstore catalogs is that they often include publishers' information, book reviews, and readers' comments about a given title. They can thus serve as a form of annotated bibliography.

Highly specialized materials and out-of-print books may also be checked in other online bookstores such as Alibris (http://www.alibris.com).

FILMS AND TELEVISION PROGRAMS

News discussion programs and movies are another way to perceive issues, with the facts conveyed through dramatizations or documentaries. The Internet Movie Database (http://www.imdb.com) contains current and past movies, along with synopses and details about the production.

A 2005 Lifetime for Women movie, *Human Trafficking,* dramatized the issue of human trafficking that heavily depends on the United States. An eloquent dramatization about a Zulu woman coping with HIV/AIDS in her rural South African village was the topic of an award-winning film made by HBO, *Yesterday,* in 2004, followed by a panel of experts who discussed the future of HIV as a national security threat.

Films and television documentaries that portray women's rights issues can be found in the annotated bibliography in chapter 10.

LEGAL RESEARCH

Legislation, or the making of laws, occurs at both the federal and state levels of government in the United States. News coverage of important cases in the general media may alert researchers about a case, but the specific court opinions or the text of decision or pending legislation is more reliable.

Federal legislation is compiled in the massive U.S. Code. The Government Printing Office (http://www.gpoaccess.gov) has links to the Code of Federal Regulations (which contains federal regulations that have been finalized), the Federal Register (which contains announcements of new federal agency regulations), the Congressional Record, the U.S. Code, congressional bills, a catalog of U.S. government publications, and other databases. It also provides links to individual agencies, grouped by government branch (legislative, executive, judicial) and regulatory agencies. Administrative decisions, core documents of U.S. history such as the U.S. Constitution, and federal Web sites are also listed.

The Internet provides ways to search laws and court cases easily by entering the name of the law, bill, or court case into a search engine. Cornell Law School (http://www.law.cornell.edu/uscode) provides a fast way to retrieve a law by its title and section citation and keywords.

U.S. treaties are equivalent in status to federal legislation, forming part of what the Constitution calls "the supreme Law of the Land." Treaties can be referred to by a number of different names: *international conventions, international agreements, covenants, final acts, charters, protocols, pacts, accords,* and *constitutions for international organizations.* Usually these different names have no legal significance in international law. Treaties may be bilateral (between two parties) or multilateral (among several parties), and a treaty is usually only binding on the parties to the agreement. Bilateral treaties usually enter into force when both parties agree to be bound as of a certain date. Treaties in force in the United States can be found online or through research indexes.

A uniform act is an act proposed by the Uniform Law. The National Conference of Commissioners on Uniform State Laws (NCCUSL) consists of lawyers and other professionals who work for the standardization of U.S. state laws but does not have any legislative power. A uniform act requires the approval of state legislatures to become legal.

The existence of uniform acts results in large part from the nature of the American federal system. The United States Congress does not have authority under the Constitution to legislate many issues, leaving many powers to state governments. At the same time, there is a desire to have consistent laws across the states.

Many state agencies have home pages that can be accessed through the Washburn University School of Law Library (http://www.washlaw.edu) or the Findlaw state resources Web site (http://www.findlaw.com). This site also has links to state law codes. These links may not provide access to the text of specific regulations, however.

To keep up with legislative changes, consult state and local advocacy groups for pending legislation. Chapter 9, "Organizations and Agencies," contains their contact information. International organizations such as UNIFEM will provide an international perspective on treaties and conventions, while groups such as the National Organization for Women or the Women's Political Caucus for legislation in the United States or the All-Women China Organization in China offer details on current national issues.

The Library of Congress Thomas Web site (http://thomas.loc.gov/home/abt_thom.html) includes files summarizing legislation by the number of the Congress (each two-year session of Congress has a consecutive number; for example, the 109th Congress was in session in 2005 and 2006). Legislation can be searched for by the name of its sponsor(s), the bill number, or topical keywords.

FINDING COURT DECISIONS

The way laws are interpreted is decided by the Supreme Court and state courts. As are laws, legal decisions are organized using a system of citations. The general form is as follows: *Party 1 v. Party 2* volume reporter [optional start page] (court, year).

Here is an example of a Supreme Court decision: *Roe v. Wade,* 410 U.S. 113(1973). The parties are Roe and Wade (the first listed is the plaintiff or appellant, the second the defendant). The plaintiff is a person who brings an action in a court of law, and the appellant is the party who challenges and appeals a decision from a lower court. The case is in volume 410 (the U.S. Supreme Court Reports), beginning on page 113, and the case was decided in 1973. (For the U.S. Supreme Court, the name of the court is omitted.)

A state court decision is identified by the state's name appearing in the title. In this example of a state court decision, 87 N.Y.2d 130, 637 N.Y.S.2d 964 (1995), two different books need to be consulted to find the case: on page 130 of volume 87 of the New York Reports, second series, and on page 964 of volume 637 of New York Supplement, second series. The case was decided in 1995.

The states call their books different names, so you may have to find out what the letters stand for in your state's case. For example, in *Aguinda et al. v. Texaco,* 142 F Supp. 2d 53 (SDNY 2001), the 142 F Supp. 2nd is the federal district court from which the case was transferred, but SDNY refers to the New York state court where it was first heard.

After the jurisdiction of a case has been decided, the researcher can then find cases by citation, names of the parties, or subject keywords on the Internet. Useful Web sites include the following:

- Justia U.S. Supreme Court Center (http://www.justia.us/index.html) offers updates of the latest Supreme Court decisions.
- The Legal Information Institute (http://www.law.cornell.edu/) has all Supreme Court decisions since 1990, plus 610 of the most important historic decisions.
- Washlaw Web (http://www.washlaw.edu) has a variety of court decisions (including states' decisions) and legal topics listed, making it a good starting place for many types of legal research.
- Visit http://www.landmarkcases.org for landmark Supreme Court case decisions.
- The OYEZ Project (http://www.oyez.org) of Northwestern University's Learning Technologies Group provides access to over 2,000 hours of

Supreme Court audio since 1995, with selective recordings from the period October 1955 to 1995.

Researchers who have access to a university or corporate library may be able to access two commercial legal databases, Lexis and Westlaw, which have extensive information and use detailed relational methods. A certain amount of training is required to use legal databases.

PLAGIARISM/CITING SOURCES/ COPYRIGHT INFRINGEMENT

With the growth of the Internet a host of plagiarism-related issues has evolved. The ability to cut and paste text from a variety of sources into a new document, though practical in the early phases of gathering research, needs to be monitored carefully.

Ultimately, the integrity of a work relies on a thoroughly researched and originally written work that cites its sources, either in the form of bibliography or some form of reference system (endnotes or footnotes), or both.

A number of court decisions have helped to develop an informal test to distinguish between fair use and infringement:

- Purpose and character of use (e.g., commercial, nonprofit educational)
- Nature of the copyrighted work
- Amount and substantiality of the portion used compared with the whole
- Impact on the market or value of the copyrighted work

Attributes that can flag a work as plagiarized from a pre-existing work:

- Similarly structured
- Slight modification of wording
- Quoted sentences without the quotes
- Citations with misleading reference information
- An assembly of citations with correct reference information, but no original thought.
- Abuse of "fair use" copyright

The quickest way to spot check one's work for originality is to enter a sentence into a search engine (e.g., Google) and see which of the research sources appear in the list. Publishers have access to even more sophisticated search engines that enable them to check whole works for plagiarism.

Web sites with useful guides on the subject include:

- http://www.plagiarism.org
- http://www.indiana.edu/~wts/pamphlets/plagiarism.shtml
- http://www.copyright.gov/fls/fl102.html

7

Facts and Figures

GLOBAL STATISTICS

1.1 Worldwide Women's Earnings as Percentage of Men's Earnings, 2006, by Region

	Female income as % of male income
East Asia and Pacific	60.0
Latin America and Caribbean	51.0
Europe and Central Asia	60.0
Middle East and North Africa	32.0
South Asia	41.0
Sub-Saharan Africa	57.0
Europe	62.0
North America	65.0
All Regions	54.2

Gender wage gaps can vary greatly according to region, country, industry, occupation, education, and age level. Values for a region can be skewed by how often countries report data and what levels of employment they are including within that region in any given year. This OECD 2009 database is working with 2006 data. Women are more likely than men to work in lower paying professions, in both rural and urban settings. Generally, women are drawn to lower-paying, part-time occupations that allow for flexible schedules for caretaking and work/home balance. They are also more likely to perform work without any benefits.

Source: Organisation for Economic Co-operation and Development (OECD). Gender, Institutions and Development Database 2009 (GID-DB). Available online. URL: http://stats.oecd.org/Index.aspx?DatasetCode=GID2.This specific query: http://stats.oecd.org/Index.aspx?QueryId=27325. Accessed January 29, 2011.

1.2 Ratio of Women's to Men's Pay
(cents to the dollar), 2008

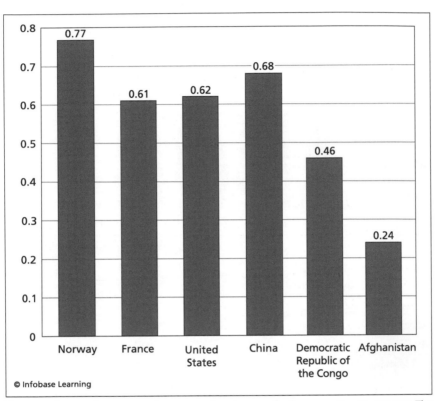

© Infobase Learning

The way the gender pay gap is measured varies greatly from country to country. The average difference in women's median earnings to men's in developed economies, such as OECD countries, is about 18 percent, which is similar to the United States' wage gap of 17 percent, when looking at the middle- to upper-income brackets. Here, the pay gap is based on all income brackets.

Source: UNDP, *Human Development Report 2009.* Table K, pp. 186–190.

1.3 Worldwide Employment Status of Women, 2008, by Region

Region	Wage & Salary Workers	Self-employed	Contributing Family Worker	Unemployed	Unemployed (% of Total Labor Market)
		% of women			
World	47.0	26.8	24.6	6.1	5.8
Developing economies and European Union	89.2	6.4	2.2	6.1	6.0
Central & Southeast Europe	80.0	11.5	7.2	8.1	8.3
East Asia	40.7	34.1	23.9	3.6	4.3
Southeast Asia and the Pacific	33.4	29.6	35.8	5.5	5.3
South Asia	14.5	33.3	51.7	5.6	4.8
Latin America and Caribbean	65.7	22.9	8.2	8.8	7.0
Middle East	52.6	23.5	22.7	14.7	9.2
North Africa	46.4	13.8	37.9	14.8	10.0
Sub-Saharan Africa	17.3	42.9	38.5	8.5	8.0

The ILO Trends Economic Models considers employment status as the combination of three categories: (1) wage and salaried workers, (2) self-employed workers, and (3) contributing family workers. Each is a proportion of the total employed. Women have traditionally been the main source for "vulnerable employment," defined as own-account (or self-employed) and contributing family workers. The percentage of women in the labor market who are unemployed is compared with the total unemployment rates to demonstrate this point. The ILO has observed a declining trend in the share of workers in vulnerable employment between 1999 and 2009, though the rate still remains high in sub-Saharan Africa.

Sources: International Labour Organization (ILO), *Global Employment Trends,* January 26, 2010; ILO, KILMnet, Table 3. Status in Employment (by sex), manuscript: Box 3a. World and regional estimates of status in employment, July 2009, p. 8 of the PDF file.

1.4 Worldwide Women Employment in Agriculture, Industry, and Services, by Region, 2008 (% of all women)

Region	Agriculture	Industry	Services
World	35.9	15.6	48.3
Developing economies and European Union	3.0	12.8	84.2
Central & Southeast Europe	17.7	17.8	64.4
East Asia	42.3	21.8	35.9
Southeast Asia and the Pacific	41.9	16.2	41.9
South Asia	64.9	15.7	19.4
Latin America and Caribbean	8.4	11.7	79.9
Middle East	34.3	7.3	58.3
North Africa	36.7	20.4	42.9
Sub-Saharan Africa	59.6	5.4	35.0

Cultural attitudes vary greatly from one region to another and can dictate which labor sector women are permitted to excel in. For instance, the growing participation of women in the labor market in developed economies accounts for the increase in the services sector. Agricultural jobs remain a significant source of employment for women in the African and Asian economies, despite the global shift from agricultural to service jobs in recent years.

Source: International Labour Organization (ILO). KILMnet beta database. Table 4a. Employment by Sector by Sex (manuscript). Available online. URL: http://kilm.ilo.org/KILMnetBeta/default2.asp. Accessed December 3, 2010.

1.5 Worldwide Top Recipients of Development Assistance, 2008, by Country (millions of 2008 dollars)

	2000 ODA receipts	2008 ODA receipts
Iraq	174	9,880
Afghanistan	232	4,865
Ethiopia	1,065	3,327
Occupied Palestinian Territory	986	2,593
Viet Nam	2,104	2,552
Sudan	359	2,384
United Republic of Tanzania	1,601	2,331
India	1,867	2,108
Bangladesh	1,716	2,061
Turkey	502	2,024
Mozambique	1,488	1,994
Uganda	1,362	1,657
Democratic Republic of the Congo	299	1,648
Pakistan	907	1,539
China	2,256	1,489
Kenya	745	1,360
Egypt	1,927	1,348
Ghana	864	1,293
Nigeria	252	1,290
Liberia	102	1,250
Subtotal, 2008 top 10	10,607	34,124
Subtotal, 2008 top 20	20,808	48,994
Memorandum Items		
Shares of total ODA (percentage of country allocable aid):		
Share of 2008 top 10	19.1	37.6
Share of 2008 top 20	37.5	53.9
Share of each year's top 10	34.5	37.6
Share of each year's top 20	51.9	53.9

ODA = Official Development Assistance

Iraq and Afghanistan continue to receive the largest amounts of aid. Still, as seen with China, amounts vary according to strategic reasons or because the countries make relatively productive use of aid. For developing countries, such as the Democratic Republic of the Congo, the challenging aid-delivery process and lack of donor policy focus can prevent them from receiving the aid they need.

Source: United Nations. MDG 8: The Global Partnership for Development at a Critical Juncture, p. 17. Available online. URL: http://www.un.org/millenniumgoals/pdf/10-43282_MDG_2010%20(E)%20WEBv2.pdf. Accessed October 23, 2010.

UNITED STATES STATISTICS

2.1 U.S. Civilian Labor Force Participation, Past, Present, and Future, 1950–2018

Group	1950	1960	1970	1980	1990	1998	2008	2018
Total population, 16 and older	59.2	59.4	60.4	63.8	66.4	67.1	66.0	64.5
Men, 16 years and older	86.4	83.3	79.7	77.4	76.1	74.9	73.0	70.6
Women, 16 years and older	33.9	37.7	43.3	51.5	57.5	59.8	59.5	58.7
Women's earnings as % of men's	63.9	60.7	59.4	60.2	71.6	73.2	79.9	NA

Men's participation in the U.S. labor force has been declining since the 1950s, while the women's rate has been steadily increasing. After peaking in 1999, women's participation has been decreasing for the past 10 years, and it is not expected to rebound to higher rates in the next 10 years.

Sources: Bureau of Labor Statistics (BLS), *Monthly Labor Review,* November 2009, p. 37, Table 3, Civilian Labor Force Participation Rates by Age, Sex, Race, and Ethnicity, 1988, 1998, 2008, and Projected 2018. Accessed December 3, 2010. U.S. Women's Bureau and the National Committee on Pay Equity.

2.2 U.S. Women's Earnings as Percentage of Men's Wages, by Age, 1979–2010

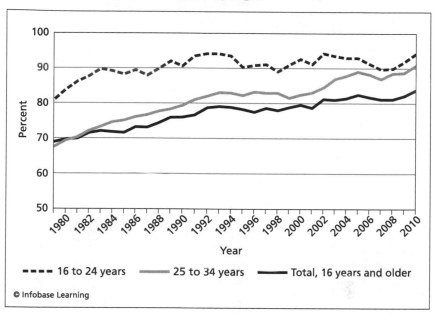

© Infobase Learning

Women's-to-men's earning ratios were first recorded in 1979 as part of the government's population survey. Rising from 62 percent in 1981 to a peak of 77 percent in 2010, earnings of women 35 years and older have averaged less than three-fourths that of their male counterparts. The gap in earnings is notably lower among younger women, with 25-to-34-year-olds earning 91 percent and 16-to-24-year-olds earning 94 percent of what men earn.

Source: U.S. Census Bureau, *The Editor's Desk,* July 22, 2011. Available online. URL: http://www.bls.gov/opub/ted/2011/ted_20110722_data.htm#chartdata1. Accessed September 26, 2011.

2.3 U.S. Leading Causes of Death in Women by Race, All Ages, 2006 (% of all deaths within that race)

Cause	All	White	Black	American Indian or Alaska Native	Asian or Pacific Islander	Hispanic
Heart disease	25.8	26.0	25.5	18.8	23.7	22.8
Cancer	22.0	22.0	21.6	19.22	26.9	21.7
Stroke	6.7	6.7	6.8	4.9	9.8	6.4
Chronic lower respiratory diseases	5.3	5.8	2.5	4.3	2.3	2.7
Alzheimer's disease	4.2	4.5	2.3	Chronic liver disease 4.2	1.8	2.7
Unintentional injuries	3.5	3.5	3.1	8.1	4.0	5.0
Diabetes	3.0	2.7	5.0	7.0	4.0	5.4
Influenza and pneumonia	2.5	2.6	2.0	2.0	3.4	2.6
Kidney disease	1.9	1.7	3.2	2.4	1.7	2.2
Septicemia	1.5	1.4	2.4	1.7	Hypertension 1.6	Perinatal conditions 2.1

Differences between racial groups in causes of death (morbidity) can reveal the health issues that are specific to each group. Data are collected from death certificates. The deaths due to the disease indicated are percentages of total deaths in the race category specified. Visit the CDC Web site for age-specific information in all these categories.

Source: Centers for Disease Control and Prevention. Leading Causes of Death in Females, United States, 2006. URL:http://www.cdc.gov/women/lcod/. Accessed December 1, 2010.

FRANCE STATISTICS

3.1 French Women's Policy Agency, 1974–2007

Time Range	Rank and Area of Concern	Head of the Department	Person in Charge
1974–1976	Secretary of state, women's condition	Prime minister	Françoise Giroud
1976–1978	Delegation, women's condition	Prime minister	Nicole Pasquier, until January 1978, then Jacqueline Nonon
1978–1981	Secretary of state, women's employment	Labor	Nicole Pasquier
1978–1980	Delegate minister, women's condition	Prime minister	Monique Pelletier
1980–1981	Delegate minister, family and women's condition	Prime minister	Monique Pelletier
1981–1985	Delegate minister, women's rights	Prime minister	Yvette Roudy
1985–1986	Minister, woman's rights	(no head of department)	Yvette Roudy
1986–1988	Delegate, women's condition	Prime minister	Hélène Gisserot
1988–1991	Secretary of state, women's rights	Prime minister	Michèle André
1991–1992	Secretary of state, women's rights and daily life	Labor	Véronique Neiertz
1992–1993	Secretary of state, women's rights and consumption	Economy and finance	Véronique Neiertz
1993–1995	Minister (women's rights are part of the minister's assignments, but don't appear in the name of the ministry)	Social affairs, health and city affairs	Simone Veil
1995	Minister (women's rights are part of the minister's assignments, but don't appear in the name of the ministry)	Intergenerational solidarity	Colette Codaccioni

(Table continues)

(Table continued)

Time Range	Rank and area of concern	Head of the Department	Person in Charge
1995–1997	Delegate, minister (women's rights are part of the minister's assignments, but don't appear in the name of the ministry)	Employment	Anne-Marie Couderc
1997–1998	Delegation, women's rights	Prime minister	Geneviève Fraisse
1998–2002	Secretary of state, women's rights and job training	Employment and solidarity	Nicole Péry
2002–2005	Delegate minister, parity and equal employment	Social affairs, labor and solidarity	Nicole Ameline
2005–2007	Delegate minister, social cohesion and parity	Employment, social cohesion and housing	Catherine Vautrin

Since the 1960s, the French government has been consolidating its policies and positions regarding women's issues within women policy agencies (WPAs). In turn, the cultural concept of family as an institution—or *familialisme*—has been a powerful force upon these agencies and the government's handling of women's rights.

Source: Anne Revillard. "Stating Family Values and Women's Rights: Familialism and Feminism within the French Republic," *French Politics*, 2007, p. 215.

3.2 European Marriage, Civil Partnership and Cohabitation, 2006–2007 (%, adult population)

	Married	Civil Partnership	Cohabitants	Singles	Total
Austria	52	.	.	.	.
Belgium	54	7	6	34	100
Denmark	57	1	13	30	100
Finland	51	0	15	34	100
France	56	2	14	28	100
Germany	54	1	8	36	100
Hungary	53	6	3	37	100
Ireland	55	0	7	37	100
Netherlands	56	6	8	30	100
Norway	50	3	14	33	100
Poland	56	0	2	42	100
Portugal	62	0	4	34	100
Slovak Rep.	56	5	1	39	100
Spain	55	3	4	38	100
Sweden	44	1	21	35	100
Switzerland	61	2	6	31	100
United Kingdom	54	4	6	36	100
OECD	54	3	8	35	100

While divorce rates have risen in most OECD countries, marriage rates have fallen to nearly a third less than in 1970. The pace of the decline in marriage rates varies by country, with declines being the greatest in the Czech Republic, Korea, and the United States, while Spain and Sweden show stable or rising rates since the late 1990s. In 2006, the crude marriage rate averaged 5.1 per 1,000 people across all countries. Data are derived from the European Social Survey (2006–2007).

Source: Organisation for Economic Co-operation and Development (OECD). *Society at a Glance 2009: OECD Social Indicators, General Context Indicators,* 4. Marriage and Divorce, p. 69.

CHINA STATISTICS

3.3 China's Population Logistics, 1978–2009

Year-end	Population (in 10,000s)				
	1978	1990	2000	2007	2009
Total	96,259	114,333	126,743	132,129	133,474
Male	49,567	58,904	65,437	68,048	68,652
Female	46,692	55,429	61,306	64,081	64,822
Urban	17,245	30,195	45,906	59,379	62,186
Rural	79,014	84,138	80,837	72,750	71,288

With emphasis being placed on urbanization and education, much of China's population—1.3 billion persons in 2009—is shifting from rural to urban locations, as seen in the above table. Women were part of the threefold growth in urban migration between 1978 and 2008, as they expanded their roles in the labor force. There still is a noticeable imbalance of men to women, at a 1.06 ratio, which could be due to underreporting of female births.

Source: National Bureau of Statistics of China. *China Statistical Yearbook 2010.* Available online. URL: http://www.stats.gov.cn/tjsj/ndsj/. Accessed September 25, 2011.

3.4 Chinese Women as Percentage of Enrollment in Higher Education, 2009

Higher Education	New Enrollment	Total Enrollment	Graduates	Females as % of Total
Postgraduates	510,953	1,404,942	371,273	47.04
Doctor's Degree	61,911	246,319	48,658	34.86
Master's Degree	449,042	1,158,623	322,615	49.63
Regular Undergraduates and College Students	6,394,932	21,446,570	5,311,023	50.48
Enrolled in Full Undergraduate Courses	3,261,081	11,798,511	2,455,359	48.89
Enrolled in Specialized Courses	3,133,851	9,648,059	2,855,664	52.42
Adult Undergraduates and College Students	2,014,776	5,413,513	1,943,893	52.33
Enrolled in Full Undergraduate Courses	815,795	2,256,662	865,421	53.93
Enrolled in Specialized Courses	1,198,981	3,156,851	1,078,472	51.19

As an emerging economy, China is gearing its population toward a more educated labor force, one that speaks English and is service- and industry-oriented. The government still benefits from workers receiving a low per capita income of about 15,781 yuan (roughly $2,395.43) in an urban household in 2008.

Source: National Bureau of Statistics of China. Table 20-2, Basic Statistics on Students by Level and Type of Education (2009). Available online. URL: http://www.stats.gov.cn/tjsj/ndsj/2010/indexteh.htm. Accessed September 25, 2011.

AFGHANISTAN STATISTICS

3.5 Afghan Women's Participation in Parliament, as Compared with Other Countries in Case Studies, 2005–2011

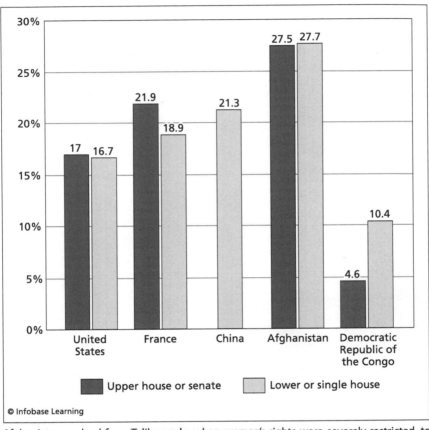

Afghanistan evolved from Taliban rule, when women's rights were severely restricted, to one that mandates gender equality by law, although still difficult to enforce. In the area of political representation, the new constitution guarantees the formal inclusion of women in political decision-making processes. Article 83 states that at least two female candidates from each province should be elected to parliament. This constitutional provision was successfully implemented.

Source: IPU Women in Parliaments: World Classification. Available online. URL: http://www.ipu.org/wmn-e/classif.htm. Accessed September 26, 2011.

3.6 Afghan Educational Enrollment by Sex (%)

	Total	Female	Male
Primary (2002/2003)	92.3	52.8 (F/M GPI ratio)	
Secondary (2002/2003)	12.5	NA	NA
2005 (ages 6-13)	37.0	29.0	43.0
Combined gross enrollment ratio in education (2007)	50.1	34.4	63.6

By 2007, the Afghanistan Ministry of Women's Affairs (MOWA) had conducted three separate countrywide campaigns to enroll girls in school following the fall of the Taliban in December 2001. With the resurgence of crimes committed by Taliban soldiers and their religious police, who beat girls to prevent them from attending school, it is difficult to have an accurate count.

Source: United Nations Development Programme (UNDP). *Human Development Report* 2009, Tables H. UNIFEM/MOWA, Women and Men in Afghanistan: Baseline Statistics on Gender, p. 51.

DRC STATISTICS

3.7 Estimated Relation between HIV Infections and AIDS, in Women and Children in the Democratic Republic of the Congo, 2008–2009

Parameters	2008			2009		
	Children 0–14 years	15 years and older	Total	Children 0–14 years	15 years and older	Total
People living with HIV	106,347	958,625	1,064,972	109,250	1,034,086	1,143,336
New HIV infections	30,046	99,379	129,425	30,521	102,681	133,202
Pregnant women living with HIV	NA	99,491	99,491	NA	101,543	101,543
Deaths from AIDS	20,289	60,581	80,870	20,856	61,934	82,790
Orphans from AIDS	NA	NA	1,008,658	NA	NA	1,025,551
Children needing pro-phylaxis cotrimoxazole	222,497	NA	NA	227,542	NA	NA
Needing anti-retroviral therapy	40,783	232,010	272,793	41,603	241,452	282,055
Prevalence (%) of HIV among adults	NA	NA	3.24	NA	NA	3.25

Women are a target population for the fight against the spread of HIV/AIDS. Despite the negligible gains seen here within each of the indicators, measured between January 2008 and December 2009, the epidemic of HIV/AIDS virus stabilized between 2006 and 2010. Antiretroviral therapy is starting to take effect, as are preventative measures in orphaned children.

Source: Programme National de Lutte contre le SIDA (PNLS). Ministry of Health. Epidemiological surveillance report of HIV in pregnant women attending CPNs in 2008. (RAPPORT NATIONAL UNGASS , République Démocratique du Congo, Période considérée : janvier 2008 – décembre 2009, March 31, 2010, p. 12.)

3.8 Map of the Democratic Republic of the Congo

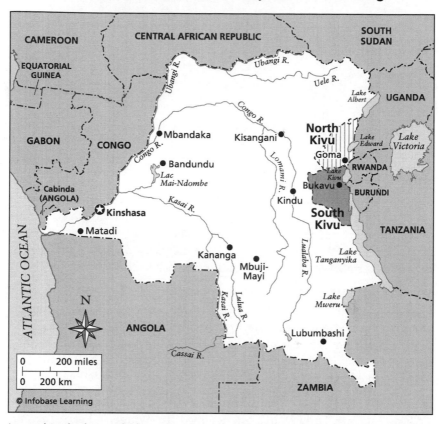

Located in the heart of Africa, the Democratic Republic of the Congo (DRC) possesses abundant natural resources, the control of which has led to violence erupting in the provinces of North and South Kivu during the First and Second Congo Wars. During this time and in these regions, women in particular suffered mass atrocities.

Sources: "The Security Dilemma in North Kiva, the Democratic Republic of the Congo," *Conflict Trends* 3 (2009): 42.

8

Key Players A to Z

BELLA SAVITSKY ABZUG (1920–1998)   U.S. politician from New York City and one of the leaders of the women's liberation movement in the 1970s, Abzug helped to found Women Strike for Peace in 1961 and the New Democratic Coalition in 1968. She was a high-profile activist, along with GLORIA STEINEM and BETTY FRIEDAN. She became the first Jewish congresswoman, known for her New York chutzpah and trademark wide-brimmed hats.

ABIGAIL ADAMS (1744–1818)   Wife of John Adams, the first vice president and second president of the United States, she rallied for women's right to education. An avid letter writer, she expressed women's demand to be included in the government when writing to her husband at the time the Founding Fathers were drafting the Declaration of Independence in 1776: "If women are not represented in this new republic there will be another revolution."

JANE ADDAMS (1860–1935)   American social activist and advocate for peace during World War I. She founded the Women's Peace Party in 1915 and later the International League for Peace and Freedom (WILPF), in Geneva, Switzerland, in 1919. She was awarded the Nobel Peace Prize in 1931, the first American woman to receive the prize.

AMENA AFZALI (1958–   )   Afghan, minister for youth affairs until the 1979 Soviet invasion of Afghanistan, during which she helped Afghan refugees settle in Iran. Afzali held senior positions on the Norwegian Afghanistan Committee and with the United Nations High Commissioner for Refugees. In 2002, she returned to Afghanistan and was appointed commissioner on the Afghan Independent Human Rights Commission.

MADELEINE ALBRIGHT (1937–   )   U.S. secretary of state from 1997 to 2001. Recognized for her talents in foreign policy, she was the first woman in the history of the U.S. government to hold the cabinet position. She also served as U.S. ambassador to the United Nations from 1993 to 1997.

SAFIA AMAJAN (1943–2006)   Head of the department of women's affairs in Kandahar, Afghanistan, she was assassinated by the Taliban on September 25, 2006. A dynamic teacher and public servant, she promoted the emancipation of Pashtun women, including the right to work, and the right of girls to go to school.

NICOLE AMELINE (1952–)   Specializing in public law, with a degree from the Institute of Political Studies in Paris, Ameline has held several high-level positions in French and international government agencies, including French minister of gender affairs and professional equality and representative of the French government to the International Labour Organization. She was active in the international initiative Beijing +10.

MATHILDA ANNEKE (1817–1884)   German writer, feminist, Social Democrat, antislavery campaigner, and editor of the *Neue Kölnische Zeitung* (New Cologne Times), which she renamed the *Frauen-Zeitung* (The woman's journal). Anneke took her family to the United States after her husband's arrest following the unsuccessful 1848 revolution. There she met SUSAN B. ANTHONY and ELIZABETH CADY STANTON and joined the women's movement.

SUSAN B. ANTHONY (1820–1906)   American reformer. Raised as a Quaker, Anthony undertook early advocacy work focused on equal pay for female teachers, coeducation, and college training for girls in New York State. In 1851, she met Elizabeth Cady Stanton, who became a lifelong friend. They formed the National Woman Suffrage Association (NWSA) in 1869 with the purpose of making changes to the U.S. Constitution that would allow women the vote. Anthony authored volumes I to III of the *History of Woman Suffrage* with ELIZABETH CADY STANTON and Matilda Joslyn Gage.

SEDIQA BALKHI (1946–)   Afghan educator, manager, and minister of martyrs and disabled. She was raised in a religious and educated family and earned a bachelor's degree in Islamic studies. She studied religion in Iran, writing and holding public seminars about the anti-Soviet invasion movement. She educated young Afghan refugees in Iran and taught business skills to women and girls.

SHUKRIA BAREKZAI (1972–)   Afghan founder and editor in chief of *Aina-e Zan* (Women's mirror weekly), which is dedicated to women's issues, and one of 68 women elected to the Afghan parliament in September 2005. During Taliban rule, she coordinated underground schools for women. She was named International Editor of the Year in 2005 by WorldPress.org.

MARY BECKENHAM (DATES UNKNOWN)   Kenyan activist who won the She Woman Award in 2005 for her work of caring for HIV-positive babies. In 1994, she opened New Life Home Trust's first home in the Loresho suburb of Nairobi. There are five homes and centers now: two in Nairobi, one in Kisumu (in western Kenya, on the shores of Lake Victoria), and two on the Indian Ocean island of Lamu (off the Kenyan northern coast, near Somalia).

MARY MCLEOD BETHUNE (1875–1955)   African-American missionary and educator, who founded the secondary school in 1904 that later became a four-year accredited college, Bethune-Cookman College. She also established the National Council of Negro Women in 1935 by uniting several major national black women's associations. Bethune remained its president until 1949 and was its representative at the founding conference of the United Nations in San Francisco, California, in 1945.

CATHIE BLACK (1944–)   Former president of Hearst Magazines, one of the largest magazine publishers in the world, Black rose through the ranks from being a sales assistant in 1966. Responsible for many of the titles, from *Good Housekeeping* and *Esquire* to *O:The Oprah Magazine*, Black is known for her ambitious lifestyle and belief in self-empowerment through self-improvement, for which she sees a role in women's magazines. She was briefly New York City Schools Chancellor in 2011.

ANTOINETTE L. BROWN BLACKWELL (1825–1921)   The first U.S. woman to be ordained to the ministry, in the 1850s. As a writer and women's rights activist, she advocated abolition, temperance, prison reform, antipoverty measures, and tried to reconcile Christianity with women's rights. She authored books on religious and philosophical issues, and even novels. She married the brother of Elizabeth Blackwell.

ELIZABETH BLACKWELL (1821–1910)   Physician, the first woman awarded an M.D. in the United States. Originally from Britain, she submitted applications to major medical schools in the United States that were rejected because of her sex, except that to Geneva Medical School (now Hobart & William Smith Colleges in Geneva, New York). In spite of hostility from professors, students, and townspeople, she earned her medical degree in 1849 and completed her medical education in Europe. Eventually, she founded the Women's Medical College.

GERTRUDE BONNIN (1876–1938)   Native American author and educator who founded the reform group the National Council of American Indians in 1926 and became its first president.

BARBARA BOXER (1940–   )   Senator Boxer (R-CA) has worked in the House of Representatives for 10 years and in the Senate for 18 years. She rallied support for the Museum of Women's History in 2005 and for an international response in 2010 to sexual violence against women in the Democratic Republic of the Congo.

MADELEINE BRÈS (1842–1925)   The first woman in France to become a physician. From her youth, she aspired to healing, having developed an interest in medicine at the Hôpital de Nimes, where her father was employed as a cartwright. She married at 15 and did not begin her medical training until 1866. The support of Empress Eugénie of France (1826–1920) and the minister of public education were critical to her gaining admission to the Faculty of Medicine. She later worked as an intern at the Hôpital de la Pitié during the Franco-Prussian War and received her medical diploma on June 3, 1875.

HALLIE QUINN BROWN (1849–1949)   African-American educator. She earned a bachelor of science degree in 1873 from Wilberforce University in Ohio, where she eventually became teacher, principal, dean, and professor. In 1893, she cofounded and presided over the Colored Woman's League of Washington, D.C., which was the forerunner to the National Association of Colored Women.

CARRIE CHAPMAN CATT (1859–1947)   U.S. suffragist and peace advocate educated in Iowa, where she became superintendent of schools in the early 1880s. Her two marriages—in 1885 to the journalist Lee Chapman and in 1890 to George Catt—left her a widow. From 1890 to 1900, she organized the National American Woman's Suffrage Association (NAWSA). Catt organized the League of Women Voters to educate women in political decision making. At the Berlin meeting of the International Council of Women, she organized the International Woman Suffrage Alliance (IWSA), over which she presided from 1904 to 1923.

JEANNE CHAUVIN (1862–1926)   First female lawyer in France. In 1897, despite having attained all the required diplomas, she was refused accreditation by the Cour d'Appel of Paris due to existing laws prohibiting women from practicing law. On December 30, 1901, the law officially changed, and Chauvin was allowed to practice.

SHIRLEY CHISHOLM (1924–2005)   The first African-American woman to be elected to the House of Representatives, in 1968. From Brooklyn, New York, Chisholm was an advocate for women and minorities during her seven terms in office, and she became the first woman to run for president in 1972.

democratic reforms. She is currently chairman and CEO of Holsman International, an investment and management company involved in domestic and international business.

ABIGAIL (ABBY) KELLEY FOSTER (1810–1887) Nineteenth-century American teacher, abolitionist, and lecturer on women's rights from Massachusetts. After teaching in Quaker schools, Abby Kelley fought against slavery in 1837 as part of the Female Anti-Slavery Society of Lynn, Massachusetts, and married a radical abolitionist and reformer in 1845. She often experienced hostility from audiences when she lectured on abolition. She turned her attention to women's rights, becoming a prominent suffragist for the rest of her life.

MARILYN FRENCH (1929–2009) A writer who published her first novel, *The Women's Room,* in 1977, around the theme of female solidarity and empowerment, using a narrative that was highly autobiographical. The story concerns Mira, a 1950s housewife, who must challenge expectations about men and herself when her daughter is raped, an event that actually occurred in French's life. Although she went on to write essays, other novels, literary criticism, and a memoir, French was best known for this work.

BETTY FRIEDAN (1921–2006) A writer and activist who in 1963 published *The Feminine Mystique,* which evolved out of a survey of colleagues at a 20-year college reunion. In the book, she documents the emotional and intellectual oppression that middle-class educated women were experiencing because of societal limitations. The best seller inspired thousands of women to seek a life beyond homemaking.

FATANA GAILANI (DATES UNKNOWN) Founder of the Afghanistan Women Council, she began her humanitarian work for human, children's, and women's rights in 1980 after fleeing the communist regime in her native Kabul for asylum in Pakistan. She represented Afghan women at the Beijing Conference on Women in 1995 and at the 1997 Post-Beijing Follow-up Conference in Thailand. She lived 20 years in Pakistan and three years in Switzerland as an Afghan refugee. After she received death threats from the Taliban, Amnesty International issued an urgent action bulletin in 1999 calling for her enhanced protection.

FAUZIA GAILANI (1971–) An Afghan women's rights campaigner and professional fitness instructor, Gailani was a candidate in the 2005 parliamentary elections. Popular among young Afghans, she was elected to Afghanistan's parliament in an upset victory. Gailani topped the ballot with nearly 17,000 votes and eclipsed powerful provincial allies of the warlord

Ismail Khan. One of Gailani's pledges is to form Afghanistan's first women's party. She opposes child marriage, a common practice in Afghanistan, to which she was herself subjected.

JULIA GILLARD (1961–) Australia's first female prime minister following a historical election in June 2010 that resulted in a hung parliament after the ousting of a fellow Labor Party incumbent who created controversy by proposing the taxation of mining companies, an important source of revenue for the country.

RUTH BADER GINSBURG (1933–) As a lawyer, Ginsburg advocated for the application of the equal protections afforded under the Fourteenth Amendment to gender as well as race. She successfully argued *Reed v. Reed* before the Supreme Court in 1971 and, thereafter, continued to argue more cases involving sex-role stereotyping. She was appointed an associate justice of the Supreme Court in 1993.

MARY GOEGG (1826–1899) Founder of the International Association of Women in Geneva, Switzerland, in 1868. She published articles advocating that women make their case known as part of the universal right of suffrage. She also contributed to *La Solidarité* in France. In 1872, she became the first woman to petition the government about women's right to higher education, an act that was followed by women's admission in the winter semester of 1872 and 1873. At 68 years old, she became vice president of l'Union des femmes de Genève, founded by a new generation of feminists in 1891.

EMMA GOLDMAN (1869–1940) American radical and feminist, who advocated free speech, birth control, women's equality and independence, and union organization. Her criticism of mandatory conscription of young men into the military during World War I led to her two-year imprisonment, followed by deportation in 1919. For the rest of her life until her death in 1940, she participated in social and political movements of her era, from the Russian Revolution to the Spanish civil war.

OLYMPE DE GOUGES (1745–1793) A French feminist, writer, and revolutionary. In her famous 1791 work "Rights of Woman," she argued for applying the new "Rights of Man" to women during the French Revolution of 1789–99. In her many pamphlets written during the Revolution, she criticized bloodshed and was outspoken against revolutionary figures such as Robespierre; she was beheaded as a traitor in 1793.

KATHARINE MEYER GRAHAM (1917–2001) Publisher of the *Washington Post,* Graham assumed leadership of the newspaper after the suicide of her husband, its president, in 1963. She also became the first female member of the board of the Associated Press in 1974. She was considered one of the most powerful women in America as a result of her role at the *Washington Post* and the disclosures by the paper of the Watergate scandal that led to the resignation of President Richard Nixon.

ANGELINA EMILY GRIMKÉ (1805–1879) American abolitionist and advocate of women's rights in the 19th century. Converted to the Quaker faith by her elder sister, Sarah Moore Grimké (1792–1873), she became an abolitionist in 1835 and wrote *An Appeal to the Christian Women of the South* as a testimony of her conversion. She began speaking to the public around New York City with her sister and developed powerful oratory skills, which led to her addresses to the Massachusetts legislative committee on antislavery petitions in 1838 on three occasions.

NASRINE GROSS (1945–) Afghan founder and president of the Roqia Center for Women's Rights, Studies and Education, Afghanistan, which provides women's rights seminars, academic information, and adult literacy classes. The organization's literacy program for couples is modeled to shape democratic behavior and experience by requiring that both husbands and wives attend classes.

FANNY LOU HAMER (1917–1977) Civil rights worker and member of the Mississippi Freedom Democratic Party who called black voting discrimination and physical abuse of African Americans to public attention at the 1964 Democratic National Convention. One of 11 children of a Mississippi sharecropping family, Hamer, who had little formal education, spoke from her heart: "I'm sick and tired of being sick and tired," she stated. A year later, President Lyndon B. Johnson signed the Voting Rights Act of 1965.

HATSHEPSUT (1508–1458 B.C.E.) Egyptian pharaoh who during her 15-year reign (ca. 1473–1458 B.C.E.) became known for her military campaigns and building projects. Upon the death of her husband, Thutmose II, Hatshepsut became regent for Thutmose III and within two years became pharaoh In her own right. Her reign was characterized by growing commerce on the Red Sea and extensive building of temples. After her death, Thutmose III discredited her rule and her memory by leaving her tomb at Deir el-Bahari in the Valley of the Kings unfinished.

ANITA HILL (1956–) African-American lawyer whose 1991 landmark testimony raised public awareness of sexual harassment. Hill received a law degree from Yale University and after working at the Equal Employment Opportunity Commission (EEOC) taught law at the University of Oklahoma.

She brought allegations of sexual harassment against Supreme Court nominee Clarence Thomas during his Senate confirmation hearings. Although Thomas's appointment was subsequently confirmed, Hill's testimony called the issue of sexual harassment to public attention.

JANET JAGAN (1920–2009)   Chicago nursing student who would became the first female president of Guyana, succeeding her deceased husband, Cheddi Jagan, a former dentist.

MASSOUDA JALAL (1962–)   Physician and politician, a member of the ethnic Tajik minority in Afghanistan. She earned her degree from Kabul Medical Institute in 1988. From 1993 to 1995, she was the women's rights director in a women's organization and was a member of the Children's Department of Kabul Medical Institute. In 1996, she worked for the United Nations High Commissioner for Refugees (UNHCR); afterward she was the health adviser and a national program officer for the World Food Program in Afghanistan. In June 2002, she became a candidate during the first post-Taliban *loya jirga* in Kabul to discuss the future of Afghanistan and its constitution. She was minister of women's affairs from 2004 to 2006 under the Afghanistan transitional administration.

RAHIMA JAMI (1961–)   Afghan educator and politician who participated in the 2005 elections in Afghanistan. As the principal of a girl's school in western Afghanistan, Jami represents the more moderate view of feminism in Afghanistan, believing women need to work within the Islamic framework, covering themselves and obeying the laws of the Qur'an.

MILDRED JEFFERSON (1926–2010)   African-American surgeon and antiabortion activist. In 1951. Jefferson became the first black woman to graduate from Harvard Medical School. She served as president of the National Right to Life Committee from 1975 to 1978.

LADY BIRD JOHNSON (1917–2007)   Wife of U.S. president Lyndon Johnson, mostly known for her environmental work. She was also instrumental in advocating on behalf of the Equal Rights Amendment.

BARBARA JORDAN (1936–1996)   Political science educator and congresswoman. She held an unprecedented reign as a black woman in the Texas state senate in 1966 and became the first black state senator to chair a committee (Labor and Management Relations), in 1967. She was the first African-American woman to give a keynote speech at the Democratic National Convention, 1976.

MALAI JOYA (1978–)   Prominent young activist elected from the province of Farah for the Afghan *loya jirga* in September 2005. Joya presented grassroots opposition through her experience working in a refugee camp and as an underground teacher during the Taliban rule. Her speech in Kabul denounced the warlords in power as criminals who should be brought to justice as well as the discrimination against women, all of which has required her to employ an armed bodyguard.

TANG JUNYING (DATES UNKNOWN)   Founding the Chinese Suffragette Society in Beijing in 1911, she modeled the organization on that of militant British suffragists and translated and published articles from the West into Chinese.

ELENA KAGAN (1960–)   American attorney, solicitor general, Supreme Court justice. After working as a prosecutor in New York City, Kagan was selected to serve for four years as associate counsel for President Bill Clinton. Though without previous judicial experience, she was nominated to the Supreme Court by President Barack Obama in 2010 and became the fourth woman and youngest person at age 50, ever to sit on the high court. With her appointment for the first time in U.S. history, three women would serve simultaneously on the Court.

JEAN KAGGIA (DATES UNKNOWN)   Antiabortion activist from Kenya. She is the chairperson of the Christian Medical Fellowship of Kenya and the leader of the Protecting Life Movement of Kenya.

ALICE KAGUNDA (FL. 1960s)   Kenya's first female senior deputy commissioner of police, appointed in 2004. She grew up in the early 1960s in Nyeri, where there were no policewomen. Seeing one while visiting a relative in Nairobi inspired her to enter the field of law enforcement.

JUSTINE KASSA-VUBU (1952–)   Writer, social scientist, and activist from the Democratic Republic of the Congo. She was nine when the former Belgian Congo gained its independence in June 1960. Her father, Joseph Kasa-Vubu, was the first president of the Republic of Congo. She went into exile with the coup d'état by Joseph Mobutu in 1965 but returned to serve as minister for the public service under President Laurent Kabila. She resigned from her position in 1998, going into exile and founding the Movement of Democrats.

BILLIE JEAN KING (1943–)   A U.S. tennis player, King fought for equal prize money for women. In 1971, she became the first female athlete to win more than $100,000. Her campaign for equality is most notably remembered for the 1973 "Battle of the Sexes" match, in which she beat 55-year-old tennis champion

Bobby Riggs, who claimed the women's game to be inferior. In 1974, Billie Jean King became the first president of the Women's Tennis Association. She was elected to the International Tennis Hall of Fame in 1987 and served as captain of the United States Fed Cup team in the 1990s. Following her marriage from 1965 to 1981, she became one of the first prominent American athletes to openly admit to having a gay relationship when it became public some 10 years later.

CORETTA SCOTT KING (1927–2006) Activist and founder of the Martin Luther King, Jr. Center for Nonviolent Social Change and wife of Dr. Martin Luther King, Jr., who was assassinated in 1968. In 1983, an act of Congress instituted the Martin Luther King, Jr. Federal Holiday Commission, which she chaired until January 1986, when she oversaw the first legal holiday in honor of her husband, one now celebrated in more than 100 countries.

IRENE MORGAN KIRKALDY (1917–2007) Civil rights pioneer whose opposition to segregation while traveling through the Upper South in the summer of 1944 led to a Supreme Court decision outlawing segregated seating on interstate bus lines.

CHRISTINE LAGARDE (1956–) Minister three times—of economy and industry, economy, and industry and employment. Known for her fluent English, in 1981 she joined the renowned international legal firm Baker & McKenzie, where she specialized in labor rights and acquisitions. She was called to serve within the French ministry of commerce in 2005 by Prime Minister Dominique de Villepin. Under President Nicolas Sarkozy, she became the first female minister of finance and economy, in 2007. In June 2011 she was named managing director of the International Monetary Fund. She is also the first woman to hold this position.

JERI LABER (1931–) Cofounder of the Human Rights Watch, which was first known as Helsinki Watch, in 1978. Laber advocated on behalf of human rights in Afghanistan in the 1980s and visited refugee settlements in Pakistan. Author of *The Courage of Strangers* (2002), and one-time editor of the *Fanny Farmer Cookbook* (1979), she pioneered the grassroots, personal level of what would later become a complex human rights movement and global bureaucracy of aid organizations.

MARINE LE PEN (1968–) After practicing penal law for several years, Le Pen became leader of France's right-wing National Front in 1998, of which she had been a member since she was 18 years old. She is considered by many to be the successor of her father, Jean-Marie Le Pen, as president of the party, her candidacy having already been approved by two-thirds of the French departmental secretariats.

DORIS LESSING (1919–)   British novelist awarded the 2007 Nobel Prize in literature. As an author, she is well known for her visionary style in depicting women's lives, a quality recognized by the Swedish Academy that awards this distinction. Her breakthrough novel, *The Golden Notebook*, inspired a generation of feminists.

LI YINHE (1952–)   Sociologist and sexologist, she advocated on behalf of the Chinese gay community, speaking publicly in favor of legalizing same-sex marriages, including during the National People's Congress in 2000 and 2004. According to Chinese law, 35 delegates' signatures are required to allow a bill to be discussed in the Congress. Li's efforts failed due to lack of support from Congress delegates. Many scholars, as well as gays and lesbians generally, believe it will be difficult to pass such a law in China in the near future.

MARY LYON (1797–1849)   Founder of Mount Holyoke College in South Hadley, Massachusetts. Educated at a female academy in Byfield, Massachusetts, Lyon cofounded Ipswich Female Seminary in Massachusetts. Perceiving the limitations of the seminary, which based its criteria on personal conduct and discipline, she conceived the idea of an educational institution for women.

SHEIKHA LUBNA (1958–)   Minister of foreign trade of the United Arabs Emirates (UAE), Lubna was voted the most powerful Arab woman by *Forbes* magazine in October 2010. She served as the UAE's first female cabinet minister in 2004 and as economic minister and is considered an inspiration to young women across the Arab world.

WANGARI MUTA MAATHAI (1940–2011)   The first African woman to win the Nobel Peace Prize, in 2004. Maathai was active in the National Council of Women of Kenya and became its chair from 1981 to 1987. She introduced the idea of planting trees and developed the Green Belt Movement as a grassroots organization that focused on conserving the environment and improving the quality of life through women's groups. Green Belt coordinated the planting of over 20 million trees on farms and school and church property. In December 2002, Professor Maathai was elected to parliament by a majority vote and was subsequently appointed by the president as assistant minister for environment, natural resources, and wildlife in Kenya's ninth parliament.

MALALAI (DATES UNKNOWN)   Afghan female leader, who inspired Afghan troops to fight the British in the Second Anglo-Afghan War of 1880. Her life and the image of her waving a veil over her head serve as a model for many girls today, and schools are named in her honor.

RONA MANSURI (DATES UNKNOWN)   Activist for Afghan refugees and daughter of a former prime minister, who moved in the 1960s to Germany, where her father was Afghanistan's ambassador. She was one of three women who took part as delegates in the United Nations talks in Bonn, Germany, to form the provisional government for post-Taliban Afghanistan.

JUDI ANN MASON (1955–2009)   Playwright and television writer who grew up in the 1960s South. She wrote episodes for the sitcoms *Good Times, A Different World,* and *Sanford and Son*—all programs that introduced television viewers to the lifestyles of African Americans. She wrote 25 plays depicting the black experience in America, including *A Star Ain't Nothin' but a Hole in Heaven,* which earned her the Lorraine Hansberry Playwriting Award in 1977. Hurricane Katrina's 2005 ravaging of her native community of Shreveport, Louisiana, provided the setting of her play *Storm Stories.*

DIANA K. MAYER (1947–)   In 1974, Mayer became Citicorp's first female vice president at the age of 27. She went on to become vice president in the money management division of the Marine Midland Bank of New York and was subsequently appointed a senior vice president in 1981.

MARGARET MEAD (1901–1978)   Pioneering sociologist, activist, and inspiration to the American women's movement who spoke the famous words "'Never doubt that a small group of thoughtful committed citizens can change the world. Indeed it is the only thing that ever has."

RIGOBERTA MENCHU (1959–)   Human-rights activist who ran for president of Guatemala in September 2007 with the support of the Encounter for Guatemala party, making her the first female Mayan to do so. She won the Nobel Peace Prize in 1992 for her work defending indigenous people.

ANGELA MERKEL (1954–)   Chancellor of Germany since 2005, the former physics researcher from East Berlin made the leap to politics when the Berlin Wall fell in 1989. Soon after, she joined the Christian Democratic Union (CDU) of East Germany and became its chairperson in 2000, but of a unified Germany; between 2002–05, she was chairwoman of the CDU-CSU (Christian Social Union) parliamentary coalition.

BARBARA MIKULSKI (1936–)   Senior U.S. senator (D-MD), she is the longest-serving female senator (since 1986) and—as of March 2012—member of Congress (since 1976), having also served in the House of Representatives. In 2009, she championed both the Lilly Ledbetter Fair Pay Act and Rosa's Law, which banned from official use the term "mentally retarded" and replaced it with "mentally challenged," "intellectual disability," and "developmental disability."

ESTHER MORRIS (1814–1902) First woman to hold a judicial position, who led the first successful state campaign for woman suffrage in Wyoming in 1869.

JAMES MOTT (1788–1868) Lucretia Mott's husband, he also worked for the antislavery and woman suffrage causes. He was a delegate to the World Anti-Slavery Convention in London and the women's rights convention at Seneca Falls. With other members of the Religious Society of Friends, a Quaker organization, he helped found Swarthmore College in 1864 as a coeducational institution.

LUCRETIA MOTT (1793–1880) Nineteenth-century American reformer and international and national figure in the women's movement. From Massachusetts, she was first known after 1818 as a lecturer for temperance, peace, the rights of labor, and the abolition of slavery. After her intervention to aid slaves and a meeting of the American Anti-Slavery Society, she organized the Philadelphia Female Anti-Slavery Society in 1833. Refusal by the 1840 World Anti-Slavery Convention in London to recognize women delegates led to her championing of the cause of women's rights. She organized the first women's rights convention in the United States with Elizabeth Cady Stanton at Seneca Falls, New York, in 1848.

EVELYN MUNRO (1914–2007) Activist and member of the Southern Tenant Farmers Union, a racially integrated union that fought on behalf of sharecroppers, often meeting with racist plantation owners and police. She supervised the Memphis headquarters and eventually became its educational director, mentoring other women in activism, and also edited a newspaper.

ANTONIA C. NOVELLO (1944–) First woman and Hispanic to be appointed surgeon general of the United States Public Health Service, in 1990. Born, raised, and educated in Puerto Rico, Novello completed her master's degree in public health at Johns Hopkins University and earned an M.D. in 1970. She worked for 12 years in the U.S. Public Health Service at the National Institutes of Health. She became the first female president of the Pan American Medical Society.

ODETTE NYIRAMILIMO (1956–) Senator, Republic of Rwanda, and a physician. She served as minister of state for social affairs in the government of Paul Kagame from March 2000 to October 2003. Nyiramilimo, an ethnic Tutsi, saw many of her family members killed in the power struggles following independence. After an eventful childhood, which included expulsion from school because she was Tutsi, she attended medical school in Butare and became a physician. She later married Jean-Baptiste Gasasira, also a physician, and the two later founded a private maternity and pediatrics practice in Kigali called Le Bon Samaritain (Good Samaritan). Nyiramilimo's life story was profiled at length in Philip Gourevitch's book *We Wish to Inform You That Tomorrow We Will Be Killed with Our Families.*

SANDRA DAY O'CONNOR (1933–   )   The Supreme Court's 102nd justice and its first female member. O'Connor grew up on a cattle ranch in El Paso, Texas, and attended Stanford University, where she received a B.A. in economics and a law degree two years later. O'Connor served as an Arizona assistant attorney general from 1965 to 1969, when she was appointed to the Arizona Senate. In 1974, she ran successfully for trial judge, a position she held until her appointment to the Arizona Court of Appeals in 1979. President Ronald Reagan nominated her 18 months later, in September 1981, to the Supreme Court. She announced her retirement from the Supreme Court on July 1, 2005.

MILLIE AKOTH ODHIAMBO (DATES UNKNOWN)   Lawyer and protector of women's rights in Kenya. She graduated from the University of Nairobi in 1990 and passed the bar exam in 1991. She worked as a state attorney until 1996, when she joined the International Federation of Women Lawyers, Kenya Chapter (FIDA (K)), a public education and advocacy organization that offers legal aid to indigent women. While there, Millie represented a Masai woman in a landmark domestic violence case that received local and international attention and became a milestone in the protection of the rights of women in Kenya.

EMMELINE PANKHURST (1858–1928)   Radical British feminist who along with her two daughters, Christabel (1880–1958), and Sylvia (1882–1960), founded the Women's Social and Political Union (WSPU) in 1903. The Pankhursts used extreme measures to promote women's suffrage, including chaining themselves to the fences of Parliament and engaging in prison hunger strikes. They inspired the radical faction of the women's movement in the United States, represented by ALICE PAUL, and in other countries.

ROSA PARKS (1913–2005)   The African-American woman who spurred the Civil Rights movement by refusing to give up her seat at the front of a bus in Montgomery, Alabama. Her arrest in December 1955 in Montgomery sparked a 13-month civil rights protest and the formation of the Montgomery Improvement Association, led by the young pastor Dr. Martin Luther King, Jr. In 1957, Mrs. Parks and her husband moved to Detroit, Michigan, where she served on the staff of U.S. Representative John Conyers. After the death of her husband in 1977, she founded the Rosa and Raymond Parks Institute for Self-Development. She was presented with the Presidential Medal of Freedom in 1996 and the Congressional Gold Medal in 1999. Rosa Parks died in 2005, and her casket was placed in the rotunda of the United States Capitol; she was the first woman in U.S. history to lie in state at the Capitol.

ALICE PAUL (1885–1977) Radical suffragist, who, in 1916, broke off from the National American Woman Suffrage Association to form the National Women's Party with Lucy Burns. Her infamous prison hunger strikes attracted national and international attention, causing President Woodrow Wilson to acknowledge the role of women in the war effort in 1919 and to prompt the states to consider a constitutional amendment. She drafted the Equal Rights Amendment.

NANCY PELOSI (1940–) The first woman to serve as Speaker of the House, she served from January 2006 to January 2011. She was the first woman to lead a political party in the history of the U.S. Congress when she was named Minority Leader in November 2002, a position she assumed for a second time in January 2011, at the age of 70.

ESTHER PETERSON (1906–1997) Director of the Women's Bureau of the Department of Labor in 1961. She encouraged President John F. Kennedy to convene the Commission on the Status of Women, naming Eleanor Roosevelt as its chair. The report issued by that commission in 1963 documented discrimination against women in virtually every area of American life. State and local governments quickly followed suit and established their own commissions for women, to research conditions and recommend changes.

LISA RANDALL (1962–) American theoretical physicist joining the ranks of Stephen Hawking with her theories about the existence of universal dimensions beyond the tangible ones. She is the first female physicist to gain tenure at Harvard University.

CONDOLEEZZA RICE (1954–) Secretary of state of the United States from January 2005 to January 2009 (the first African-American woman to hold that position), Dr. Rice was formerly the national security advisor to President George W. Bush. Prior to that, she was a professor of political science on the Stanford University faculty, where she received distinguished awards for teaching. She received the third annual Woman of Valor Award in May 2006 from the Independent Women's Forum (IWF).

SALLY RIDE (1951–) Nominated in 2005 by the National Women's History Museum for the "35 Who Made a Difference," Dr. Ride was the first

U.S. female astronaut in the 1983 flight on the *Challenger*. Her current work encourages girls to participate in the field of science with the Sally Ride Science Club. She is among the few women to be inducted into the Women's Hall of Fame at a young age and while still alive.

MARY ROBINSON (1945–)   President of Ireland from 1990 to 1997, Robinson brought to bear her legal and political experience from a local to a national level. Early in her career, she advocated on behalf of women, such as for their right to sit on juries, to remain in civil service jobs after marriage, and to access contraceptives legally. She was the first Labor Party nominee for the presidency and the first female candidate ever in the history of Ireland. Appointed UN High Commissioner for Human Rights from 1997 to 2002, she campaigned on behalf of homosexual law reform and on behalf of lesbian, gay, bisexual, and transgender (LGBT) human rights. In 2009, President Barack Obama awarded her with the Presidential Medal of Freedom.

ELEANOR ROOSEVELT (1884–1962)   Wife of President Franklin D. Roosevelt; she was active in political and reform work, redefining the role of first lady by advocating rights for women, blacks, and union workers. She was among the first to join the League of Women Voters in 1920. After her husband's death in 1945, she was named the U.S. delegate to the newly established United Nations; she presented the *Universal Declaration of Human Rights* to the General Assembly for adoption in 1948.

ERNESTINE ROSE (1810–1892)   One of the first women to speak publicly for women's rights in America. A rabbi's daughter, born in Poland, she arrived in New York in May 1836, with a petition for married women's property rights. After 12 years of activism, New York became the first state to pass a married women's property law and was followed by other states. The campaign led to lifelong association with Elizabeth Cady Stanton and Paulina Wright Davis. Susan B. Anthony, who joined the movement in 1852, and Stanton credited Rose's pioneering role.

YVETTE ROUDY (1953–)   French politician who implemented the law prohibiting sexual discrimination in the workplace in 1983, known as *la Loi Roudy* (the Roudy law) during her tenure as minister for women's rights, from 1981 to 1986. A former journalist, her political platform favored women's rights. After being a member of Comité Directeur of the Socialist Party, she became National Secretary for Action Féminine in 1977 and was subsequently elected to the European Parliament in 1979.

MARIE-SÉGOLÈNE ROYAL (1953–)   French politician, born in Dakar, Senegal (then part of French West Africa), promotive of family and social issues. She was the first woman in France to be nominated by a major party, as the Socialist candidate in the 2007 French presidential elections, which she lost to Nicolas Sarkozy on May 6, 2007. In November 2008, Royal declared her intended candidacy for the next presidential elections in 2012.

ZAINAB SALBI (1970–) Iraqi-American writer, activist, and cofounder of Women for Women International. Her father was a pilot employed by Iraqi dictator Saddam Hussein, who imposed much psychological abuse on her family. When she was 19, she and her family moved to the United States, where she earned a degree in sociology and women's studies. She went on to the London School of Economics for a master's degree in development studies. Her experience with the Iran-Iraq War made her outspoken about women as victims of sexual violence in wars worldwide. Since 1993, her organization has provided humanitarian aid to more than a quarter of a million women, including microcredit loans, training in rights awareness, and assistance to female survivors of wars in Bosnia and Herzegovina, Rwanda, Kosovo, Nigeria, Colombia, Afghanistan, Iraq, the Democratic Republic of the Congo, and Sudan.

SIMA SAMAR (1957–) Chairwoman of the Independent Human Rights Commission from Afghanistan. Dr. Samar was selected as the John Humphrey Freedom Award recipient for her efforts to strengthen the human rights of women and girls in Afghanistan and in refugee camps on the northern border of Pakistan in 2001.

MARGARET SANGER (1879–1966) Nurse and advocate for *birth control*, she is credited with coining the term. In her work as a public health nurse in New York City, she was aware of the effects of unplanned pregnancies. In 1912, Sanger gave up nursing work to distribute birth control information; she was challenged by the Comstock Act of 1873, which forbade distribution of birth control devices and information, and she was arrested numerous times. In 1914, she founded the National Birth Control League and set up the first clinic in the United States. In 1942, after several organizational mergers and name changes, Planned Parenthood Federation emerged. In 1927, Sanger helped organize the first World Population Conference in Geneva.

ANNA HOWARD SHAW (1847–1919) American ordained Methodist minister, physician, temperance lecturer, woman's suffrage orator, and peace advocate. The second woman to graduate from Boston University School of Theology, in 1878, Shaw was a friend and colleague of Susan B. Anthony. She also became the first woman to receive the highest civilian presidential citation, the Distinguished Service Medal, for her work as chair of the Women's Committee of the National Council of Defense during World War I.

SUHAILA SIDDIQ (1941–) Afghanistan's woman general and surgeon, who became the minister of health in 2002. She spent two decades working in Kabul's 400-bed military hospital, and her abdominal surgery is credited with saving hundreds of lives. She played a pivotal role in keeping hospitals functioning in the 1990s during rocket attacks.

SONIA SOTOMAYOR (1954–) American lawyer and judge, nominated by President Barack Obama to be the first Hispanic justice on the United States Supreme Court. Raised in a housing project in the Bronx, New York, she earned a degree in law at Yale University and went on to be a prosecutor in Manhattan. President George H. W. Bush nominated her in 1991 to serve as a federal judge.

ELIZABETH CADY STANTON (1815–1902) A pioneer of women's rights in the United States, organizer of the Seneca Falls Conference, and founder of the National Woman Suffrage Association (NWSA), with Susan B. Anthony. With her husband, Henry Brewster Stanton, a journalist and abolitionist, she tried to attend the international slavery convention in London. Women delegates were excluded from the floor of the convention, arousing indignation in both Stanton and Lucretia Mott and moving them to organize women and win greater equality with men.

GLORIA STEINEM (1934–) Writer, activist, and leader in the women's rights movement in the early 1960s. Steinem began her career as a freelance writer with an interest in politics, which was considered novel at the time. She founded *Ms.* magazine, the National Women's Political Caucus, the Women's Action Alliance, and the Ms. Foundation for Women. Then, in the 1980s and 1990s, Steinem became a best-selling author with books such as *Outrageous Acts and Everyday Rebellions, Revolution from Within: A Book of Self-Esteem, Doing Sixty, and Moving beyond Words.*

LUCY STONE (1818–1893) American reformer and leader in the women's rights movement. In 1847, she gave her first lecture on women's rights, and the following year, she was engaged by the Anti-Slavery Society as one of their regular lecturers. Her eloquent speaking often captivated even difficult audiences. She married Henry Brown Blackwell in 1855 but continued, as a matter of principle, to use her own name and was known as "Mrs. Stone." In 1870, she founded the *Woman's Journal,* which represented AWSA and NAWSA for 50 years.

DORA JEAN DOUGHERTY STROTHER (1921–) U.S. military pilot. Her military flying career began in 1942, when she entered the Women's Air Force Service Pilots (WASP). Her piloting jobs included flight training, target towing for antiaircraft gunnery, ferrying, and radio control piloting. Established primarily to relieve male pilots who were needed in combat roles, the WASPs flew almost every type of plane used by the Army Air Forces, including liaison, training, cargo, fighters, attack bombers, dive bombers, and very heavy bombers.

MARIA W. STUART (1803–1879) An 1830s black orator who spoke about women's rights in the United States. She spoke against African colonization and stirred public sentiment with her speeches about self-determination. She published two collections of essays and speeches: *Religion and the Pure Principles of Morality* (1831) and *Meditations from the Pen of Mrs. Maria W. Stuart* (1832).

HABIBA SURABI (1956–   ) Surabi, a hematologist, represented moderate views as Afghanistan's minister of women's affairs from 2003 to 2004. She went on to become Afghanistan's first female provincial governor, of Bamiyan, in 2005.

HELEN BROOKE TAUSSIG (1898–1986) Physician whose groundwork changed the face of cardiac surgery when she teamed with the surgeon Dr. Alfred Blalock in 1945 to perform the first "blue baby" operation in the United States. Blue babies were often left to die because they lacked oxygen exchange as a result of arterial constriction between the heart and lungs until Taussig proposed a novel technique, creating a new vessel.

MARY CHURCH TERRELL (1863–1954) African-American women's and civil rights activist from Tennessee. Educated at Oberlin College in Ohio and well traveled, Church Terrell received multiple honorary doctorates during her life. In Washington, D.C., she founded in 1892 the Colored Women's League, which merged four years later with the National Federation of Afro-American Women to become the National Federation of Colored Women. Church Terrell became its first president. She was appointed to the District of Columbia Board of Education in 1895. A lecturer and writer on equal rights for women and blacks and related social issues, she served as a U.S. delegate to international women's rights conferences.

HELEN THOMAS (1920–   ) American author, journalist, and reporter, who started working in 1943 for the United Press. A member of the White House Press Corps, she covered every presidency from John F. Kennedy to Barack Obama.

TZ'U-HSI (CIXI) (1835–1908) Concubine of Emperor Hs'en Feng, she was de facto ruler of China in 1861 after his death. She held the reins of power until 1889. She ruled against foot binding and legitimized intermarriage between ethnic Chinese and Manchus. She also gave girls access to state educational facilities.

SIMONE VEIL (1927–   )   French lawyer and minister of health who championed the French law legalizing abortion in 1974. Daughter of an Auschwitz-Birkenau concentration camp survivor, she would become a forerunner for women's rights across Europe.

SIMA WALI (DATES UNKNOWN)   Activist for Afghan women's rights, who settled in the United States after the Russians invaded Afghanistan in 1979. She worked to improve the lives of Afghan women and was one of three women who took part as delegates in the United Nations talks on a provisional government for post-Taliban Afghanistan. Wali is head of the Washington, D.C.–based agency Refugee Women in Development.

MARY WOLLSTONECRAFT (1759–1797)   Author of *A Vindication of the Rights of Men,* with which she established her reputation as a writer in 1790. Two years later, she wrote *A Vindication of the Rights of Woman,* which inspired the international women's movement. Her second daughter. Mary Wollstonecraft Shelley, authored *Frankenstein.*

FRANCES "FANNY" WRIGHT (1795–1852)   Socialist and free-thought advocate in 1830s America. The first American woman to speak publicly against slavery and for the equality of women, she also advocated birth control and liberalized divorce laws, among other rights. As a rebel, she inspired Susan B. Anthony and Elizabeth Cady Stanton. She joined a utopian community, New Harmony, in Indiana, created by Robert Owen. In 1825, she published a plan for the gradual emancipation of American slaves and created a settlement, Nashoba, in Memphis, Tennessee, to train slaves for freedom, which was not successful financially.

MARGUERITE YOURCENAR (1903–1987)   Novelist who in 1980 became the first female admitted to the renowned Académie française. Her work, characterized by its classical humanism, which suited the academy, contrasted with her explorations in literature—translating spirituals, blues and gospel tunes and Japanese Noh plays—and lesbianism.

ZOYA (1981–   )   Afghan activist. The daughter of activists in Kabul, Zoya was raised by her grandmother after her parents disappeared. She was a child during the 1979 Russian invasion and a teen when the Taliban took power in 1994. She is now a member of the Revolutionary Association of the Women of Afghanistan (RAWA) and lives and works in a refugee camp near the Afghan-Pakistani border. She also travels abroad to raise funds for the organization.

9

Organizations and Agencies

Afghan Independent Human Rights Commission
URL: http://www.aihrc.org.af
Pul-i-Surkh, Karti 3
Kabul, Afghanistan
Phone: (93) (20) 2500676, (93) (20) 2500677, (93) (20) 2500197
E-mail: aihrc@aihrc.org.af

The women's rights unit of the commission monitors the situation of women in Afghanistan. It also attempts to eliminate and reduce the discriminatory attitudes toward women in Afghan society.

Afghan Women's Council (AWC)
URL: http://www.afghanistanwomencouncil.org
House # 117, Str. 6, Sector H-4, Phase II, Hayatabad
P.O. Box 1215 GPO
Peshawar, Pakistan
Phone: (92) (91) 811261
Fax: (92) (91) 812138

Founded in 1986, AWC started its activities for human rights, women's rights, children's rights, and peace building in 1993. As a nongovernmental, nonprofit, nonsectarian organization, it runs the Ariana School, the Mother and Child Health Clinic, in Peshawar, where it provides education and medical care to refugee families. Its 20-bed Nazo Ana Clinic in Kabul stayed open during the five years of the Taliban regime. AWC also manages humanitarian relief efforts for newly arrived refugees and publishes the monthly journal *Zan-e-Afghan* (Afghan women) to encourage women to act as a resource for peace and stability in the country.

Afghan Women's Network (AWN)
URL: http://www.afghanwomensnetwork.org
H#193, Street-3 Qalai Fathullah
Kabul, Afghanistan
Phone: (93) 2200691
E-mail: awnkabul@hotmail.com

Established in 1995, this nonpartisan network of women and women's NGOs is committed to empowering Afghan women and ensuring their equal participation in society. Currently, there are 70 NGO members and over 3,000 individual members in Afghanistan and in Pakistan. The Web site provides current reports on legislation and elections in Afghanistan and announcements for women's training programs.

African Women's Development Fund (AWDF)
URL: http://www.awdf.org
25 Yiyiwa Street
Abelenkpe
Accra, Ghana
Phone: (233) (21) 780477
Fax: (233) (21) 782502
E-mail: awdf@awdf.org

AWDF supports work in women's human rights, political participation, peace building, health, reproductive rights, HIV/AIDS, and economic empowerment. It offers grants that range from $1,000 to a maximum of $25,000.

The Alice Paul Institute (API)
URL: http://www.alicepaul.org
128 Hooton Road
Mt. Laurel, NJ 08054
Phone: (856) 231-1885
Fax: (856) 231-4223
E-mail: info@alicepaul.org

A not-for-profit corporation established in 1984 with the goal to enhance public awareness of the life and work of Alice Paul as author of the Equal Rights Amendment. The organization also develops and presents educational programs to empower women and girls to accept leadership in their communities and workplaces.

All-China Women's Federation (ACWF)
URL: http://www.women.org.cn/english/index.htm

The Chinese Women's Delegation on Africa
Phone: (010) 65211639
Fax: (010) 65211156

Founded on April 3, 1949, the All-China Women's Federation (ACWF) has as its main task helping women out of poverty and illiteracy. It works closely with the Chinese government to create approved means for advancing Chinese women of different ethnic groups in all professions through a variety of training programs.

American Civil Liberties Union (ACLU)
URL: http://www.aclu.org
125 Broad Street, 18th Floor
New York, NY 10004-2400
Phone: (800) 775-2258

Founded in 1920, this nonprofit and nonpartisan organization has grown from a roomful of civil liberties activists to an organization of more than 500,000 members and supporters. The ACLU handles nearly 6,000 court cases annually through offices in almost every state in America. Its mission is to preserve all of the protections and guarantees stated in the Constitution's Bill of Rights. The ACLU's Women's Rights Project, founded in 1972 by Ruth Bader Ginsburg, also focuses on low-wage Latina workers' rights in the New York area, tackling the issues of sexual harassment, gender discrimination, pregnancy discrimination, and full and fair wages for working Latina women's labor. The project conducts know-your-rights workshops for working women at these organizations and work related to translating rights legislation and literature into Spanish.

Amnesty International
URL: http://www.amnesty.org
322 8th Avenue
New York, NY 10001
Phone: (212) 807-8400

This NGO is a worldwide movement of 1.8 million members, supporters, and subscribers in over 150 countries and territories in every region of the world, who campaign for internationally recognized human rights. AI upholds the *Universal Declaration of Human Rights* and other international human rights standards and undertakes research and action focused on preventing and ending grave abuses of the rights to physical and mental integrity, freedom of conscience and expression, and freedom from discrimination, within the context of its work to promote all human rights.

Asia-Japan Women's Resource Center (AJWRC)
URL: http://www.aworc.org/org/ajwrc/ajwrc.html
14-10-311 Sakuragaoka
Shibuya-ku
Tokyo 150-0031, Japan
Phone: (81) (0)3 3780 5245
Fax: (81) (0)3 3463 9752
E-mail: ajwrc@jca.apc.org

The Asia-Japan Women's Resource Center (AJWRC) was formed in 1995; its foundations are in the Asian Women's Association (AWA), which pioneered from the 1970s the development of a strong gender, a North-South perspective within the Japanese progressive mass movements in general, and the women's movement. The founding of AJWRC is a response to the challenge of creating an alternative society for the 21st century: a society that is based on gender justice, ecological sustainability, as well as local and global democracy.

Asian Centre for Women's Human Rights (ASCENT)
URL: http://www.achrweb.org
P.O. Box AC 662 Cubao 1135
Quezon City, Philippines
Phone: (632) 928-4973; (632) 410-1512
Fax: (632) 533-0452; (632) 928-4973
E-mail: ascent@csi.com.ph

ASCENT was set up to respond to the training needs of women's organizations in Asia on human rights standards. ASCENT uses the human rights system to monitor, investigate, document, report, and enforce women's human rights. It has developed a women's human rights defenders program that gives women's rights training including understanding of and access to UN systems and international human rights standards and mechanisms.

Association des Femmes du Kivu (UWAKI), DRC
URL: http://www.oxfamsol.be/fr/Union-des-femmes-paysannes-du-sud.html

In October 2002, the Association des Femmes du Kivu (UWAKI) organized a workshop that brought together 90 women from Burundi, the DRC, Kenya, and Rwanda in Butembo in eastern DRC's war-torn province of North Kivu. The objective was to discuss and share experiences on ways to promote the integration of women in decision-making.

Center for Health and Human Rights
URL: http://www.hsph.harvard.edu/fxbcenter
Harvard School of Public Health
8 Story Street
Cambridge, MA 02138
Phone: (617) 496-4370
Fax: (617) 496-4380

The François-Xavier Bagnoud Center for Health and Human Rights is the first academic center to focus exclusively on health and human rights. The center combines research and teaching with a strong commitment to service and policy development, with its faculty working at international and national levels through collaboration and partnerships with health and human rights practitioners, governmental and nongovernmental organizations, academic institutions, and international agencies.

The Center for Reproductive Rights
URL: http://www.crlp.org
120 Wall Street
New York, NY 10005
Phone: (917) 637-3600
Fax: (917) 637-3666
E-mail: info@reprorights.org

The Center for Reproductive Rights provides national and international reports on reproductive law.

The Center for Women's Global Leadership (CWGL)
URL: http://www.cwgl.rutgers.edu
Douglass College
Rutgers, The State University of New Jersey
160 Ryders Lane
New Brunswick, NJ 08901-8555
Phone: (732) 932-8782
Fax: (732) 932-1180
E-mail: cwgl@igc.org

The CWGL develops and facilitates women's leadership for human rights and social justice worldwide. Founded as a project of Douglass College in 1989, it is a unit of the Institute for Women's Leadership (IWL)—a consortium of six women's programs at Rutgers University—created to study and promote how and why women lead, and to develop programs that prepare women of all ages to lead effectively.

The Center for Women Veterans
URL: http://www1.va.gov/womenvet
Department of Veterans Affairs
810 Vermont Avenue NW
Washington, DC 20420
Phone: (202) 273-6193

In fulfillment of Congress's Public Law 103-446, the center assesses women veterans' services within and outside the department to assure that Veterans Administration (VA) policy and planning practices address the needs of women veterans and foster VA participation in general federal initiatives focusing on women's issues. It identifies policies, practices, programs, and related activities that are unresponsive or insensitive to the needs of women veterans. It also recommends changes and initiatives designed to address these deficiencies.

Chinese Academy of Social Science (CASS)
URL: http://bic.cass.cn/english
Bureau of International Cooperation
Hong Kong Maco and Taiwan Academic Affairs Office

The National Academy of the People's Republic of China for the Social Sciences, CASS is an institution of the State Council of China, founded in 1977. It develops scholarship in the fields of social sciences and the humanities and carries out theoretical exploration and policy studies, which include women's rights.

Coalition Against Trafficking in Women (CATW)
URL: http://www.catwinternational.org/
P.O. Box 7427, Jaf Station
New York, NY 10116 USA
Phone: (212) 643-9896 (fax)
E-mail: info@catwinternational.org

A nongovernmental organization that promotes women's human rights, working internationally to combat sexual exploitation in all its forms, especially prostitution and trafficking in women and children, in particular girls. The organization operates in countries around the world by launching and supporting anti-trafficking projects in areas that few programs address: the links between prostitution and trafficking, challenging the demand for prostitution that promotes sex trafficking, and protecting the women and children who are its victims by working to curb legal acceptance and tolerance of the sex industry.

Committee on the Elimination of Discrimination against Women (CEDAW)
URL: http://www2.ohchr.org/english/bodies/cedaw/index.htm
c/o Office of the United Nations High Commissioner for Human Rights (OHCHR)
Palais Wilson
52 rue des Pâquis
CH-1201 Geneva, Switzerland

The committee acts as a monitoring system to oversee the implementation of the convention of the same name by those states that have acceded to the convention through reports submitted by those states' parties. The committee considers these reports and makes suggestions and recommendations based on their consideration. It may also invite United Nations specialized agencies to submit reports for consideration and may receive information from nongovernmental organizations. The committee reports annually on its activities to the General Assembly through the Economic and Social Council, and the council transmits these reports to the Commission on the Status of Women.

The Committee on Women in the NATO Forces (CWINF)
URL: http://www.nato.int/issues/women_nato/index.html
NATO Headquarters
Blvd Leopold III
1110 Brussels, Belgium
E-mail: natodoc@hq.nato.int

CWINF is a mission to advise NATO leadership and member nations on critical issues affecting women in the Alliance's Armed Forces that has been in effect since 1961.

Danish Women's Society (Dansk Kvindesamfund)
URL: http://www.kvindesamfund.dk
Niels Hemmingsensgade 10, 3
1153 Copenhagen, Denmark

Phone: (45) 33157837
E-mail: kontor@kvindesamfund.dk

The first women's suffrage organization in Denmark, formed in 1871, the Danish Women's Society works for establishing real equality of liberties, responsibilities, and opportunities of women and men. It is a nonpartisan organization affiliated with the International Alliance of Women (IAW).

End Child Prostitution, Child Pornography and Trafficking of Children for Sexual Purposes (ECPAT)
URL: http://ecpatusa.org/ECPAT-USA
157 Montague Street
Brooklyn, NY11201
Phone: (718) 935-9192
E-mail: ecpat@ecpatusa.org

A network of organizations and individuals created in 1991 in Asia during the End Child Prostitution in Asian Tourism campaign. The group of NGO employees and other private individuals work together to eliminate the global commercial sexual exploitation and illegal trafficking of children and protect their rights through educational programs and research for law-enforcement and travel agencies. The organization also funds the medical needs of individual child victims of sex trafficking and monitors the border between Haiti and the Dominican Republic to mitigate the exploitation of victims from the 2010 earthquake.

Equal Employment Opportunity Commission (EEOC)
URL: http://www.eeoc.gov
1801 L Street NW
Washington, DC 20507
Phone: (202) 663-4900

The EEOC has five commissioners and a General Counsel appointed by the president and confirmed by the Senate. The commission makes equal employment opportunity policy and approves most litigation. The General Counsel is responsible for conducting EEOC enforcement litigation under Title VII of the Civil Rights Act of 1964 (Title VII), the Equal Pay Act (EPA), the Age Discrimination in Employment Act (ADEA), and the Americans with Disabilities Act (ADA).

EMILY's List
URL: http://www.emilyslist.org

1120 Connecticut Avenue NW, Suite 1100
Washington, DC 20036
Phone: (202) 326-1400
Fax: (202) 326-1415

Founded in 1985, EMILY's List is a financial resource for women seeking federal office. Before it existed, no Democratic Party woman had ever been elected to the U.S. Senate in her own right, no woman had ever been elected governor of a large state, and the number of Democratic women in the U.S. House had declined to 12—less than 3 percent of the chamber's 435 members. Since then, the grassroots network has helped elect 61 Democratic members of Congress, 11 senators, and eight governors.

FemAid
URL: http://www.femaid.org
33, rue Guy Moquet
92240 Malakoff, France
E-mail: info@femaid.org

FemAid is an unaffiliated, independent nonprofit organization based in Paris, run by a team that has worked in humanitarian aid in war zones. They were active in Bosnia with the Enfants de Bosnie, an NGO that helped women and children in the suburb of Sarajevo, culminating in the reconstruction of a major primary school in Dobrinja. Since late 1999, they have been working mainly but not exclusively with the Revolutionary Association of Women of Afghanistan (RAWA), the only secular feminist group in Afghanistan. FemAid also aided victims of the earthquake in Kashmir, both Pakistani and Indian, at the end of 2005.

Feminenza International
URL: http://www.feminenza.org
P.O. Box 271
Welwyn Garden City, Herts AL7 1WJ, England
Phone: (44) 7985 171949
E-mail: info.uk@feminenza.org;
P.O. Box 24381
Fort Lauderdale, FL 33307
Phone: (561) 451-0141
info.fna@feminenza.org

An international women's network that holds self-development workshops, courses, talks, seminars, and retreats for personal and spiritual growth for women. It also has North American chapters, headquartered in Fort Lauderdale, Florida. Teachings are based on original research concerning the three inner lives of the woman—referred to as female, woman, and lady—and how understanding these three aspects can enrich and improve women's lives, relationships, and choices.

Feminist Majority Foundation
URL: http://www.feminist.org
1600 Wilson Boulevard, Suite 801
Arlington, VA 22209
Phone: (703) 522-2214
Fax: (703) 522-2219

Advocacy group that provides news feeds about the latest legislation that may impact women's rights in the United States and abroad. Areas of particular concern to the organization are human trafficking, Afghanistan women's rights, domestic violence, and reproductive rights.

FEMNET
URL: http://www.femnet.or.ke
The African Women's Development and Communication Network
P.O. Box 54562
00200 Nairobi, Kenya
Fax: (254) (20) 3742927
E-mail: admin@femnet.or.ke

The African Women's Development and Communications Network (FEMNET) is a pan-African network addressing African women's development, equality, and other human rights. Set up in 1988 and based in Nairobi, Kenya, FEMNET works on advocacy at the regional and international levels and training on gender analysis, mainstreaming, and communications.

Femmes Afrique Solidarité (FAS)
URL: http://www.fasngo.org/
Representative Office in NY
777 United Nations Plaza, 5th Floor
New York, NY
Phone: (212) 687-1369
Fax: (212) 661-4188
E-mail: infony@fasngo.org

Experience in the field of gender, conflict resolution, peace building, and security through networking and communication activities of women in their communities. Promotes women's rights and initiatives in Africa; strengthening women's leadership capacity, including at the grassroots, to restore and maintain peace in their countries; develop policies, structures, programs, and the peace process for the attainment of durable peace and human security in Africa. Advocates at the national, regional, and international levels for African women's rights and concerns and their critical role in peace and security issues.

The Foundation for Women's Health, Research and Development (FORWARD)
URL: http://www.forwarduk.org.uk
Unit 4, 765–767 Harrow Road
London, United Kingdom NW10 5NY
Phone: (44) (0)20 8960 4000
Fax: (44) (0)20 8960 4014

An international nongovernmental organization, FORWARD is pursuing the elimination of human trafficking, especially of women and girls, and unsafe traditional practices such as female genital mutilation.

Girlup.org
URL: http:// girlup.org
UN Foundation
1800 Massachusetts Avenue NW, Suite 400,
Washington, DC 20036
Phone: (202) 887-9040
E-mail: adielsi@unfoundation.org

A United Nations Foundation's initiative offering intersupport by American girls, age 10 to 19, to girls in other countries—developed and developing.

Global Peace Initiative of Women
URL: http://www.gpiw.org
301 East 57 Street, 3rd Floor
New York, NY 10022
Phone: (212) 593-5877
Fax: (646) 792-3871
E-mail: info@gpiw.org

This global network includes women and men in all walks of life.

Green Belt Movement (GBM Kenya)
URL: http://greenbeltmovement.org/index.php
P.O. Box 67545
Kilimani Lane (off Elgeyo Marakwet Road)
Adams Arcade
Nairobi, Kenya
Phone: (254) (20) 3873057, (254) (20) 3871523
E-mail: gbm@wananchi.com

The Nobel Prize laureate Professor Wangari Muta Maathai established the Green Belt Movement in 1977, under the auspices of the National Council of Women of Kenya. A grassroots nongovernmental organization, Green Belt focuses on environmental conservation, community development, and capacity building through women's efforts.

The Guttmacher Institute
URL: http://www.guttmacher.org
1301 Connecticut Avenue NW, Suite 700
Washington, DC 20036
Phone: (202) 296-4012, (877) 823-0262
Fax: (202) 223-5756
E-mail: info@guttmacher.org

A nonprofit organization that focuses on sexual and reproductive health research, policy analysis, and public education. The institute's mission is to protect the reproductive choices of all women and men in the United States and throughout the world. It supports people's ability to obtain the information and services needed to achieve their full human rights, safeguard their health, and exercise their individual responsibilities in regard to sexual behavior and relationships, reproduction, and family formation.

Heritage Foundation
URL: http://www.heritage.org
214 Massachusetts Avenue NE
Washington, DC 20002
Phone: (202) 546-4400

A research and educational think tank whose mission is to formulate and promote conservative public policies based on the principles of free enterprise, limited government, individual freedom, traditional American values, and a strong national defense.

Human Rights Watch
URL: http://hrw.org/women
485 Fifth Avenue
New York, NY 10017
Phone: (212) 972-8400
Fax: (212) 972-0905

Human Rights Watch has portals specific to different regions of the globe, including Afghanistan, China, and Tibet. Originally founded in 1978, as Helsinki Watch, the Human Rights Watch Asia office was opened in 1985 and the Watch Committees became Human Rights Watch in 1988. A special division devoted to women now surveys their rights across all regions.

Institute for Women's Policy Research (IWPR)
URL: http://www.iwpr.org
1707 L Street NW, Suite 750
Washington, DC 20036
Phone: (202) 785-5100
Fax: (202) 833-4362
E-mail: iwpr@iwpr.org

A research organization founded in 1987 to meet the needs for women-centered policy-oriented scientific research, IWPR focuses on issues of poverty and welfare, employment and earnings, work and family issues, health and safety, and women's civic and political participation.

International Labour Organisation's Bureau for Gender Equality
URL: http://www.ilo.org
4, route des Morillons
CH-1211, Geneva 22, Switzerland
Phone: (41) (22) 799 6090
Fax: (41) (22) 799 7657
E-mail: genprom@ilo.org

The role of the Bureau for Gender Equality, part of the Geneva-based Secretariat of the International Labour Organisation, is to advocate gender equality throughout the organization. It produces a yearly document, monitoring global employment trends.

Inter-Parliamentary Union (IPU)
URL: http://www.ipu.org
5, chemin du Pommier

Case postale 330, CH-1218
Le Grand-Saconnex
Geneva, Switzerland
Phone: (41) (22) 919 4150
Fax: (41) (22) 919 4160

The IPU is the international organization of parliaments of sovereign states (Article 1 of the Statutes of the Inter-Parliamentary Union). Established in 1889, the union is the focal point for worldwide parliamentary dialogue and works for peace and cooperation among peoples and for the firm establishment of representative democracy.

KULU—Women and Development
URL: http://www.kulu.dk/in_english.htm
Rosenoerns Allé 12, st. 1634
Copenhagen V, Denmark
Phone: (45) 3315 7870
Fax: (45) 3332 5330
E-mail: kulu@kulu.dk

KULU is an umbrella NGO for 25 women's organizations, with three local organizations and an individual membership base. It is also part of the Network on Indigenous Peoples, Gender and Natural Resource Management (IGNARM), a Danish NGO network collaboration that is active in African nations and China.

League of Women Voters
URL: http://www.lwv.org
1730 M Street NW, Suite 1000
Washington, DC 20036-4508
Phone: (202) 429-1965
Fax: (202) 429-0854

The voluntary nonpartisan public service organization was organized in 1920 in Chicago as an outgrowth of Carrie Chapman Catt's National American Woman Suffrage Association. The league was organized to educate American women in the intelligent use of their newly won suffrage. Formerly limited to female membership, the league voted in 1974 to accept men as full members and now has over 110,000 members.

Muslim Women's League (MWL)
URL: http://www.mwlusa.org

3010 Wilshire Boulevard, Suite #519
Los Angeles, CA 90010
Phone: (626) 358-0335
E-mail: mwl@mwlusa.org

MWL is a nonprofit American Muslim organization working to implement the values of Islam and thereby reclaim the status of women as free, equal, and vital contributors to society.

National Abortion Federation (NAF)
URL: http://www.prochoice.org
1755 Massachusetts Avenue NW, Suite 600
Washington, DC 20036
Phone: (202) 667-5881
Fax: (202) 667-5890
E-mail: naf@prochoice.org

A professional association of abortion providers in the United States and Canada that believes women should be trusted to make private medical decisions in consultation with their health care providers. NAF offers training and services to abortion providers and information and referral services to women.

National Coalition against Domestic Violence (NCADV)
URL: http://www.ncadv.org
1120 Lincoln Street, Suite 1603
Denver, CO 80203
Phone: (303) 839-1852
Fax: (303) 831-9251
E-mail: sbaca@ncadv.org

NCADV was formally organized in January 1978 when over 100 battered women's advocates from all parts of the nation attended the U.S. Commission on Civil Rights hearing on battered women in Washington, D.C., to address common problems these programs usually faced in isolation. NCADV is the only national organization with grassroots shelter and service programs for battered women.

National Coalition of 100 Black Women (NCBW)
URL: http://www.nc100bw.org/
1925 Adam C. Powell Jr. Blvd., Suite 1L,
New York, New York 10026
Phone: (212) 222-5660

Fax: (212) 222-5675
E-mail: ExecutiveDirector@nc100bw.org

NCBW empowers African-American woman through greater access to education, political strength, business opportunities and civic responsibility.

National Commission on the Status of Women (NCSW)
URL: http://www.ncsw.gov.pk
House # 39, Street 56, F-6/4
Islamabad, Pakistan
Phone: (51) 922 4875
Fax: (51) 922 4877

Founded in 2000 by the president of Pakistan, under the Ordinance of July 17, 2000, the commission has as its main objectives the emancipation of women, equalization of opportunities and socioeconomic conditions of women and men, and elimination of all types of discrimination against women. Functions of the commission include the examination of the policy, programs, and other measures taken by the government for women's development and the review of all policies, laws, rules, and regulations affecting the status and rights of women and gender equality in accordance with the country's constitution.

National Council of Negro Women, Inc. (NCNW)
URL: http://www.ncnw.org
633 Pennsylvania Avenue NW
Washington, DC 20004
Phone: (202) 737-0120
Fax: (202) 737-0476

Mary McLeod Bethune founded NCNW in 1935, forming it out of several major national black women's associations. She remained its president until 1949 and was its representative at the founding conference of the United Nations in San Francisco, California, in 1945. NCNW helps women of African descent to improve the quality of life for themselves, their families, and their communities with an outreach to 4 million women and has consultative status at the United Nations.

National Council of Women's Organizations (NCWO)
URL: http://www.womensorganizations.org,
http://www.equalrightsamendment.org
1050 17th Street NW, Suite 250

Washington, DC 20036
Phone: (202) 293-4505
Fax: (202) 293-4507
E-mail: ncwo@ncwo-online.org

NCWO is a nonpartisan, nonprofit umbrella organization of about 200 groups, which collectively represent over 10 million women across the country. The national coalition grew out of an informal group of women's organizational leaders after defeat of the Equal Rights Amendment in 1983. Capitalizing on the energy and inspiration that followed the 1995 Beijing Conference, NCWO has taken an active role in the policy arena, uniting women's groups across the country to work together to advance the progressive women's agenda and the Equal Rights Amendment.

National Organization for Women (NOW)
URL: http://www.now.org
1100 H Street NW, 3rd Floor
Washington, DC 20005
Phone: (202) 628-8669
Fax: (202) 785-8576

The National Organization for Women (NOW) is the largest organization of feminist activists in the United States. NOW has 500,000 contributing members and 550 chapters in all 50 states and the District of Columbia. Since its founding in 1966, NOW has had the goal of taking action to bring about equality for all women. NOW works to eliminate discrimination and harassment in the workplace, schools, the justice system, and all other sectors of society; secure abortion, birth control, and reproductive rights for all women; end all forms of violence against women; and eradicate racism, sexism, and homophobia.

The National Women's History Project (NWHP)
URL: http://www.nwhp.org, http://www.legacy98.org
3343 Industrial Drive, Suite 4
Santa Rosa, CA 95403
Phone: (707) 636-2888
Fax: (707) 639-2909

A nonpartisan, nonprofit educational organization dedicated to promoting the historic contributions and the rich, diverse experiences of women to mainstream culture and society. Founded in 1996, the National Women's History Museum is scheduled to open in Washington, D.C., in 2007.

National Women's Law Center (NWLC)
URL: http://www.nwlc.org
11 Dupont Circle NW, Suite 800
Washington, DC 20036
Phone: (202) 588-5180
Fax: (202) 588-5185
E-mail: info@nwlc.org

NWLC is a nonprofit organization that has been working since 1972 to expand the possibilities for women and their families at work, in school, and in virtually every aspect of their lives. NWLC focuses on major concerns to women and girls, including family economic security, education, employment opportunities, and health, with special attention given to low-income women.

National Women's Political Caucus
URL: http://www.nwpc.org
1712 Eye Street NW, Suite 503
Washington, DC 20006
Phone: (202) 785-1100
Fax: (202) 370-6306
E-mail: info@nwpc.org

The National Women's Political Caucus is a multicultural, intergenerational, and multiissue grassroots organization dedicated to increasing women's participation in the political process and creating a true women's political power base to achieve equality for all women. NWPC recruits, trains, and supports pro-choice women candidates for elected and appointed offices at all levels of government regardless of party affiliation.

Office on Violence against Women, U.S. Department of Justice
URL: http://www.usdoj.gov/ovw
145 N Street NE, Suite 10W.121
Washington, DC 20530
Phone: (202) 307-6026
Fax: (202) 307-3911

Since its inception in 1995, the Violence against Women Office, now the Office on Violence against Women, has worked closely with components of the Office of Justice Programs, the Office of Legal Policy, the Office of Legislative Affairs, the Office of Intergovernmental Affairs, the Immigration and Naturalization Office, the Executive Office for United States Attorneys, U.S. Attorneys' Offices, and state, tribal, and local jurisdictions to implement the mandates of the Violence against Women Act and subsequent legislation.

PeaceWomen Project
URL: http://www.peacewomen.org
WILPF, UN Office
777 United Nations Plaza, 6th Floor
New York, NY 10017
Phone: (212) 682-1265
Fax: (212) 286-8211
E-mail: info@peacewomen.org

In response to the unanimous adoption of UNSC Resolution 1325, the Women's International League for Peace and Freedom (WILPF) United Nations Office in New York City developed the PeaceWomen Project in 2001 to monitor and advocate its full and rapid implementation.

Pennsylvania Women Work
URL: http://www.pawomenwork.org/
411 Seventh Avenue - Suite 925
Pittsburgh, PA 15219
Phone: (412) 281-9240, (866) 729-6636

The network, now hosted by the Pennsylvania chapter, publishes the *Economic Equity Insider* monthly while Congress is in session and is a beneficiary of membership with Women Work! The National Network for Women's Employment.

Planned Parenthood Federation of America (PPFA)
URL: http://www.plannedparenthood.org
434 West 33rd Street
New York, NY 10001
Phone: (212) 541-7800
Fax: (212) 245-1845
E-mail: actioncenter@ppfa.org

PPFA's affiliated health centers provide reproductive health care and sexual health information to nearly 5 million women, men, and teens each year through family planning counseling, testing, and referrals. Its sexual education community programs include a wide range of information resources and materials about a variety of topics concerning family planning. The organization also sponsors a range of advocacy events to defend reproductive freedom.

Rape, Abuse & Incest National Network (RAINN)
URL: http://www.rainn.org
635-B Pennsylvania Avenue SE
Washington, DC 20003
Phone: (202) 544-1034, (800) 656-4673, ext. 3
Fax: (202) 544-3556
E-mail: info@rainn.org

The nation's largest anti–sexual assault organization has been ranked as one of America's 100 Best Charities by *Worth* magazine. RAINN was founded in 1994 by Scott Berkowitz, who continues as the organization's president.

Réseau des Femmes pour la Defense des Droits et de la Paix
URL: http://www.societecivile.cd/node/789
72, avenue maniema
Kivu region, DRC
Phone: (243) 0813181854
E-mail: rfdp1999@yahoo.fr

Human rights organization that has been training and mobilizing women for peace-making missions in Africa since 1999.

Revolutionary Association of the Women of Afghanistan (RAWA)
URL: http://www.rawa.org
P.O. Box 374
Quetta, Pakistan
Phone: (92) (300) 8551638
E-mail: rawa@rawa.org

RAWA is the oldest political/social organization of Afghan women involved in education, health, income generation, and politics. It was established in Kabul, in 1977, by a number of Afghan woman intellectuals under the leadership of Meena (1956–87), who was assassinated in 1987 in Quetta, Pakistan. RAWA's objective is to involve an increasing number of Afghan women in social and political activities aimed at acquiring women's human rights and contributing to the struggle for the establishment of a government based on democratic and secular values in Afghanistan.

Roqia Center for Women's Rights, Studies and Education
URL: http://www.kabultec.org
Kabultec
P.O. Box 2079

Falls Church, VA 22042
Phone: (703) 536-6471
E-mail: Kabultec@erols.com

Founded by the Afghan women's rights advocate Nasrine Gross in 2002, the Roqia Center provides women's rights seminars, academic information, and adult literacy in Kabul, Afghanistan. The innovative literacy program requires husbands and wives to attend class, thereby leveling the playing field for women and helping men experience models of democratic behavior and experience. The organization is the partner of Kabultec, a charity organization in the United States.

Run for Congo Women
URL: http://www.runforcongowomen.org/index.html
See Women for Women International for contact information.

Founded by photographer Lisa Shannon to raise money to sponsor women in the DRC through running events. Shannon raised nearly $28,000 on her first run in 2006. The movement has since expanded to runs and walks throughout the United States, raising more than $600,000, enough to sponsor 1,444 women in the DRC.

Society for Women's Health Research (SWHR)
URL: http://www.womenshealthresearch.org
1025 Connecticut Avenue NW, Suite 701
Washington, DC 20036
Phone: (202) 223-8224
Fax: (202) 833-3472

Founded in the late 1980s by women's health professionals who were convinced that the health of American women was at risk because of biases in biomedical research, SWHR is a not-for-profit research organization that also produces reports on sex-based medicine and identifies areas in which women differ from men in their health care needs. It guarantees that women's health has a voice in the federal government by supporting the women's health offices within agencies such as the Department of Health and Human Services, the Food and Drug Administration, and the Centers for Disease Control and Prevention.

Soroptimist International
URL: http://www.soroptimist.org
1709 Spruce Street
Philadelphia, PA 19103-6103

Phone: (215) 893-9000
Fax: (215) 893-5200
E-mail: siahq@soroptimist.org

Founded in 1921, Soroptimist is an international organization for business and professional women who provide volunteer service to their communities. Almost 100,000 Soroptimists in about 120 countries and territories contribute time and financial support to community-based and international projects benefiting women and girls. The name *Soroptimist* means "best for women." Club projects range from renovating domestic violence shelters, to providing mammograms to low-income women, to sponsoring self-esteem workshops for teenage girls.

Third Wave Foundation
URL: http://www.thirdwavefoundation.org
511 West 25th Street, Suite 301
New York, NY 10001
Phone: (212) 675-0700
Fax: (212) 255-6653
E-mail: info@thirdwavefoundation.org

The Third Wave Foundation is a feminist activist foundation working nationally to support young women ages 15 to 30. Third Wave creates initiatives, operates specific grant and public education programs, and facilities networking and leadership development opportunities. It is led by a board of young women, men, and transgender activists striving to combat inequalities they face as a result of their age, gender, race, sexual orientation, economic status, or level of education.

United Nations Development Fund for Women (UNIFEM)
URL: http://www.unifem.org, http://www.unifem-eseasia.org
304 East 45th Street, 15th Floor
New York, NY 10017
Phone: (212) 906-6400
Fax: (212) 906-6705

UNIFEM was created in 1976 after the 1975 UN First World Conference on Women in Mexico City. Placing the advancement of women's human rights at the center of all of its efforts, it has worked to help improve the living standards of women in developing countries by providing financial and technical assistance to innovative programs and strategies to foster women's empowerment and gender equality. UNIFEM focuses its activities on four strategic areas: (1)

reducing feminized poverty, (2) ending violence against women, (3) reversing the spread of HIV/AIDS among women and girls, and (4) achieving gender equality in democratic governance in times of peace as well as war. UNIFEM also has an East and Southeast Asia Regional Office that covers 13 countries.

United Nations Division for the Advancement of Women (DAW)
URL: http://www.un.org/womenwatch/daw
2 UN Plaza, DC2-12th Floor
New York, NY 10017
Fax: (212) 963-3463
E-mail: daw@un.org

Located within the Department of Economic and Social Affairs of the United Nations, DAW advocates the improvement of the status of women of the world and the achievement of their equality with men, both within and outside the United Nations system. DAW also provides oversight to the Commission on the Status of Women (CSW), established on June 21, 1946, to prepare recommendations and reports to the council on promoting women's rights in political, economic, civil, social, and educational fields. The commission is the vehicle by which the UN is monitoring the Beijing Platform for Action on a yearly basis.

United Nations International Research and Training Institute for the
 Advancement of Women (INSTRAW)
URL: http://www.un-instraw.org
102-A Santo Domingo, DN, Dominican Republic
Phone: (809) 685-2111
Fax: (809) 685-2117

INSTRAW is a United Nations entity mandated at the international level to promote and undertake research and training programs to contribute to the advancement of women and gender equality worldwide. By stimulating and assisting the efforts of intergovernmental, governmental, and nongovernmental organizations, INSTRAW plays a critical role in advancing the global agenda of gender equality, development, and peace. INSTRAW is funded entirely through voluntary contributions from UN member states and donor agencies; the institute does not have a regular UN budget.

United Nations Population Fund (UNFPA)
URL: http://www.unfpa.org
220 East 42nd Street

New York, NY 10017
Phone: (212) 297-5000

An international development agency that promotes the right of every woman, man, and child to enjoy a life of health and equal opportunity. UNFPA supports countries in using population data for policies and programs to reduce poverty and to ensure that every pregnancy is wanted, every birth is safe, every young person is free of HIV/AIDS, and every girl and woman is treated with dignity and respect.

UN Women
URL: http://www.unwomen.org
New York, NY

Created in July 2010 by the UN General Assembly, UN Women is part of a reform agenda by the UN that seeks to accelerate its goals for gender equality and women's empowerment through existing UN agencies and intergovernmental bodies. UN Women coordinates resources, policy making, standards, and their implementation in member states and provides a system of accountablility and progress.

Vital Voices Global Partnership
URL: http://www.vitalvoices.org
1150 Connecticut Avenue NW, Suite 600
Washington, DC 20036
Phone: (202) 861-2625
Fax: (202) 861-4290

This nonprofit organization grew out of the U.S. government's successful Vital Voices Democracy Initiative, which was established in 1997 by then–first lady Hillary Rodham Clinton and former secretary of state Madeleine Albright after the United Nations Fourth World Conference on Women in Beijing. With the U.S. foreign policy goal to promote the advancement of women, Vital Voices invests in women who are leading social, economic, and political progress in their countries through development and training initiatives and a global network.

The White House Project
http://www.thewhitehouseproject.org
110 Wall Street, 16th Floor
New York, NY 10005
Phone: (212) 785-6001

Fax: (212) 785-6007
E-mail: admin@thewhitehouseproject.org

The White House Project, a national nonpartisan, not-for-profit organization, aims to advance women's leadership in all communities and sectors, up to the U.S. presidency. Through multiplatform programs, it is trying to create a culture in which women can succeed in all realms and become the critical mass needed to make American institutions, businesses, and government representative of the American population.

Women as Partners for Peace in Africa (WOPPA)
URL:http://www.peacebuildingportal.org/index.asp?pgid=9&org=2617
Bld du 30 Juin, Galerie du Centenaire, 2e Etage
Kinshasa-Limete, DRC
Phone: (011) 243-9907586
E-mail: eldim20@hotmail.com or aninginab@yahoo.fr (NY)

WOPPA strengthens organizations that support women's participation in peace-building through networking and also transforms conflict, not only through nonviolence, but also by promoting peaceful solutions. WOPPA organized a meeting in Nairobi, Kenya, in February 2002 to bring together women from across the DRC and representatives of the warring parties, government, and civil society prior to the start of the Inter-Congolese Dialogue.

Women for Afghan Women
URL: http://www.womenforafghanwomen.org/queens.php
Queens, New York office: 158-24 73rd Ave.
Fresh Meadows, New York 11366
Phone: (718) 591-2434 Fax: (718) 591-2430

Afghanistan office:
Women for Afghan Women
Behind Park E Baharistan
Karte Parwan, Kabul, Afghanistan
Phone: (93)700974986
E-mail: office@womenforafghanwomen.org

A New York City–based organization that advocates for Afghan women and girls through a variety of programs in the two countries. Volunteers provide individual assistance, education, and counseling to Afghan adults and children, including field trips, tutoring, summer camps, and women's circle and girls' empowerment meetings.

Women for Women International
URL: http://www.womenforwomen.org
4455 Connecticut Avenue NW, Suite 200
Washington, DC 20008
Phone: (202) 737-7705
E-mail: general@womenforwomen.org.

Founded by Zainab Salbi, the organization pairs women willing to provide a year's support (at a cost of $27 per month) with "sisters" in eight war-torn countries, including Afghanistan and the DRC. The 2006 Conrad N. Hilton Humanitarian Prize recipient develops programs in financial aid, job training, rights awareness, and leadership education.

Women's Alliance for Peace and Human Rights in Afghanistan (WAPHA)
URL: http://www.wapha.org/index.html
P.O. Box 77057
Washington, DC 20012-7057
E-mail: info@wapha.org

WAPHA is a nonpartisan, nonprofit, and independent organization founded by Zieba Shorish-Shamley, a cultural anthropologist who obtained her degree from the University of Wisconsin–Madison. She is a proponent of Afghan women and girls' human rights and their full participation in the peace processes and future government of Afghanistan. She also advocates women's full participation in every aspect of Afghan sociocultural systems, including education, politics, economics, and medicine.

Women's Environment & Development Organization (WEDO)
URL: http://www.wedo.org
355 Lexington Avenue, 3rd Floor
New York, NY 10017
Phone: (212) 973-0325
Fax: (212) 973-0335
E-mail: wedo@wedo.org

WEDO is an international organization that advocates women's equality in global policy. It seeks to empower women as decision makers to achieve economic, social, and gender justice; a healthy, peaceful planet; and human rights for all.

Women's International League for Peace and Freedom (WILPF)
URL: http://www.wilpfinternational.org/

1, rue de Varembé
Case Postale 28
1211 Geneva 20, Switzerland
Phone: (41) (22) 919 70 80
Fax: (41) (22) 919 70 81
E-mail: info@wilpf.ch

Founded in April 1915 in the Hague, Netherlands, among 1,300 women from Europe and North America, among countries at war against each other and neutral ones, WILPF joined in a Congress of Women to protest the killing and destruction of the war then raging in Europe. Led by the Dutch physician Aletta Jacobs, the women issued 20 resolutions, some of immediate importance to end the conflict, negotiate the differences, and others with long-term aims to reduce conflict, prevent war, and lay the foundations for permanent peace. It is recognized as an international NGO with national sections in 37 countries and a New York UN office.

Women's Research and Education Institute (WREI)
URL: http://www.wrei.org
3300 North Fairfax Drive, Suite 218
Arlington, VA 22201
Phone: (703) 812-7990
Fax: (703) 812-0687
E-mail: wrei@wrei.org

WREI identifies issues affecting women and their roles in the family, workplace, and public arena, to inform and help shape public policy on these issues. It is a resource for federal legislators and administrators, and for state and local government officials, women's advocates, corporate policy makers, the media, teachers, and students. It promotes the informed scrutiny of policies regarding their effect on women and encourages the development of policy options that recognize the circumstances of women and their families.

10

Annotated Bibliography

This annotated bibliography consists of selected books, articles, Web documents, audiovisual materials, and media agencies organized by subject area. Listings are grouped in the following categories:

Abortion
Affirmative Action
Afghanistan
Africa
China
Contraceptives
Democratic Republic of the Congo (DRC)
Document Research
Education
Employment
Encyclopedias
European Union
Family Planning
Female Genital Mutilation
Feminist Literature
Finance for Women
France
Gender Roles
Health Care
History
HIV/AIDS

Human Trafficking
International Women's Movement
Islam
Leadership
Lesbian, Gay, Bisexual, Transgender Issues
Literacy
Literature
Military
Monitoring
Multicultural Issues
Politics
Population
Poverty
Property Rights
Racism
Statistics
Suffrage
Violence
Women's Studies

Within each category, items are listed by type of reference: books, articles, Web documents, television/film/video, or media. Articles include both newspapers and magazines. Articles and reports that are accessible in partial or full-text form on the Internet are listed under Web documents. An item is only listed once, where it is most germane to the subject of women's rights, although it may be relevant to several categories.

ABORTION
Books

Faux, Marian. *Roe v. Wade: The Untold Story of the Landmark Supreme Court Decision That Made Abortion Legal,* New York: Cooper Square Press edition, 2001 (republication of 1988 edition with new introduction). The 1973 U.S. Supreme Court decision that legalized abortion was one of the most stunning and far-reaching decisions the high court ever made. This work re-creates the case that prompted the decision and the story about the young lawyers involved in the showdown with the state. The updated edition follows the path the United States has been on since, detailing the challenges and erosions to the decision and the impact on policy and public attitude.

Hull, N. E. H., William James Hoffer, and Peter Charles, eds. *The Abortion Rights Controversy in America: A Legal Reader.* Chapel Hill: University of North Carolina Press, 2004. This is a compendium of primary sources related to the abortion controversy. The editors, who are also law professors, have collected relevant briefs, news articles, statutes, and first-person accounts with a strong focus on the development of abortion law in the 1990s.

Torr, James D, ed. *Opposing Viewpoints Series: Abortion.* Farmington Hills, Mich.: Greenhaven Press, 2006. As the title suggests, the Opposing Viewpoints Series is an excellent resource for researching controversial topics. Viewpoints in the abortion book include "Is Abortion Immoral?" "How Does Abortion Affect Women?" and "Should Abortion Rights Be Restricted?"

Articles

Childress, Sarah. "Abortion Wars: From Internet Campaigns to Cookie Boycotts, Small Pro-Life Groups Are Adopting a Range of Tactics to Fight the Nation's Largest Pro-Choice Organization." *Newsweek,* Web edition (April 13, 2004). Childress chronicles the efforts of pro-life organizations as they mobilize in their fight against legal abortion. Available online. URL: www.newsweek.com/2004/04/12/abortion-wars.html. Accessed June 2, 2011.

Chinni, Dante. "A Shift in Antiabortion Strategy?" *Christian Science Monitor,* 26 July 2005, 9. After years of arguing that *Roe* is a life-or-death issue, antiabortion activists are beginning to argue that the real issue is letting the voter decide about abortion. Abortion opponents can now argue they are not interested in overriding the voters' will but simply want to restore power to the voters.

Mayes, Tessa. "Do Politicians Know the Facts?" *New Statesman*, 21 March 2005, 14. Mayes focuses on various aspects of the topic of abortion and politics in Great Britain. Includes suggestions that politicians decide before election not to make abortion an issue, in reference to the personal views of party leaders, which were published in *Cosmopolitan* magazine. It remains questionable as to whether politicians know their facts. In addition to statistics from the British Pregnancy Advisory Service (BPAS), the survival rates for premature babies are discussed. The safety of early abortions and observations that women do not discover they are pregnant until late are also mentioned, as are the reasons the BPAS turns away 100 women a year.

Sullivan, Andrew. "Life Lesson," *New Republic*, 7 February 2005, 6. Sullivan focuses on the politics and morality of abortion. Although the priority is to reduce the number of unwanted pregnancies, reference is made to a speech by New York senator Hillary Rodham Clinton in which she affirms that abortion should remain legal. She acknowledges the role religious communities have played in encouraging women not to have abortions. The article highlights ways in which the pro-choice movement has damaged its image by not focusing on the moral aspects of abortion.

Web Documents

Ahman, Elisabeth, and Iqbal Shah. "Unsafe Abortion: Global and Regional Estimates of Unsafe Abortion and Associated Mortality in 2000." World Health Organization (WHO), 2004. Available online. URL: http://www.who.int /reproductive-health/ publications/unsafe_abortion_estimates_04/index.html. Accessed December 30, 2010. The report takes the position that unsafe abortion is preventable but persists as a significant cause of maternal morbidity and mortality rates in the developing world, where nearly all unsafe abortions occur. Since 1995, the World Health Organization has estimated the regional and global incidences of unsafe abortion and associated mortality rate. Estimates based on figures for the year 2000 indicate that 19 million unsafe abortions take place each year, indicating that approximately one in 10 pregnancies ends in an unsafe abortion, giving a ratio of one unsafe abortion to about seven live births. Unplanned pregnancies, family planning, and the legal framework of abortion as it applies from a global perspective, are also topics covered in this report.

Feldmann, Linda. "A New Federal Move to Limit Teen Abortion." *Christian Science Monitor* (April 27, 2005). Available online. URL: http://www.csmonitor. com/2005/0427/p01s02-uspo.html. Accessed December 30, 2010. Feldmann reports on Congress's latest abortion-related legislation. The Child Interstate Abortion Notification Act, or CIANA, makes it a crime to transport a minor across state lines to obtain an abortion.

Johnsen, Jennifer. "The Difference between Emergency Contraception Pills and Medication." Planned Parenthood, 2006. Available online. URL: http://www. plannedparenthood.org/resources/research-papers/difference-between-emergency-contraception-medication-abortion-6138.htm. Accessed January 14, 2011.

Contains basic facts and documents that describe the differences in current abortion methods.

Sowti, Naseem. "Abortion: Just the Data: With High-Court Debate Brewing, New Report Shows Procedure's Numbers Down." *Washington Post*, p. HE01 (July 19, 2005). Available online. URL: http://www.washingtonpost.com/wp-dyn/content/article/2005/07/18/AR2005071801164.html. Accessed May 5, 2006. Offers a demographic snapshot about how many abortions are being performed in the United States and who is obtaining them.

Television/Film/Video

Abortion Clinic. 53 minutes. *Frontline*, Public Broadcasting System, 1983, television documentary (May 2006). Information and documentary are available online. URL: http://www.pbs.org/wgbh/pages/frontline/twenty/watch/abortion.html?utm_capaign=searchpage&utm_medium=videosearch&utm_source=videosearch. The program examines the successes of the pro-life movement and its efforts to lobby for and help pass state legislation restricting access to abortion. It was filmed at a clinic in Chester, Pennsylvania, a small city with a 30 percent unemployment rate at that time, as a common example of an abortion clinic in the United States. The clinic offered individual counseling in which the reasons behind the decision are explored. As are most women who have had abortions in the United States in the past 30 years, the two whose abortions are shown in this film are single, white, and young. A 1983 National Academy of Television Arts and Sciences Emmy Award winner for Outstanding Background/Analysis of a Single Current Story, the story touches upon the balance between state and federal authority over Americans' lives and state legislative measures by pro-life advocates to restrict access to abortion.

The Last Abortion Clinic. Written, produced, and directed by Raney Aronson-Rath. 52 minutes. *Frontline*, Public Broadcasting Station, 2005, television documentary (May 2006). More information and documentary are available online. URL: http://www.pbs.org/wgbh/pages/frontline/clinic/. In 2005, the *Frontline* documentary team interviewed abortion providers and their patients, staff at a pro-life pregnancy counseling center, and key legal strategists on both sides of the national debate in the South, where a growing number of states with regulations limiting access to abortion states have been trying to restrict abortion. Raney Aronson-Rath documents the success of the pro-life movement and its beginning with a critical 1992 U.S. Supreme Court ruling in a case called *Planned Parenthood v. Casey.* While the Court upheld *Roe v. Wade*, it changed the standard by which abortion laws would be judged. It allowed states to regulate abortion so long as they did not place an "undue burden" on the women seeking the procedure. The page also offers additional tools—statistics, commentaries, a map of state legislation, and access to the documentary itself.

Vera Drake. Directed by Mike Leigh. 125 minutes. Fine Line Features, 2004, film (May 2006). More information is available online. URL: http://www.veradrake.com. For 20 years, an Englishwoman (Imelda Staunton) "with a heart of gold" performs abortions for fellow working-class girls and women who are pregnant, without her family's knowledge. Often the women are young girls or are already mothers of several children. She does this at no charge, although her friend, Lillian Clark, brokers the appointments for a fee without Drake's knowledge until 1950, when a girl nearly dies.

AFFIRMATIVE ACTION
Books

Jain, Harish C., Peter Sloane, Frank Horwitz, Simon Taggar, and Nan Weiner. *Employment Equity and Affirmative Action: An International Comparison.* Armonk, N.Y.: M. E. Sharpe, 2003. Compares similarities and differences of affirmative action/employment equity practices in six countries (the United States, Canada, Great Britain/Northern Ireland, India, Malaysia, and South Africa).

Articles

Alverson, Marchel. "The Call to Manage Diversity," *Women in Business* 50 (4) (July/August 1998): 34. The author discusses diversity in the workplace and the need for the management of diversity. In his exploration of how minorities, women, seniors, and the disabled can add diversity to the workplace, he includes comments from Connie Aden, president of Aden Management Resources. The article defines diversity training and its importance to a business and what management can do to overcome the differences that divide individuals. He distinguishes between affirmative action and "Equal Employment Opportunity."

Casey, Susan, Albert Kim, and Kostya Kennedy. "The Games Women Play," *Sports Illustrated,* 24 June 2002, 21. The authors focus on how the Title IX legislation has affected the number of athletic opportunities allotted to women in the United States and addresses the controversy surrounding the law 30 years after its passage and details about the law, which enforces equal opportunity for both sexes in sports that receive federal funding. Opponents attribute the gradual elimination of men's wrestling programs to the bill.

Poltenson, Norman. "Diversity (a.k.a. Affirmative Action) Splits Courts and Country," *Business Journal* (Central New York), 20 April, 2001, 35. Poltenson writes an overview on court rulings in different legal disputes arising from racial diversity issues. He discusses factors that promote racial diversity in U.S. education institutions, which he believes will broaden intellectual and life experiences, but criticizes affirmative action programs.

AFGHANISTAN
Books

Abirafeh, Lina. *Gender and International Aid in Afghanistan: The Politics and Effects of Intervention.* Jefferson, N.C.: McFarland & Co., 2009. Women are barometers by which aid agencies measure social change. This book studies the relationship between social indicators and aid dynamics and the progress of the gender agenda in the 2005 parliamentary elections. It examines the roots of Afghan society and how Islamic traditions do not always lend themselves to the social indicators by which international agencies measure progress.

Coleman, Isobel. *Paradise Beneath Her Feet : How Women Are Transforming the Middle East.* New York: Random House, 2010. Coleman journeys through the strategic crescent of the greater Middle East—Saudi Arabia, Iraq, Iran, Afghanistan, and Pakistan—to reveal how activists are working within the tenets of Islam to create economic, political, and educational opportunities for women. Coleman argues that these efforts are critical to bridging the conflict between those championing reform and those seeking to oppress women in the name of religious tradition.

Ellis, Deborah. *Women of the Afghan War.* Westport, Conn.: Praeger, 2002. The author, an antiwar and women's rights activist in Toronto, Ontario, Canada, writes an oral history account of the Afghan War as told by women victims. As personal snapshots of the news reports of the Taliban activities in Afghanistan, the accounts provide a historical background to the growth of the Taliban and reveal circumstances of the daily life women must survive in a closed society.

Sunita Mehta, ed. *Women for Afghan Women—Shattering Myths and Claiming the Future.* New York: Palgrave Macmillan, 2002. An attempt to write history, to increase awareness of the issues of Afghanistan and Afghan women, and to promote the agency of Afghan women in issues that impact their lives, the book includes a variety of female voices, highlighting a unifying desire to join as women and share, network, and strategize for change. This desire is focused on Afghan women but is also about global sisterhood and about the importance of feminist activism on an international level. The group of Afghan and non-Afghan women formed in April 2001 and is still committed to the struggle for women's human rights.

Zoya, James R. Follain, John Follain, and Rita Cristofari. *Zoya's Story: An Afghan Woman's Battle for Freedom.* New York: HarperCollins, 2002. Zoya is a young activist who describes how the Taliban publicly cut hands and lashed sick women at hospitals. She chronicles the oblique and subtle resistance of the Kabulites, as women wore makeup under the veils and cursed Taliban under their breath at public places. She also describes the pitiable conditions at the refugee camps in Peshawar, where she was assigned to work by RAWA. She describes the difficulty in operating a school in a camp where most fathers thought a daughter was more useful weaving carpets than acquiring education, which would make her an "infidel." Zoya also speaks about the dangers faced by RAWA members from Taliban supporters in Pakistani cities.

Articles

Nijhowne, Diya, and Lauryn Oates. "Violence against Women in Afghanistan: Documenting Prevalence, Organizing for Change," *Peacework* 35, no. 391 (December 2008/January 2009): 18. The article is an excerpt of a report by the same authors, "Living with Violence: A National Report on Domestic Abuse in Afghanistan," published by Global Rights Partners for Justice (http://www.globalrights.org). Of the 4,600 households surveyed in 2006, about 17 percent of women in Afghanistan have experienced some form of violence—physical, sexual, and psychological.

Web Documents

Amowitz, Lynn L. "Women's Health and Human Rights in Afghanistan. A Population-Based Assessment." Physicians for Human Rights (PHR), 2001. Available online. URL: http://physiciansforhumanrights.org. Accessed December 26, 2005. Based on research undertaken by PHR over a three-month period in the year 2000, the report offers background information and current statistics on humanitarian aid to Afghanistan with the chapter "The Status of Women." It also includes a useful glossary of common terms.

Asmar, Abdul Razaq. "Four-Year Period Main Achievements of MoWA." Ministry of Women's Affairs (MoWA), January 2007. Available online. URL: http://mowa.gov. af/files/pdf/what_we_do_english.pdf. Accessed December 30, 2010.

Associated Press. "New Rights, but Afghan Women Still May Face Forced Marriages." *International Herald Tribune* (March 15, 2005). Available online. URL: http://www.iht.com/articles/2005/03/14/news/afghan.php. Accessed December 30, 2010. The story takes as an example of forced marriages 14-year-old Bibi, an Afghan girl who has never seen the father who may earn as much as $7,000 from selling her into marriage with a stranger.

Haidari, M. Ashraf. "Afghanistan's Parliamentary Election Results Confirm Stunning Gains for Women." Eurasianet (October 27, 2005). Available online. URL: http://www.eurasianet.org/departments/civilsociety/articles/eav102805b.shtml. Accessed June 2, 2011. Haidari highlights with statistics the challenges overcome in Afghanistan's first parliamentary elections on September 18, 2005, as the fulfillment to the Bonn Agreement, signed after Afghanistan was liberated from Taliban rule in November 2001. She also speaks of women's returning to political leadership roles.

Human Rights Watch. "Afghan Election Diary." Human Rights Asia (September 19, 2005). Available online. URL: http://www.hrw.org/legacy/campaigns/afghanistan/blog1.htm Accessed January 14, 2011. Daily posts from the division researchers Sam Zarifi and Charmain Mohamed that are informative and candid about the challenges in the field during the election process.

———. "The Status of Women in Afghanistan, October 2004." Human Rights Asia. 2004. Available online. URL: http://www.hrw.org. Accessed December 19, 2005. A list of facts about women in Afghanistan two years after the end of the Taliban rule.

Kolhatkar, Sonali. "Afghan Women Continue to Fend for Themselves." Foreign Policy in Focus (FPIF) Special Report (March 2004). Available online. URL: http://www. fpif.org. Accessed December 15, 2010. Kolhatkar points out the various measures and promises by international organizations and the United States to establish equality, democracy, and economic, civil, and political rights for women and for the Afghan population, but "there is little about creating the institutions to uphold or implement these provisions."

Nawa, Fariba. "Afghan Women Debate the Terms of Their Future." Women's E-News (June 30, 2002). Available online. URL: http://www.feminist.com/news/news61. html Accessed January 14, 2011. Afghan women agree that they should play a role in the rebuilding of their country. They are divided, however, on what role Islam should play in the new nation—integral to the new government or a belief system guiding a secular state.

UNIFEM. "Gender Budgeting in Afghanistan." UNIFEM Afghanistan (2008). Available online. URL: http://afghanistan.unifem.org/docs/pubs/07/toolkits/ toolkit4_ EN.pdf. Accessed December 30, 2010. This report by UNIFEM demonstrates the role national budgets play, despite their appearance as a "gender-neutral policy instrument," in achieving development objectives and their impact on women's lives.

Television/Films/Video

Afghanistan: Exporting the Taliban Revolution. Reported by Mark Corcoran and Ashraf Ali. 24 minutes. Films for the Humanities & Sciences, Princeton, N.J., 1998, documentary. In Afghanistan, the Taliban—militant Sunni fundamentalists schooled in Pakistan—have taken over almost all of the country. Will their jihad spread to the Sunni minority of Iran, igniting a rebellion against that country's Shiite government? Or will Iran strike first, through the Shiite minority living in Afghanistan? This compelling report, filmed by the first crew to enter Afghanistan after America's antiterrorist air strikes in 1998, takes a firsthand look at both the results and the implications of the escalating tensions between Afghanistan and its neighbors.

Afghanistan Revealed. 45 minutes. National Geographic, 2001, documentary film. A vivid portrait of the tumultuous country during the Taliban rule, when it was no longer accessible to journalists and filmmakers. Features in-depth interviews by the author Sebastian Junger and the photographer Reza Deghati of the late Afghan resistance leader Ahmad Shad Massoud, who was assassinated two days before the September 11 terrorist attacks in the United States. Includes exclusive interviews with Taliban soldiers being held by the Northern Alliance. Looks at refugees who speak plainly of their suffering from the effects of Taliban rule and the decrees that are especially harsh for women.

Afghanistan Unveiled. Produced by Aïna Women Filming Group and directed by Brigitte Brault and Aïna. 52 minutes. Public Broadcasting System, 2003, film. Information available online. URL: http://www.pbs.org/independentlens/afghanistan unveiled/film.html AINA is a nongovernmental organization led by the accomplished photojournalist Reza Deghati, who from July 2002 to August 2003 oversaw the training of 14 young women, several still in their teens, as camera operators and video journalists at the Aïna Afghan Media and Culture Center in Kabul. The first female journalists to be trained in Afghanistan for more than a decade and the first ever to be trained in digital media, most of the trainees had never traveled outside Kabul and had not been able to study or pursue careers while the Taliban controlled their country. Created as the culmination of this unique training program, the film contrasts the harsh lives of the rural women of Afghanistan with those of the film's young camerawomen, who are experiencing newfound freedom and opportunity while attempting to use their work to change the condition of women in their country.

Behind the Veil: Afghan Women under Fundamentalism. 26 minutes. Films Media Group, 2001, documentary film. Information available online. URL: http://www. films.com/id/1860/Behind_the_Veil_Afghan_Women_under_Fundamentalism. htm#. For women living in Afghanistan under repressive Taliban rule, beatings, rape, and enslavement were commonplace occurrences. This program, filmed during the Taliban's regime, describes the human rights abuses that escalated after the withdrawal of Soviet forces, as seen through the eyes of women who survived years of rampant gender and religious intolerance. Resistance activities carried out by women's groups as they fought for freedom and democracy inside the country are also documented. Some content may be objectionable, but check the educational standards scores and view the online media clip.

AFRICA

Media

Feminist Africa. Available online. URL: http://www.feministafrica.org. Accessed December 15, 2010. Feminist Africa is a publication of the African Gender Institute and the continental Feminist Studies Network. Initiated in 2001, and currently hosted at the African Gender Institute at the University of Cape Town, it is produced by an editorial team in conjunction with an international editorial advisory group drawn from the feminist scholarly community.

CHINA

Books

Gilmartin, Christina Kelley. *Engendering the Chinese Revolution: Radical Women, Communist Politics, and Mass Movements in the 1920s.* Berkeley and Los Angeles: University of California Press, 1995. A detailed history of the radical women involved in the revolution and Communist politics from 1920 to 1927.

National Bureau of Statistics of China. *China Statistical Yearbook.* Beijing: China Statistics Press, 2010. This annual statistical publication covers data in historically important years and the most recent 25 years at the national level and at the local levels of provinces, autonomous regions, and municipalities directly under the control of the central government. It houses key statistical indicators to China's social and economic development, which can also be directly searched in their databases located online at http://www.stats.gov.cn/english/statisticaldata.

Web Documents

"Fact Sheet: The China Gender Facility for Research and Advocacy (CGF)." Available online. URL: http://www.un.org.cn/public/resource/CGF_en.pdf. Accessed December 30, 2010. Aiming to advance gender equality, the fact sheet describes China's 2004 launch of the UN Theme Group on Gender (UNTGG), China Gender Facility for Research and Advocacy. Eight specific areas have been identified as priorities for women; they include: gender mainstreaming, political participation, migration/trafficking, violence, aging, sex ratio, HIV/AIDS, and disaster management.

"Population and Family Planning Law of the People's Republic of China." Legislative Affairs Commission of the Standing Committee of the National People's Congress of the People's Republic of China, 2002 (February 2005). Available online. URL: http://www.unescap.org/esid/psis/population/database/poplaws/law_china/ch_record052.htm. Accessed January 14, 2011. The official translation of the law adopted on December 29, 2001, which took effect September 2002, enforces family planning as a "fundamental state policy."

"Women and Gender in Chinese Studies Network." University of Warwick. Available online. URL: http://www.wagnet.ox.ac.uk. Accessed April 15, 2006. Women's activism in China. The Women and Gender in Chinese Studies Network (WAG) was inaugurated on August 12, 2001, in Berlin. The international network on gender studies offers links to papers, publications, and reading lists specific to Chinese women.

Television/Films/Video

Through Chinese Women's Eyes. Produced and directed by Mayfair Yang. 52 minutes. 1997, documentary film. Distributed by Women Make Movies, New York. The Chinese-American anthropologist Mayfair Mei-hui Yang visits Shanghai to study Chinese women's changing social roles from a Communist to a consumer culture. The documentary includes footage that spans the 20th century, of traditional gender roles, propaganda films from the 1950s, Chinese feminism during the UN world conference on women in Beijing, and recent television shots of teachers and women's rights organizers.

CONTRACEPTIVES

Books

Tone, Andrea. *Devices and Desires: A History of Contraceptives in America.* New York: Hill & Wang, 2001. Tone addresses how the complex story around unwanted pregnancies, quack remedies, and backstreet abortions led to the need for contraceptive choices—from the condoms, pessaries, and douches available in the Victorian era, to the custom-fitted diaphragm and the development of the Pill. Activist Margaret Sanger gained legitimacy for the movement and nurtured the demand for it. The book also deals with related issues: the Pill's health risks, religious objections to it, alleged racism in birth control policy, and the Dalkon Shield tragedy, in which business decisions contributed to the marketing of an unsafe intrauterine device (IUD) in the 1970s.

Articles

Thottam, Jyoti. "A Big Win for Plan B: Wal-Mart's About-Face Expands Access to the 'Morning After' Pill," *Time*, 13 March 2006, 41. Thottam evaluates Wal-Mart's decision to stock the controversial emergency contraceptive Plan B, also known as the morning-after pill, in its 3,700 pharmacies nationwide and what it means for both sides of the abortion debate.

Web Documents

"The Pill: How It Is Affecting U.S. Morals, Family Life." *U.S. News & World Report* (July 11, 1966). Available online. URL: http://www.pbs.org/wgbh/amex/pill/filmmore/ ps_revolution.html. Accessed April 21, 2006. The article reflects how the Pill caused a dramatic change in female attitudes in its first few years on the market.

Television/Films/Video

The Pill. Produced and directed by Chana Gazit. 90 minutes. PBS Home Video, 2004, documentary film. Information available online. URL: http://www.pbs. org/wgbh/amex/pill/filmmore/index.html. In May 1960, the U.S. Food and Drug Administration approved the sale of the contraceptive pill, a drug that would have an unprecedented impact on American culture. Within five years, more than 6 million American women would make it part of their daily lives; in contrast, a decade earlier, the concept of an aspirin-like pill to prevent pregnancies was inconceivable to the general public. Laws criminalizing the sale of contraceptive devices were still on the books in 30 states around the country. The documentary tells the story of Margaret Sanger and Katharine McCormick, older, defiant women activists who hired and paid the bills of Gregory Pincus, an unknown biologist, to research contraceptive options. He persuaded a pharmaceutical company to risk a possible boycott to put "the Pill" on the market with the aid of John Rock, a well-respected Catholic gynecologist, to conduct the field studies.

DEMOCRATIC REPUBLIC OF THE CONGO (DRC)
Books

Shannon, Lisa. *A Thousand Sisters: My Journey of Hope into the Worst Place on Earth to Be a Woman*. Berkeley, California: Seal Press, 2010. After watching a 2006 television episode of *The Oprah Winfrey Show* about the atrocities and genocide in DRC, the author was compelled to start a foundation, Run for Congo Women, to raise awareness and funds. The book (URL: http://athousandsisters.com/)

describes Shannon's visit to DRC in 2007, where she realized the scope of the devastation that women are facing.

Editors, Ralph Hamann, Stu Woolman, Courtenay Sprague. *The Business of Sustainable Development in Africa: Human* Rights, Partnerships, Alternative Business Models. Pretoria, South Africa: Unisa Press, 2008. Exemplifies economic initiatives in Africa, including DRC.

Web Documents

Human Rights Watch. "Democratic Republic Congo." Available online. URL: http://www.hrw.org/africa/democratic-republic-congo. Accessed December 30, 2010. Overview of issues of human rights specific to DRC and archive of news releases.

U.S. State Department. "2009 Human Rights Report: Democratic Republic of the Congo" (March 11, 2010). Available online. URL: http://www.state.gov/g/drl/rls/hrrpt/2009/af/135947.htm. Accessed December 30, 2010. The report provides detailed facts, figures, recent legislation, and current issues concerning DRC.

United States Institute of Peace. "Special Report: Conflict-Business Dynamics in the Democratic Republic of Congo" (October 2009). Available online. URL: http://www.usip.org/files/resources/confict_business_drc_sr234.pdf. Accessed September 2, 2010. Survey responses by the business community in DRC identify obstacles to doing business in conflict-affected environments.

Media/Newspapers

CBS *60 Minutes*. "War against Women" (January 13, 2008). Available online. URL:http://www.cbsnews.com/stories/2008/01/11/60minutes/main3701249.shtml. Accessed August 11, 2010. Transcript of segment covering the civil war in DRC as an ethnic conflict with women being used as weapons.

Conflict Trends. "Women in Peace Processes: Lessons from the Democratic Republic of the Congo and Uganda." 2009, pp. 34–41. Available online. URL: http://www.accord.org.za/downloads/ct/ct_2009_3.pdf. Accessed December 30, 2010. This article analyses women's participation in the ICD, the Goma Peace Conference, and the Juba Peace Process and offers lessons for donors to further more effective support for women's participation in peace processes.

Television/Films/Video/Theater

Ruined. Written by Lynn Nottage. 2 hours, 30 minutes. Play, 2008. A 2009 Pulitizer Prize–winning play about sexual violence in wartime conflicts in DRC. The piece premiered in November 2008 at the Goodman Theater in New York City.

The Greatest Silence: Rape in the Congo. Directed, written, edited by Lisa F. Jackson, produced by HBO. 76 minutes. 2008. About the war crimes committed against women in DRC. Jackson interviews women about the violence—specifically rape and torture by rebel, government, and peacekeeping soldiers—physicians, caregivers. The film offers insights as to why the violence continues. Winner of a special jury prize at the Sundance Film Festival.

Other

Simu-doc. *Pax Warrior*. 2003. This interactive training tool for collaborative conflict resolution is designed for field workers and educators. For information, contact http://www.paxwarrior.com.

Fernando, Priyanthi, et al. "Discovering Technologists: Women and Men's Work at Village Level in East Africa." Nairobi: Intermediate Technology Development Group, Eastern Africa, 2000. This is a training package designed to increase the skills of field workers involved in the processes of technology development, working with women and men in local communities. It aims to improve the capacity of men and women field workers to recognize and work with women's existing technical skills. Field workers involved in technology development will find this package a useful reference on methods and tools for developing more gender-sensitive technology interventions. The materials are based on Do It Herself case studies—an ITDG research program that focuses on grassroots technical innovation for women. The program took place in Asia, Africa, and Latin America.

USAID. "Portraits of War: the Democratic Republic of Congo." An internationally touring photography exhibition and educational campaign to raise awareness of the widespread sexual violence facing women and girls in the DRC. The exhibition features powerful photographs by award-winning photojournalists Lynsey Addario, Marcus Bleasdale, Ron Haviv and James Nachtwey that convey the strength and courage of Congolese women. Accompanying essays contextualize the impact of the crisis from a range of perspectives. Available online. URL: http://congo-women.org. Accessed January 22, 2011.

DOCUMENT RESEARCH

Non-Governmental Organizations at the United Nations. Available online. URL: http://habitat.igc.org/ngo-rev/index.html. Accessed December 30, 2010. Links to UN resolutions and International Synergy documents.

United Nations. "United Nations Documentation: Research Guide." Resolutions Adopted by the General Assembly at Its 53rd Session (May 9, 2006). Available online. URL: http://www.un.org/Depts/dhl/resguide/r53.htm. Accessed December 30, 2010. Provides a searchable database of General Assembly resolutions and additional documents.

EDUCATION

Articles

Thornburgh, Nathan. "Dropout Nation," *Time*, 17 April 2006, 30–40. The number of high school students who leave school before graduation is higher than believed. Thornburgh looks inside one town's struggle to reverse the tide and an impressive statistic: Nearly one out of three public high school students will not graduate, and for Latinos and African Americans, the rate approaches 50 percent.

Web Documents

"College Enrollment and Work Activity of High School Graduates." Bureau of Labor Statistics, Current Population Survey (March 24, 2006). Available online. URL: http://www.bls.gov/news.release/hsgec.toc.htm. Accessed December 30, 2010. News releases and data tables with information regarding college enrollment and work activity of 2005 high school graduates. The college enrollment rate for recent high school graduates was a historical high for the series dating back to 1959.

"Digest of Educational Statistics Tables and Figures." National Center for Education Statistics, 2004 (April 2005). Available online. URL: http://nces.ed.gov/programs/digest/d04/tables/dt04_102.asp. Accessed December 30, 2010. With data on educational enrollment at all levels of education between 1995 and 2004, the site also has statistics from 1989 to 2005 in other areas of education, such as the use of libraries and their cooperation with day care services and schools.

"State of the World's Mothers 2005: The Power and Promise of Girls' Education." Save the Children (May 2005). Available online. URL: http://www.ungei.org/resources/index_603.html. Accessed May 3, 2006. The report explores the connection between girls' education and a more healthy and prosperous future for all children. It highlights the need to reach the 58 million girls who are not attending school. By shining a spotlight on countries that are succeeding in getting and keeping girls in school, it shows that effective solutions to this challenge are affordable, even in the world's poorest countries.

"Title IX: 25 Years of Progress." U.S. Department of Education, June 1997 (July 9, 1997). Available online. URL: http://www.ed.gov/pubs/TitleIX/index.html. December 30, 2010. Reviews the impact Title IX legislation has had on women in education, sports, and related areas.

Television/Films/Video

Mona Lisa Smile. Directed by Mike Newell. 117 minutes, 2003. A freethinking art professor (Julia Roberts) teaches conservative 1950s Wellesley College girls (including Julia Stiles) to question their traditional societal roles.

EMPLOYMENT
Books/Reports

Giele, Janet Zollinger, and Leslie F. Stebbins. *Contemporary World Issues: Women and Equality in the Workplace: A Reference Handbook.* New York: ABC-CLIO, 2003. In spite of notable progress for women in the workplace, why do men continue to have better pay, benefits, status, and opportunities, while working women are still overlooked? This guide to gender equity in the workplace details legal and social progress and the inequalities from World War II to the present and examines sociological and economic implications of inequity. The authors focus mostly on the United States, with comparisons with global issues, to describe the impact of laws and social policies on sex discrimination, equal pay law, affirmative action, and issues of comparable worth.

Shriver, Maria. *The Shriver Report: A Woman's Nation Changes Everything*. Center for American Progress. October 16, 2009. A comprehensive study examining the social transformation caused by female workers. For the first time in American history, one-half of all U.S. workers are women, and mothers are the primary breadwinners or co-breadwinners in two-thirds of American families in 2009.

Web Documents

Bureau of Labor Statistics (BLS). "NLS Overview." National Longitudinal Study (NLS): Mature and Young Women Cohort Data (March 10, 2004). Available online. URL: http://www.bls.gov/nls/overview.htm. Accessed March 1, 2006. The four groups of men and women in the NLS Original Cohorts were first interviewed in the mid- to late 1960s. These cohorts were selected because each faced important labor market decisions, which were of special concern to policymakers. The men's cohort was retired, while respondents in the mature women's and young women's cohorts continue to be interviewed on a biennial basis and have been interviewed for over three decades.

———. "Women in the Labor Force: A Databook." U.S. Department of Labor (annual). Available online. URL: http://www.bls.gov. Accessed December 15, 2010. Background information and statistical tables on the status of women in the American labor force from 1970 and after.

———. "Women's Bureau." U.S. Department of Labor. Available online. URL: http://www.dol.gov/wb. Accessed December 15, 2010. Includes quick facts: 20 leading occupations of employed women; hot jobs for the 21st century; older women workers, ages 55 and over; women in the labor force; saving for retirement; women in nontraditional jobs; women in nursing.

Institute for Women's Policy Research. "The Gender Wage Gap: 2009:" (September 2010). Available online. URL: http://www.iwpr.org/pdf/C350.pdf. The most recent fact sheet measuring and tracking women's weekly earnings from 1955 to 2009. There is a wealth of U.S. research reports on the status of women and employment at the national and state levels at the IWPR Web site.

International Labour Organization (ILO). "Gender Equality Tool." Available online. URL: http://www.ilo.org/dyn/gender/gender.home. Accessed December 30, 2010. Lists international events, resources, and highlights about the status of women and gender equality in management and the workplace, including tools for men and boys.

———. Employment Strategy Department. Global Employment Trends Brief. A yearly report produced by the ILO that monitors global employment trends.

———. "LABORSTA Internet." Available online. URL: http://laborsta.ilo.org. Accessed December 30, 2010. View and extract data and metadata for more than 200 countries or territories from the ILO Bureau of Statistics database on labor.

Television/Films/Video

Made in Dagenham. Directed by Nigel Cole. 113 minutes, 2010. Dramatization of the landmark 1968 British strike by Rita O'Grady and female sewing machinists protesting unequal pay at the Ford Dagenham plant (stars Sally Hawkins and Bob Hoskins).

ENCYCLOPEDIAS
Books

Hannam, June, Mitzi Auchterlonie, and Katherine Holden, eds. *International Encyclopedia of Women's Suffrage.* New York: ABC-CLIO, 2000. This encyclopedia covers the history of women's suffrage throughout the world, enabling the reader to make comparisons among individual countries. The book includes biographies of individual activists and thematic entries covering issues such as suffrage periodicals and newspapers.

Walter, Lynn, editor in chief. *The Greenwood Encyclopedia of Women's Issues Worldwide.* 6 vols. Westport, Conn: Greenwood Press, 2003. Europe, edited by Lynn Walter. Sub-Saharan Africa, Aili Mari Tripp, volume editor. North Africa, Bahira Sherif-Trask, volume editor. North America and the Caribbean, Cheryl Toronto Kalny, volume editor. Central and South America, Amy Lind, volume editor. Asia and Oceania, Manisha Desai, volume editor. Covers education, employment, family and sexuality, health, politics and law, religion and spirituality, and violence.

EUROPEAN UNION
Books

García-Ramon, Maria Dolors, and Janice Monk. *Women of the European Union: The Politics of Work and Daily Life.* London and New York: Routledge, 1996. Collects studies to raise questions about the implications of the European Union policies for women. Focusing on different scales of analysis, it includes comparative multinational chapters as well as national case studies and in-depth examinations of urban and rural contexts. The book shows how work, family, and the state function differently in Spain, Italy, Greece, and Portugal than in the countries of northern Europe. Additional perspectives on diversity are provided in chapters addressing discrimination against lesbian women in Denmark and middle-class and suburban couples in the Netherlands.

Snyder, Paula, ed. *The European Women's Almanac.* London: Scarlet Press, 1992. A useful legal reference with statistics and commentary on the socioeconomic position of European women. Indexed by country.

Web Documents

European Commission. "The European Institute for Gender Equality." Available online. URL: http://ec.europa.eu/social/main.jsp?catId=732&langId=en. Accessed December 30, 2010. Based in Lithuania, the institute is housed within the Employments, Social Affairs, and Inclusion part of the European Commission. It is a repository of practices, policies, and legislative action pertaining to gender equality throughout European Union member countries. As of January 2011, this agency will be transitioned to the Justice, Fundamental Rights and Citizenship office.

FAMILY PLANNING

Books

Lief, Michael S., and H. Mitchell Caldwell. *And the Walls Came Tumbling Down: Closing Arguments That Changed the Way We Live—from Protecting Free Speech to Winning Women's Suffrage to Defending the Right to Die.* New York: A Lisa Drew Book/Scribner, 2004. Closing arguments of several trials presented in this book are relevant to the issues of sexual reproduction and suffrage rights.

Web Documents

"Family Law." Uniform Law Commissioners (June 18, 2002). Available online. URL: http://www.nccusl.org/nccusl/uniformacts-subjectmatter.asp#family. Accessed December 30, 2010. The National Conference of Commissioners on Uniform State Laws has worked for the uniformity of state laws since 1892. It is a nonprofit unincorporated association, which comprises state commissions on uniform laws from each state, the District of Columbia, the Commonwealth of Puerto Rico, and the U.S. Virgin Islands. Each jurisdiction determines the method of appointment and the number of commissioners actually appointed. Most jurisdictions provide for their commission by statute.

Gillespie, Duff G. "Whatever Happened to Family Planning and, for That Matter, Reproductive Health?" *International Family Planning Perspectives* 30 (March 2004): 34–38. Available online. URL: http://www.guttmacher.org/pubs/journals/3003404. pdf. Accessed December 30, 2010. Under the auspices of the Bill and Melinda Gates Institute, senior scholar Gillespie surveys the conspicuous absence of reproductive health issues from major international conferences in recent years.

FEMALE GENITAL MUTILATION

Books

Dirie, Waris, and Cathleen Miller. *Desert Flower: The Extraordinary Journey of a Desert Nomad.* New York: William Morrow, 1998. The journey of a young Somali woman who fled her country's traditional tribal practices to become a supermodel in New

York City. As special ambassador to the United Nations, she has as her mission to create awareness of female genital mutilation.

Articles

Hakim, L. Y. "Impact of Female Genital Mutilation on Maternal and Neonatal Outcomes during Parturition." *East African Medical Journal* 78 (2001): 255–258. This article evaluates the impact of female genital mutilation on parturition and to create awareness of its implications for women's and neonates' health. This cross-sectional study took place at the Tikur Anbessa, St. Paul's, and Ghandhi Memorial Hospitals, between January and December 1997.

FEMINIST LITERATURE
Books

Anderson, B. S. *Joyous Greetings: The First International Women's Movement, 1830–1860.* New York: Oxford University Press, 2000. Emphasizes the dramatic impact of the Industrial Revolution on western Europe and the United States and the way it ignited an international feminist movement—not just a series of discrete feminist activities in various countries, as other historians have posited. The narrative centers on the contributions of a core group of 20 feminists—American, English, Scottish, French, German, and Swedish—who shared ideas, platforms, and organizing techniques to create political change throughout the United States and western Europe.

Beauvoir, Simone de. *The Second Sex.* New York: Vintage Books, 1989. Originally published in French in 1949, translated into English in 1953. Text on the history of feminism that gives a sense of how far the movement has advanced in the last 50 years and what constituted "radical" feminist thought around 1950.

Freedman, Estelle. *No Turning Back: The History of Feminism and the Future of Women.* New York: Ballantine Books, 2002. Originally published in 1963. Examines issues related to politics, economics, race, relationships, health, sexuality, and violence within the context of feminist history and the creation of different forms of feminism within various cultures.

French, Marilyn. *The Women's Room.* New York: Ballantine Books, 1977. French's first novel explores the themes of female solidarity and empowerment using a narrative that is considered highly autobiographical. It's the story of Mira, a 1950s housewife, who has to challenge expectations about men and herself when her daughter is raped—a situation that French actually experienceed.

Friedan, Betty. *The Feminine Mystique.* New York: W. W. Norton, 1997. Originally published in 1963. A classic and insightful feminist text that voiced the unhappiness felt by women in the West in the 1950s. It is still valued for the way it exposed society's shaping of women's lives and questioned what women take for granted.

Greer, Germaine. *The Female Eunuch.* New York: Farrar, Straus & Giroux, 2001. Originally published in 1970. Greer believed sexual liberation was the key to lifting women's oppression. The book had an impact on sexual relations between men and women that generated debate both outside and inside the women's liberation movement.

Lessing, Doris. *The Golden Notebook.* New York: Harper Collins, 1962. Lessing's breakthrough novel exposed gender relations in a different light and fueled the women's movement. Anna Wulf, the novel's protagonist, is a woman who wants to live freely. The notion of not having to abandon personal aspirations in the name of having a family and children was considered radical at the time.

Peters, Julie Stone, and Andrea Wolper, eds. *Women's Rights, Human Rights: International Feminist Perspectives.* New York and London: Routledge, 1995. The transformation of human rights from a feminist perspective is crucial to addressing global challenges to human rights in the 21st century.

Rosen, R. *The World Split Open: How the Modern Women's Movement Changed America.* New York: Penguin Books, 2000. A thorough introduction to the modern American women's movement.

Wollstonecraft, Mary. *A Vindication of the Rights of Woman* (1792). Amherst, N.Y.: Prometheus's Great Books in Philosophy Series, 1996. Written during a time of revolutionary fervor, when the principle of inalienable rights for all men had caused and was causing political turmoil in the United States, France, and Britain. Wollstonecraft applied the concept of inalienable rights to women as well as men. She addressed the power struggle between the sexes, pointing out that, as with governments, it causes imbalance in both the oppressed and the oppressor. She sought instead an education for women and men that will endow individuals with reason, knowledge, and virtue.

Web Documents

Documents from the Women's Liberation Movement—An On-Line Archival Collection. Special Collections Library, Duke University" (April 1997). Available online. URL: http://scriptorium.lib.duke.edu/wlm. Accessed December 30, 2010. Documents are arranged by the following categories: general and theoretical, medical and reproductive rights, music, organizations and activism, sexuality and lesbian feminism, socialist feminism, women of color, women's work and roles.

FINANCE FOR WOMEN
Books

Black, Cathie. *Basic Black: The Essential Guide for Getting Ahead at Work (and in Life).* New York: Three Rivers Press (Random House imprint), 2007. Life lessons from Cathie Black, one of *Forbes* magazine's 100 Most Powerful Women and *Fortune's* 50 Most Powerful Women in Business, on how to land a job, promotion, or project; how to handle interviews; which rules to break and why to make life a "grudge-free zone."

Orman, Suze. *Women and Money: Owning the Power to Control Your Destiny.* New York: Spiegel & Grau, 2007. Money management and life lessons for women.

FRANCE

Books

Allwood, Gill, and Khursheed Wadia. *Gender and Policy in France.* Basingstoke, U.K.: Palgrave Macmillan, 2009. Reviews gender mainstreaming and other gender parity–based policies (e.g., quotas) in French society. Takes a close look at the pros and cons of the Roudy Law of 1983, the Parity Law of 2000, the 2006 Ameline Law on equal employment, as well as at "gender-neutral" employment politics. Includes chapters on abortion, prostitution, domestic violence, the Islamic head scarf (hijab) debate, and a close look at the concept of *laïcité* (separation of church and state), as well as the lack of funding to support progressive policies.

Articles

Bloch, Pascale. "Diversity and Labor Law in France" *Vermont Law Review* 30 (2006): 717–747. Looks at the legal and judicial reactions to equal pay and treatment in the workplace.

Gervais-le Garff, Marie-Marthe. "Liberté, Egalité, Sororité: A New Linguistic Order in France?" *Women and Language* 25, no. 2 (Fall 2002): 1–7. Linguistic discrimination is a sensitive topic in France, one that has met much resistance, especially within the national body that provides oversight. This article explores the reasons for the opposition to the feminization of the language in the 1980s and the role of the Ministry for Women Rights.

Macknight Elizabeth C. "Why Weren't They Feminists?: Parisian Noble Women and the Campaigns for Women's Rights in France, 1880–1914." *The European Journal of Women's Studies* 14, no. 2 (May 2007): 127. An examination of the responses of Parisian noblewomen to campaigns for women's rights in France of the early Third Republic. Based on the works of Pierre Bourdieu, this article analyzes the effects of class and gender in aristocratic women's attitudes to French feminism before World War I. The conditioning of Parisian noblewomen explains their resistance, indeed often outspoken opposition, to feminists' demands. These female aristocrats supported their own oppression within a social order governed by the state, the scientific and medical establishments, the expectations of family and the Catholic Church of the time.

Revillard, Anne. "Work/Family Policy in France: From State Familialism to State Feminism?" *International Journal of Law, Policy and the Family* (2006): 133–150. French work/family policies are paradoxical: They recognize women's right to work for the prime interest and well-being of the family and economy, rather than for women's personal esteem. Familialism, as an ideology, promoted the family as an institution, which often played against individual women's rights. Yet, French women's labor force participation eventually led to their representation by a government ministry and public office quotas.

Annotated Bibliography

Web Documents

Bajos, Nathalie, Caroline Moreau, Henri Leridon, and Michèle Ferrand. "Why Has the Number of Abortions Not Declined in France over the Past 30 Years?" *Population & Societies* 407 (December 2004). Institut National d'Études Démographiques (INED). Available online. URL: http://www.ined.fr/en/publications/pop_soc/bdd/publication/69/. Accessed October 16, 2010. Abortion is a final resort after contraception has failed. When the Veil Act legalizing abortion in France was passed in 1974, the frequency of abortion was expected to decrease as modern contraception methods spread. Though the number of unplanned pregnancies has gone down, the number of abortions has not. Women with unplanned pregnancies more frequently resort to elective abortion.

Colin, Christel, Zohor Djider, and Claire Ravel. "La parité à pas comptés." March 2005, National Statistical Institutes (INS), Paris, France. Available online. URL: http://www.insee.fr/fr/ffc/docs_ffc/ip1006.pdf. Accessed September 8, 2010. Women and their impact on society, reviewing factors such as their life expectancy, socio-professional choices, use of leisure time, and other lifestyle choices.

Revillard, Anne. "Stating Family Values and Women's Rights: Familialism and Feminism within the French Republic." *French Politics, 2007*, pp. 210–228. Available online. URL: http://www.palgrave-journals.com/fp. Accessed December 30, 2010. A comprehensive English-language symposium article analyzing the triadic relationship between women, family, and the labor force and its influence on women's policy agencies within France.

Media/Newspapers

Hugo, Victor. "Victor Hugo on Women's Rights" (April 18, 1875). *New York Times.* The French literary scholar publicly announced his position on women' rights in the *New York Times.* Available online. URL: http://query.nytimes.com/gst/abstract.html?res=F70617FC345D147A93C7A9178DD85F4D8185F9. Accessed May 24, 2011.

Other

European Union. "Europa: Gateway to the European Union." English version of a dedicated Web site that offers resources about the European Union, organized by policies, life and civil rights, active participation opportunities, publications and important documents, media services. Available online. URL: http://www.europa.org. Accessed November 19, 2010.

GENDER ROLES

Books

Ackmann, Martha. *The Mercury 13: The Untold Story of Thirteen American Women and the Dream of Space Flight.* New York: Random House, 2003. In 1961, 13 women were secretly tested in a program to prepare America's first female astronauts, yet it would be 20 years before Sally Ride rode the shuttle into space and another decade before Eileen Collins piloted the shuttle. This is a fascinating and frustrating account of how qualified women were denied their chance by the "Boy's Club" in NASA and on Capitol Hill.

Dowler, Lorraine, Josephine Carubia, and Bonj Szczygiel, eds. *Gender and Landscape: Renegotiating Morality and Space.* London and New York: Routledge, 2005. This volume examines the effect of landscape on women and the "gendering of the landscape," bridging the feminist discussion "of space and place as something 'lived' and landscape interpretations as something 'viewed.'"

Gaughen, Shasta. *Contemporary Issues Companion: Women's Rights.* Westport, Conn.: Greenwood Press, 2003. Explores the transformative force of the modern women's movement, from history, to issues, to its international implications. The book includes writings and speeches by notable individuals, including Margaret Sanger, Gloria Steinem, and Hillary Rodham Clinton. Chapter 1 examines the historical perspective of the movement through these writings, while chapter 2 explores workplace issues for women. Chapter 3 surveys medical and reproductive right concerns, and chapter 4 looks at international rights issues, including female circumcision, sex trafficking, and the changes and challenges for women of Islamic faith.

Hardill, Irene. *Gender, Migration and the Dual Career Household.* London and New York: Routledge, 2002. Addresses labor mobility primarily in Great Britain and examines work and family and dual-career families.

Macy, Sue, and Jane Gottesman. *Play Like A Girl.* New York: Henry Holt, September 1999. Macy, an award-winning young adult author, and Gottesman, a sportswriter, present a collection of quotations, photographs, and excerpts from hundreds of sports books celebrating women in sport; for young adult readers.

Markham, Beryl. *West with the Night.* Boston: Houghton Mifflin, 1942. This part-autobiography, part-memoir describes Markham's exploits as an African bush pilot in 1930s Kenya and as the first person to fly solo across the Atlantic from east to west.

Web Documents

Commission of the European Communities. "Report from the Commission to the Council, the European Parliament, the European Economic and Social Committee and the Committee of the Regions on Equality between Women and Men" (February 14, 2005). Available online. URL: http://www.daadcenter.wisc.edu/events/gende%20equality%20report%202006_71_en.pdf. Accessed December 30, 2010. This second annual report on equality of women and men is the first to cover the enlarged European Union of 25 member states. Equality of women and men is reinforced by the new treaty establishing a constitution for Europe. In addition to the provisions of the current treaty on gender equality, the constitution expressly states that equality is a value of the Union, which should be promoted not only inside the Union but also in its relations with the rest of the world.

HEALTH CARE

Books

Dyck, Isabel, Nancy Davis Lewis, and Sara McLafferty, eds. *Geographics of Women's Health.* London and New York: Routledge, 2001. The book focuses on a range of issues: health and hygiene, women's health services, medical geography, world health, and case studies. Includes bibliographical references and index.

Web Documents

The Henry J. Kaiser Family Foundation (March 2006). Available online. URL: http://www.kff.org/womenshealth/index.cfm. Accessed December 30, 2010. Resources and fact sheets on female health care and contraception, with additional information by ethnicity.

The Office on Women's Health. Quick Health Data Online. U.S. Department of Health and Human Services. Available online. URL: http://www.healthstatus2010.com/owh/index.html. Accessed December 30, 2010. This system permits those interested in the health status of women and the entire population of the United States to have access to comparative, county-level data for all 50 states, the District of Columbia, and U.S. territories and possessions. Data in the system are available by gender, race and ethnicity, and, to the extent possible, age. Data have been collected from local, state, regional, and national sources, from credible sources at both the national (CDC, U.S. Census Bureau) and local (state health departments) levels. Definitions are consistent across the sources and the data have been compared to other references.

World Health Organization (WHO). "The World Health Report 2009." Available online. URL: http://www.who.int/whosis/whostat/EN_WHS09_Full.pdf. Accessed October 2, 2010. WHO's annual compilation of data from its 193 Member States. Reports on global public health and key statistics.

———. "Countries." Available online. URL: http://www.who.int/countries/en. Accessed December 30, 2010. The site, updated regularly, provides statistics by country, including country indicators, health expenditures, health services, current legislation, life summary tables, status of specific disease conditions, and human resources.

———. "International Digest of Health Legislation (IDHL)." Online Database. Available online. URL: http://apps.who.int/idhl-rils/frame.cfm?language=english. Accessed January 15, 2011. Contains a selection of national and international health legislation. Texts of legislation are summarized in English or mentioned by their title. Where possible, links are provided to other Web sites that contain full texts of the legislation in question. The electronic version of the digest supersedes the printed version, which was published from 1948 to 1999. It represents the latest stage in the evolution of a service that began in 1909 with the publication of the first issue of the *Bulletin mensuel de l'Office international d'Hygiène publique.* Query the database by country, subject, volume, and issue, or specific keywords.

HISTORY

Books

Chapman, Anne. *Women at the Heart of War: Soldiers without Guns.* Los Angeles: National Center for History in the Schools, UCLA, 1997. This primary source unit documents the multiple ways in which women of diverse regions were affected by World War II. Sections are German Women and Hitler's Ideology, Women's Employment in the United States, Gender Equality in Soviet Combat Forces, and Women's Attitudes about the War in China. Includes activities and discussion ideas, charts, introduction activities, and a time line.

Crawford, Vicki L., et al., eds. *Women in the Civil Rights Movement: Trailblazers and Torchbearers, 1941–1965 (Blacks in the Diaspora).* Bloomington: Indiana University Press, October 1993. This book describes specific times in history when black women played a deciding role in the fight for civil rights, from the Mississippi Delta, Montgomery bus boycott, and the Cambridge movement, to the Boston YWCA.

Gross, Susan, and Marjorie Bingham. *Women in World Area Studies Series.* St. Louis Park, Minn.: Glenhurst, 1983–87. This series of 13 units is now out of print, but some can still be found through used book outlets. This series describes the life of women in different regions and countries of the world and how their social status has changed in history. "Women in Japan," "Women in Latin America from Pre-Columbian Times to the 20th Century—Vols. I and II," "Women in Ancient Greece and Rome," and "Women in Medieval/Renaissance Europe" are recommended.

Himmell, Rhoda. *The Role of Women in Medieval Europe.* Los Angeles: The Regents, National Center for History in the Schools, UCLA, 1992. This work, intended for grades 10 through 12, uses primary sources to establish a historic dramatic moment for students to read, followed by teacher background information and more readings enhanced by questions, role playing, and simulation lessons. Emphasizes Germanic tribes. One section illustrates male attitudes that determined women's place within the framework of medieval society.

Hunter, Lisa, ed. *Sources of Strength: Women and Culture.* Newton, Mass.: Education Development Center, 1980. These individual units provide background information, first-person accounts, and activities that ask students to evaluate the degree of economic, political, and personal power a woman may exercise in a given culture. They look at women's lives in traditional settings and then what happens during periods of change. The Women in Nigeria unit gives information on village life and changes that occurred during European colonization and national independence. The Women in China unit looks at traditional life and continuity and change during the revolutionary years. Other units examine similar themes for women in Chinese-American and African-American history, concluding with a student oral history project.

Ladd, Doris. *Mexican Women in Anahuac and New Spain: Three Study Units.* Austin: Institute of Latin American Studies, University of Texas, 1979. The study unit topics are Aztec roles of women, Women in Mexico City in the 16th century, and the life and writing of Sor Juana Ines de la Cruz. For each, a short introduction is followed by primary documents illustrating the content points. Reflective questions and writing activities end the section.

Mertus, Julie, Nancy Flowers, and Mallika Dutt. *Local Action/Global Change: Learning about the Human Rights of Women and Girls.* New York: UNIFEM, 1999. Each chapter provides information, statistics, and illustrative examples of both human rights abuses and victories and culminates with an exercise in which participants can create a "document" that would protect that right for women. There also are numerous consciousness-raising activities and role playing that draw attention to the issues around women and their universal rights.

Osolina, Elena, and Ruth Tudor. *Teaching 20th Century Women's History: A Classroom Approach.* Strasbourg: Council of Europe Press, 2000. The historian Elena Osolina uses topics in European women's history to integrate historical skills with knowledge in comparing and contrasting the experiences of women in different political systems across Europe in this high school teacher's guide.

Porter, Cathy. *Women in Revolutionary Russia.* Cambridge: Cambridge University Press, 1987. This is about women active in the revolutionary movement, notably in the Bolshevik Party. It is a thorough look, starting with a descriptive outline of women's place before the revolution, astounding changes during the revolution's early period, and the weakening of women's gains during the 1920s and 1930s. Maps, key dates, and a glossary make this a highly recommended resource.

Read, Phyllis J., and Bernard L. Witlieb. *The Book of Women's Firsts.* New York: Random House, 1992. A book of first achievements by women in the United States and the prerevolutionary colonies that provides a record of lives and events unheralded until the early 1990s.

Reese, Lyn, and Rick Clarke. *Two Voices from Nigeria: Nigeria through the Literature of Chinua Achebe and Buchi Emecheta.* Stanford, Calif.: Stanford Program of International and Cross-Cultural Education (SPICE), Stanford University, 1985. Many teachers use Chinua Achebe's novel *Things Fall Apart* to teach about changes in village society during Western colonial contact. This unit provides excerpts from that novel and others by Achebe, which are coupled with those found in the works of the female author Buchi Emecheta. Through this approach, both male and female views are represented in an exploration of specific Nigerian themes and periods. Critical thinking questions accompany the excerpts. Activities using African proverbs and poems by Nigerian students are included.

Ross, Mandy. *The Changing Role of Women (20th Century Perspectives).* Chicago: Heinemann, 2002. Examines the changing role of women throughout the 20th century in politics, human rights, education, domestic life, work, health care, the arts, fashion, and sports. Primary source materials are included.

Rowland, Debra. *Boundaries of Her Body: A Troubling History of Women's Rights in America.* Naperville, Ill.: Sphinx Publishing, Sourcebooks Inc., August 2004. The legal journalist Rowland analyzes how women's rights have, and have not, evolved since the signing of the Mayflower Compact in 1620. Until the late 19th century, women's rights derived from husbands, fathers, and sons. It was believed that their biology made women incapable of thinking rationally—hence they could not own property, vote, or work as many hours or for as much pay as men, until 1965, when the Supreme Court legalized contraception and other aspects of women's legal lives.

Smith, Bonnie G., ed. *Women's History in Global Perspective.* Vols. 1, 2, and 3. Champaign: University of Illinois Press, 2004–05. These essays, written by some of the pioneering figures in women's history, provide background information, with chronological historical overviews and changing perspectives in the research on women in the era of their expertise. Volume 1: Theory and Practice of Women's History, Family History in Global Perspective, Women and Gender in Judaism, Christianity, and Islam; Gender and Work; Race and Ethnicity; Gender and Nation; and Worlds of Feminism. Volume 2: Women in Ancient Civilizations; Women in China, Japan, and Korea; Women and Gender in South and Southeast Asia; Medieval Women; Women and Gender in Colonial Latin America; Women in the United States to 1865. Volume 3: Sub-Saharan Africa; The Middle East; Early and Modern Europe; Russia and the Soviet Union; Latin America; North America after 1865.

Sproule, Anna. *Solidarity: Women Workers.* London: Macdonald Press, 1987. Sproule features women who fought for social justice for workers in Britain, the United States, and Japan from the 19th to early 20th centuries, with first-person quotes, "action" sections that raise questions allowing one to interact with the material, "focus" pieces on key personalities, and a useful time chart.

Stanton, Elizabeth Cady, et al. *History of Woman Suffrage.* 6 vols. (1881–1922). Reprint, Salem, N.H.: Ayer, 1985. Many of the activities of the late 19th-century women's movement, including the campaigns of the postbellum years, are recorded in a multivolume work, *History of Woman Suffrage*, authored by Stanton, Susan B. Anthony, and Matilda Josyln Gage. The volumes were later published in 1881, 1882, 1886, and 1902.

Von Drehle, David. *Triangle: The Fire That Changed America.* New York: Grove/ Atlantic, 2003. Of the 146 workers who died in the Triangle Shirtwaist Factory fire in 1911, 123 were young women. This narrative examines the fire and the Jewish and Italian immigrants who poured into New York City and provided the cheap female labor required by the garment industry.

Weiss, Ellen. *Voting Rights Days.* New York: Simon & Schuster, 2002. After going to live with nine-year-old Emily and her family in Washington, D.C., in 1916, Hitty, a well-traveled wooden doll, witnesses the efforts of Emily's aunt and other suffragists to win women the right to vote.

Web Documents

National Women's History Project. News & Events. Available online. URL: http:// www.nwhp.org. Accessed December 15, 2010. The News & Events alerts readers to special events, such as the Women's History Auction.

Find Your Female Ancestors. Available online. URL: http://www.female-ancestors.com. Accessed December 30, 2010. Several databases of female ancestors, including the entries from the Daughters of Genius (1886); Kansas Women in Literature (1915); a directory of women in New York Women's Clubs published in 1906; early female physicians from "Daughters of America or Women of the Century" by Phebe A. Hanaford, published in 1883; and "History of Stanislaus County California with Biographical Sketches of the Leading Men and Women of the County" by George H. Tinkham, published in 1921.

Gale Free Resources. Women's History. Available online. URL: http://www.gale.cengage.com/free_resources/whm. Accessed December 30, 2010. Thomson Gale has assembled a collection of activities and information to complement classroom topics on women's history. Within this site, teachers and students can read biographies of significant women throughout time, take a quiz based on women and their achievements, follow a time line of significant events in women's history, and enjoy activities to celebrate women's history.

Women in World History Curriculum's Web site. Available online. URL: http://www.womeninworldhistory.com/index.html. Accessed December 30, 2010. Focuses on information about women's history beyond the borders of the United States. This project began in 1985 as the result of a U.S. Department of Education grant to create a secondary-level classroom resource bibliography about women in World History and Global Studies.

Television/Films/Video

Charles Dana Gibson: Portrait of an Illustrator. Directed by Josiah Emery. 28 minutes. Acre Island Productions, 1997, documentary. Explores a popular image of the American woman, the Gibson Girl.

The Flapper Story. Directed by Lauren Lazin. 29 minutes. The Cinema Guild, 1985, documentary. Examines the social phenomenon of the flapper during the 1920s in America.

HIV/AIDS

Television/Films/Video

Yesterday. Produced and directed by Darrell Roodt. 96 minutes. HBO, 2004, television movie. About a Zulu women (Leleti Khumalo) who copes with the AIDS virus in her rural South African village. After falling ill, Yesterday (Khumalo) learns that she is HIV positive. With her husband in denial and a young daughter to tend to, Yesterday has one goal: to live long enough to see her child go to school.

Web Documents

Human Rights Watch. "Women and HIV/AIDS." Available online. URL: http://www.hrw.org/en/news/2008/05/16/women-and-hivaids. Accessed January 14, 2011. The link between women's rights abuses and the spread of HIV/AIDS is slowly gaining recognition, but not before millions of women have lost their lives to the disease. The Web page provides links to the latest news, publications, and related resources.

Joint United Nations Programme on AIDS (UNAIDS). "UNAIDS/WHO AIDS Epidemic Update: December 2005." Available online. URL: http://www.unaids.org/ epi/2005/doc/report_pdf.asp. Accessed December 30, 2010. Although the precise number of people living with HIV is unknown, the report estimates the global penetration of the AIDS epidemic by using a variety of sources—population surveys, medical reports, and the like. The ranges reflect the uncertainty that still surrounds the virus that has been infecting people worldwide since the early 1980s. The report, illustrated with maps and data tables, discusses the impact of HIV/AIDS by region and has a chapter on prevention as a key strategy for coping with the deadly virus.

HUMAN TRAFFICKING
Web Documents

Human Rights Watch. Search with the term *trafficking*. Available online. URL: http:// hrw.org. Accessed December 30, 2010. This watchdog organization tracks trends in global sexual trafficking.

United Nations Children's Fund (UNICEF). "Child Protection from Violence, Exploitation and Abuse." Available online. URL: http://www.unicef. org/protection/index_ exploitation.html. Accessed December 30, 2010. In its work, UNICEF upholds the Convention on the Rights of the Child. This Web site specifies the conventions and protocols established, in addition to facts and figures.

United Nations Office of Drugs and Crime. "Global Report on Trafficking in Persons." February 12, 2009. Available online. URL: http://www.unodc.org/unodc/en/front page/unodc-report-on-human-trafficking-exposes-modern-form-of-slavery-. html. Accessed December 30, 2010. Summarizes the protocol and issues concerning trafficking of women and children, collected from information furnished by 155 countries. A global assessment of human trafficking and the measures being taken to fight it. The page also links to collections of documents about human trafficking that include other UN and non-UN organizations coping with trafficking of human beings and background information about the 2003 United Nations Protocol against Trafficking in Persons.

U.S. Department of Justice—Human Trafficking. Available online. URL: http://www. justice.gov/olp/human_trafficking.htm. Accessed December 30, 2010. DOJ resources.

U.S. Department of State's Office of Global Women's Issues. Available online. URL: http://www.state.gov/s/gwi/index.htm. Accessed December 30, 2010. The office, led by Ambassador-at-Large Melanne Verveer, looks after the political, economic, and social empowerment of women.

U.S. Immigration and Customs Enforcement [ICE]—Human Trafficking. Available online. URL: http://www.ice.gov/human-trafficking/. Accessed December 30, 2010.

ICE was established in March 2003 as the largest investigative arm of the Department of Homeland Security. It works with state and local law officials to identify human trafficking rings entering and exiting the United States.

Television/Films/Video

Human Trafficking. Directed by Christian Duguay. 240 minutes with commercials. Lifetime for Women movie, 2005, television miniseries. Mira Sorvino and Donald Sutherland play U.S. officers who crack down on an international human-trafficking ring. The story follows several girls and women all over the world who have been abducted and sold into prostitution.

INTERNATIONAL WOMEN'S MOVEMENT
Books

Fraser, Arvonne S., and Irene Tinker, eds. *Developing Power: How Women Transformed International Development.* New York: City University of New York, Feminist Press, 2004. Two activists from the 1970s encourage 27 women who are pioneers from a wide variety of countries and fields to write personal accounts. Through the collection of inspiring and revealing memoirs, they document women's historical accomplishments from the 1970s, from educational development to challenging of international development institutions, and ways women have learned to integrate work and family. Information about the UN conferences for women, the expansion of women's international nongovernment organizations, and major global women's issues is also discussed.

Kahn, Janet, and Susan Bailey. *Shaping a Better World: Global Issues, Gender Issues.* Wellesley, Mass.: Center for Research on Women, 2000. A teaching guide for grades seven to 12 that places women at the center of contemporary concerns about human rights, the global economy (notably sweatshop labor), ethnic conflicts, sustainable development, the environment, and cultural diversity.

Neft, Naomi, and Ann D. Levine. *Where Women Stand: An International Report on the Status of Women in 140 Countries, 1997–1998.* New York: Random House, 1998. This easy-to-read book offers background information, clear charts, and ways to compare the progress of women's issues and status in the global community using United Nations documents.

Pietilä, Hilkka. *Engendering the Global Agenda: The Story of Women and the United Nations.* New York: UN Non-Governmental Liaison Service, 2004. Available online. URL: http://www.unsystem.org/ngls/documents/publications.en/ develop.dossier/dd.06/contents.htm. Accessed December 30, 2010. Accessible for downloads in five parts, the book describes how the International Women's Day began with women's roles in the League of Nations and the evolution into a global movement.

Smith, Bonnie, ed. *Global Feminism since 1945.* London: Routledge, 2000. From the West, East, North and South, Smith describes the similarities and differences in women's activism on behalf of equality, liberation, and humane conditions across different countries. Fourteen reprinted essays appear in analyses of nation building, sources of activism, women's liberation, and new waves in the 1980s and 1990s. The collection offers perspectives from 19th- and 20th-century Egypt, Vietnam, South Africa, Brazil, Kenya, Korea, Britain, Japan, Russia, Iran, Germany, and the United States. Of notable interest are discussions of contemporary international movements dealing with women's human rights, Amnesty International, and the "NGO-ization" of feminism, as well as reflections on the world conference on women in Beijing.

Podcasts

Organization for Economic Co-operation and Development (OECD). "Gender Equality." Podcast (2010). 3:12 minutes. Available online. URL: http://www.oecd.org/document/16/0,3343,en_2649_33935_39323280_1_1_1_1,00.html. Accessed on December 3, 2010. OECD's Dennis Drechsler speaks about the OECD Gender, Institutions and Development Database (GID-DB) and its usefulness as a tracking device to hold countries accountable for their progress in promoting gender equality. Other features and podcasts are available at this Web site.

ISLAM

Books

Mernissi, Fatima. *The Forgotten Queens of Islam.* Translated by Mary Jo Lakeland. Minneapolis: University of Minnesota Press, 1993. A Moroccan author analyzes the lives of little-known female leaders within the context of Islamic beliefs about women's place in society. Fascinating stories reveal the meaning of *caliph* and *queen* and the criteria of sovereignty in Islam. A survey of the queens—from those who ruled "behind the throne"; to those, such as the Arab queen Arwa of Yemen, who held great power; to the most numerous, the sultanas of Persia and India—is discussed.

Web Documents

University of Alberta, Canada. "Women, Class, and Islam." Available online. URL: http://www.humanities.ualberta.ca/ottoman/module2/tutorial2a.htm. Accessed on December 30, 2010. A tutorial on women, class, and Islam during the Ottoman Empire.

Television/Films/Video

Not without My Daughter. Directed by Brian Gilbert. Written by Betty Mahmoody and William Hoffer, 1991. About the American Betty Mahmoody's (played by Sally Fields) escape from Iran, where her Iranian husband has reaffirmed his faith in

Islam and will not allow her to leave with her daughter. The film provides a vivid portrayal of women's lives during Ayatollah Khomeini's rule and their attempts to defy tribal customs, beliefs, and manners of living.

LEADERSHIP

Book

Earnshaw, Doris, ed. *International Women Speak: The Emergence of Women's Global Leadership.* Palo Alto, Calif.: AltaVista Press, 2000. This book is part of Earnshaw's Women's Speak series, which highlights influential women with excerpts from their speeches or writings to present their perspectives on a variety of topics. The author presents 20 women, including Queen Noor (Jordan), Benedita da Silva (Brazil), and Mary Robinson (Ireland), who represent different countries and interests. Each has become a leader, speaking authoritatively on issues such as children, housing, war, peace, and health.

Skaine, Rosemarie. *Women Political Leaders in Africa.* Jefferson, North Carolina: McFarland & Company, Inc., 2008. An examination of African women leaders who have been elected or appointed to national leadership positions. This book analyzes the progress made by women leaders in individual countries and provides an overview of the historical role of women in African governments. Eleven women in high office are profiled, including Liberian president Ellen Johnson-Sirleaf and Prime Minister Luisa Diogo of Mozambique.

LESBIAN, GAY, BISEXUAL, TRANSGENDER ISSUES

Books

Bullough, Vern L., ed. *Before Stonewall: Activists for Gay and Lesbian Rights in Historical Context.* New York, London, and Oxford: Harrington Park Press, 2002. A collection of 49 short biographies of activists in the gay and lesbian rights movement, including Henry Gerber, Pearl Hart, Lisa Ben, and Phyllis Leon.

Curry, Hayden, Denis Clifford, and Frederick Hertz. *A Legal Guide for Lesbian and Gay Couples.* 12th ed. Berkeley, Calif.: Nolo Law for All Series, National Center for Lesbian Rights, April 30, 2005. This guide has been updated frequently since its first edition in 1980 and offers state-by-state legal guidance and information about the forming of domestic partnerships, money management, parenting, health care, and estate planning for gay and lesbian couples.

Donahue, David M. *Lesbian, Gay, Bisexual, and Transgender Rights: A Human Rights Perspective.* Minneapolis: University of Minnesota, Human Rights Resource Center, Human Rights Education Series, 2000. This curriculum guide includes nine lessons that set the struggle for lesbian, gay, bisexual, and transgender (LGBT) rights in a human rights perspective. Using the Universal Declaration of Human Rights as a standard, the lesson plans take students from a gay-straight alliance in

Salt Lake City to a prison in Romania in order to improve understanding of the issues confronting LGBT people in today's world.

Endean, Steve, and Vicki Lynn Eaklor, eds. *Bringing Lesbian and Gay Rights into the Mainstream: Twenty Years of Progress.* New York, London, and Oxford: Harrington Park Press, 2006. First-person account of the lesbian and gay movement's early progress in the 1970s and the 1980s, and the legislative and political struggles Endean, the author, endured.

Kranz, Rachel, and Tim Cusick. *Gay Rights.* Library in a Book Series. New York: Facts On File, 2000. A concise treatment of the major issues in the gay rights movement. The text has been updated throughout to reflect developments through early 2005.

Web Documents

Human Rights Watch. Search "Lesbian, Gay, Bisexual, and Transgender Rights." Available online. URL: http://hrw.org/doc/?t=lgbt. Accessed December 30, 2010. The Web site is updated regularly with the latest international news stories relative to LGBT rights. It offers links to information by country and related materials.

International Gay and Lesbian Human Rights Commission. Available online. URL: http://www.iglhrc.org/cgi-bin/iowa/home/index.html. Accessed December 30, 2010. Regularly updated with current international news stories pertaining to gays and lesbians.

The National Center for Lesbian Rights. Available online. URL: http://www.nclrights. org. Accessed December 30, 2010. Daily updates on news stories and legislation pertaining to lesbian rights.

The Pew Forum on Religion and Public Life. "State Policies on Same-Sex Marriage." Available online. URL: http://pewforum.org/Gay-Marriage-and-Homosexuality/ State-Policies-on-Same-Sex-Marriage.aspx. Accessed January 7, 2011. Graphs and statistics about state policies permitting same-sex marriage.

———. "Gay Marriage Research Package." Available online. URL: http://pewforum. org/Gay-Marriage-and-Homosexuality/Gay-Marriage-Research-Package-Navigation-page.aspx. Accessed January 19, 2011. An overview of the same-sex marriage debate, which examines public opinion and religious groups' viewpoints, as well as legal and international perspectives.

U.S. State Department. "Human Rights Reports." Available online. URL: http://www. state.gov/g/drl/rls/hrrpt. Accessed December 30, 2010. Annual reports on human rights since 1999 that document violations against lesbian, gay, bisexual, and transgender people and people with HIV/AIDS. A number of human rights issues are addressed in a variety of countries.

"World Timeline on Same-Sex Rights." CBS News In-Depth. Available online. URL: http://www.cbc.ca/world/story/2009/05/26/f-same-sex-timeline.html. Accessed December 30, 2010. In addition to an international time line of events related to the gay and lesbian movement, the Web page links to newscasts and current legislation.

LITERACY

Web Documents

United Nations Educational, Scientific and Cultural Organization (UNESCO). "Global Monitoring Report 2006." Available online. URL: http://www.unesco.org/new/en/education/themes/leading-the-international-agenda/efareport/reports/2006-literacy/. Accessed January 14, 2011. The 2006 report aims to shine a policy spotlight on the more neglected goals of literacy—a foundation not only for achieving "education for all" but, more broadly, for reaching the goal of reducing human poverty. The 2006 report is based on data for the 2002–03 school year.

LITERATURE

Books

Cahill, Susan, ed. *Wise Women: Over 2000 Years of Spiritual Writing by Women.* New York: W. W. Norton, 1996. One place to find the ancient and modern voices of women is within the realms of the spiritual. Even in established religious institutions, women have often been "allowed" to express themselves. The writings vary from poems, songs, stories, prayers, letters, excerpts from novels, excerpts from the transcripts of a trials, to short essays. A short biography of the author introduces each piece.

Frederick, Bonnie, and Susan McLeod, eds. *Women and the Journey: The Female Travel Experience.* Pullman: Washington State University, 1993. A series of essays about women travelers or women whose journeys are notably different from men's. A global and historic view includes a discussion of Victorian women's travel dress and how white women prisoners in Argentina and Uruguay were used to heighten colonial and 19th-century fear of Indians, as well as tales of Chinese women in the American West, Ibn Battuta's account of travel by medieval women in Islamic culture, and English women's 20th-century plays. In the section Women and Traditions of Narrative, the editors offer gender perspectives on literature such as the *Faerie Queen, Pilgrim's Progress*, D. H. Lawrence's books, *The Handmaid's Tale*, and stories from the American frontier.

Hirshfield, Jane, ed. *Women in Praise of the Sacred: 43 Centuries of Spiritual Poetry by Women.* New York: HarperCollins, 1994. Hirshfield's anthology of world history poetry contains background information on the author and her times from the hymns of the world's earliest identified author, the Sumerian priest Enheduanna, to a poem written by a Korean Buddhist nun in the 1950s. The poems express major religious traditions from the East and West and several indigenous cultures.

Television/Films/Video

In Black and White. Volume 2: *Gloria Naylor.* Produced by RTSI Swiss TV and directed by Matteo Bellinelli. 22 minutes. California Newsreel, 1992. Information available online. URL: http://www.newsreel.org/nav/title.asp?tc=CN0048-

2&s=women. Naylor explains her exploration across the social spectrum of what it means to be black in America in *The Women of Brewster Place* and *Mama Day.*

MILITARY

Books

Carl, Ann Baumgartner. *A WASP among Eagles.* Washington, D.C.: Smithsonian Press, 1999. An account by a test pilot who was among the thousand Women Airforce Service Pilots (WASPs) to ferry and test aircraft or instruct others during World War II for American troops, with little or no publicity and very low status within the force. Includes specifications and costs of the airplanes flown.

Cochran, Jacqueline, and Brinley Maryann Bucknum. *Jackie Cochran: An Autobiography.* New York: Bantam Books, 1987. Excerpts from the late Cochran's own accounts of her flying and life overcoming challenges from poverty to a childhood as an orphan.

Holden, Henry M., with Lori Griffith. *Ladybirds: The Untold Story of Women Pilots in America.* Mt. Freedom, N.J.: Black Hawk, 1993. A history of American women in every aspect of aviation from a woman balloonist of 200 years ago, to the early days of Anne Morrow Lindbergh and Amelia Earhart, to today's commercial women airline pilots (coauthor Lori Griffith is a Boeing 737 captain with USAir).

Articles

Darr, Ann. "The Women Who Flew, but Kept Silent," *New York Times Magazine,* 7 May 1995, SM70–71. Darr describes her experience flying military planes under the director, Jacqueline Cochran, in the early 1940s (and the quest for the Women Airforce Service Pilots (WASPs) to be recognized for their early feats) by the U.S. Air Force. They won veteran status only after much labor in 1977.

Dickerson, Debra. "Was Abu Ghraib Her Fault?" *Elle,* November 2005, 248. Dickerson, who served in the army for 12 years, interviews Janis Karpinski, the first female general to command in a combat zone in the 2002 war in Iraq.

McGirk, Tim. "Crossing the Lines: Though Barred from Combat, Female Troops in Iraq Often Find Themselves in Full-Fledged Battle," *Time,* 27 February 2006, 38–43. An intimate look at the lives of the real "G.I. Janes."

Web Documents

About.com. "Women and World War II." Women's History, Military & War: Women. Available online. URL: http://womenshistory.about.com/od/warwwii/ Women_and_World_War_II.htm. Accessed December 30, 2010. Provides information about international and American women's roles during World War II.

U.S. Bureau of Census. "Department of Defense Manpower." Available online. URL:http://www.allcountries.org/uscensus/577_department_of_defense_manpower.html. Accessed December 30, 2010. Data from 1960 to 1999 by corps.

Annotated Bibliography

Williams, Rudi. "Military Women Take 200-Year Trek toward Respect, Parity." American Forces Information Service News Articles. August 1998. Available online. URL: http://www.defense.gov/news/newsarticle.aspx?id=43226 Accessed January 14, 2011. Williams describes the 220 years of trials, tribulations, and indignities women experienced to reach, and benefit, from their present-day positions within the military.

Television/Films/Video

Fly Girls. Written, produced, and directed by Laurel Ladevich. 60 minutes. PBS movie, 1999, documentary. Full transcript available online. URL: http://womenshistory. about.com. Information about the film available online. URL: http://www.pbs. org/wgbh/amex/flygirls/tguide/index.html. During World War II, more than 1,000 women signed up to fly with the U.S. military. Wives, mothers, actresses, and debutantes who joined the Women Airforce Service Pilots (WASPs) test-piloted aircraft, ferried planes, and logged 60 million miles in the air. Thirty-eight women died in service. But the opportunity to play a critical role in the war effort was abruptly canceled by politics and resentment, and it would be 30 years before women would again break the sex barrier in the skies.

The Life and Times of Rosie the Riveter. Directed by Connie Fields. 65 minutes. Video of motion picture by Clarity Productions, 1980, documentary. During World War II, an unprecedented number of American women responded to government encouragement to enter the high-paying world of war production heavy industry. Women who had worked at pink-collar jobs or in lower-paying women's industrial jobs flocked to war production work as an opportunity to learn new skills and make higher wages. The documentary *The Life and Times of Rosie the Riveter* presents these women's experiences as they developed throughout the war years, and after, when the men came marching home. Some of the valuable elements of the film are interviews with several of the women who entered war production work. When watching the film, pay attention to the juxtaposition of their stories and experiences with government propaganda films that encouraged women to become war workers, described their work on the lines, and then encouraged them to "return to their homes" after the war. The film has been deemed "culturally significant" by the Library of Congress, thereby allowing it to be preserved in the U.S. National Film Registry.

Swing Shift. Directed by Jonathan Demme and written by Nancy Dowd. 100 minutes. 1984, film. A woman (Goldie Hawn) finds romance when she takes a job at an airport plant to help make ends meet after her husband goes off to war. This comedy entertains while it reveals some of the aspects of life for women on the domestic front during World War II.

Podcasts

PBS Newshour. *Women Veterans Face Unique Obstacles, Needs.* Podcast (November 30, 2010). 7:10 minutes. Available online. URL: http://www.pbs.org/newshour/

bb/military/july-dec10/womenvets_11-30.html. Accessed on December 30, 2010. How women's experience in the military and afterward is different from men's is explored. Risk factors they face make them more susceptible in dealing with PTSD, single parenthood, sexual violence, and homelessness.

National Public Radio. Panel to Recommend Allowing Women in Combat. Podcast (January 13, 2011). 3:58 minutes. Available online. URL: http://www.npr. org/2011/01/13/132882277/Panel-To-Recommend-Allowing-Women-In-Combat. Accessed on January 14, 2011. Women are often in support of combat troops but are not assigned to combat duty. A high-level congressional commission is preparing to recommend that the Pentagon reverse this rule, thus giving women the opportunity for promotion within the ranks.

MONITORING

Books

Flexner, Eleanor, and Ellen Fitzpatrick. *Century of Struggle: The Woman's Rights Movement in the United States.* Cambridge, Mass.: Harvard University Press, 1996. Betty Friedan's review: "A book to be read by every student in this country . . . this account will help us to maintain a truer image of ourselves as we try to finish up the struggle first launched so long ago." The book documents the movement as one of the great social processes in American history.

Mezey, Susan Gluck. *Elusive Equality: Women's Rights, Public Policy, and the Law.* Boulder, Colo.: Lynne Rienner, 2003. This book documents the history of the concerted efforts to equalize women's status in the law—a story marked both by major steps forward and by movement backward, and even inertia. It is in this sense that equality remains elusive.

Van Der Gaag, Nikkie, and Nawal el Saadawi. *The No-Nonsense Guide to Women's Rights.* Market Marborough, U.K.: New Internationalist/Verso, 2004. Although women have progressed—in legal rights, political representation, employment, education, and health—the statistics indicate otherwise. Testimonies from women and men around the world explain why, especially in this postfeminist age, women's rights are still very much an issue for men and women alike.

Women's Rights Project. *Women's Human Rights Step by Step: A Practical Guide to Using International Human Rights Law and Mechanisms to Defend Women's Human Rights.* Washington, D.C.: Women, Law & Development International and Human Rights Watch, 1997. About women's human rights in practice, the analysis describes the concept and content of human rights law and its application to women and to the rights issues of concern to them. As a basic guide to the operation of human rights mechanisms and the strategies at national, regional, and international levels, the manual explains how to use these strategies and mechanisms to uphold women's human rights in different cultural, legal, and political contexts.

Annotated Bibliography

Web Documents

The President's Interagency Council on Women (January 8, 2001). Available online. URL: http://secretary.state.gov/www/picw. Accessed December 30, 2010. Launched in 1995 on the eve of the UN Fourth World Conference on Women in Beijing, to "make sure that all the effort and good ideas actually get implemented when we get back home" by presidential executive order. The council was chaired by the Health and Human Services secretary Donna Shalala with first lady Hillary Rodham Clinton as honorary chair. The activities supporting the agency were discontinued when President Clinton left office in 2001, but the Web site still exists for archival purposes.

United Nations. "The World's Women 2005 Progress in Statistics" (January 18, 2006). Available online. URL: http://unstats.un.org/unsd/demographic/products/indwm/wwpub.htm. Accessed December 30, 2010. A report prepared by the Statistics Division of the UN Department for Economic and Social Affairs (UNDESA) at five-year intervals starting in 1991. The 2005 issue compiles and analyzes data from national reporting of sex-disaggregated statistics in such areas as demographics, health, education, work, violence against women, poverty, human rights, and decision making. Five years ago, the World's Women report emphasized that the improvement of national statistical capacity—the ability to provide timely and reliable statistics—is essential for improving gender statistics.

———. Division for the Advancement of Women. Available online. URL: http://www.un.org/womenwatch/daw/csw. Accessed December 30, 2010. The Commission on the Status of Women (CSW) was established by UN Economic and Social Council Resolution 11(II) of June 21, 1946, to prepare recommendations and reports to the council on promoting women's political, economic, civil, social, and educational rights. CSW now monitors on a yearly basis progress made in emerging issues from the Beijing Platform for Action.

———. United Nations Millennium Development Goal Indicators. Available online. URL: http://millenniumindicators.un.org/unsd/mdg/Default.aspx. Accessed December 30, 2010. This Web site provides access to the database with the current metadata on the Millennium Development Goal Indicators.

MULTICULTURAL ISSUES

Books

Kramarae, Cheris, and Dale Spender, eds. *Routledge International Encyclopedia of Women: Global Women's Issues and Knowledge.* 4 vols. New York: Routledge, 2000. Provides comprehensive global, multicultural coverage of women's issues and concerns with references and further reading. Selections are cross-referenced. Check the Web site to explore the four-volume resource, from an A–Z list of entries to an extensive selection of excerpts.

Web Documents

The American Civil Liberties Union of Southern California. "ACLU/SC Announces Launch of Latina Rights Project on International Women's Day." Teaching to Change LA. Available online. URL: http://www.tcla.gseis.ucla.edu/rights/features/5/attorneylatinarights.html. Accessed December 30, 2010. On International Women's Day, the American Civil Liberties Union of Southern California announced the launch of its Latina Rights Project. The project, a pilot initiative of the ACLU Foundation of Southern California, will utilize model litigation, bilingual/bicultural public education and public advocacy to address priority civil rights issues facing Latina women and girls in Southern California. The article offers interesting statistics about the Latina population in California.

Escobar-Haskins, Lillian, and George F. Haskins. "The AIDS Crisis in Pennsylvania: The Hidden Epidemic among African American and Latina Women." Lulu. com. Available online. URL: http://www.lulu.com/content/136980. Accessed December 30, 2010. Study commissioned by the Philadelphia AIDS Coalition that documents the evolution of the AIDS epidemic and issues related to prevention efforts. It focuses on the two segments of the population who are the fastest-growing and highest-risk groups in the HIV/AIDS population: African-American women and Latinas.

MANA, A National Latina Organization. Available online. URL: http://www.hermana.org/homfrm.htm. Accessed December 30, 2010. The mission of this nonprofit advocacy organization established in 1974 is to empower Latinas through leadership development, community service, and advocacy. MANA fulfills its mission through programs designed to develop the leadership skills of Latinas, promote community service by Latinas, and provide Latinas with advocacy opportunities. Support for these programs is derived from members, corporations, foundations, and government grants.

Mujeres Latinas en Acción. Available online. URL: http://www.mujereslatinasen accion.org. Accessed December 30, 2010. This long-established Chicago organization is a bilingual/bicultural agency that seeks to empower women, their families, and youth. Mujeres Latinas offers counseling, leadership development, and advocacy for program participants. Mujeres Latinas worked with the Chicago Women's Liberation Union (CWLU) to form the Committee to End Sterilization Abuse.

National Organization for Women (NOW). "On Equal Pay Day, NOW Wants Women to 'Get Even.'" Available online. URL: http://www.now.org/press/04-06/04-25. html. Accessed January 14, 2011. April 25 is Equal Pay Day—the day in 1966 when women's average earnings finally catch up with the amount men earned on average in the previous calendar year alone. NOW identified the wage gap and its negative impact on women. Over 40 years later, the gap remained wide and progress had slowed to a crawl. Now, women working full time, year-round, are paid only about three-quarters as much as men, and African-American women and Latinas receive even less.

Pew Research Center. "The New Demography of America's Motherhood." August 2010. Available online. URL: http://pewsocialtrends.org/files/2010/10/754-new-demography-of-motherhood.pdf. Accessed December 30, 2010. This research report examines the changing demographic characteristics of U.S. mothers by comparing women who gave birth in 2008 with those who gave birth in 1990. It is based on data from the National Center for Health Statistics and the Census Bureau.

United Nations Division for the Advancement of Women (DAW). "Women, Nationality, and Citizenship." Available online. URL: http://www.un.org/womenwatch/daw/public/jun03e.pdf. Accessed December 30, 2010. This UN report discusses the issue of nationality and women and the significance of the Convention on the Nationality of Women signed at Montevideo, Uruguay, in 1933.

Urban League. "Race, Ethnicity, Gender." Available online. URL: http://www.urban.org/race/index.cfm. Accessed December 30, 2010. Web site with a variety of resources for the family, including child support, and immigration information. Sample topics include women and minorities in science fields, the Native American health system, and graduation rates.

Television/Films/Video

Real Women Have Curves. Directed by Patricia Cardoso. 90 minutes. 2002, film. The story of a first-generation, Mexican-American teenager living in East Los Angeles on the threshold of womanhood. Encouraged by a Latino high school teacher, Ana receives a full scholarship to Columbia University, but her traditional Latino parents feel that now is the time for Ana to help provide for the family, and not go off to college. Ana's yearning to fulfill her potential as a woman and sense of dignity is tempered by her mother's concerns over her portly female attributes. Based on the play by Josefina Lopez.

POLITICS

Book

Reese, Lyn. *I Will Not Bow My Head: Documenting Political Women*. Berkeley, Calif.: Women in the World Curriculum Resource Project, 1995. Over 60 primary sources reveal defiant political acts and the resisting voices of women in diverse periods and places. Background information, follow-up questions, research and activity suggestions, illustrations, and selected bibliography accompany each document.

POPULATION

Web Documents

Population Reference Bureau (PRB). "2010 World Population Data Sheet." Available online. URL: http://www.prb.org/Publications/Datasheets/2010/2010wpds.aspx. Accessed January 14, 2011. PRB's annual World Population Data Sheet reveals persisting global inequalities in health and well-being. The data and frequently asked questions about them can be downloaded directly from the Web site.

United Nations Population Fund (UNFPA). "State of World Population 2010." 2010. Available online. URL: http://www.unfpa.org/swp. Accessed December 30, 2010. How do we improve the lives of the nearly 3 billion individuals living on less than two dollars a day? How can we enable all individuals—male and female, young and old—to protect themselves from HIV? How can we save the lives of more than 500,000 women who die each year in childbirth? What will it take to show young people living in poverty that they have a stake in development and a hope for the future? For perhaps the first time in history, questions such as these are not simply rhetorical. They have answers: answers that go to the very heart of what it means to be a woman or a man, wealthy or poor. This annual, comprehensive overview of the state of the world includes a critical examination of poverty, the significant role of human rights, reproductive health issues, implications for youth of all of these aspects, the role men and boys can play, gender-based violence, humanitarian strategies, and empowerment of women and youth to achieve the Millennium Development Goals.

POVERTY
Web Documents

Integrated Public Use Microdata Series Census. Available online. URL: http://www.ipums.org. Accessed December 30, 2010. Microdata for national and international social and economic research. The national census database spanning 1850 to the present is maintained by the University of Minnesota and receives major funding by the National Institute of Child Health and Human Development and the National Science Foundation.

World Bank. "World Development Report." Available online. URL: http://www.worldbank.org. Accessed December 30, 2010. The annual WDR (since 1978) describes how the opportunities to live a healthy life, learn, work, invest, and innovate vary widely within and across countries on the basis of predetermined characteristics, such as gender, race, and family background. These differences are a clear indication that the world today is far from realizing the ideal of equal opportunities for all. Online database is now available.

The World Bank Group. "06 World Development Indicators." Available online. URL: http://devdata.worldbank.org/wdi2006/contents/Section1.htm. Accessed December 30, 2010. Database of progress on poverty and other Millennium Development Goals by country.

PROPERTY RIGHTS
Web Documents

Kameri-Mbote, Patricia. "The Law of Succession in Kenya: Gender Perspectives in Property Management and Control." Report, Nairobi: Women and Law in East

Africa, 1995. Available online. URL: http://www.ielrc.org/content/b9501.pdf. Accessed December 30, 2010. Women's property ownership within a marriage circumstance has evolved as a controversial area in gender research and development. The report surveys the history of property ownership; the complex laws of inheritance in Kenya, which are based on four religious systems of marriage; and their relationship to the 1981 Law of Succession Act.

RACISM
Book

Blee, Kathleen M. *Women of the Klan: Racism and Gender in the 1920s.* Berkeley and Los Angeles: University of California Press, 1991. A groundbreaking work about the women of the Ku Klux Klan (WKKK), which enrolled hundreds of thousands of recruits in the 1920s and 1930s. The author examines the historical, cultural, and symbolic contexts of the Klan in the United States. From interviews of surviving Klan members, Blee looks at activities of the women's Klan in Indiana and gives biographical sketches of some of the more prominent women in the Indiana WKKK.

STATISTICS
Web Documents

Eurostat. "Your Key to European Statistics." Available online. URL: http://epp.eurostat. ec.europa.eu/portal/page/portal/eurostat/home/. Accessed January 21, 2011. Statistical agent for the European Union, domiciled in Luxembourg, which enables comparisons between countries and regions.

Organisation for Economic Co-operation and Development (OECD). "The Gender, Institutions and Development Database (GID)." Available online. URL: http://www. oecd.org and http://stats.oecd.org/index.aspx. Accessed December 30, 2010. A tool offered to researchers and policy makers to determine and analyze obstacles to women's economic development. It covers indicators on gender for OECD countries and selected nonmember states. The database has been compiled from various sources and combines in a systematic and coherent fashion the current empirical evidence that exists on the socioeconomic status of women. Its true innovation is the inclusion of institutional variables, which range from intrahousehold behavior to social norms. Information on cultural and traditional practices that impact women's economic development is coded to measure the level of discrimination. Such a comprehensive overview of gender-related variables and the database's specific focus on social institutions make the GID unique, providing a toolbox for a wide range of analytical queries and allowing case-by-case adaptation to specific research or policy questions.

United Nations, Department of Economic and Social Affairs, Population Division. "World Marriage Data 2008." Available online. URL: http://www.un.org/esa/ population/publications/WMD2008/WP_WMD_2008/Data.html. Accessed

January 7, 2011. Statistics and indicators on marital status, marriages, and divorces by country, 1970s to present.

United Nations Statistics Division. "Statistics and Indicators on Women and Men." Available online. URL: http://unstats.un.org/unsd/demographic/products/ indwm/default.htm. Accessed December 30, 2010. This Web site provides statistics and indicators on women and men in six specific fields: population, health, work, families, education, decision making.

———. "Millennium Development Goal Indicators Database." Available online. URL: http://unstats.un.org/unsd/mi/mi_goals.asp. Accessed December 30, 2010. A framework of eight goals, 18 targets, and 48 indicators to measure progress toward the Millennium Development Goals was adopted by a consensus of experts from the United Nations Secretariat and IMF, OECD, and the World Bank. Each indicator is linked to millennium data series as well as to background series related to the target in question.

The World Bank. "Gender and Development." Available online. URL: http:// go.worldbank.org/A74GIZVFW0. Accessed January 21, 2011. Statistical surveys and databases with indicators on women's entrepreneurship and impact of labor laws and policies on women in developing economies.

Books

Organisation for Economic Co-operation and Development (OECD). *OECD Factbook*. This annual edition provides more than 100 indicators—from population, economic production, foreign trade and investment, energy, labor force, information and communications, public finances, innovation, the environment, foreign aid, agriculture, taxation, education, health to quality of life—for OECD member countries with area totals and for select non-member economies. The 2010 OECD Factbook features a chapter on the financial crisis and beyond.

SUFFRAGE

Books

Pankhurst, Emmeline. *My Own Story.* New York: Hearst International Library, 1914 and Kraus Reprints, 1971. Pankhurst's autobiography briefly speaks of her childhood and married life to Dr. Pankhurst, who was considerably older, died, and left her with several children. Mrs. Pankhurst became the leading figure in the British suffragist movement from the turn of the 20th century to World War I, when agitation was suspended for the sake of the war effort, without yet, however, gaining women in Britain the vote, the point where the book's account ends.

Web Documents

Jamieson, Amie, with Hyon B. Shin and Jennifer Day. "Voting and Registration in the Election of November 2000." Current Population Report, U.S. Census Bureau, February 2002. Available online. URL: http://www.census.gov/prod/2002pubs/

p20-542.pdf. Accessed December 30, 2010. The report discusses voting and registration of the citizen voting-age population in the November 2000 presidential election. Voting and registration rates historically have been higher in years with presidential elections than in the "off" years. In this report, the 2000 (a presidential election year) data are compared with data for previous presidential election years (1996, 1992, 1988, etc.).

Television/Films/Video

Iron-Jawed Angels. Directed by Katja von Garnier. 125 minutes. 2004, film. Hillary Swank portrays the life of the suffragist Alice Paul from her beginnings in the movement, to her hunger strike, to winning of enfranchisement in 1920.

VIOLENCE

Web Documents

National Institute of Justice. *Compendium of Research on Violence against Women, 1993–Present* (June 2010). Available online. URL: http://www.ojp.usdoj.gov/nij/pubs-sum/vaw-compendium.htm. A regularly updated compendium that lists and briefly describes all of the projects funded under the National Institute of Justice's Violence Against Women and Family Violence Program.

Tjaden, Patricia, and Nancy Thoennes. *Full Report of the Prevalence, Incidence, and Consequences of Violence against Women.* U.S. Department of Justice. Office of Justice Programs, National Institute of Justice (November 2000). Available online. URL: http://www.ncjrs.gov/pdffiles1/nij/183781.pdf. Accessed January 14, 2011. These findings from the National Violence Against Women Survey provide a comprehensive overview of violence against women in the United States.

World Health Organization. *WHO Multi-Country Study on Women's Health and Domestic Violence against Women* (November 29, 2005). Available online. URL: http://www.who.int/gender/violence/who_multicountry_study/en/. Accessed January 14, 2011. From 24,000 interviews with women in 10 countries, this study analyzes data and sheds new light on the prevalence of violence against women in countries where few data were previously available. It also uncovers the forms and patterns of this violence across different countries and cultures, documenting the consequences of violence for women's health. This study on domestic violence reveals that intimate partner violence is the most common form of violence in women's lives—much more common than assault or rape by strangers or acquaintances. The study reports on the enormous toll physical and sexual violence by husbands and partners has on the health and well-being of women around the world and the extent to which partner violence is still largely hidden.

World Health Organization. *World Report on Violence and Health.* Available online. URL: http://www.who.int/violence_injury_prevention/violence/world_report/en/. Accessed January 14, 2011. Since 2002, WHO examines the types of violence that occur worldwide in the everyday lives of people and that generate much of the health burden imposed by violence. Accordingly, the information has been arranged in nine chapters, covering the following topics: violence—a global public health problem, youth violence, child abuse and neglect by parents and other caregivers, violence by intimate partners, abuse of the elderly, sexual violence, self-directed violence, collective violence, and the way forward: recommendations for action.

Television/Film/Video

No! Produced and directed by Aishah Shahidah Simmons. 94 minutes. 2006, documentary film. Information available online. URL: http://www.newsreel.org/nav/title.asp?tc=CN0187&s=women. Accessed December 30, 2010. About the impact of sexual violence on black women and girls. As the incidents of violence and sexual assault continue on campuses and in communities across the country, this film can be used to support both women and men, regardless of race, as they learn to negotiate the challenging terrain of sexuality—without violence.

WOMEN'S STUDIES

Books

Walker, Mary Edwards, M.D., and Mercedes Graf. *Essays on Women's Rights.* Amherst, N.Y.: Humanity Books, Classics in Women's Studies, 2003. The only woman to receive the Congressional Medal of Honor for her service during the Civil War, Dr. Mary Edwards Walker (1832–1919) was a surgeon, a public lecturer, and an outspoken champion of women's rights. One of the first women in the country to be awarded a medical degree, she served as an assistant surgeon for the Fifty-second Ohio Infantry and was cited for her valor in working behind enemy lines to attend to the sick and wounded.

Articles

Fish, Cheryl J., with Yi-Chun and Tricia Lin. "Women's Studies Then and Now," *Women's Studies Quarterly,* December 2002. Since the launch of the first women's studies courses in the early 1970s, more than 600 programs in the field have been established in the United States and throughout the world. In this special edition, teachers, scholars, activists, and poets examine the historical impact and the new struggles in this dynamic field. Contributors explore intergenerational differences, the effect of new technologies on women's studies curricula, and the challenges of teaching women's studies since September 11, 2001. They speak from community college, undergraduate, and doctoral programs in urban and rural settings.

Chronology

1780 B.C.E.

- The Egyptian queen Sobeknefru (ca. 1787–1783 B.C.E.) rules without a king. She is portrayed wearing the royal head cloth and a kilt over female dress.

1750 B.C.E.

- The Babylonian Code of Hammurabi protects a woman's right to hold and inherit property.

1500 B.C.E.

- During Egypt's Golden Age (the New Kingdom, ca. 1550–1069 B.C.E.), Ahhotep is awarded for bravery in support of her two sons, King Kamose and King Ahmose, and her husband, King Seqnenre-Taa.

1472 B.C.E.

- Hatshepsut becomes one of Egypt's most famous queens.

1400 B.C.E.

- Queen Tiy becomes the wife of Amenhotep III (1390–1352 B.C.E.) in spite of her provincial origins.

1336 B.C.E.

- Queen Nefertiti assists her husband, King Akhenaten, in his restructuring policies. Some believe she ruled as king after her husband died.

1200 B.C.E.

- After the death of her husband, Seti II, in 1194 B.C.E., Tawosret takes the throne.

51 B.C.E.

- The last of Egypt's female pharaohs, the great Cleopatra VII, restores fortune to Egypt until her eventual suicide in 30 B.C.E., marking the end of ancient Egypt.

61‡63 C.E.

- Boadicea, a Dark Ages hero in the United Kingdom, leads the Iceni Celts to a glorious, but not victorious, war against the Romans in East Anglia.

415

- Hypatia, the first noted woman mathematician, is a brilliant lecturer. Her Neo-Platonist philosophy, with religious undertones, leads to her killing by a Christian mob.

527

- Theodora, a renowned stage performer, made empress by Justinian in Constantinople, legalizes property inheritance by women and divorce laws and attempts to outlaw prostitution.

1141

- Hildegard von Bingen, a German nun and magistra (teacher), has a vision that gives her instant understanding of the meaning of religious texts and commands her to record in writing everything she observes in her visions.

1100s

- Mahasty is jailed for speaking her mind about the role women could play in Afghan society.

1327

- Twinslayer's Case for abortion in England.

1348

- Abortionist's Case in England.

1400s

- Queen Gowhar Shad of Heart, ruler of the Afghan empire for 50 years, supports the arts, founds colleges, and enacts laws.

1412‡31

- Joan of Arc leads French forces in chasing the English out of France.

Chronology

1558

- *November 17:* Queen Elizabeth succeeds to the throne in England.

1694

- The British author and feminist Mary Astell pleads for greater opportunities for women in her *Serious Proposal to the Ladies,* written in two parts between 1694 and 1697. Her work offers a scheme for a women's college, an idea well before its time and the subject of public ridicule.

1700s

- Nazo, Zainab, and Zarhgoona are three Afghan wise women who advise the state on various matters. Zainab advocates educational rights of women in harems.

1701

- The first sexually integrated jury—six men and six women—hears cases in Albany, New York.

1747

- In Afghanistan, King Ahmad Shah discontinues the practice of divorce that shames women. Marriage and property rights for widowed women are also protected under his reign, which encourages widows to remarry.

1769

- American colonies base their laws on the English common law, summarized in Sir William Blackstone's *Commentaries on the Laws of England* (1765–69): "By marriage, the husband and wife are one person in the law. The very being and legal existence of the woman is suspended during the marriage, or at least is incorporated into that of her husband under whose wing and protection she performs everything."

1777

- During the American Revolution, state constitutions bar women from political process. New York passes laws that take away women's right to vote. By 1807, all states disenfranchise women.

1788

- Women win the right in the United States of America to stand for election.

1789

- The United States Constitution is ratified so the terms *persons, people,* and *electors* can be interpreted to include men and women.

WOMEN'S RIGHTS

1792

- Mary Wollstonecraft's *A Vindication of the Rights of Woman* is published in Britain. Educated women begin to promote the equal rights of women to education and work.

1806

- Divorce is prohibited in France.

1839

- The first Married Women's Property Act is enacted in Mississippi, allowing women the right to hold property in their own name, but with their husband's permission.

1840

- The World's Anti-Slavery Convention is held in London, England, but the female delegates from the United States, Lucretia Mott and Elizabeth Cady Stanton, are not allowed to participate. They decide to have a women's rights convention when they return home.

1845

- Danish women are permitted to take the examination to be heads of schools, allowing them the opportunity to improve teaching and education of girls.

1847

- Mary Blackwell attains full status as a physician in the United States.

1848

- The New York Married Women's Property Law replaces Mississippi's as a model for other states. The law provides for a married woman to be a sole owner of land and protected from a husband's creditors.
- At the Women's Convention in Seneca Falls, New York, 100 people (68 women and 32 men) of the 300 attendees sign the Declaration of Sentiments, to cease discrimination against women in all aspects of society.
- The Boston Female Medical College in Massachusetts opens and eventually merges with Boston University School of Medicine, making it the first coeducational medical school in the United States.

1852

- Antioch College in Yellow Springs, Ohio, is the first nonsectarian college to grant women equal rights with men.

Chronology

1855

- In *Missouri v. Celia*, a black female slave is defined as property and without the right to defend herself against a master's act of rape.
- Woman's Hospital opens in New York City as the first institution in the world established by women "for the treatment of diseases peculiar to women." It becomes known as the "birthplace of gynecology" and is now part of the St. Luke's hospital complex.

1860s

- Indiana State College becomes the first state college to grant equal privileges to women in the 1860s.

1861

- Empress Tz'u-hsi (Cixi) becomes de facto ruler of China when her husband dies. She holds the reins of power until 1889.
- Julie Daubie is the first female high school graduate in France.

1862

- The Morrill Act of 1862 grants land in the west of the United States for colleges.

1863

- French minister of public instruction Victor Duruy creates secondary school classes specific to girls, until then prohibited.

1866

- The Fourteenth Amendment is passed by Congress to be later ratified by the states in 1868. It is the first time *citizens* and *voters* are defined as "male" in the Constitution.
- The American Equal Rights Association (AERA) is founded in New York City with the purpose of securing for all Americans their civil rights irrespective of race, color, or sex. Lucretia Mott is elected president and Susan B. Anthony as secretary.
- To test women's constitutional right to hold public office, Stanton runs for Congress, receiving 24 of 12,000 votes cast.

1869

- The first U.S. woman suffrage law is passed in the territory of Wyoming.

- John Stuart Mill, an English philosopher and economist, addresses the rights of women in his book *The Subjection of Women*, which is immediately translated into Danish.
- AERA splits in 1869 as a result of disagreements about the status of equal suffrage rights for blacks, creating three organizations: the National Woman Suffrage Association (NWSA), the American Woman Suffrage Association (AWSA), and the National American Woman Suffrage Association (NAWSA). Anthony and Stanton organize NWSA.
- Washington University School of Law (then, St. Louis Law School) in Missouri becomes the first law school to admit women.
- The first women's labor organization, Daughters of St. Crispin, holds its first convention at its founding in Lynn, Massachusetts. Chaired by Carrie Wilson, delegates from lodges across New England and the Northeast attend. An economic depression in 1873 causes the organization to disband in 1876.

1870

- The Fifteenth Amendment receives final ratification. Its wording does not specifically prevent women from voting: "The right of citizens of the United States to vote shall not be denied or abridged by the United States or by any State on account of race, color, or previous condition of servitude."
- The first sexually integrated grand jury hears cases in Cheyenne, Wyoming.

1871

- 1871, the Dansk Kvindesamfund (Danish Women's Society) is founded, envisioned at first as a division of the International Association of Women, in the Bajer's home in Copenhagen.

1872

- Anthony leads a group of women to the polls in Rochester, New York, to test the right of women to the franchise under the terms of the Fourteenth Amendment. Her arrest, trial, and sentence to a fine propel the high-profile case to the U.S. Supreme Court, which decides against her.

1873

- In (Myra Colby) *Bradwell v. Illinois*, the U.S. Supreme Court rules that a state has the right to exclude a married woman from practicing law.
- The Comstock Act makes it a federal crime to use the U.S. mail to distribute anything considered "obscene, lewd, lascivious, indecently filthy, or vile." The law classifies information about contraception, abortion, and sexual health as obscene in the United States.
- The Woman's Crusade of 1873–74 protests alcohol and saloons.

Chronology

1874

- Nielsine Nielsen is among the first women to apply to and be accepted in medical school at the University of Copenhagen in Denmark.

1875

- In *Minor v. Happersett,* the U.S. Supreme Court declares that despite the privileges and immunities clause, a state can prohibit a woman from voting. The Court declares women as "persons" but holds that they constitute a "special category of nonvoting citizens."
- Danish universities become open to women who successfully pass the physical fitness exams with the same scores as men.

1878

- The U.S. Congress passes a constitutional amendment enfranchising women, which the states do not ratify until 41 years later.
- The first women's medical society is formed. Later renamed the New England Women's Medical Society, it is initially chaired by Dr. Marie E. Zakrzewska.

1879

- Through special congressional legislation, Belva Lockwood becomes the first woman admitted to try a case before the Supreme Court.

1880

- Malalai, a Pashtun woman, leads Afghans into war while waving a veil over her head, during the Second Anglo-Afghan War.

1881

- Volume 1 of a multivolume series, *History of Woman Suffrage*, written by Susan B. Anthony, Elizabeth Stanton, and Matilda Gage, is published. Volumes are published in 1882, 1886, and 1902.
- Teacher's College in Sèvres, France, opens to train female professors for secondary education.

1885

- Bryn Mawr College in Pennsylvania opens and offers graduate programs to women.

1886

- The Young Women's Christian Association (YWCA) is founded as a national group in the United States. It began in Britain in 1855.

WOMEN'S RIGHTS

- The Young Women's Hebrew Association (YWHA) is founded for women and girls of Jewish descent. The YWHAs eventually become Jewish community centers.

1888

- The International Council for Women is founded in Chicago, Illinois, and holds its first meeting in Washington, D.C.

1890

- The first U.S. state (Wyoming) grants women the right to vote in all elections.
- The Daughters of the American Revolution is established in the United States as the first women's patriotic group based on heredity.

1892

- French women are not permitted to work at night.

1893

- New Zealand grants women the right to vote in all elections.
- Johns Hopkins Medical School in Baltimore, Maryland, begins to admit women. By 1903, the drive to make medical school coeducational causes a majority of the women-only medical colleges to close.

1896

- The National Association of Colored Women is formed, uniting more than 100 black women's clubs. Leaders of the clubs include Josephine St. Pierre Ruffin, Mary Church Terrell, and Anna Julia Cooper.

1897

- By 1897, the Women's Suffrage Organization in Copenhagen merges with the Danish Women's Society.

1899

- The Danish Women's National Council is founded and associates itself with the Chicago-based International Council of Women (ICW).

1900

- Every state has passed legislation modeled after New York's Married Women's Property Act, granting American married women some control over their property and earnings.
- Following a change in the law, the first French female lawyer, Jeanne Chauvin, is permitted to practice.

Chronology

1902

- Australia grants women the right to vote in all elections but excludes aboriginal women.
- ICW holds its board meeting in Copenhagen.

1904

- The International Women's Suffrage Alliance (IWSA) is founded to focus on the struggle for suffrage across the globe.

1906

- Finland grants women the right to vote in all elections.
- Copenhagen is host to an IWSA meeting for suffragists from many countries.

1907

- Norway grants women the right to stand for election, which is subject to conditions and restrictions.
- Married French women are allowed to control their salaries without husbands' oversight.

1908

- The U.S. Supreme Court rules in favor of Oregon's 10-hour workday for women in *Muller v. State of Oregon.*

1909

- The IWSA Congress takes place in London.

1910

- The Camp Fire Girls is founded as the first national nonsectarian, interracial organization promoting character development for girls through indoor and outdoor activities. It holds its first meeting in Maine with a focus on Native American lore. The organization now includes boys and girls.

1912

- The Women's Suffragette Alliance is formed in Nanking (Nanjing), China, with women from 18 provinces who rally for equal rights before the national legislature.

1913

- In Norway, restrictions are lifted and women can now vote in all elections.
- Lucy Burns and Alice Paul organize a demonstration on March 3, 1913, in Washington, D.C., the day President Woodrow Wilson is inaugurated.

1915

- Denmark grants women the right to vote in all elections. Iceland also grants women the right to vote in all elections, subject to restrictions.
- The Women's Peace Party is formed and chaired by the sociologist Jane Addams, an Illinois native, who goes on to become the first American woman to win the Nobel Peace Prize in 1931 for her work for international peace.

1916

- The birth control advocate Margaret Sanger tests the validity of New York's anticontraception law by establishing a clinic in Brooklyn.
- The Congressional Union for Woman Suffrage, founded by Alice Paul and Lucy Burns in 1913, splits from the National American Women Suffrage Association (NAWSA), after differences with its president, Carrie Chapman Catt, and becomes the National Women's Party (NWP).

1917

- Canada grants women the right to vote, with restrictions; Netherlands grants women the right to stand for election.
- During the Russian Revolution, the February Revolution is triggered by an International Women's Day demonstration.
- Russia grants women the right to vote.

1918

- Austria and Canada grant women the right to vote, although Canada excludes the Inuit and Indians. In Estonia, Georgia, Germany, and Hungary, women are granted the right both to vote and to stand for election. Ireland grants women the right to vote with restrictions. Kyrgyzstan, Latvia, Lithuania, Poland, the Russian Federation, and the United Kingdom grant women the right to vote with restrictions.
- Margaret Sanger wins her suit to allow doctors to advise their married patients about birth control for health purposes in the state of New York.

1919

- Belarus grants women the right to vote; Belgium grants women the right to vote, with conditions; Luxembourg grants women the right to vote; the Netherlands grants women the right to vote; New Zealand grants women the right to stand for election; Sweden grants women the right to vote (with conditions); and Ukraine grants women the right to vote.
- Women in Denmark win the right to equal pay in the civil service.

Chronology

- The delegates to the International Women's Congress form a new organization, the Women's International League for Peace and Freedom (WILPF), in Geneva, Switzerland.
- At the end of World War I, the Paris Peace Conference in 1919 provides proposals for the newly formed Covenant of the League of Nations and the International Labour Organisation (ILO).

1920

- Albania grants women the right to vote; Canada grants women the right to stand for election with conditions; the Czech Republic grants women the right to vote; Iceland lifts restrictions; and Slovakia grants women the right to vote.
- American women are granted the right to vote with the ratification of the Nineteenth Amendment to the U.S. Constitution. It declares: "The right of citizens of the United States to vote shall not be denied or abridged by the United States or by any State on account of sex."

1921

- Armenia grants women the right to vote, and Azerbaijan women are granted the right both to vote and to stand for election. Belgium grants women the right to stand for election, with conditions; Georgia grants women the right to vote; and Sweden lifts conditions on women's right to vote.

1922

- In Denmark, the marriage reform acts of 1922 and 1923 establish equal child custody, property, and divorce rights.
- The Republic of Ireland grants women the right to vote.
- Grace Abbott is the first woman to serve as an unofficial U.S. delegate—the United States is not an official member—to the League of Nations. She serves on the organization's Advisory Committee on Traffic in Women and Children until 1934.

1923

- The National Woman's Party proposes a constitutional amendment: "Men and women shall have equal rights throughout the United States and in every place subject to its jurisdiction. Congress shall have power to enforce this article by appropriate legislation (The Equal Rights Amendment)."
- The Afghan constitution is amended to guarantee equal rights for men and women.

1924

- In Kazakhstan, Mongolia, Saint Lucia, and Tajikistan, women are granted the right both to vote and to stand for election.

- A New York State case (*Radice v. New York*) upholds a law that forbids waitresses to work the night shift but makes exception for entertainers and ladies' room attendants.

1925

- American Indian suffrage is granted by an act of Congress.
- The Women's World Fair is organized by Grace Coolidge, wife of President Calvin Coolidge, in Chicago, Illinois. The fair is a demonstration of what women have accomplished up to that time.

1927

- During an International Women's Day celebration on March 8, tens of thousands of Russian women gather around a statue of Lenin in Bukhara, near the Afghan border, and throw their burqas into a bonfire. The event is inspired by an earlier one that took place in the 1920s, when Russian women went to Bukhara to introduce revolutionary ideas to the women there.
- In Turkmenistan, women are granted the right both to vote and to stand for election.
- Involuntary sterilization of Carrie Buck and others occurs under the Virginia Supreme Court decision on its 1924 eugenics law.

1928

- Restrictions are lifted on women's right to vote in Ireland. In the United Kingdom, the second passage of the Representation of the People Act leads to suffrage for both men and women.
- Emmeline Pankhurst, the British pioneer of the women's suffrage movement, dies shortly after suffrage is granted in Great Britain.
- The École de Mannequins opens in Chicago, becoming the first institution to train young women to be models. At the time, they earn a dollar an hour. Eventually the 6,000 models in Chicago form a union and rally for better pay and hours.

1929

- Ecuador and Romania grant women the right to vote (both with conditions).

1930

- South African white women are granted the right both to vote and to stand for election. Turkey grants women the right to vote.

1931

- Chile and Portugal grant women the right to vote (with conditions). Spain grants women the right to vote. Sri Lankan women are granted the right both to vote and to stand for election.

Chronology

- The All-Asian Women's Conference unites representatives in Lahore from Afghanistan, Burma, Japan, Ceylon (Sri Lanka), and Persia (Iran) with observers from Britain, New Zealand, the United States, and Java (Indonesia) about the achievement of equality and adult franchise.

1932

- Creation in France of the Allocations Familiales, which oversees family services, social benefits, disbursements, and reimbursements by the government.
- In Maldives, Thailand, and Uruguay, women are granted the right both to vote and to stand for election.

1933

- The U.S. National Industrial Recovery Act forbids more than one family member from holding a government job; as a result, many women lose their jobs.

1934

- Brazil and Cuba grant women the right both to vote and to stand for election. Portugal grants women the right to vote (with conditions); Turkey grants women the right to stand for election.

1935

- Myanmar grants women the right to vote.
- Mary McLeod Bethune organizes the National Council of Negro Women, a coalition of black women's groups that lobbies against job discrimination, racism, and sexism.

1936

- In *United States v. One Package of Japanese Pessaries* (vaginal suppositories), a Manhattan judge, Augustus Hand, rules that the package ("containing 120 rubber pessaries, more or less, being articles to prevent conception") can be delivered, giving judicial approval of medicinal use of birth control. The ruling weakens the federal Comstock Law, which has prevented dissemination of contraceptive information and supplies since 1873.

1937

- The U.S. Supreme Court upholds Washington State's minimum wage laws for women.
- Filipino women are granted the right both to vote and to stand for election.
- July: The American female pilot Amelia Earhart disappears over the Pacific.

WOMEN'S RIGHTS

1938

- Women of Bolivia and Uzbekistan are granted the right both to vote and to stand for election.
- The Fair Labor Standards Act establishes minimum wage without regard to sex in the United States.

1939

- In El Salvador, women are granted the right both to vote and to stand for election.
- June: The Civilian Pilot Training Program (CPTP) is established by the U.S. government. The program provides pilot training across the country and allows for one woman to be trained for every 10 men.

1940

- *September:* Jackie Cochran writes to Eleanor Roosevelt suggesting the establishment of a women's flying division of the Army Air Forces.

1941

- *June:* Jackie Cochran becomes the first woman to ferry a bomber across the Atlantic.
- *June:* Women are banned from participating in the CPTP.
- In Panama, women are granted the right both to vote and to stand for election (with conditions).

1942

- Abortion is considered a state crime, punishable by death, in France.
- In the Dominican Republic, women are granted the right both to vote and to stand for election.
- In response to the need for workers in shipbuilding during the war, the International Brotherhood of Boilermakers, Iron Shipbuilders and Helpers, a union of the American Federation of Labor (AFL), opens to women.

1944

- France and Bulgaria grant women the right to vote; in Jamaica, women are granted the right both to vote and to stand for election.

1945

- Croatia grants women the right to vote; Guyana grants women the right to stand for election. Women in Indonesia, Trinidad, Italy, Japan, Panama, Senegal, Slovenia, and Tobago are granted the right both to vote and to stand for election.

1946

- Cameroon, the Democratic People's Republic of Korea, and Djibouti grant women the right to vote. Guatemala, Liberia, and Myanmar grant women the right to stand for election. Restrictions are lifted in both Panama and Romania. The former Yugoslav Republic of Macedonia, Trinidad and Tobago, Venezuela, Vietnam, and Ecuador grant women the right to vote. In Yugoslavia, women are granted the right both to vote and to stand for election.

1947

- Germaine Poinso-Chapuis is the first female in France to be nominated for a cabinet-level post.
- In *Fay v. New York*, the U.S. Supreme Court rules that women are equally qualified with men to serve on juries but are free to be exempted from service.
- Women are granted the right both to vote and to stand for election in Argentina, Japan, Malta, Mexico (to vote only), Pakistan, and Singapore.

1948

- Belgium lifts restrictions on voting. Women in Israel, Niger, Republic of Korea, Seychelles, and Suriname are granted the right both to vote and to stand for election.
- *The Universal Declaration of Human Rights* is adopted by the General Assembly at the United Nations.

1949

- Bosnia and Herzegovina grant women the right to vote. Chile lifts restrictions. In China and Costa Rica, women are granted the right both to vote and to stand for election. The Syrian Arab Republic grants women the right to vote with conditions.
- Simone de Beauvoir's 1949 *The Second Sex* explores Marxist, Freudian, and Hegelian themes to uncover the sources of the definition of *woman* as the "other" of man.

1950

- Susan B. Anthony is elected to the Hall of Fame for Great Americans at Bronx Community College, New York, of the City University of New York.

- Barbados and Canada grant women the right to vote. Restrictions are lifted in Haiti and India.

1951

- Women of Antigua and Barbuda, Dominica, Grenada, Nepal, Saint Kitts and Nevis, Saint Vincent, and the Grenadines are granted the right both to vote and to stand for election.
- Paula Ackerman performs her husband's function as a rabbi of a reform congregation in Meridian, Mississippi, and acts as an interim spiritual leader after he dies.

1952

- Restrictions are lifted in Bolivia, and women in Côte d'Ivoire, Greece, and Lebanon are granted the right both to vote and to stand for election.
- The General Assembly adopts a resolution urging all member nations to extend suffrage rights to women.

1953

- Bhutan and Guyana give women the right to vote. In Mexico, they can stand for election. In the Syrian Arab Republic, restrictions are lifted.
- Daoud becomes Afghanistan's prime minister and encourages women to participate in government and employment.
- Women's names are used to designate hurricanes in the Atlantic, Caribbean, and Gulf of Mexico. *Alice* is the first female moniker used to name a hurricane.

1954

- In Belize, Colombia, and Ghana, women are granted the right both to vote and to stand for election.

1955

- In Cambodia, Eritrea, Ethiopia, Honduras, Nicaragua, and Peru, women are granted the right both to vote and to stand for election.
- Rosa Parks's arrest in December prompts a 13-month civil rights protest, later dubbed the Montgomery bus boycott.
- The Daughters of Bilitis (DOB), the first lesbian organization in the United States, is founded. Although DOB originates as a social group, it later develops into a political organization to win basic acceptance of lesbians in the United States.

1956

- In Benin, Comoros, Egypt, Gabon, Mali, Mauritius, and Somalia, women are granted the right both to vote and to stand for election.

Chronology

1957

- In Malaysia, women are granted the right both to vote and to stand for election. Zimbabwe grants women the right to vote and lifts restrictions.

- **March 25:** The Treaty of Rome establishes the European Economic Community (EEC) with France, West Germany, Italy, Belgium, the Netherlands, and Luxembourg as the initial members. The name is later changed in 1993 and 2002 to the *EC Treaty*.

- Conference for Asian Women takes place in Ceylon, and women from Afghanistan attend.

1958

- In Burkina Faso, Chad, Guinea, Lao People's Democratic Republic, and Nigeria (South), women are granted the right both to vote and to stand for election.

- Afghanistan sends a female delegate to the United Nations.

1959

- Madagascar and San Marino grant women the right to vote. In Tunisia and the United Republic of Tanzania, women are granted the right both to vote and to stand for election.

1960

- The Democratic Republic of the Congo (Zaire) becomes independent following a violent nationalist uprising.

- Canada lifts restrictions for women to stand for election; in Cyprus, Gambia, and Tonga, women are granted the right both to vote and to stand for election. Benin, Burkina Faso, Cameroon, Central African Republic, Chad, Comoro Islands, the Republic of the Congo, the Democratic Republic of the Congo (Zaire), Equitorial Guinea, Gabon, Gambia, Guinea, Ivory Coast, Madagascar, Mali, Niger, Nigeria, and Senegal grant women the right to vote.

- The Food and Drug Administration approves the sale of birth control pills.

1961

- Bahamas grants women the right to vote (with restrictions). Burundi and El Salvador grant women the right to stand for election. In Malawi, Mauritania, Paraguay, Rwanda, and Sierra Leone, women are granted the right both to vote and to stand for election. Somalia and Tanzania grant women the right to vote.

- The U.S. Supreme Court upholds a rule adopted by the state of Florida that makes it less likely for women than men to be called for jury service on the grounds that a "woman is still regarded as the center of home and family life."

- In 1961, the first North Atlantic Treaty Organization (NATO) Conference of Senior Women Officers of the Alliance takes place in Copenhagen, Denmark.
- President John Kennedy establishes the President's Commission on the Status of Women and appoints Eleanor Roosevelt chairperson until her death in 1962. The report issued by the commission in 1963 documents substantial discrimination against women in the workplace and makes specific recommendations for improvement, including fair hiring practices, paid maternity leave, and affordable child care.

1962

- Algeria grants women the right to vote. Australia lifts restrictions, and aboriginal women are allowed to vote. In Monaco, Uganda, and Zambia, women are granted the right both to vote and to stand for election.

1963

- In Afghanistan, Congo, Equatorial Guinea, Fiji, Iran (the Islamic Republic of Iran), Kenya, and Morocco, women are granted the right both to vote and to stand for election. Papua New Guinea grants women the right to stand for election.
- The Equal Pay Act is passed by Congress, promising equitable wages for the same work, regardless of the race, color, religion, national origin, or sex of the worker.
- Betty Friedan publishes her highly influential book *The Feminine Mystique*, which describes the dissatisfaction felt by middle-class American homemakers with the narrow role imposed on them by society. The best seller is a boon to the contemporary women's rights movement.

1964

- Bahamas lifts restrictions on women's right to vote. The Libyan Arab Jamahiriya, Papua New Guinea, and Sudan grant women the right to vote.
- Title VII of the Civil Rights Act passes; it includes a prohibition against employment discrimination on the basis of race, color, religion, national origin, or sex.
- The Equal Employment Opportunity Commission (EEOC) is established to investigate complaints and impose penalties.

1965

- Marriage reform laws (countering the laws of 1804) are enacted in France permitting women to manage their income, open bank accounts, and practice a profession without the permission of a husband.

Chronology

- In Botswana and Lesotho, women are granted the right both to vote and to stand for election.
- The decision in *Weeks v. Southern Bell* challenges labor laws and company regulations, making former men-only jobs available to women, with improved hours and work conditions.
- In *Griswold v. Connecticut*, the Supreme Court overturns one of the last state laws prohibiting the prescription or use of contraceptives by married couples.

1966

- The National Organization for Women (NOW) is founded by a group of feminists including Betty Friedan. The largest women's rights group in the United States, NOW seeks to end sexual discrimination, especially in the workplace, by means of legislative lobbying, litigation, and public demonstrations.
- The International Covenant on Civil and Political Rights (ICCPR) and the International Covenant on Economic, Social and Cultural Rights (ICESCR) are two major international human rights treaties drafted by the United Nations in 1966 but not enforced until 1976.
- Indira Gandhi becomes prime minister of India; she rules until 1977 and again from 1980 to 1984.

1967

- The Democratic Republic of the Congo grants women the right to vote. Restrictions are lifted in Ecuador.
- The Neuwirth Law permits contraception in France.

1968

- Nauru and Swaziland women are granted the right both to vote and to stand for election.
- Executive Order 11246 prohibits sex discrimination by government contractors and requires affirmative action plans for hiring of women.
- *July 22:* Afghan women protest Kabul University's possible prohibition of study in universities abroad by women.

1969

- In *Bowe v. Colgate-Palmolive Company*, the court rules that women meeting the required physical requirements can work in many jobs formerly reserved for men only.
- California adopts the nation's first "no fault" divorce law, allowing divorce by mutual consent. (Note: By 1985, every state has adopted a similar law. Laws are also passed regarding the equal division of common property.)

WOMEN'S RIGHTS

1970

- In Andorra, women are given the right to vote. In the Democratic Republic of the Congo, women are allowed to stand for election. In Yemen (Arab Republic), women are granted the right both to vote and to stand for election.
- In *Schultz v. Wheaton Glass Co.*, a U.S. court of appeals rules that jobs held by men and women need to be "substantially equal" but not "identical" to fall under the protection of the Equal Pay Act. An employer cannot, for example, change the job titles of women workers in order to pay them less than men.
- The North American Indian Women's Association, the first of its kind, is founded by Marie Cox.

1971

- Women in Switzerland are granted the right both to vote and to stand for election.
- The U.S. Supreme Court outlaws the practice of private employers' refusing to hire women who have preschool-age children (*Phillips v. Martin Marietta Corporation*).
- Idaho's state law establishing automatic preference for males as administrators of wills is ruled unconstitutional in *Reed v. Reed*. This is the first time a court strikes down a law treating men and women differently. The U.S. Supreme Court finally declares women as *persons*. "Reasonableness" is the criterion rather than making sex a "suspect classification," under the Fourteenth Amendment.
- *Ms.* magazine is first published as a sample insert in *New York* magazine. Over 300,000 copies are sold in eight days. The first regular issue is published in July 1972. The magazine becomes the major forum for feminist voices, and its cofounder and editor, Gloria Steinem, is launched as an icon of the modern feminist movement.
- Veil Law (named after its advocate, Simone Veil) authorizes abortions under certain conditions in France.

1972

- Title IX (Public Law 92-318) of the Education Amendments prohibits sex discrimination in all aspects of education programs that receive federal support.
- The Supreme Court decision in *Eisenstadt v. Baird* extends the right to privacy to unmarried persons' right to use contraceptives.
- In Bangladesh, women are granted the right both to vote and to stand for election.

Chronology

1973

- Andorra and San Marino grant women the right to stand for election; in Bahrain, women are granted the right both to vote and to stand for election. Syria grants women the right to vote.
- The U.S. Supreme Court bans sex-segregated "help wanted" advertising as a violation of Title VII of the Civil Rights Act of 1964 as amended, on the basis of its decision in *Pittsburgh Press v. Pittsburgh Commission on Human Relations*.
- *Roe v. Wade* and *Doe v. Bolton* are two cases in which the U.S. Supreme Court declares that the Constitution protects women's right to terminate an early pregnancy, making abortion legal in the United States.
- "Call Off Your Old Tired Ethics (COYOTE)" is established to protect rights of women prostitutes and former prostitutes in San Francisco, California. Initially, the organization seeks legalization of prostitution, protection against arrests, and proper legal counsel for arrests.

1974

- Jordan, Solomon Islands, and Guinea-Bissau grant women the right both to vote and to stand for election.
- Housing discrimination on the basis of sex and credit discrimination against women are outlawed by Congress.
- The decision in *Cleveland Board of Education v. LaFleur* asserts the illegality of forcing pregnant women to take maternity leave on the assumption they are incapable of working because of their physical condition.
- The Women's Educational Equity Act funds the development of nonsexist teaching materials and model programs that encourage full educational opportunities for girls and women.
- The Equal Employment Opportunity Commission, the Justice and Labor Departments, and AT&T sign a consent decree banning AT&T's discriminatory practices against women and minorities.
- The Equal Credit Opportunity Act prohibits discrimination in consumer credit practices based on sex, marital status, age, or receipt of public assistance. It is later amended to include race, religion, national origin, and age.
- The first women's professional football league is founded, consisting of seven teams coached by men. Players are paid $25 per game.

1975

- International Women's Year is initiated by the United Nations.
- March 8 is chosen by the United Nations as International Women's Day in recognition of women's fight for universal rights.

411

- The first of four UN world conferences on women in Mexico City takes place.
- The court's decision in *Taylor v. Louisiana* denies the state the right to exclude women from juries.
- Angola, Cape Verde, Mozambique, São Tomé and Príncipe, and Vanuatu grant women the right to vote.
- On August 1, leaders of 35 nations gather in Helsinki to sign the Final Act of the Conference on Security and Co-operation in Europe (CSCE); the organization will eventually focus on human trafficking and terrorism.
- Women can no longer be excluded from juries because of their sex in the United States.
- The French Law of 1975 of Divorce makes it legal for women not to live in the same household as their husbands and allows for mutual consent as grounds for divorce. Adultery is less reprimanded.

1976

- Following International Women's Year in 1975, the UN announces the Decade for Women.
- Portugal lifts restrictions on women's right to vote.
- In *General Electric Company v. Gilbert,* the Supreme Court upholds women's right to unemployment benefits during the last three months of pregnancy.
- The U.S. Supreme Court declares unconstitutional a state law permitting 18- to 20-year-old females to drink beer while denying the rights to men of the same age in *Craig v. Boren*. The Court establishes a new set of standards for reviewing laws that treat men and women differently.
- The Equal Pay Act is passed in Denmark.
- Barbara Jordan addresses the Democratic National Convention in the United States as the first African-American woman to give the keynote speech.

1977

- In Guinea-Bissau, women are granted the right both to vote and to stand for election.
- In November 1955, Eritrea was part of Ethiopia when women there were enfranchised. The constitution of sovereign Eritrea adopted on May 23, 1997, stipulates that "all Eritrean citizens, of eighteen years of age or more, shall have the right to vote."
- RAWA is founded in Afghanistan by Meena Keshwar.
- *November 3:* The U.S. House of Representatives votes to give the Women's Airforce Service Pilots (WASPs) veteran status.

- *November 23:* President Jimmy Carter signs a bill into law "officially declaring the WASPs as having served on active duty in the Armed Forces of the United States for purposes of laws administered by the Veterans Administration."

1978

- In the United States, the Pregnancy Discrimination Act bans employment discrimination against pregnant women. Under the act, a woman cannot be fired or denied a job or a promotion because she is or may become pregnant; nor can she be forced to take a pregnancy leave if she is willing and able to work.
- The Equal Treatment Act of 1978 prohibits job discrimination on the basis of sex and provides recourse, such as access to the Equal Status Council, in Denmark.
- The National Aeronautics and Space Administration (NASA) names six females of 35 candidates for the space shuttle program, including Margaret Seddon, M.D., from Tennessee, and Sally K. Ride, from California. NASA acknowledges the important role of the women's movement in causing more women to be qualified for the space program.
- In Nigeria (North), the Republic of Moldova, and Zimbabwe, women are granted the right both to vote and to stand for election.
- Civil war begins in Afghanistan. One reason cited is the Communist Party's fight for women's literacy rights.

1979

- In the Marshall Islands, Micronesia (Federated States), and Palau, women are granted the right both to vote and to stand for election.
- The Soviet Union invades Afghanistan. Women are emancipated, especially in the cities, and allowed to pursue education and professional opportunities. Other women choose to fight against the Russians with the mujahideen.
- **December:** The UN Convention on the Elimination of All Forms of Discrimination against Women (CEDAW) is adopted by the General Assembly. It becomes known as the "Women's Rights" treaty.
- Margaret Thatcher is elected as prime minister of England.
- *May:* The U.S. Air Force issues the first honorable discharges for women serving in the WASPs during World War II.
- The U.S. government issues a silver dollar bearing the image of Susan B. Anthony.

1980

- In Iraq and Vanuatu, women are granted the right both to vote and to stand for election.

- The second of four world conferences on women convened by the United Nations is host to 145 representatives of member states in Copenhagen in 1980. CEDAW is introduced.
- *April 21:* High school girls mount a massive protest in Kabul against Soviet occupation of Afghanistan in what comes to be known as the Children's Revolt.

1981

- The U.S. Supreme Court rules that excluding women from the draft is constitutional.
- *Kirchberg v. Feenstra* overturns state laws designating a husband "head and master" with unilateral control of property owned jointly with the wife.
- The Law of Succession Act of 1981 proclaims equal consideration of inheritance rights by male and female children in Kenya.
- French government creates the Ministry of Women's Rights.
- The U.S. Congress passes a resolution establishing National Women's History Week. The week is chosen to coincide with International Women's Day on March 8.

1983

- Roudy Law, named after its advocate, politician Yvette Roudy, prohibits all forms of professional discrimination in France due to sex.
- In the United States, the antiporn activist Catherine MacKinnon drafts the Minneapolis antiporn ordinance, which states that all women forced to work in porn can bring a civil lawsuit against producers and distributors.

1984

- The Democratic Party presidential candidate Walter Mondale selects Geraldine Ferraro as his vice presidential running mate.
- In *Roberts v. U.S. Jaycees,* membership policies of organizations are forbidden to discriminate by sex, giving women access to many previously all-male organizations (Jaycees, Kiwanis, Rotary, Lions).
- The state of Mississippi belatedly ratifies the Nineteenth Amendment, granting women the vote.
- In *Hishon v. King and Spaulding,* the U.S. Supreme Court rules that law firms may not discriminate on the basis of sex in promoting lawyers to partnership positions.
- EMILY's List (Early Money Is Like Yeast) is established as a financial network for pro-choice Democratic Party women running for national political office.

The organization has a significant impact on the increasing numbers of women elected to Congress.

- Women in Liechtenstein and South Africa (black and Indian) are granted the right both to vote and to stand for election.

1985

- The third of four world conferences on women takes place in Nairobi.

1986

- Women in the Central African Republic and Djibouti are permitted to stand for election.

- In *Meritor Savings Bank v. Vinson,* the U.S. Supreme Court holds that a hostile or abusive work environment can prove discrimination based on sex.

- Liberia grants women the right to vote.

1987

- A U.S. Supreme Court case decision (*Johnson v. Santa Clara County*) rules sex and race can be deciding factors for employment when the number of women or minorities holding a position is in question.

- The U.S. Congress expands National Women's History Week to a month. Every year since then, Congress has passed a resolution for Women's History Month, and the U.S. president has issued a proclamation.

1988

- The Equity Act for equal opportunities for men and women is passed in Denmark.

1989

- In *Webster v. Reproductive Health Services,* the Supreme Court affirms the right of states to deny public funding for abortions and to prohibit public hospitals to perform abortions.

- In Namibia, women are granted the right both to vote and to stand for election.

1990

- In Samoa, women are granted the right both to vote and to stand for election.

- Antonia C. Novello, M.D., is appointed surgeon general of the United States Public Health Service. She is sworn in by the Supreme Court justice Sandra Day O'Connor. She is also distinguished as the first Hispanic and first woman to be appointed surgeon general.

- The Convention on the Rights of the Child is established as an international treaty.

1991

- Senator Robert Dole introduces the Glass Ceiling Act.

1992

- In *Planned Parenthood v. Casey,* the Supreme Court reaffirms the validity of a woman's right to abortion under *Roe v. Wade.* The case successfully challenges Pennsylvania's 1989 Abortion Control Act, which sought to reinstate restrictions previously ruled unconstitutional.
- The Year of the Woman in the United States promotes female political candidates.
- The communist regime in Afghanistan gives way to the Islamic State of Afghanistan, a conservative regime that does not approve of women's education and employment. Women are required to wear headdresses and are forbidden to laugh or wear makeup in public.
- *February 7:* The European Union Treaty (or Maastrict Treaty) is signed in the Netherlands, where the adoption of a single currency is proposed for the member states.
- Laws against domestic violence and sexual harassment in the workplace are implemented in France.

1993

- Kazakhstan and the Republic of Moldova grant women the right both to vote and to stand for election.
- In *Harris v. Forklift Systems, Inc.,* the U.S. Supreme Court rules that the victim does not need to show that she suffered physical or serious psychological injury as a result of sexual harassment.
- In the United States, the Family and Medical Leave Act goes into effect.
- The Islamic State of Afghanistan's Supreme Court rules that women need to be completely covered by the veil when not in their home.
- The Treaty on European Union is signed at Maastricht.

1994

- *April:* Following the death of the Hutu president of Rwanda, Juvénal Habyarimana, killed when his airplane is shot down, the Rwanda genocide occurs, led by Hutus against an estimated 800,000 civilians, mostly Tutsi and pro-peace Hutus.
- *July:* Tutsi-led insurgency, under the Rwandan Patriotic Front, defeats the government and establishes a new national administration. An estimated 1.2 million Hutus flee over the border to North Kivu in DRC in three days.

- Black South African women and men win suffrage rights.

- The African Centre for Women (ACW) organizes a meeting in Kampala, Uganda, to evaluate the establishment of an African bank for women.

- The U.S. Congress adopts the Gender Equity in Education Act to train teachers in gender equity, promote math and science learning by girls, counsel pregnant teens, and prevent sexual harassment.

- The Violence against Women Act funds services for victims of rape and domestic violence, allows women to seek civil rights remedies for gender-related crimes, provides training to increase police and court officials' sensitivity, and establishes a national 24-hour hotline for battered women.

- *May 26:* Responding to violence against abortion clinics, President Clinton signs the Freedom of Access to Clinic Entrances (FACE) Act, which has become an important legal defense against antiabortion terror.

- The Taliban take over Kandahar in November, closing schools for girls and forbidding women to work outside their homes.

1995

- The fourth UN world conference on women takes place in Beijing.

- The Beijing Declaration and Platform for Action is introduced at the UN conference.

- *September:* The Taliban captures the strategic town of Herat in Afghanistan.

1996

- DRC's First Congo War (1996–97) is triggered by a Tutsi-led insurgency from neighboring Rwanda and Uganda that seeks to end 32-year reign, of Mobuto Sese Seko, who had supported Rwandan Hutu extremists.

- In *United States v. Virginia,* the decision acknowledges that the admissions policy of the state-supported Virginia Military Institute, which favors men, violates the Fourteenth Amendment.

- The Taliban capture Kabul in September.

1997

- With respect to Title IX, the Supreme Court rules that similar numbers of men and women must be involved in college sports programs to qualify for federal support.

- Eritrea extends women the right to vote.

- In the Bamiyan region of Afghanistan, women fight Islamic fundamentalists and establish a university for women.

- *May*: In DRC, Laurent Désiré Kabila topples President Mobutu Sese Seko, who ruled the country, then known as Zaire, since 1965, and changes its name to DRC.

1998

- Mitsubishi Motor Manufacturing of America agrees to pay $34 million to settle an EEOC lawsuit contending that hundreds of women have been sexually harassed.
- In *Burlington Industries, Inc. v. Ellerth* and *Faragher v. City of Boca Raton*, the Supreme Court addresses the balance between employee and employer rights.
- War in Congo breaks out in 1998 when Congolese rebels backed by neighboring Rwanda and Uganda try to overthrow Laurent Kabila, accusing him of harboring armed militias that threatened their own security. Angola, Namibia, and Zimbabwe step in on the side of the government.

1999

- The Amsterdam Treaty is entered into force on May 1, 1999, making substantial changes to the Treaty on European Union and defining the contemporary framework of the European Union, which implements a new currency, the euro dollar.
- *July*: Lusaka Cease-fire Agreement is reached, but territorial and ethnic conflict between rebel groups persists in DRC.

2000

- The Equal Status Council and new Equal Status Act are catalysts for further change for women in Denmark.
- The United Nations identifies the ambitious Millennium Development Goals to combat poverty, hunger, disease, illiteracy, environmental degradation, and discrimination against women, by the year 2015.
- The Dakar Framework for Action is adopted at the World Education Forum in 2000, emphasizing the role UNESCO can play in eradicating poverty through education.
- CBS Broadcasting agrees to pay $8 million to settle a sex discrimination lawsuit by the EEOC on behalf of 200 women.
- The U.S. Supreme Court renders invalid sections of the Violence against Women Act that allow rape and domestic violence victims to sue their attackers in federal court (*United States v. Morrison*).
- *September 28:* The Food and Drug Administration approves the use of the early abortion pill RU-486 (mifepristone), already available to women in 13 countries. Abortion opponents try to impose restrictions on use of the drug.

- *October:* UN Resolution 1325 on Women, Peace and Security is adopted. The UN International Day for the Elimination of Violence against Women is now celebrated on November 25 each year.
- The Trafficking Victims Protection Act is passed by Congress, launching a new visa system for victims of trafficking.

2001

- *November 27:* Afghan women NGOs participate in UN talks on a transitional government for Afghanistan in Bonn, Germany.
- *December 4–5:* The Afghan Women's Summit for Democracy in Brussels convenes at the request of Afghan NGO women's groups, in collaboration with the Office of the Special Adviser on Gender Issues and Advancement of Women and the United Nations Development Fund for Women (UNIFEM).
- In DRC, Joseph Kabila (1971–), son of Laurent Kabila, takes over command of the government following his father's assassination.
- In China, the Population and Family Planning Law of the PRC is adopted to take effect in September 2003.
- The Society for Women's Health Research calls attention to sex-based differences in health care by initiating the landmark study *Exploring the Biological Contribution to Human Health: Does Sex Matter?*
- The Children Act of 2001 asserts the rights and welfare of children and guarantees their protection against exploitation for economic purposes in Kenya.
- In Kenya, female genital mutilation is outlawed for girls under the age of 16.
- Hillary Rodham Clinton is the first former first lady to win elected office when she is sworn in as U.S. senator from New York.

2002

- *February:* Inter-Congolese Dialogue (ICD) in Nairobi, Kenya, brings together warring factions, the DRC government, and women's groups to negotiate a peaceful settlement for DRC. The outcome from the ICD includes the Nairobi Declaration, a cease-fire, the formation of the Women's Caucus, and adoption of a 30 percent quota for women at all levels of government.
- *April:* The Women's League of the African National Congress (ANC) meets with the women from the ICD.
- *October:* The Association des Femmes du Kivu hosts a workshop in Butembo (North Kivu) for 90 women from Burundi, DRC, Kenya, and Rwanda.
- *November/December:* Despite continued fighting in some regions of the DRC, the war officially ends with the signature of the December 2002 Pretoria Agreement at the Sun City meetings in South Africa. Only 10 women are permitted

to participate at the meetings. Kabila is part of the transitional government from 2003 to 2005.

- The Domestic Violence Family Protection Bill offers legislation to defend women against violent treatment in Kenya.
- President George W. Bush signs the ban against partial birth abortions.
- The U.S. government issues a memorandum reminding employers that active duty time of reservists and National Guard members is eligible for benefits under the Family Medical Leave Act.

2003

- *January:* National Council of Women's Organizations publishes statement on the potential war with Iraq ensuing from a disarmament disagreement with Saddam Hussein in late 2002.
- *March 20:* The war of Iraq begins with an invasion by a coalition of multinational military forces against the Iraqi military; the Iraqi government and Saddam Hussein's regime are deposed by April 15.
- *September 25:* A Nigerian court of appeals throws out the case against Amina Lawal, a 32-year-old single mother sentenced to death by stoning for committing adultery.
- A crisis is recognized in Darfur, Sudan, where severe forms of violence are being used against women.

2004

- *July:* At the International Conference on Peace, Security, Democracy and Development in Kenya, female parliamentarians from the Great Lakes region announce their intentions to take a prominent role to end fighting in DRC.
- *September:* U.S. Senate Department awards $10 million in grant money through the Iraqi Women's Democracy Initiative to organizations to train Iraqi women to stand for election, vote, develop media and business skills, and establish resource centers for networking and counseling for their upcoming election.
- *November 25:* A worldwide campaign called "16 Days of Activism Against Gender Violence" begins on the International Day for the Elimination of Violence Against Women, and ends on December 10, International Human Rights Day.
- The French government bans the wearing of head scarfs in public buildings, state schools, and institutions.

2005

- *March:* The Beijing + 10 Conference takes place in New York.

Chronology

- **September:** Afghanistan's first election since the end of Taliban rule takes place.
- In Kuwait, women are granted the right both to vote and to stand for election, to take effect in 2007.
- In Saudi Arabia, men take part in the first local elections ever held in the country. Women are not allowed, however, to exercise their right to vote or to stand for election on that occasion.
- **September:** The United Nations World Summit convenes with member states' reaffirming their intention to fulfill objectives of the 1995 Beijing Platform of Action and the 2000 Millennium Development Goals.
- The U.S. Senate approves the National Women's History Museum Act of 2005 to create a national women's history museum in Washington, D.C. The museum is expected to attract 1.5 million visitors a year.
- French laws are reformed to make it easier for French couples to divorce.

2006

- **January:** 60,000 to 150,000 march in Milan, Italy, to maintain abortion laws, which had been legal since 1978, countering measures by the Vatican to curb such rights.
- **June:** Kuwaiti women vote and stand in national and local elections for the first time.
- **July:** Presidential and parliamentary elections take place concomitantly in DRC, following months of voter registration and electoral-process negotiations between different parties. Of 33 presidential candidates, four are women; of 9,584 legislative candidates, 13.5 percent are women. In the new National Assembly, women hold 42 of the 500 seats.
- **August:** National and international petitions for women, activists, and groups cause the Iranian government to halt the execution of a mother of four, who had been sentenced to death by stoning for having extramarital sex.
- **August:** U.S. Food and Drug Administration announces the approval of over-the-counter status of Plan B emergency contraception for women age 18 years and older.
- U.S. Tennis Association renames the National Tennis Center in New York City after American tennis athlete and women's sports pioneer Billie Jean King at the opening ceremonies of the U.S. Open competition.
- Amal Abdullah al-Kubaissi, an Arab female architect, is elected in the United Arab Emirates's first national election, to serve on the Federal National Council. She was one of 438 candidates, including 62 other women, who ran in the election.

- *Le Livre Noir de la Condition Feminine* (The black book on the condition of women), by French sociologist and UN and CEDAW expert François Gaspard, Sandrine Treiner, and Christine Ockrent, is published.

2007

- Representative Nancy Pelosi from Illinois becomes the first female Speaker of the U.S. House of Representatives.
- Senator Hillary Clinton from New York seeks the presidency by announcing her campaign for the 2008 presidential election.
- New Jersey becomes the third state, after Vermont and Connecticut, to legally permit civil unions for same-sex couples.
- U.S. study finds one-third of American women by age 24 and one in four American females age 14 to 59 are carriers of the human papilloma virus (HPV), some strains of which cause cervical cancer.
- Governor Ricky Perry issues an executive order to make Texas the first state to require girls entering sixth grade to receive the HPV vaccine, starting in September 2008. (The order is later rescinded.)
- New medical guidelines issued about preventing heart disease and stroke in women, with specific information about the appropriate use of aspirin in young women.

2008

- *January 6–17:* Women are under-represented at the Goma Peace Conference, which assembled armed groups from the Kivus, the DRC government, and church representatives.
- *November:* Barack Obama wins the 2008 presidential election and names former first lady and New York senator Hillary Clinton as the Secretary of State.
- More U.S. states, including Massachusetts and Connecticut, acknowledge same-sex couples.

2009

- *January 29:* Lilly Ledbetter Fair Pay Act of 2009, sponsored by Sen. Barbara Mikulski (D-MD) is signed into law by President Barack Obama.
- *August 8:* Sonia Sotomayor (1954–   ) assumes the position of associate justice of the U.S. Supreme Court.
- *September:* Afghan women vote for a second time in national elections, but lose seats.
- For the first time in history, half of all U.S. workers are women, and mothers are the primary breadwinners (or co-breadwinners) in two-thirds of Ameri-

can families. This is documented in "The Shriver Report: A Woman's Nation Changes Everything."

- The Military Leadership Diversity Commission is established by Congress to look at ways to diversify the force and boost recruiting, including of women.

2010

- First Afghan female army officers graduate.

- *February:* The International Violence Against Women Act of 2010 is introduced as a bill to the U.S. Congress. It will direct the secretary of state to establish an Office for Global Women's Issues. It is currently "in committee."

- *May 19:* U.S. District Court for the Southern District of New York orders Novartis Pharmaceuticals to pay $3.4 million to 12 former female sales representatives for discrimination in pay and promotions *(Velez et al. v. Novartis Pharmaceuticals Corporation).* This case is considered the second-largest gender discrimination class-action suit in the United States, *Dukes v. Wal-Mart Stores* being the first.

- *July:* The UN General Assembly creates UN Women to accelerate its goals on gender equality and empowerment of women.

- *August 7:* Elena Kagan (1960–) becomes an associate justice of the U.S. Supreme Court. It is the first time in history that three women, along with Sonia Sotomayor and Ruth Bader Ginsburg (1933–), sit on the Court.

- *September:* The French government bans wearing the Muslim burqa in all public places.

- *November 4:* U.S. mid-term elections result in the departure of Nancy Pelosi as Speaker of the House (though she is subsequently elected House Minority Leader) and a reduced number of women in Congress.

- *November 17:* Paycheck Fairness Act defeated in U.S. Senate. The bill would have made it easier for workers to sue their employers for pay discrimination. Considered an extension of the Equal Pay Act of 1963, conservative business groups viewed it as being a potential job killer.

- *November 19:* First Judiciary Committee hearings, chaired by Sen. Dick Durbin (D-IL), on United States ratification of the UN human rights treaty, CEDAW, in eight years. The treaty was signed by President Jimmy Carter in 1979, but remains unratified. Among the issues causing reservations are women's access to medical care, expanded maternity leave, and sex-based pay discrimination.

2011

- *January 14:* A congressionally appointed commission is examining the Pentagon rule that excludes U.S. women from what would be opportunities for promotion within the ranks—combat assignments.

- *January:* The French constitutional court upholds a ban on same-sex marriage as constitutional.

- *January–February:* A popular uprising in Egypt, mobilized through social networking, ends the 30-year reign of President Hosni Mubarak. Female activists call for reforms in women's rights as part of Egypt's rebuilding.

- *March:* Release of the White House Council on Women and Girls report, *Women in America: Indicators of Social and Economic Well-Being.* The report, which is the first comprehensive analysis on women released by the federal government since 1963, focuses on five topic areas: people, families, and income; education; employment; health; and crime and violence.

- Al Qaeda launches a woman's magazine, *Al-Shammikha* ("The Majestic Woman"). The cover of the inaugural issues shows a woman clad in traditional, conservative, Muslim attire holding a machine gun.

- Groups of undergraduate and graduate students at Yale University file a Title 9 complaint alleging the university's tolerance of incidents of sexual harassment and assault between 2008 and 2010.

- *April:* The first completely female Air Force combat unit ("Dudette 7") conducts a mission in Afghanistan to support ground troops.

- *June 13:* Three-term Minnesota Congresswoman Michele Bachmann announces on television during a Republican presidential debate in New Hampshire her formal entry into the Republican primary race as a 2012 presidential candidate.

- *June 20:* The Supreme Court rules in favor of the retailer Wal-Mart in a class-action suit brought by three former female Wal-Mart employees, who are seeking damages for $1.5 million for current and former employees, alleging wage and promotion discrimination. The decision affirms that the company does not have a policy of gender discrimination in its employment practices, despite protests that discrimination occurs on more subtle levels. This decision sets precedence in how class action suits can be brought before the higher court and how sex discrimination cases will be handled by corporations with no specific discriminatory policies.

- *June 28:* French finance minister Christine Lagarde is named managing director of the IMF. She is the first woman to hold this position.

- *September 25:* In Saudi Arabia, King Abdullah announces that women have the right to vote and run for municipal elections, beginning with the next elections, scheduled for 2015.

Glossary

abolitionist   A person who believes that there should be no slavery.

abortion   The intentional intrauterine killing of a fetus.

active duty   Full-time duty in a uniformed service, including duty on the active list, full-time training duty, annual training duty, and attendance while in the active service at a school designated as a service school by law or by the secretary concerned.

affirmative action   Action taken by a government or private institution to compensate for past discrimination in education, work, or promotion on the basis of gender, race, ethnic origin, religion, or disability.

appeal   A legal proceeding by which a decision of a lower court is brought before a higher court for review.

Armed Forces of the United States   Includes the United States Army, Navy, Air Force, Marine Corps, and Coast Guard, and all components thereof.

burqas   Part of the head-to-toe caftan, with a slit left open for the eyes, originally mandated by the Taliban to safeguard women from leering eyes. Made of wool or cotton, often of dark cloth, worn wrapped around the head and usually with a cloak.

civil and political rights   The rights of citizens to liberty and equality; sometimes referred to as first-generation rights. Civil rights include freedom to worship, to think and express oneself, to vote, to take part in political life, and to have access to information.

codification, codify   The process of putting customary international law in written form.

collective rights   The rights of groups to protect their interests and identities.

Commission on Human Rights   Body formed by the Economic and Social Council of the United Nations to deal with human rights. It is considered one of the first and most important international human rights bodies.

concede   Give over; surrender or relinquish to the physical control of another; acknowledge defeat.

conscription military   A military force based on draft or required registration and participation of soldiers from the general population.

convention   Binding agreement between states that is used synonymously with *treaty* and *covenant.* Conventions are stronger than declarations because they are legally binding for governments that have signed them. When the UN General Assembly adopts a convention, it creates international norms and standards. Member states can then ratify the convention, promising to uphold it. Governments that violate the standards set forth in a convention can then be censured by the United Nations.

covenant   Binding agreement between states; used synonymously with CONVENTION and TREATY. The major international human rights covenants are the International Covenant on Civil and Political Rights (ICCPR) and the International Covenant on Economic, Social and Cultural Rights (ICESCR), both passed in 1966.

coverture   Legal concept dating back to feudal Norman customs in England. When a woman married, she became one with her husband and ceased to exist in the eyes of the law. She could not contract for wages, could not own property in her own name, could not sign contracts, and did not have the right to decisions about her own children. In Elizabeth Cady Stanton's words, "with marriage a woman is civilly dead." This concept was the driving force in the subordination of women. To understand it is to understand the roots of the women's rights revolution.

customary international law   Law that becomes binding on states although it is not written but rather adhered to out of custom. When enough states have begun to behave as though something is law, it becomes law "by use." This is one of the main sources of international law.

declaration   Document that states agreed upon standards but that is not legally binding. UN conferences, such as the 1993 UN Conference on Human Rights in Vienna and the 1995 world conference on women in Beijing, usually produce two sets of declarations: one written by government representatives and one by nongovernmental organizations (NGOs). The UN General Assembly often issues influential but legally nonbinding declarations.

domestic violence   A pattern of coercive behavior, including physical, sexual, and psychological attacks, as well as economic coercion, that adults or adolescents use against their intimate partners.

Economic and Social Council (ECOSOC)   A UN council of 54 members primarily concerned with population, economic development, human rights, and criminal justice. This high-ranking body receives and issues human rights reports in a variety of circumstances.

Glossary

economic, social, and cultural rights   Rights that concern the production, development, and management of material for the necessities of life. The rights to preserve and develop one's cultural identity, which give people social and economic security, sometimes referred to as security-oriented or second-generation rights. Examples are the right to food, shelter, and health care.

educational attainment   The highest diploma or degree, or level of work toward a diploma or degree, an individual has completed.

emergency contraception pills (ECPs)   (See MEDICATION ABORTION) ECPs prevent pregnancy. They contain hormones that reduce the risk of pregnancy if started within 120 hours of unprotected intercourse. The treatment is more effective the sooner it begins. Plan B is currently the only product marketed specifically as emergency contraception. Certain oral contraceptives taken in increased doses may also be used as ECPs.

empowerment   In feminist literature, sense of personal control over one's destiny.

enfranchisement   A statutory right or privilege granted to a person or group by a government (especially the rights of citizenship and the right to vote).

enlisted   A person enrolled or conscripted into the military service. Also includes personnel who are officer candidates currently enrolled in an officer training program.

environmental, cultural, and developmental rights   Sometimes referred to as third-generation rights, these rights recognize that people have the right to live in a safe and healthy environment and that groups of people have the right to cultural, political, and economic development.

equality   The most common definition of equality is that of "formal equality" or "Aristotelian equality." Formal equality requires the same treatment if one is the same but allows different treatment if one is different. Under the formal equality model, men and women should be treated identically because they are considered the same. The formal equality model is problematic for feminists because it does not allow for consideration of the particular role of women in society and therefore often reproduces the inequalities faced by women when treating them as men.

equity   Another term for EQUALITY.

eugenics   A social philosophy that advocates selective breeding of human beings by improving human hereditary traits through intervention to create healthier, more intelligent people; save society's resources; and prevent human suffering. Methods include prenatal testing and screening, genetic counseling, birth control, selective breeding, in vitro fertilization, sterilization, and genetic engineering. Its scientific reputation tumbled in the 1930s because of the racial policies of Nazi Germany. Although the public and science associated eugenics with abuse, many regional and national governments upheld eugenic programs until the 1970s.

evangelism   Zealous preaching and advocacy of the gospel.

familialism   Institution of the family, particularly in France.

female genital mutilation (FGM)   Female circumcision, also referred to as clitoridectomy or excision. Infibulation is the most extreme form of FGM, involving complete excision of the clitoris, labia minora, and most of the labia majora—followed by stitching to close up most of the vagina.

female infanticide   The killing of female babies, mainly prevalent in China and India and among the North American Inuit. Historically, this was done with both genders in Greek, Roman, French, British, Japanese, Chinese, and Inuit civilizations to fulfill sacrificial purposes; to ward off evil; or to dispose of illegal offspring.

feminist   A man or a woman who supports the development and equality of women in all aspects of living.

gay   Someone who is sexually attracted to persons of the same sex. Homosexual.

gender   The characteristics society expects a person to have on the basis of his or her sex. Economic, social, and cultural roles associated with behavior, attitudes, and characteristics associated with being female or male.

gender mainstreaming   Defined by the United Nations as "the process of assessing the implications for women and men of any planned action, including legislation, policies or programs, in any area and at all levels. It is a strategy for making the concerns and experiences of women as well as of men an integral dimension of the design, implementation, monitoring and evaluation of policies and programs in all political, economic and societal spheres, so that women and men benefit equally and inequality is not perpetuated. The ultimate goal [of mainstreaming] is to achieve gender equality."

gender studies   The theoretical analysis of how gender identities are constructed.

Generation X, Gen X   The generation after the post–World War II baby boom, especially Americans and Canadians, born in the 1960s and 1970s.

Generation Y, Gen Y   The associated labels *millennial* and *echo boomer* are used to describe three types of generational spans: those born in the mid-1970s through early 1980s, the late 1970s through early 1990s, and the early 1980s to the early 2000s.

genocide   The systematic killing of people because of their race or ethnicity.

glass ceiling Term coined in the 1990s to describe an artificial barrier based on attitudinal or organizational bias that prevents qualified individuals from advancing in their organization into management-level positions.

Global Gag Rule At the International Conference on Population in Mexico City in August 1984, the U.S. delegation, headed by James Buckley, announced that the United States will no longer fund foreign nongovernmental organizations (NGOs) that provide, refer, counsel, or advocate abortion. These restrictions were an executive branch policy in effect until 1993 but never became part of the permanent foreign assistance statute. It became known as the Mexico City Policy and was later dubbed the "Global Gag Rule" by its opponents.

human rights The rights people are entitled to simply because they are human beings, irrespective of their citizenship, nationality, race, ethnicity, language, gender, sexuality, or abilities; human rights become enforceable when they are codified as conventions, covenants, or treaties, or as they become recognized as customary international law.

human rights treaties Binding international legal documents outlining the responsibilities of states in regard to the protection, promotion, and fulfillment of human rights. Human rights treaties perform three functions: They guarantee specific rights to individuals, they establish state obligations or responsibilities related to these rights, and they create mechanisms to monitor state compliance with these obligations and/or allow individuals to seek redress for violations of their rights. Since human rights treaties are based on international law, they are only binding when a state voluntarily accepts their terms. In becoming a party to a treaty or ratifying it, a state accepts obligations to apply the provisions of the treaty and to accept international supervision of this compliance. Examples of international human rights treaties are the Convention on the Elimination of All Forms of Discrimination against Women (CEDAW); the International Covenant on Economic, Social and Cultural Rights (ICESCR); and the International Convention on the Elimination of All Forms of Racial Discrimination (ICERD).

human trafficking Refers to the illegal transport of human beings, in particular women and children, for the purpose of selling them or exploiting their labor. Exploitation can include prostitution of others or other forms of sexual exploitation, forced labor or services, slavery or practices similar to slavery, servitude, or the removal of organs.

inalienable Refers to rights that belong to every person and cannot be taken from a person under any circumstances.

indigenous peoples   People who are original or natural inhabitants of a country. Native American Indians, for example, are the indigenous people of the United States.

indivisible   Refers to the equal importance of all human rights laws. A person cannot be denied a right because someone decides it is "less important" or "nonessential."

infibulation   (See FEMALE GENITAL MUTILATION) When the clitoris, labia minora, and most of the labia majora are removed and the labia majora (the outer lips of the vagina) then stitched together to cover the vaginal entrance.

interdependent   Refers to the complementary framework of human rights law. For example, persons' ability to participate in government is directly affected by their right to express themselves, to obtain an education, and even to obtain the necessities of life.

intergovernmental organizations (IGOs)   Organizations sponsored by several governments that seek to coordinate their efforts. Some are regional (e.g., the Council of Europe, the Organization of African Unity), some are alliances (e.g., the North Atlantic Treaty Organization [NATO]), and some are dedicated to a specific purpose (e.g., the UN Centre for Human Rights and the United Nations Educational, Scientific and Cultural Organization [UNESCO]).

International Bill of Human Rights   The combination of the Universal Declaration of Human Rights (UDHR), the International Covenant on Civil and Political Rights (ICCPR) and its optional Protocol, and the International Covenant on Economic, Social and Cultural Rights (ICESCR).

International Labour Organization (ILO)   Established in 1919 as part of the Versailles Peace Treaty to improve working conditions and promote social justice, the ILO became a specialized agency of the United Nations in 1946.

justiciable   Liable to trial in a court of justice.

legal rights   Rights laid down in law that can be defended and brought before courts of law.

lesbianism   Sexual orientation of a woman toward other women.

loya jirga   Afghan general assembly. It is a traditional decision-making body dating from the 18th century. Prior to the establishment of the Afghan transitional administration, the government of Afghanistan consisted of the interim administration established by the Bonn Agreement.

medication abortion   (See EMERGENCY CONTRACEPTION) Medication that terminates an unwanted pregnancy. Medication abortion is the use of medication that can induce abortion. There are currently two drugs available in the United States for this purpose—mifepristone and methotrexate. Mifepristone can be taken up to 56 days after the first day of the last menstrual period, and methotrexate can be taken up to 49 days after the first day of the last menstrual period. Both are used in conjunction with misoprostol, which is taken after either mifepristone or methotrexate to complete the abortion.

member states   Countries that are members of the international body being referred to, such as the United Nations or the European Union.

misogynism   Hatred of women.

moral rights   Rights that are based on general principles of fairness and justice; they are often but not always based on religious beliefs. People sometimes feel they have a moral right even when they do not have a legal right. For example, during the Civil Rights movement in the United States, protesters demonstrated against laws forbidding blacks and whites to attend the same schools on the premise that these laws violated their moral rights.

national liberation movement   A worldwide movement that began between the first two world wars, growing to massive proportions after 1945, in favor of national self-determination for the colonies of the imperialist powers. The national liberation movement grew out of the resistance of workers in the colonies in the wake of the Russian Revolution, generally inspired and led by the Comintern, and swept across the "third world" after the Second World War, culminating in the defeat of the United States in Vietnam in 1975.

natural rights   Rights that belong to people simply because they are human beings.

neologism   A new word or expression in a language or a new meaning for an existing word or expression.

New Woman   A phrase coined in late 1890s novels and magazines to describe confident women who were seeking emancipation in all ways of living, to be self-sufficient.

nonbinding   A document, such as a declaration, that carries no formal legal obligations. It may, however, carry moral obligations or attain the force of law as customary international law.

nongovernmental organizations (NGOs)   Organizations formed by people outside government. NGOs monitor the proceedings of human rights bodies such as the Commission on Human Rights and are the "watchdogs" of human rights that fall within their mandate. Some are large and international (e.g., the Red Cross, Amnesty International, the Girl Scouts), while others may be small and local (e.g., an organization that is an advocate for people who have disabilities in a particular city or a coalition that promotes women's rights in a refugee camp). NGOs play a major role in influencing UN policy, and many of them have official consultative status at the United Nations.

nonpartisan   Orientation of an organization that neither supports nor opposes candidates for office at any level of government.

parity   Another term for equality.

parochial   Relating to or supported by or located in a parish, such as schools; narrowly restricted in outlook or scope.

partial-birth abortion   A late-term abortion in which a physician vaginally delivers, euthanizes, and extracts an unborn child's body.

patrilineal   Based on or tracing descent through the male line.

patrilocal   Of or relating to residence with a husband's kin group or clan.

political rights   (See CIVIL AND POLITICAL RIGHTS) The rights of people to participate in the political life of their communities and society, for example, the right to vote for their government or run for office.

postbaccalaureate   Adjective describing coursework or a degree program in which a bachelor's degree is a prerequisite.

poverty line   The level of personal income defining the state of poverty. The World Bank uses reference lines set at $1 (extreme poverty) and $2 a day.

Prohibition   The period from 1920 to 1933 when the sale of alcoholic beverages was prohibited in the United States by a constitutional amendment.

protocol   A treaty that modifies another treaty by adding procedures or substantive provisions.

quickening   The stage of pregnancy at which the mother first feels movement of the fetus, usually around the 21st week.

race   A social attribute based on skin color and other physical characteristics. The Current Population Survey provides data by race, as specified by the household respondent. Since 2003, respondents are allowed to choose more than one race; previously, multiracial persons were required to select a single primary race. Persons who select more than one race are classified separately in the category *two or more races.* Persons who select one race only are classified in one of the following five categories: (1) white, (2) black or African American, (3) Asian, (4) Native Hawaiian and other Pacific Islander, and (5) American Indian or Alaska Native. Only data for whites, blacks, and Asians are currently published because the number of survey respondents for the other racial categories is not large enough to produce statistically reliable estimates.

ratification, ratify Process by which the legislative body of a state confirms a government's action in signing a treaty. The formal procedure by which a state becomes bound to a treaty after acceptance.

reservation The exceptions made by state parties to a treaty, such as provisions that they do not agree to follow. Reservations, however, may not undermine the fundamental meaning of the treaty.

secular Not religious-based, nor part of the clergy.

Selected Reserve The Selected Reserve consists of those units and individuals within the Ready Reserve designated by their staff as so essential to initial wartime missions that they have priority over all other Reserves. All Selected Reservists are in an active status.

self-determination Determination by the people of a territorial unit of their own political future without coercion from powers outside that region.

secularism Indifference to—or rejection or exclusion of—religion and religious considerations. Often referred to in discussing issues related to the separation of church and state.

sex The biological characteristics that make a person male or female, with the distinction that only females become pregnant and menstruate.

sexist Biased toward one sex or the other.

sexual harassment Unwanted sexual attention that intrudes on a person's integrity. This includes requests for sexual favors, unwelcome or demeaning remarks, or touching. It is a form of discrimination and constitutes abuse of power.

signing, sign In human rights the first step in ratification of a treaty; signing a declaration, convention, or one of the covenants constitutes promising to adhere to the principles in the document and to honor its spirit.

Soroptimist The word *Soroptimist,* from the Latin words *soror,* meaning "sister," and *optima,* meaning "best," loosely translates as "best for women." It is in the name of an international organization that acts as a sisterhood.

stand for election When a person can be a candidate in an election.

state Often synonymous with *country.* A group of people permanently occupying a fixed territory, deploying common laws and government, and capable of conducting international affairs.

states party Those countries that have ratified a covenant or a convention and are thereby bound to conform to its provisions.

suffragette The term originated in Britain and was first used to insult members of the suffrage movement. It then became the term to describe the more radical branch of the British suffrage movement.

suffragist A woman or man who is an advocate for a woman's right to vote.

surrogate mother   Also called *gestational carrier*. A woman's carrying and giving birth to a child for another woman, by prearrangement. Full surrogacy occurs when the infertile mother's egg is fertilized by the father's sperm and inserted into the surrogate mother's womb. Partial surrogacy occurs when the surrogate mother's egg is fertilized by the father's sperm.

Taliban   Islamic fundamentalists who controlled Afghanistan from 1994 to 2002. The literal translation of *Taliban* is "seminary student."

temperance   A movement that evolved in the late 1800s to advocate living without destructive excesses such as alcohol; a precursor to the Prohibition era (1920–33) in the United States. Women's groups were strong advocates of both temperance and prohibition.

tenure   The right to hold property. Part of an ancient hierarchical system of holding lands.

traumatic fistula   Tearing in the vagina, anus, or urinary tract.

treaty   Formal agreement between states that defines and modifies their mutual duties and obligations; used synonymously with CONVENTION and COVENANT. When conventions are adopted by the UN General Assembly, they create legally binding international obligations for the member states that have signed them. When a national government ratifies a treaty, the articles of that treaty become part of its domestic legal obligations.

United Nations Charter   Initial document of the United Nations adopted in San Francisco in 1945 that set forth its goals, functions, and responsibilities.

United Nations General Assembly   One of the principal organs of the United Nations, consisting of representatives of all member states. The General Assembly issues declarations and adopts conventions on human rights issues, debates relevant issues, and censures states that violate human rights. The actions of the General Assembly are governed by the United Nations Charter.

Index

Page numbers in **boldface** indicate major treatment of a subject. Page numbers followed by *b* indicate biographical entries. Page numbers followed by *c* indicate chronology entries. Page numbers followed by *f* indicate figures. Page numbers followed by *g* indicate glossary entries. Page numbers followed by *m* indicate maps. Page numbers followed by *t* indicate tables.

435

Index

Index

Index

National Consumer's
  League 64
National Council of Negro
  Women 73, 76, 335,
  403c
National Council of
  Women's Organizations
  335–336, 420c
National Crime
  Victimization Survey
  97–98
National Institute of Justice
  97–98
national liberation
  movement 431g
National Organization for
  Women 27, 72, 76, 88,
  103, 208, 336, 409c
National Woman Suffrage
  Association 41, 61, 62,
  396c
National Women's Health
  Network 75
National Women's History
  Museum Act (2005) 105,
  421c
National Women's History
  Project 336
National Women's Law
  Center 88, 337
National Women's Political
  Caucus 70, 103, 277, 337
National Women's Studies
  Association 105
Native Americans
  leading causes of death
    for 288t
  poverty rate for 87
  suffrage for 402c
natural rights 431g
Nauru 409c
neologism 431g
Neopaganism 36
Nepal 16, 406c
Netherlands 24, 33, 291t,
  400c, 407c, 416c
networking 42–46
"new age" spirituality 36
New Culture movement
  123–124

New Democratic Coalition
  70
New Partnership for
  Africa's Development 152
newspapers 275
New Woman 431g
New York Women's
  Property Act (1848) 186–
  187, 394c, 398c
New Zealand 4, 14, 28, 52,
  398c, 400c
Nicaragua 17, 30, 406c
Nielsen, Nielsine 397c
Niger 9, 10, 405c, 407c
Nigeria 16, 21, 285t, 407c,
  413c, 420c
Nineteenth Amendment
  44, 63–64, 188–189, 401c,
  414c
nonbinding 431g
nongovernmental
  organizations 431g–432g
nonpartisan 432g
North Atlantic Treaty
  Organization 17, 408c
Norway 17, 26, 117, 282f,
  291t, 399c
Novartis 220–221, 423c
Novello, Antonia C. 312b,
  415c
Nyiramilimo, Odette
  312b–313b

O

Obama, Barack 69, 78, 81,
  422c
obscenity 99
occupations 11, 82–83,
  126–127, 284t
O'Connor, Sandra Day 94,
  313b, 415c
Odhiambo, Millie Akoth
  313b
Office on Violence against
  Women 337–338
Oman 5
one-child policy (China)
  xiv, xvii, 25, 32, 127–129
online resources 267–273
opium trade 136

Organisation for Economic
  Co-operation and Devel-
  opment 9–10, 52, 122
organizations 272–273,
  320–346

P

pacifism 45
Pakistan 32, 285t, 405c
Palau 413c
Palin, Sarah 78, 102
Panama 404c, 405c
Pan American Health
  Organization 30
Pankhurst, Emmeline 42,
  44, 63, 313b, 402c
Papua New Guinea 15, 408c
Paraguay 407c
Paris Peace Conference
  (1919) 44, 401c
parity 432g
Parks, Rosa 313b–314b,
  406c
parochial 432g
partial-birth abortion 94,
  213–220, 420c, 432g
Partial-Birth Abortion Ban
  Act (2003) 213
Pasque law (France, 2002)
  121
patrilineal 11, 432g
patrilocal 11, 432g
Paul, Alice 34, 43, 63, 64,
  76, 189, 314b, 399c
Paycheck Fairness Act 82,
  423c
peace-building 50, 151,
  152, 243–247, 261, 419c
PeaceWomen Project 338
Pelosi, Nancy 78, 314b,
  422c, 423c
Pennsylvania Women Work
  338
periodical indexes 273
Perry, Ricky 422c
Peru 30, 406c
Peterson, Esther 71, 314b
Pittsburgh Press v.
  Pittsburgh Commission on
  Human Relations 411c

445

Index